AF887445

Enterprise Systems

The Cornerstone for Seamlessly Integrating Robust Business Processes and Driving Organizational Excellence

Robert Szymanski

and

Pierre Hadaya

Library and Archives Canada Cataloguing in Publication

Hadaya, Pierre, 1970-, author

Enterprise Systems: The Cornerstone for Seamlessly Integrating Robust Business Processes and Driving Organizational Excellence / Robert Szymanski and Pierre Hadaya.

ISBN: 978-1-7772049-9-0 (softcover)

Table of Content

Introduction

What is an Enterprise System?

While there are many definitions of "Enterprise Systems", we'll take a very broad approach to defining what it is. Enterprise Systems are very large-scale software systems that are designed to manage enterprise-wide functions and related business processes in an integrated manner. An enterprise system provide real-time data into a single integrated database to business users to support decision making. Contrary to traditional software, once installed enterprise systems also need to be configured to the needs of the organization prior to use. (Configuration discussed in more details in Chapter 2).

Some examples of enterprise systems include Enterprise Resource Planning systems (ERP), Customer Relationship Management systems (CRM), Supply Chain Management systems (SCM), and Supplier Relationship Management systems (SRM). SAP is a global leader in enterprise systems software.

A benefit to implementing enterprise systems is that they integrate across various business functions of an enterprise. From our perspective, we use the term "business function" to broadly represent different areas of business in an enterprise. Examples of business functions include accounting, purchasing, production, sales, human resources, and inventory management. As a matter of fact, enterprise systems refer to these business functions as "modules". You'll find there are specific modules in enterprise systems to match the business functions mentioned above.

Since integration is a key benefit of an enterprise system, it might be worth defining what is meant by "integration". In simple terms, integration occurs when an activity on one business function impacts another. As an example, if we purchase materials to be placed into inventory for later use, the business function of purchasing will impact the inventory management function. Not only do materials need to be purchased, but the enterprise must now determine how it will physically manage the quantity purchased in inventory and accurately store those materials. As a matter of fact, you'll learn when reading this book, that purchasing these materials for storage also integrates with accounting. Receiving the purchased materials into inventory assumes we have taken ownership of the materials, thus we must record that increase in assets in our balance sheet. This is just one of many examples we will cover in this book.

You will also find that this book focuses heavily on business processes, specifically the sequence of steps in these processes. To put this in context, a business process is a very specific sequence of steps to carry out a very specific part of one or more business functions. If we refer back to the previous example of the business function of purchasing, we'll find that there are many different ways to carry out purchasing. In our earlier example, we purchased materials to be stored in inventory. What if we are purchasing materials to be shipped directly to a customer? Or what if the materials we purchase are not going to go into inventory for storage, but rather go directly to production? Additionally, what if we have to pay for the materials prior to receiving them or we aren't purchasing materials, but instead purchasing services from a vendor? These are all different processes related to the business function of purchasing and each one has a very specific sequence of steps to carry out the process. That then begs the question, what do we mean by steps?

Steps are individual actions that must be completed to carry out a process. Some steps are informal, while others are considered formal and are documented in the enterprise system. The formal steps that are documented are considered "transactions". To put this in perspective, let's consider one of the steps in our original example of the purchasing of materials for inventory. Once we have determined that we want to purchase the materials, the next step in the process is called "sourcing". Sourcing could be formal or informal. If it is a formal step, then it might include sending requests for quotation (RFQ) to several vendors so a decision can be made regarding a valid source of supply. This formal step requires a transaction. In this case, a specific transaction is entered in the enterprise system and a document is generated for the RFQ. This document serves as an electronic record for that transaction.

However, if sourcing is informal, a buyer might already know which vendor to use when purchasing the materials. In this case, sourcing is still a required step as you can't purchase materials without identifying from which vendor those materials will be purchased. But because this informal step did not require a formal action within the system, no document was created in the system. In this case it is not considered a transaction in the enterprise system. It might be worth noting that all transactions in the system result in the creation of at least one document, which is an electronic record of that transaction and it serves as part of the audit trail for the process.

SAP as an Exemplar

This book covers the core business processes and their realization within SAP. SAP is chosen as the exemplar for the concepts we cover in this book because it is the global leader in enterprise systems software. As of July 2025, SAP has published that its customers who use their enterprise systems generate 84% of the total global commerce.[1] That is an astounding statistic! In addition, SAP University Alliances is a branch of SAP that provides faculty and students at colleges and universities with resources for higher education. For decades, faculty at SAP University Alliances programs have been using SAP in their classrooms to educate the next generation of business professionals.

The book emphasizes the integration of business functions and between business functions through business processes. More specifically it addresses how SAP S/4HANA models the business processes tied to each of the following business functions and highlights their integration:

- At the very least, companies are required by law to do Financial Accounting. (Discussed in details in Chapter 3)
- To operate efficiently, we can imagine that companies will also perform Management Accounting to make good decisions based on accounting information. (Discussed in details in Chapter 4)
- Most companies, especially manufacturing and trading companies, deal with materials and must handle Inventory, Warehouse Management, and Procurement. (Discussed in details in Chapters 5, 7 and 8)
- Any company with a reasonable number of employees must also perform Human Resources Management. (Discussed in details in Chapter 6)

1 See *https://www.sap.com/about/company.html*

- Manufacturing and trading companies generate revenue by selling goods to customers. These companies must also effectively manage the shipment of these goods to their customers. Therefore, these companies must manage Sales and Distribution. (Discussed in details in Chapter 9)
- Companies can also generate revenue by servicing goods sold to their customers. Such service arrangements often generate revenue via service contracts and maintenance plans (as is often the case in the automobile industry). This is accomplished using Sales for Service. (Discussed in details in Chapter 11)
- A company with manufacturing facilities certainly must perform Plant Maintenance or Enterprise Asset Management. This will encompass both routine Preventive Maintenance to reduce the risk of mechanical breakdowns (like oil changes for cars), as well as Breakdown Maintenance when things do go wrong. (Discussed in details in Chapter 10)
- In addition, companies often execute projects like constructing new manufacturing facilities, conducting sales conferences, and building new information systems. Companies therefore need to do Project Management as well. (Discussed in details in Chapter 12)

If we were to cover every possible unique business process in this book, we would not have enough time nor space. Therefore, we are going to use a best-practice approach to these business processes. A best-practice approach means the processes we cover will not conform to managing exceptions or customizing process steps.

Although the sheer volume of material covered appears daunting, pure common sense can help us to navigate it quite easily. Much of the complexity actually arises from terminology.

You will encounter numerous terms, but as long as you can clearly associate the terms with common-sense business activities, you will progress smoothly through the material. In this chapter, we provide a bird-eyed view of some of the important business processes and the associated SAP terms.

We cover a lot of ground and get down to very minute details about many things. It might seem complex but grasping everything well only requires you to attach a common-sense meaning to the numerous terms that you will encounter. This chapter has already introduced many terms and will introduce some more before we are done.

Why Study Enterprise Systems?

Previously, we mentioned that integration is a key benefit to implementing enterprise systems. For students of business and for those who are already active in the business world, having a complete view of the business is essential to success. Often you'll hear others describe this as an enterprise view of the business. This isn't a coincidence.

From the perspective of a student studying business, for better or worse, the business programs at their institutions are traditionally structured in silos. There is an academic department for almost every business function. Unfortunately, this structure doesn't always support an enterprise view of the business. Students are typically siloed into their field of study, often resulting in them lacking a solid foundation as to how their field of study impacts other parts of the business. Student who elect to study enterprise systems have a better understanding of many business processes and their impacts on the entire enterprise. Their level of knowledge extends beyond their field of study and they can make an immediate impact on companies that hire them. These students generally find early success in their business careers.

For those with industry experience, understanding enterprise systems and their integrated nature results in better decision making. Business activities that drive key performance indicators are better understood and the enterprise knowledge allows them to become more agile and able to respond quickly and effectively to various scenarios. In reality, knowledge of the integrated nature of an enterprise systems put power in the hands of the business decision makers. It provides the business users with real-time data to all parts of the business.

How to use this Book?

The amount of material contained in this book seems daunting just in terms of volume. Keep in mind, the information contained in this book is also designed to adequately prepare you for an SAP certification in the integration of business processes. Tackling everything covered in this book will be a challenge to you, so we offer recommendations for success.

This book is broken down into chapters which, as mentioned previously, mostly reflect the various business processes and modules in SAP S/4HANA. Except for two overview chapters, each chapter will contain related discussions about the following concepts:

- Enterprise Structure (Organizational Data/Levels that specify how the data is structured in the S/4HANA system)
- Master Data (entities needed to complete business transactions)
- Business Processes (steps and transactions to complete various end-to-end processes)
- Impacts of Transactions (integration within S/4HANA and other intelligent technologies).

In this section we suggest a sequence of activities that will help you to best absorb the material. Figure I.1 shows the suggested study strategy

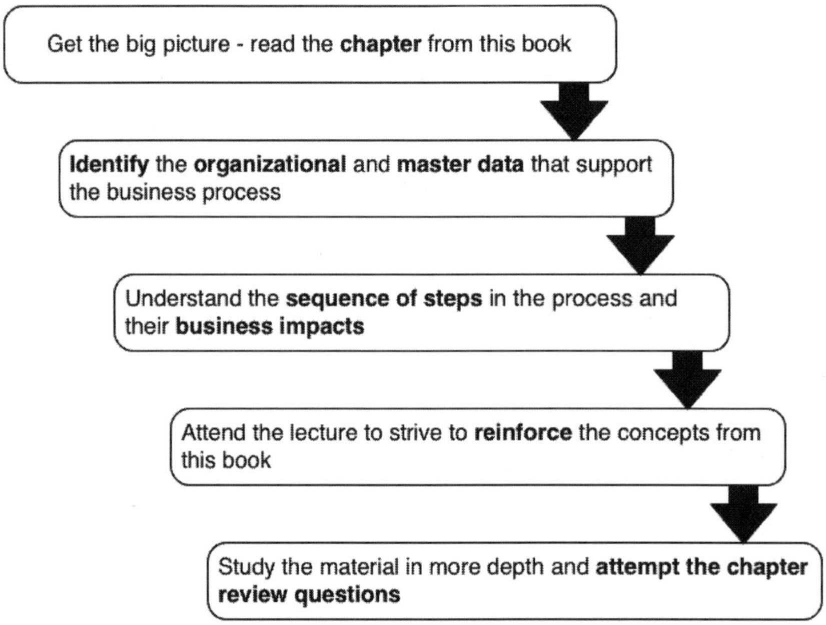

Figure I.1: Suggested Study Strategy

Certification

To pass SAP certification exams related to business processes, you need to clearly understand the above business processes and their integration. Rather than just seeing each process and term we cover as something abstract that you need to memorize, you should be able to relate everything we talk about to concrete real-world occurrences.

As of July 2025, the latest SAP certification in the integration of business process is the "End-to-End Business Processes for the Intelligent Enterprise". Because SAP changes with advances in technology, the name of this certification may also change in a future release. However, if you are using this book as a guide to prepare for that specific SAP certification, it's important to know that not all chapters in this book are included in that certification. As of the date this book was published (August 2025), the following chapters are not covered in this certification: Chapter 7, Chapter 10, and Chapter 12.

While these chapters are not directly included on this certification, it's possible you may find them a valuable resource when preparing for the exam. For example, Chapter 11 - Sales for Service, includes concepts from Chapter 10 - Enterprise Asset Management.

Chapter 1: The Big Picture

Setting the Stage

Manufacturing organizations purchase raw materials and convert them into finished products for sale. Such organizations need to plan carefully for materials to ensure that material availability meshes properly with production plans. Otherwise, they may realize they are short of some of the required materials just as they are about to begin a production shift. That could be disastrous.

Manufacturing organizations also cannot just play safe and have huge quantities of materials either – because that would mean holding a lot of inventory and incurring working capital costs. The material can also get spoiled or even go to waste if they decide to discontinue making some products. You can see how proper material planning plays a big role in profitability. With very stiff competition among companies, even a 2-3% increase in costs can hurt.

We consider a trivial example to unveil some of the main issues involved in Material Planning.

TablesRUs (TRUS) produces and sells study tables. TRUS buys the legs and the top as raw materials, assembles them into tables and then paints them to ready them for sale. TRUS makes only one kind of table.

To make one table, they need:

- Four legs
- One top
- 2 liters of primer
- 2 liters of paint

We see a very simple list above because of our simplifying assumptions. The list would be more complex in more realistic situations. Business organizations use the term Bill of Materials – or just BOM for short – to refer to such lists. In SAP terms, a BOM is considered Master Data. Table 1.1 shows the BOM for a TRUS study table.

Table 1.1: BOM for a TRUS Table

Item #	Material	Quantity	Units
1	Leg	4	Ea.
2	Top	1	Ea.
3	Primer	2	Liters
4	Paint	2	Liters

Manufacturing organizations deal with raw materials (RM), finished goods (FG), and often semi-finished goods (SF). These three (RM, FG, and SF) are examples of Material Types. We will discuss material types in more detail later in this book. For now, in our example we will assume TRUS uses only raw materials to make a single finished good.

As Table 1.1 shows, a BOM for a material includes the raw materials and the quantity of each one needed to manufacture or assemble the finished good.

BOMs play an important role in determining how much of each material a company should buy (or make) while considering the production plans, current inventory, anticipated deliveries, how much time suppliers need to deliver the materials, and many other such factors. When companies deal with thousands of materials, the task becomes large and complex. Enterprise systems like SAPS4HANA help companies to efficiently manage this complexity.

Let us consider another example to make one unit of a material A, we need 3 each of material B and one each of material C (Table 1.2).

However, in this example let's assume material B is an item which is also produced and therefore it needs its own BOM to make one unit of material B we might require 2 each of material D and 5 each of material E (Table 1.3). Material B is thus considered a semi-finished good. A semi-finished good is a material that is produced and used in the further production of another material. In this case, material B is produced in order to produce material A.

Table 1.2: Another BOM for A

Item #	Material	Quantity	Units
1	B	3	Ea.
2	C	1	Ea.

Table 1.3: BOM for Item B from Table 2

Item #	Material	Quantity	Units
1	D	2	Ea.
2	E	5	Ea.

Let us assume that materials C, D and E are atomic and not assemblies – that is, they do not need their own BOMs. We do not need to assemble any other parts to make materials C, D or E. Therefore materials C, D, and E are considered raw materials.

The above example shows a multi-level BOM, that is, one in which materials that form a part of a BOM for one material could themselves be assemblies – and therefore have their own BOMs. SAP uses the term BOM exactly in the sense that we have used it above. However, BOM is a generic term used in industry and is not SAP specific.

BOMs help in material planning. Let us also understand an important SAP-specific term that often goes along with BOMs – Routing. Routings are also considered Master Data. Whereas a BOM specifies the materials and their quantities needed to make a product, a Routing specifies the operations to be carried out to make a finished good or semi-finished good. Table 1.4 shows the routing for the same study table.

Table 1.4: Routing for TRUS Study Table

Opn. no	Description	Material Needed	Work Center	Standard Time
10	Fix legs to table	Top and four legs	Assembly area	20 min
20	Sand and apply primer	Primer	Finishing area	15 min
30	Paint	Paint	Finishing area	15 min
40	Dry	-	Finishing area	2 hrs

Because all of the needed materials are raw materials, TRUS buys table legs and the tops from vendor Country Lumber. The primer and paint are purchased from another vendor, Village Depot. While purchasing these raw materials from vendors, let us suppose that the vendors cannot supply the materials immediately and that there is a delay between ordering these and their arrival at the factory. We refer to this delay as Purchasing Lead Time.

Companies also do not usually buy items in arbitrary quantities. Instead they buy most materials in multiples of certain quantities – called the lot size – which could differ from material to material (and also from vendor to vendor). For example, it might be the case that TRUS has a lot size of 100 each for legs. In this case, if the company needed 360 legs, it would buy four lots of 100 each. This represents an example of fixed lot size. Table 1.5 shows the lead times and lot sizes for the materials that TRUS uses.

Table 1.5: Purchasing Lead Times and Lot Sizes for TRUS Materials

Material	Vendor	Purch Lead Time	Lot Size
Legs	Country lumber	1 month	100 ea.
Tops	Country lumber	2 months	25 ea.
Primer	Village depot	2 weeks	100 ltrs
Paint	Village depot	3 weeks	25 ltrs

TRUS buys raw materials from these vendors regularly. To do so, TRUS places Purchase Orders with these vendors. Let us suppose that TRUS prints and sends out Purchase Orders by regular mail. Since TRUS does business regularly with several vendors, it might be beneficial for them to be able to pull up vendor information on demand. Assuming TRUS uses a computerized system to generate the Purchase Orders, the program can pull relevant information about a vendor automatically. Some items of information that companies might store about their vendors include, among many others, Vendor name and Vendor address. Of course, companies need to maintain such information for all the vendors with whom they do business. Obviously, the same situation applies to customers as well – companies maintain information about all their registered customers – same with materials and lots of other things.

You have already been exposed to the term Master Data during the above discussion on BOMs and Routings. In general terms, Master Data represents entities needed to support business processes. Therefore, in order to purchase materials from vendors, Master Data would need to be created for each vendor. Each vendor would then have its own Master Record. If a company does business with 1,000 vendors, then it would need to create unique Master Data for each of those 1,000 vendors, meaning there would be 1,000 vendor Master Records. Table 1.6 shows an example of a vendor master data.

Table 1.6: Vendor Master, Containing One Vendor Master for Each Vendor

Vendor no	Name	Address	Email	...	...
1	Country Lumber	100 Main st, ...	...	...	...
2	Village Depot	150 South ave, ...	...	...	...
3	Ace Hardware	95 Brooklyn st, ...	...	...	...
4	...	...	...	...	...

Similarly, companies maintain Customer Master Data for each individual customer and Material Master Data for each material it uses.

To generate a Purchase Order, TRUS would obviously need information about the materials that it wants to order. You can easily see that some of this information would come from the Material Master Data of the corresponding materials. In this sense, we are encountering one of the most important concepts in this book. That is, Master Data is required to carry out business transactions.

Recall, we talked about the various material types that TRUS deals with. The study table that TRUS sells is a Finished Good while the materials that TRUS uses to make the table are Raw Materials. Sometimes, companies do not manufacture any of the products that they sell. They simply buy from vendors and sell them to end customers without any additional processing. Amazon's book and digital media business is an example. WalMart would be another. Sometimes companies do both. That is, they make and sell some materials and also simply resell others. SAP refers to materials that a company simply buys and sells without further processing, that is, material that a company trades in, as Trading Goods. Trading Goods then, would be another example of a Material Type.

If in addition to manufacturing and selling tables, TRUS also sells chairs, but does not manufacture them. Instead, TRUS buys chairs from another manufacturer and simply resells them (at a profit). In this case, we would not treat chairs as finished goods. These chairs would then be considered Trading Goods.

The Material Master Data contains information for all material types. The Material Type is the most important characteristic of a material. As we have seen, different material types mean the material will have different touch-points on the business. To further emphasize this, you can see from our discussion above, different material types will integrate with different business functions, and therefore different business processes. When creating Material Master Data, choosing the correct material type is essential in ensuring the information needed to support the various business processes is properly maintained.

Armed with this basic information about TRUS, we can readily imagine the following business processes that would absolutely be essential for it to operate:

- purchasing raw materials (procurement processing)
- producing finished goods (manufacturing execution)
- selling finished products (sales order processing)

Would these processes alone suffice? Think of what else the company would need to do in order to function. Looking closer, we can see that, in addition to the above processes, TRUS also needs to perform various other activities. For example:

- Integrated Business Planning (IBP): How much of finished goods should the company produce in various time periods: next week, the following week, and so on. TRUS will need to base this on several things:
  - forecasted demand for its products
  - finished goods already in stock
  - production capacity constraints
  - supply chain bottle necks
- Materials Requirement Planning (MRP): Once TRUS has an IBP, it needs to then translate that into raw material requirements and prepare a plan for how much of each material to buy at specific times. In more complex situations, companies may buy raw materials to produce semi-finished goods (sometimes referred to as sub-assemblies) which they incorporate into their final products. In such cases, they would also need to plan when to make these sub-assemblies as well and determine the timing and quantities of raw material purchases accordingly. When companies deal with many raw materials and finished products, all this can become too complex to track manually. Furthermore, these processes happen continuously with prior plans being changed often to accommodate changes in the environment.

Suppose, for example, that TRUS needs to produce 140 study tables on March 31 and has nothing in stock (i.e., no raw materials and no finished goods). How much raw materials would they need to purchase and by when should the purchase orders be sent out to the vendors? Assume, for simplicity, that all the study tables will be produced on a single day and that we are concerned with planning for just that one day of production.

Given a BOM for a material M – which could be a finished good or a subassembly –, the process of finding out how much of various other materials we need for producing a certain quantity of M is called BOM Explosion. This might look trivial, but when we have complex BOMs with several levels of nesting and numerous materials, BOM Explosion can be tedious. Automating it can increase efficiency. When we consider that companies often make many finished goods, with several of them having at least some common raw materials and sub-assemblies, you can see how useful automated BOM explosion can be for Materials Requirement Planning or MRP.

Key Process Flows

After that overview of the book's topics, let us turn our attention to some key process flows in SAP. You will grasp the upcoming chapters much better once you have this broad picture.

In this section, we want to expose some common themes that underly many business processes in SAP. Before we look at that, let us look at a concrete process. We start with Sales Order Processing, also known as the Lead-to- Cash Process.

The Lead-to-Cash process covers all the steps involved in customers ordering products from a company, the company fulfilling the order and the customer paying for the products. The formal process starts when a customer places a firm Sales Order with the company. However, in a business-to-business (B2B) situation some steps will usually precede the formal step of placing a Sales Order. The unit that covers the Sales Order Fulfillment or Lead-to-Cash process in detail will discuss many possible preliminary steps. We discuss one of them next.

A customer could initiate the process with a Sales Inquiry. Through a Sales Inquiry, a prospective customer merely seeks some information about the products, pricing and availability, with no contractual obligation involved. After getting the information, the customer could decide not to buy and that will end the process.

Alternatively, the customer might proceed to place a Sales Order which is a more binding document. The company will start the process of shipping the product and the customer will be bound to pay for the shipped products. Note the key difference between a Sales Inquiry and a Sales Order.

As we mentioned above, instead of using a Sales Inquiry, the overall Lead-to- Cash process might begin in other ways as well. For example, a prospective buyer might send an RFQ – Request for Quotation. The Quotation can also initiate the process. We will cover this in a later chapter.

Once the company generates a Sales Order for the customer, it will need to start the process of fulfilling the order. That is, the sales department must give the green signal to initiate the process of picking the materials from the warehouse and shipping them out to the customer.

Although the Sales department might have initiated the Sales Order, other departments will take care of many of the subsequent steps. The finished goods stock from which the company will fulfill the order might be in a warehouse in some other part of the country or even elsewhere around the globe. Therefore, someone in the warehouse will need to see that they have a new delivery to fulfill and initiate the steps to pick the materials from the warehouse shelves. In some cases, after verifying that everything about the Sales Order is correct, the Sales Department may initiate the shipping process by creating a document called the Outbound Delivery. In other cases, this document may be created by warehouse personnel. In either case, this Outbound Delivery document authorizes the subsequent steps to take place.

In large companies, picking an item out of a warehouse shelf might not be as trivial an operation as it sounds. The warehouse could be huge – the size of several football fields – and so someone with a forklift, or a robot, will need to go to the correct location and pick out the material. In large warehouses, picking materials each time an order comes in could be woefully inefficient and hence warehouse operators will need to optimize the whole process. For example, they might accumulate orders for a while and then determine an optimal routing through the warehouse to pick out the materials while expending as little energy as possible in the process (and incurring as little wear and tear on the equipment as possible). Given all these intricacies in warehouse operations, companies typically use complex software to manage warehouse operations. SAP S/4HANA also supports warehouse operations. Thus, the picking step involves an integration between the Sales Order Processing system and the Warehouse Management system.

Once the warehouse completes the operation of taking a material off the shelves (i.e., picking), the material can then be formally removed from the company's stock. Suppose the company had 1000 laptops of a certain model in stock for sale and some customer ordered 90 of these. Once the 90 units are allocated to the customer sales order, the company now has only 910 units in stock. Which department tracks this?

Warehouse management is only concerned with the warehouse logistics of efficiently putting materials away and retrieving them. Inventory Management is the business entity that tracks the quantities of various materials in stock at various storage locations. We are beginning to see how certain transactions impact other parts of the business. In this case, fulfilling a Sales Order will have an impact on more than just Warehouse Management. It also affects Inventory Management.

The step of reducing the inventory once the warehouse operation is completed is called Posting of Goods Issue. At this step, the company allocates the picked materials to the concerned sales order and records the fact that it now has fewer units of the concerned material in stock. The company does not own these materials anymore. Who owns them?

At this point, the customer who ordered the items owns the material and therefore owes the company the money they agreed to pay in return for these items. To initiate the process of receiving payment, the company Posts an Invoice in the system and sends it to the customer for payment. This step shows an interface between the sales process and Financial Accounting. From the perspective of the company, this is considered a receivable, which is an asset to the company.

Eventually, the customer sends a payment and the company's Accounting department will post the payment to the customer's account, which will clear the receivable. The posting of this payment completes the process. The terms, "posting" or "post" were used three times in this example (posting a goods issue, post an invoice, and post the payment). This term is often used in transactions that will have an impact on accounting. If you understand this now, it will help you get a clearer picture as we uncover other transactions in other business processes which have accounting impacts.

Figure 1.1 shows the major steps in the Lead-to-Cash process.

Enterprise Systems strive to provide smooth integration across departmental boundaries. Individual steps of business processes are initiated within some module of the enterprise system. However, completing a step in all but the most trivial business processes involve interfacing with one or more other modules of the enterprise system. Again, we will learn later that cloud solutions and other intelligent technologies may also be involved in the process steps.

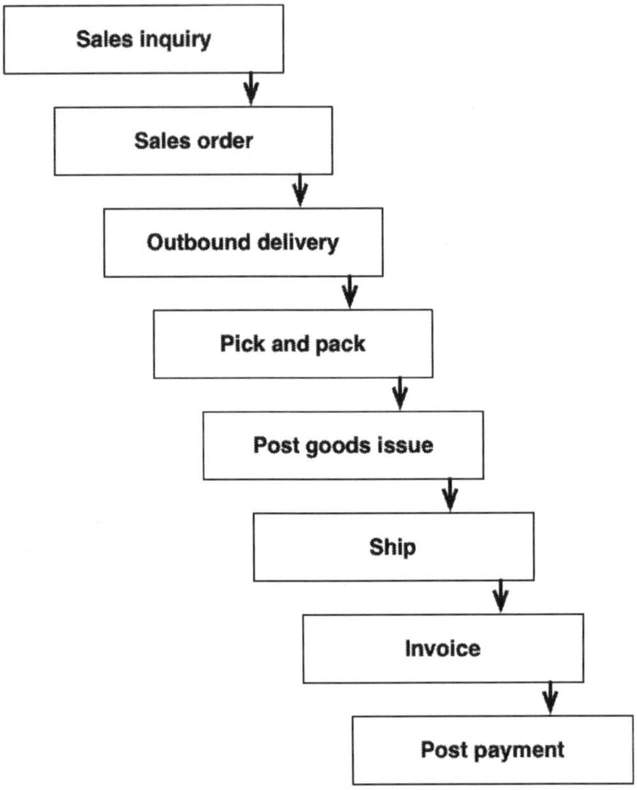

Figure 1.1: Lead-to-Cash Business Process

Table 1.7 shows the Lead-to-Cash process with additional details about the module in which each step might be initiated and the other key modules with which each step might integrate.

Table 1.7: Lead-to-Cash Business Process With Integration Details

Step	Initiated in SAP Module	Integration
Sales Inquiry	Sales and Distribution	Inventory, Procurement, Production
Sales Order		
Outbound Delivery		Inventory, Warehouse
Pick and Pack		Warehouse
Post Goods Issue		Inventory, Financial Accounting
Ship		Transportation
Post Invoice		Financial Accounting
Post Payment	Financial Accounting	

Generic Process Structure in SAP

Several SAP business processes share a common structure and you might find it useful to understand this basic structure.

Many important processes begin with a preliminary step to initiate the process, like Sales Inquiry in the Lead-to-Cash process.

This preliminary step is usually tentative, with no firm requirement for further action. For example, a customer could initiate a Sales Inquiry, but then not follow it up with a Sales Order. However, once the Sales Order is created, then the process goes forward.

Figure 1.2 shows the generic structure of many important processes in SAP and shows how the Lead-to-Cash process maps to that generic structure. Table 1.8 shows a similar mapping for other business processes, with Lead-to-Cash included for reference. Later chapters go into further details on these processes, but we briefly describe each one below.

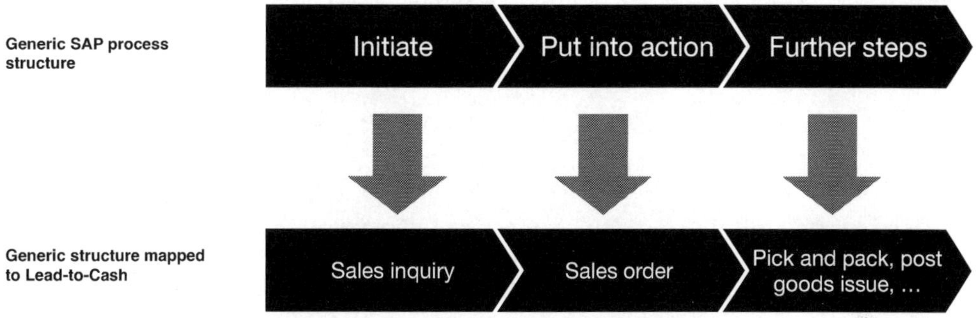

Figure 1.2: SAP Generic Process Structure and its Mapping to the Lead-to-Cash Process

We see that each business process that Table 1.8 covers has a preliminary step to initiate the process (e.g., Sales Inquiry, Purchase Requisition, Planned Order, Transfer Request, and Maintenance Notification). All of these represent preliminary steps do not guarantee that the process will be executed to completion. The formal step occurs when these informal steps result in a corresponding Order (e.g., Sales Order, Purchase Order, Production Order, Transfer Order, or Maintenance Order).

Table 1.8: SAP Generic Process Structure and its Mapping to Several Key Processes

	Initiative	Put Into Action	Further Steps
Lead-to-cash	Sales inquiry	Sales order	Outbound delivery, Pick and pack, Post goods issue, Ship, Invoice, Post customer payment
Purchasing	Purchase requisition	Puschase order	Goods receipt, Invoice verification
Manufacturing	Planned order	Production order	Goods issue, Confirmation, Goods receipt, Order settlement
Warehouse	Transfer request	Transfer order	Confirmation
Plant maintenance	Maintenance notification	Maintenance orders	Goods issue, Confirmation, Settlement

The subsequent steps differ from process to process.

Not all the steps in the above process template occur all the time. It is entirely possible that the process stops with the informal step itself (i.e., an Order might never be created). For example, a Sales Inquiry might never be converted into a Sales Order and a Purchase Requisition might not be converted into a Purchase Order.

The informal step is not mandatory. For example, it is possible for the Lead-to-Cash process to start with the creation of a Sales Order directly and for the Purchasing process to begin with the creation of a Purchase Order.

We now provide a thumbnail description of each of the above processes. Be sure to see the common-sense nature of these processes and to memorize the steps and the documents in each one. That will significantly ease the process for you of integrating more intricate details in later chapters.

Figure 1.3 shows the steps in the Source-to-Pay business process (purchasing) and re-emphasizes their mapping to our generic process template.

The Purchasing or Source-to-Pay business process starts with some department requesting the purchasing department to buy some materials. The department needing the materials does this by creating a Purchase Requisition. Assuming this requisition progresses further, the purchasing department might create a Purchase Order and send it to a vendor. You will see the details of vendor selection as well as other options for initiating the purchasing process in the corresponding course unit.

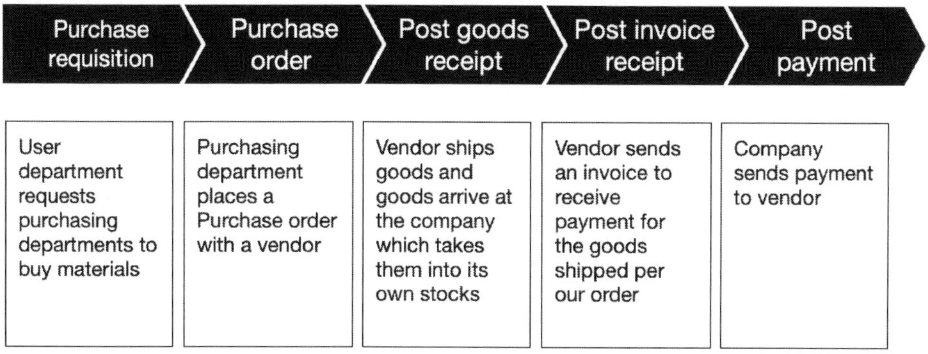

Figure 1.3: Outline of the Source-to-Pay Process

After receiving the Purchase Order, the vendor eventually ships the ordered materials, and these materials show up at our company's warehouse. Thus far, the materials do not belong to our company, and we execute the step of Posting a Goods Receipt to formally receive the goods into our possession. Naturally this increases our stock of the materials received. We might often have additional steps(e.g., like quality inspection) before we take in the goods. We again see the term, "post" which is an indication this step will integrate with accounting. We will cover these aspects later in the book.

The vendor will then send an invoice for the materials shipped and the company will Post an Invoice Receipt. This step covers the process of verifying the invoice. After all we have to make sure that the invoice is for materials that we have actually ordered and received, as well as creating a Payable to the vendor. Again, we have another accounting impact.

Finally, our company sends out a payment by posting the payment to the vendor, completing the process and clearing the payable in Financial Accounting.

Figure 1.4 briefly describes the steps in the Manufacturing business process.

The Manufacturing business process begins with the creation of a Planned Order; just a plan and not yet anything that causes any action. Planned Orders can be created manually but are usually automatically generated by the material requirements planning (MRP) process.

Once the company decides to go ahead and execute the Planned Order, it creates a Production Order that authorizes actual manufacturing work.

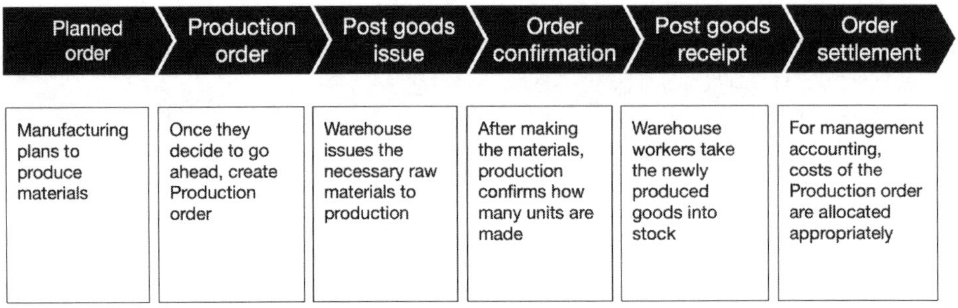

Figure 1.4: Outline of the Manufacturing Process

In SAP, the term "release" has a special connotation from a cost accounting viewpoint. From the viewpoint of production, a company would clearly be interested in tracking production costs. Let us suppose that a company has created a Production Order to produce 1000 units of some material. The company will surely want to track the production cost for this batch of 1000 units. The company should therefore accurately track all costs that go into this Production Order. In SAP, so-called Cost Objects can accumulate costs. To do this, whenever we record an expense, we can indicate the Cost Object to which the expense applies.

To facilitate this tracking, once the Production Order is released, SAP treats it as a Cost Object. This applies not just to Production Orders, but to all other orders for which we want to track costs. To do this, these orders are released, and it is now that the orders become cost objects. They are called Order-Related Cost Objects (discussed in greater detail in the Management Accounting chapter).

Once the Production Order is released, and not before that, the manufacturing department can go ahead and issue the materials needed for the Production Order via the step, Post Goods Issue. By now, you should immediately be recognizing this step as having an accounting impact.

As production progresses, the manufacturing department confirms the number of units of the materials produced. Why would they need to do this. Did they not start out to make a specific quantity of the material anyway? Well, actual production could come out quite different from what was intended. This could be because of quality or productivity issues. For management accounting, the company will need to know the exact quantity produced. This would be needed for computing the unit cost of manufacturing, and for other purposes.

In SAP, you will come across the term confirmation in a few different contexts. In manufacturing it denotes the completion of manufacture of some materials. In general, it confirms that some activity that was started has been completed and often causes other dependent activities to start.

Once manufacturing has produced the goods, the resulting materials must go into our company's stock. Let us suppose our company had 200 tables in stock and manufacturing just completed making 50 more, we need to take those new tables into stock by executing the Post Goods Receipt step. Yes, that is correct. There will again be an accounting impact.

Although this seems to complete the manufacturing process, the process is not complete until the corresponding management accounting steps are complete. In the process of manufacturing some materials, the company has incurred some costs and these costs must be allocated to the appropriate entities in the company. That whole process is called Order Settlement. You will also encounter the term Settlement quite a bit in SAP and it represents the step of bringing the balance of costs in an order to zero by transferring those costs to one or more entities responsible.

Figure 1.5 briefly describes the steps in the Warehouse logistics process. Notice, there are no "postings" which occur in a simple warehouse transaction and this figure needs no further elaboration. However, later in this book we will address Extended Warehouse Management where things differ considerably.

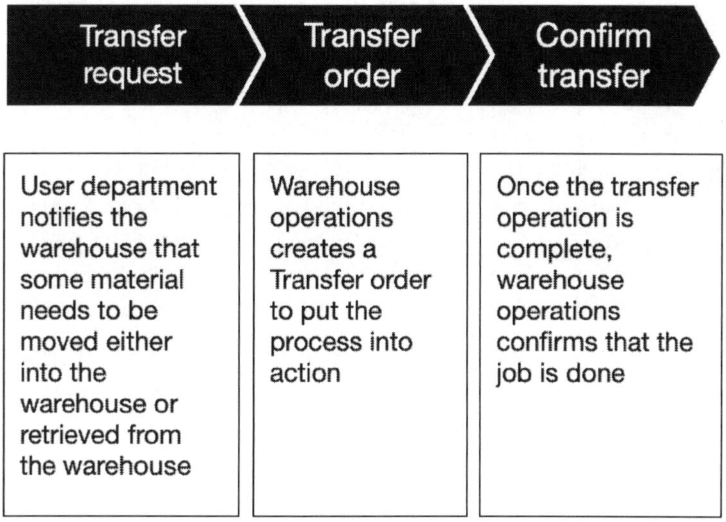

Figure 1.5: Outline of the Warehouse Business Process

Figure 1.6 describes the steps in the Plant Maintenance process (Enterprise Asset Management). You will notice much similarity between this process and the Manufacturing business process as both processes are managed with the use of an Order-related Cost Object.

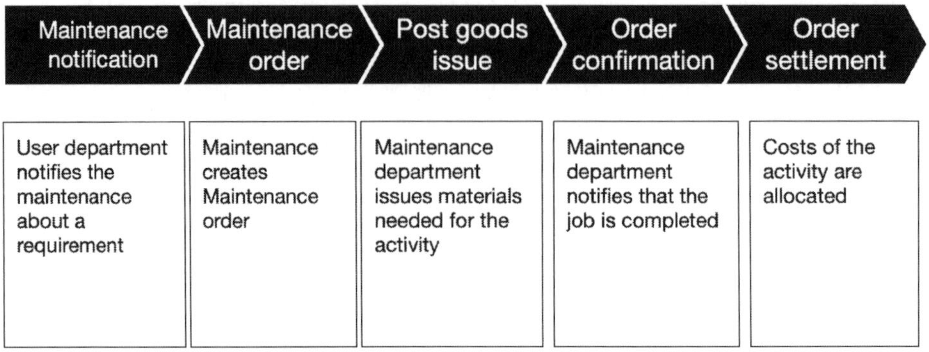

Figure 1.6: Plant Maintenance or Enterprise Asset Management Business Process

Organization Levels in SAP (Enterprise Structure)

You already know that SAP is a packaged solution that is intended to meet the needs of many different organizations. Each organization adopts a structure to suit its own requirements. For example, one organization might divide its sales function in one way and another one might do it differently.

However, a packaged solution like SAP cannot possibly reflect the thousands of variations on how organizations could be structured. The SAP ERP system has its own structure. Mapping the structure of a user organization to those in the SAP system forms a key part of configuration.

SAP calls this concept the Enterprise Structure and the basic components of these structures as Organization Levels – do not confuse this with the common use of the term to represent levels in an organization's managerial reporting structure. Consider SAP Organizational Levels as a means for organizing data in the enterprise system that support the various business processes

To properly understand SAP, you need to master the concept of the Enterprise Structure and how the various Organization Levels are assigned to ensure data integrity and integration.

In SAP, a Client represents a conglomerate company (i.e., a company that has several subsidiary companies within it). Ideally, it represents the entire enterprise. Take for example, the pharmaceutical giant Johnson and Johnson (J&J). Although J&J is a company in the legal sense of the term, internally it has several companies as legal entities, and it is thus a conglomerate consisting of many companies.

Consider Google or Microsoft. These companies have their foreign subsidiaries (e.g., Google UK, Google China, Google India, etc.), with each of these being legal entities in their own right, registered in the respective countries.

Most large companies are conglomerates made up of other companies (legal entities). SAP uses the term Client to represent such a conglomerate entity. In SAP, Client is the highest organizational level. In this sense, the Client organizational level contains all the data in an enterprise. The SAP use of the term Client as an organizational level has no relationship to our normal use of the term.

SAP calls the individual companies that exist within a Client as Company Codes. Each company code is a separate legal entity. In general terms, wherever a separate set of financial records is required by law, it is represented with a Company Code (CoCd). At a minimum, each country in which an enterprise operates, will need a separate CoCd because each country will have its own legal financial reporting requirements.

A company code is the smallest SAP entity to support a full set of books – or legal financial records. We will discuss this further in a later chapter. Figure 1.7 illustrates these ideas.

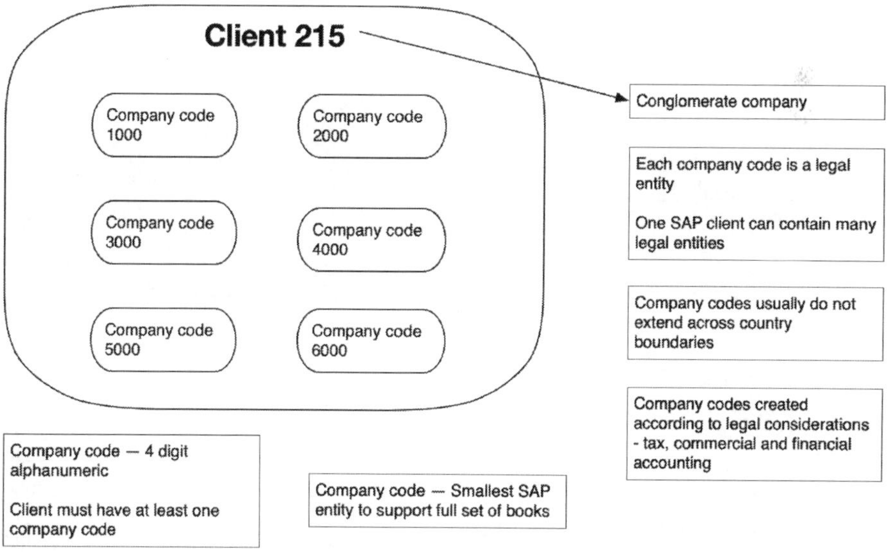

Figure 1.7: Client and Company Codes in SAP

Company Codes represent legal entities from the viewpoint of statutory reporting requirements and other legal considerations. Thus, each company code has a Chart of Accounts and a General Ledger and can generate financial statements like the Balance Sheet and Income Statement.

Consider a conglomerate called ERPI with eight company codes as Figure 1.8 shows. Each company code of conglomerate ERPI operates in one or more of the following market segments: Automotive, Pharmaceutical, Consumer Electronics and Medical Electronics.

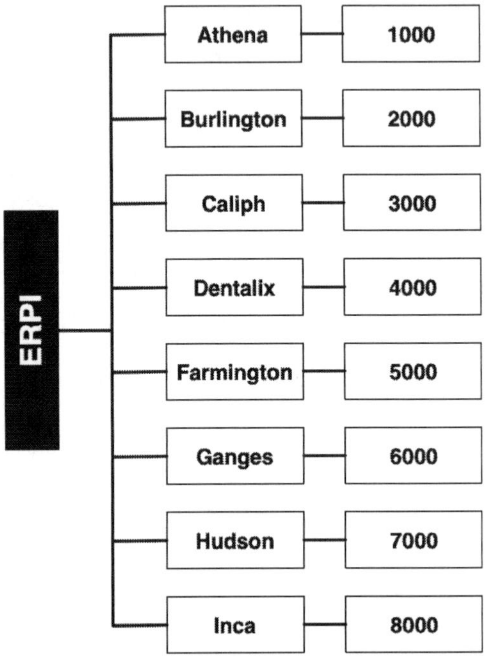

Figure 1.8: ERPI - A Conglomerate With Eight Company Codes

Furthermore, large companies who do business in multiple countries often need to track the financial information for each of these segments. Since the company would create a company code for each of the countries in which it operates, there may be additional legal requirements to generate financial reports for each of these Business Segments. Using our ERPI example, Figure 1.9 shows how these Business Segments can span across one or several company codes. As an example, notice the Medical Electronics business segment spans across every company code, while the Automotive Business Segment spans across all but company codes 1000 and 8000. Should company code 2000 (Burlington) require segment reporting, ERPI would be required to generate separate financial statements for each of the four business segments.

		Business Segments			
		Atutomotive	Pharmaceutical	Consumer electronics	Medical electronics
Company codes	1000	☐	☒	☒	☒
	2000	☒	☒	☒	☒
	3000	☒	☒	☐	☒
	4000	☒	☐	☒	☒
	5000	☒	☐	☒	☒
	6000	☒	☐	☐	☒
	7000	☒	☒	☒	☒
	8000	☐	☐	☒	☒

Figure 1.9: ERPI - Four Business Segments Across Eight Company Codes

Each company code has individual financial reporting capabilities. However, companies may often need to generate financial statements for each business segment that spans across several company codes. To facilitate such a need, SAP makes use of business segments to support this process. If ERPI were to generate a set of financial statements for its overall Automotive business segment, it would include the relevant financial information from company codes 2000, 3000, 4000, 5000, 6000, and 7000. Likewise, the company could also generate financial information specific to one company code and one business segment. There is a great deal of flexibility for reporting using Business Segments. Some of this flexibility is possible by implementing the Group Ledgers and the Ledger Solution in SAP S/4HANA. Group Ledgers allow for consolidating financial information into a single ledger. While the Ledger Solution supports parallel accounting by taking advantage of multiple ledgers to satisfy various accounting standards. More on this later in this book.

In a conglomerate scenario, different company codes often share certain activities for efficiency. For example, ERPI could perform centralized purchasing for some company codes that use the same material. In such situations, the costs of shared activities need to be divided properly across the company codes that use these activities. Once again, we see the need to cut across company codes.

SAP uses the organization level called Controlling Area to facilitate management accounting across company codes. Only those companies belonging to the same Controlling Area can participate in cost sharing. We will see this in greater detail in the chapter on Management Accounting.

Figure 1.10 shows an example of controlling areas and their mapping to company codes.

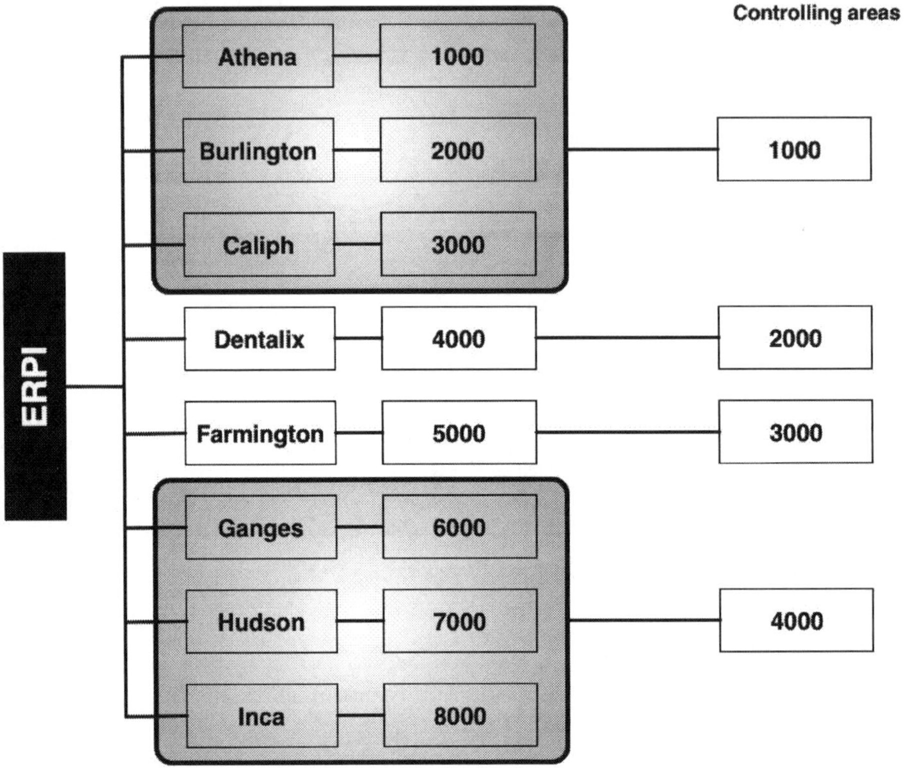

Figure 1.10: ERPI - Controlling Areas and their Mapping to Company Codes

SAP uses four-digit characters to represent company codes as well as controlling areas. Thus, a company code and a controlling area could have the same number. Do not let this confuse you. For example, company code 1000 is completely different from controlling area 1000.

Company codes 1000, 2000 and 3000 all belong to the controlling area 1000 and thus they can share some costs.

Likewise, company codes 6000, 7000 and 8000 all fall under controlling area 4000 and can share costs. Each of the company codes 4000 and 5000 has its own controlling area and therefore cannot share costs with any other company codes.

Chapter 2: SAP Basics

SAP has been around since 1972 and has undergone significant changes concurrently with the numerous momentous evolutions in hardware and software technologies. In this chapter, we cover the important stages in this evolution.

The Evolution of SAP ERP

In 1979 SAP came out with their first ERP software product. At that time, it was known as SAP R/2. The goal and design of this software was to integrate business processes in a single software package and to do so in real-time. The architecture for R/2 was mainframe computing. In the early 1990's, R/2 was succeeded by R/3, in part because the technological architecture transitioned from mainframe to client/server. The year 2004 brought a growing business environment and the introduction of SAP NetWeaver. It also meant another change in architecture. The growing business environment and change in architecture is a common thread in the evolution of SAP ERP. MySAP ERP was not enough to meet the increasing demands of business. Businesses realized the need for software that extended beyond the enterprise. Additional applications such as CRM (Customer Relationship Management), SCM (Supply Chain Management), SRM (Supplier Relationship Management), and PLM (Product Lifecycle Management) were included alongside SAP ERP. This suite of applications was called the SAP Business Suite. In 2004, SAP NetWeaver was introduced as an integration and application platform to support the SAP Business Suite as well as previous SAP products, and non-SAP products. The new technological architecture for MySAP ERP and its successor

(ECC) was Service-Oriented Architecture (SOA). Figure 2.1 shows the evolution of SAP ERP.

Figure 2.1: Evolution of SAP ERP

In the late 2000's, convergence of various technologies – multi-core processors, large affordable memory capabilities, cloud computing, optimized cache – and critical mass (i.e., use of new technologies to create big data, social media, mobile users, Internet of Things, cloud usage) led to innovative advancements at SAP (Figure 2.2 and Figure 2.3). Initially, SAP introduced HANA as a database which was SAP's first advancement in hardware. But the introduction of HANA alone wasn't enough to meet the growing demands of business. SAP began to leverage the capabilities of SAP HANA and soon developed SAP S/4HANA. (Note: SAP HANA as an ERP database was first available to SAP ECC 6.07)

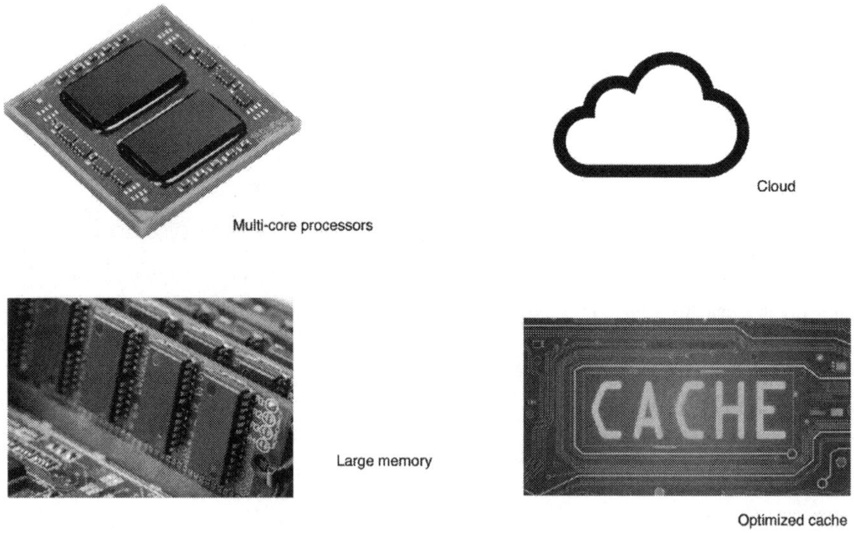

Figure 2.2: Convergence of Technologies

Changes in technologies resulting from SAP HANA led SAP to even more innovation. SAP ERP and the traditional SAP Business Suite were redesigned to leverage all the capabilities of SAP HANA. As noted above, prior to S/4HANA the SAP Business Suite included CRM, SRM. SCM, and PLM. These made up a suite of applications which were essentially add-on applications to SAP ERP. With the introduction of SAP S/4HANA, these applications are now co-deployed with ERP and are natively embedded in SAP S/4HANA. What was traditionally referred to as ERP, is now called “Enterprise Management” in SAP S/4HANA. All the applications available in SAP S/4HANA have been rebranded to some degree as “Line of Business” (LOB) applications.

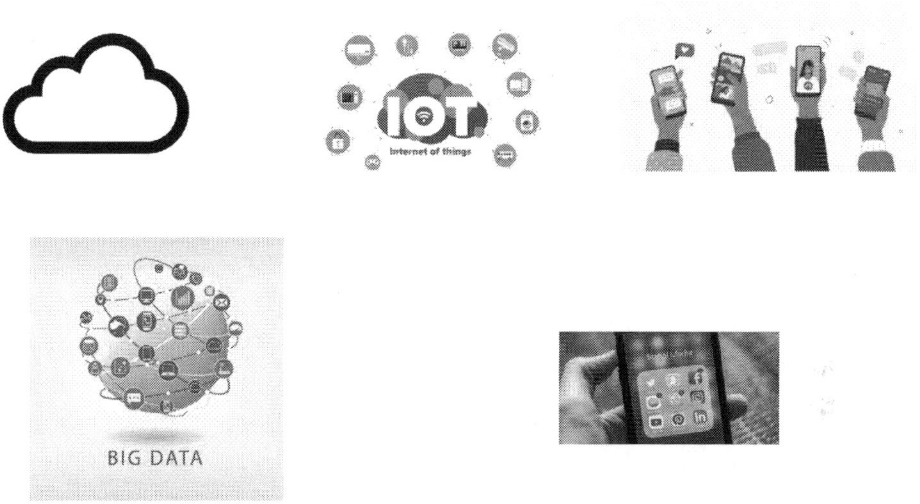

Figure 2.3: Critical Mass

With the advent of Digital Transformation, business continued to seek ways to automate transactions and reduce manual paper trail for end-to-end processes. SAP has led the way regarding Digital Transformation and leveraged it to create what they call the Digital Core. The Digital Core includes SAP S/4HANA as a means for managing business processes through digitization while serving as a foundation for integrating with cloud solutions and Intelligent Technologies such as Artificial Intelligence (AI), Robotic Process Automation (RPA), and Machine Learning (ML). All of this is made possible because SAP S/4HANA runs on the SAP HANA database.

The Intelligent Enterprise

Digital Transformation paved a path to the Intelligent Enterprise. In short, the Intelligent Enterprise brings together Intelligent Technologies, Intelligent Processes, Collaborative Networks, Cloud capabilities, and a Technology Platform that supports innovation. One example of SAP Intelligent Technologies is SAP Fieldglass (Figure 2.4). SAP Fieldglass is a cloud-based solution which supports vendor and contract management. Another Intelligent Technology is SAP SuccessFactors which is a cloud-based Human Resource solution. And there are others. SAP Concur is a cloud-based travel management solution. SAP Ariba is the collaborative network and will be discussed in more detail in our chapter covering the Procurement Process. For now, know that SAP Ariba is a marketplace for buyers and sellers that provides resources to satisfy sourcing needs during external procurement. Finally, SAP Customer Experience is a cloud-based solution supporting the sales and marketing needs of an enterprise.

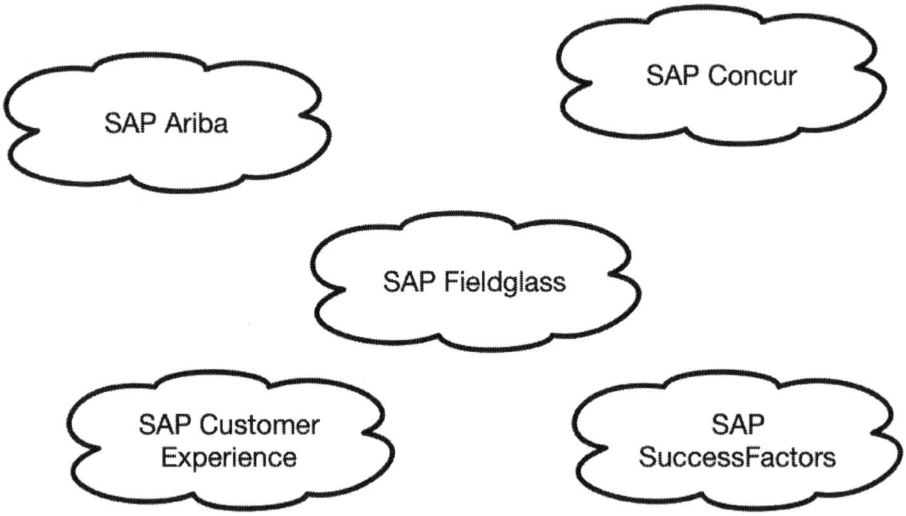

Figure 2.4: Sampling of SAP Cloud Solutions

SAP Business Technology Platform

Supporting business processes in a digitized world requires a technology platform that enables the integration of the end-to-end business processes. Now that we've been introduced to some intelligent technologies, let's address the platform that supports these technologies through innovation, enabling intelligent processes. SAP has developed the SAP Business Technology Platform (BTP) to do exactly this.

Generally speaking, SAP BTP has four areas of functionality (Figure 2.5):

- DevApps
- Integrations: includes standard Application Programming Interfaces (API's) that allow integration of SAP Cloud solutions as well as the integration of non-SAP solutions with SAP S/4HANA).
- Data and Analytics: ensures data integrity and a single source of truth across the organization).

- Artificial Intelligence: includes Machine Learning, Robotic Process Automation, Internet of Things, and AI).

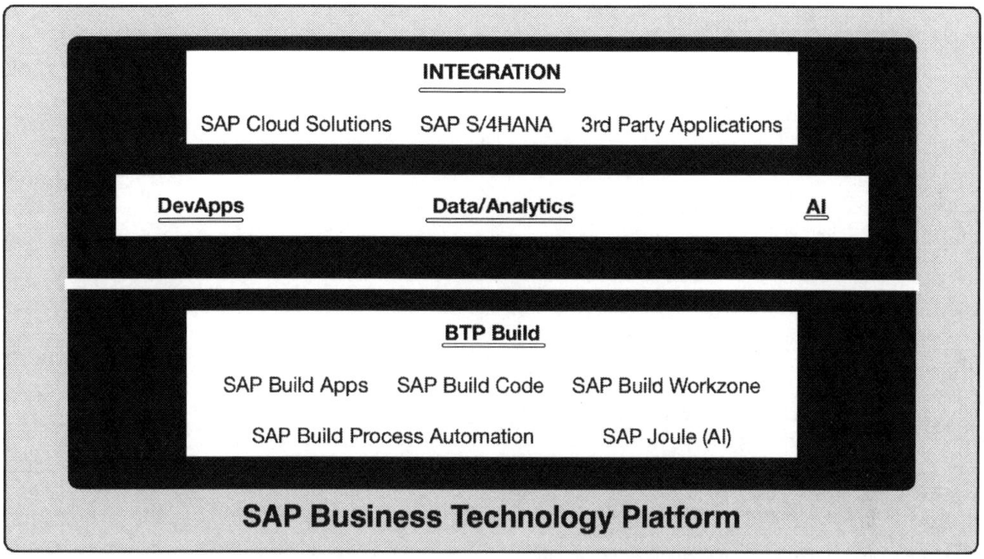

Figure 2.5: SAP Business Technology Platform

In addition, SAP BTP includes SAP Build. SAP Build has several components (Figure 2.5):

- SAP Build Apps An application development tool supporting low-code/no-code app development.
- SAP Build Code: a more advanced set of coding tools designed for developers).
- SAP Build Workzone: an ability for users to develop personalized websites to meet their specific needs.
- SAP Build Process Automation: provides technologies to automate repetitive tasks associated with several business processes.
- SAP Joule: SAP's artificial intelligence assistance tool

Intelligent Processes

Below is a list of Intelligent Enterprise business processes. These have been rebranded because they encompass more than the traditional processes whose transactions were typically managed only by ERP. With the emergence of intelligent technologies in the Intelligent Enterprise, the processes can be decomposed into steps that can be managed using a myriad of technologies and cloud solutions and are no longer restricted to being managed solely in ERP. Here are some examples of intelligent processes.

- Lead-to-Cash (Sales Order Fulfillment)
- Source-to-Pay (Purchasing)
- Record-to-Report (Financials)
- Recruit-to-Retire (Human Resources)
- Design-to-Operate (Manufacturing)
- Request-to-Service (Maintenance and Customer Service)

SAP S/4HANA Characteristics

As noted earlier, the Digital Core is made possible because SAP S/4HANA resides on the SAP HANA database. The in-memory capability of SAP HANA has the advantage of processing data many times faster than a traditional hard-disc database. As a result, SAP S/4HANA is much faster than prior SAP products. This increase in speed is not linear, it's exponential. SAP estimates that reporting and analytics in SAP S/4HANA is up to 1800 times faster than before. Another major advantage of using SAP HANA is the coming together of separate Online Transaction Processing (OLTP) and Online Analytical Processing (OLAP) databases into a single database (Figure 2.6). This, along with simplifications in the data model (to be discussed a little later) leads to a massive decrease in data footprint.

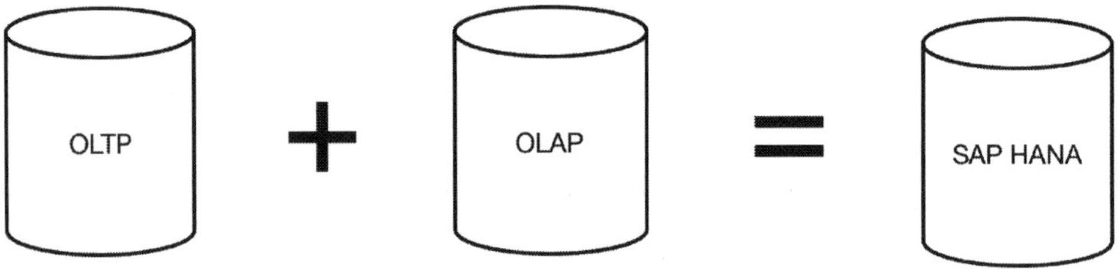

Figure 2.6: Coming Together of OLTP and OLAP

Additional benefits of using SAP S/4HANA include:

- Higher throughput
- Less process steps
- Unlimited workload capacity

- SAP HANA multi-tenancy
- New User Experience (SAP Fiori)
- Choice of deployment (on-premise, cloud, hybrid)

Deployment Options

SAP S/4HANA offers several options for deployment (Figure 2.7). SAP customers can run SAP S/4HANA on-premise. This means SAP customers are not only managing the data but managing the entire infrastructure of their SAP S/4HANA solution. Though this book does not get into recommended deployment, we will discuss differences between the deployment options and why an SAP customer may opt for one over another. As an example, an on-premise deployment is not considered suitable for small to medium size businesses as the costs are generally higher. As discussed in the opening chapter of this book, many larger-sized SAP customers are opting for the on-premise deployment to retain control over their data and the infrastructure.

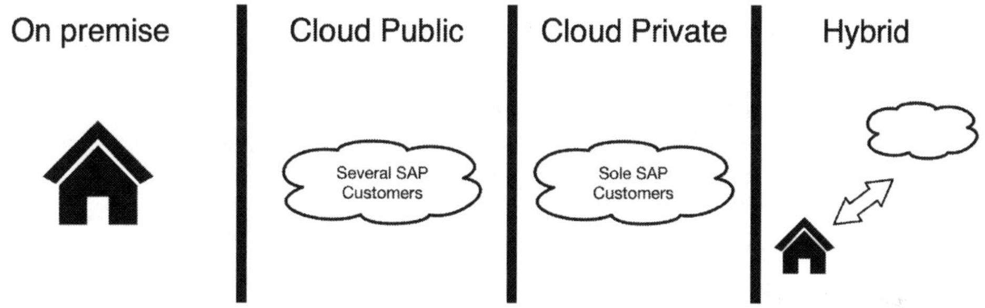

Figure 2.7: SAP S/4HANA Deployment Options

SAP S/4HANA can also be deployed in the cloud, SAP S/4HANA Cloud. Customers who deploy SAP S/4HANA in the cloud still manage and own the data in the cloud, but don't have the worries of managing and owning the infrastructure. There are essentially two options for cloud deployment: Cloud-public and cloud-private. In a cloud-public scenario, SAP customers are sharing space in the cloud with others. Their data is maintained separately, but they share the infrastructure with other SAP customers. In cloud-private, SAP customers manage and own the data, do not share space with other SAP customers, but also do not manage nor own the infrastructure.

Cloud deployment was previously addressed in the opening chapter of this book as well. Keep in mind, cloud deployment involves sourcing the infrastructure through hyperscalers, such as Microsoft Azure, Amazon Web Services, Google Cloud and

Alibaba Cloud. SAP customers who opt for cloud deployment are subject to bi-annual releases of updates to the SAP S/4HANA software. These updates are pushed to SAP customers who have thirty days to complete testing of these updates to ensure their business processes and data are not affected. This can be demanding for larger organizations who may require customizations of their SAP S/4HANA system. Small to medium-sized organizations are encouraged to avoid customizations to the software, leaving them with a "Clean Core" which helps to ensure that update releases have no negative impact on their business processes and data.

Additionally, SAP offers two additional options for organizations seeking to implement SAP S/4HANA in the cloud. They are SAP RISE (or RISE with SAP) and SAP GROW (or GROW with SAP). These two options are intended for different audiences, but both provide organizations with accelerators to ease implementing their SAP S4/HANA solution in the cloud. Though we won't go into detail, SAP RISE is generally described as more adaptable and intended for larger organizations who may be current SAP customers. SAP GROW is generally intended for net new customers who are medium-sized organizations whose business processes are mostly standardized.

Finally, SAP customers can opt for a hybrid deployment option. In this scenario, the SAP customer keeps some data on-premise, while the rest is maintained in the cloud. SAP RISE also supports hybrid scenarios.

S/4HANA Simplified Data Model

To make SAP S/4HANA successful, SAP not only re-branded their applications, they changed the entire data model. To accomplish this, SAP looked at their existing data model, which they found to be quite complex. Perhaps the first generation of a simplified data model for SAP HANA was SAP Simple Finance (S/4HANA Finance). In S/4HANA Finance, the data model needed to be redesigned to leverage the benefits of running on the SAP HANA database. As we discussed in Chapter 1, many SAP transactions will have various impacts, especially from an accounting perspective. Often these impacts are on Financial Accounting (FI). But they are not limited to FI. Many postings in FI will also impact Management Accounting (CO). There are also many situations where there will be impacts in CO, but not FI. Profitability, material valuation, and assets can also be impacted from an accounting perspective. In traditional SAP ERP products, the data created from these impacts were maintained in separate tables in the SAP system.

To simplify the data model, SAP developed the Universal Journal (ACDOCA table). We will discuss this in more detail in the next chapter, but Figure 2.8 demonstrates how various accounting impacts are now stored in a single table (Universal Journal).

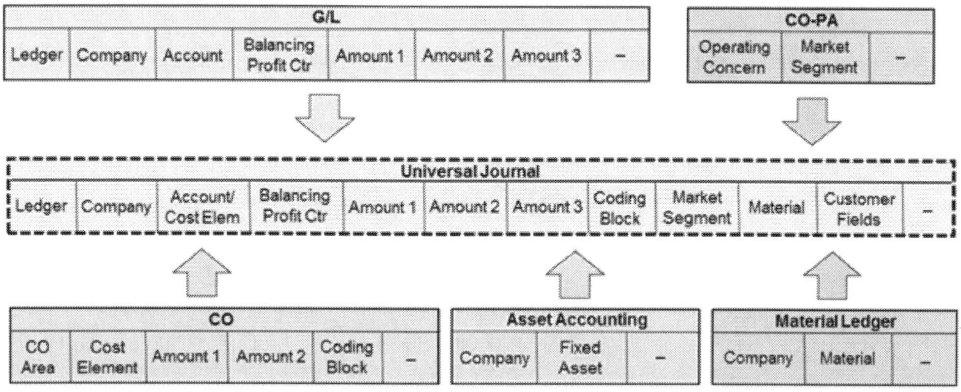

Figure 2.8: Universal Journal[1]

Another example of the simplified data model in SAP S/4HANA can be found by looking at how SAP traditionally managed master data for vendors and customers. Traditionally, this data was stored in two separate master data records. There was a record for the vendor and a separate record for the customer. Using the simplified approach, SAP realized that certain types of data stored for vendors and customers were maintained similarly. Figure 2.9 shows two separate records (one each for vendor and customer), however you can see that general and accounting data need to be maintained for both. The only data that was truly unique, was the data relevant for purchasing (vendor) or sales (customer).

This new simplified approach led to a new way to maintain vendors and customers using the Business Partner approach. Whereby a business partner may be a vendor, customer, or both. The Business Partner approach is not unique to SAP S/4HANA. It was also available in SAP ECC but required that SAP customers activate the Customer/Vendor Integration (CVI) functionality. This is a critical piece of information as the Business Partner approach is mandatory in SAP S/4HANA. As customers begin migrating from their ECC systems to SAP S/4HANA, they need to ensure the CVI functionality is activated in ECC.

---

[1] Image source: *https://blogs.sap.com/2017/04/21/moving-to-the-universal-journal-how-does-the-new-gl-fit-in/*

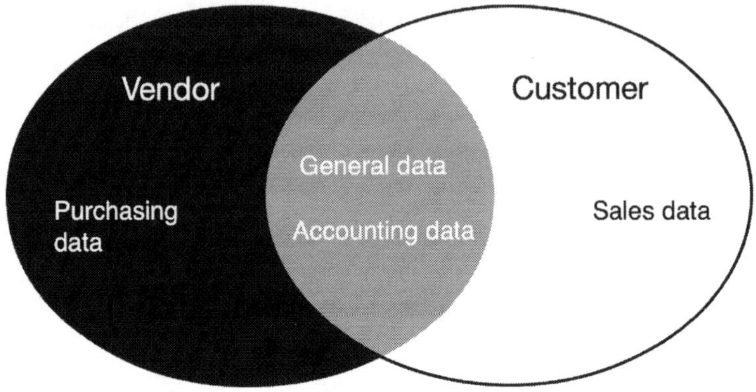

Figure 2.9: Commonalities Between Customer and Vendor Masters

To further demonstrate the Business Partner approach, Figure 2.10 shows how a single business partner record can now be created to manage all types of data, dependent on the role of the business partner. As you can see in the example, Business Partners are managed in roles. The roles define the data that must be maintained. Because the Business Partner is maintained in roles, it's possible to maintain different data dependent on the role. For instance, if the Business Partner is both a vendor and a customer, different address and contact information can be maintained for each.This simplified data model is not exclusive to vendors and customers. It is a common thread used to create a simpler and more unified data model throughout the entirety of SAP S/4HANA and was instrumental in establishing a Digital Core containing the Enterprise Management (ERP) application as well as the new Line of Business applications (SCM, CRM, etc.).

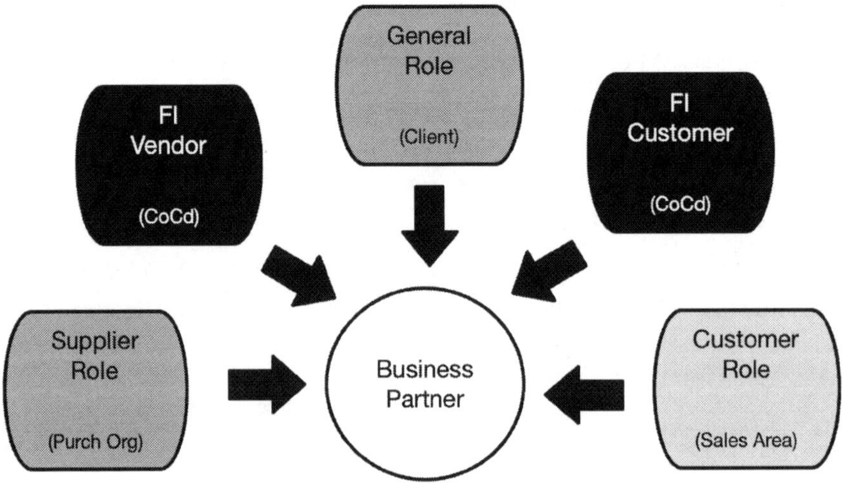

Figure 2.10: Simplified Business Partner Data Model

Data in SAP S/4 HANA and the Intelligent Enterprise

As we briefly discussed in the Introduction, data takes on several forms in SAP S/4HANA. The three types of data are listed below:

- Organizational Levels (Enterprise Structure)
- Master Data
- Transactional Data

Organizational Levels (or Enterprise Structure), often referred to as configuration data represents how data is organized and stored according to business functions. As an example, data that applies across the entire enterprise is stored at the Client organizational level, while data associated with a legal entity from a financial accounting view is called a Company Code. Operational data is stored at the Plant organizational level and inventory data is maintained at the Storage Location organizational level. Examples of some Organizational Levels (Enterprise Structure) was introduced at the end of Chapter 1. Please feel free to review that information again if you feel a need to refresh your memory.

Master Data represents data about entities that are needed to carry out business transactions. We saw some examples of master data earlier in this book when we discussed Materials/Product master data, Bill of Materials, Routings, and Customers and Vendors as Business Partners. It's important to note, because master data is used for managing business processes, aspects of that data are relevant to different organizational levels. As a reminder, while discussing the simplified data model in an earlier section of this chapter, we saw how SAPS4HANA manages vendor and customer master data as Business Partners. As an example, a vendor master record has general data at the Client level, while also storing financial accounting relevant data in the Company Code level and purchasing relevant data at the Purchasing Organization level.

Transactional data is fluid data that is created every time a business transaction occurs in the SAP S/4HANA system. Examples of transactions include creating a purchase order, posting a goods receipt or a goods issue, creating a sales order, or creating a transfer order in the warehouse. As discussed earlier, transactions are typically formal steps within a business process.

Every transaction in the SAP S4/HANA system will require both master data and organizational levels from the Enterprise Structure to successfully process. The system will also generate an electronic document in each module that is impacted by that transaction. An example of how this works was also addressed in Chapter 1, but at a much higher level. We may now have a clearer picture as to how all of this comes together

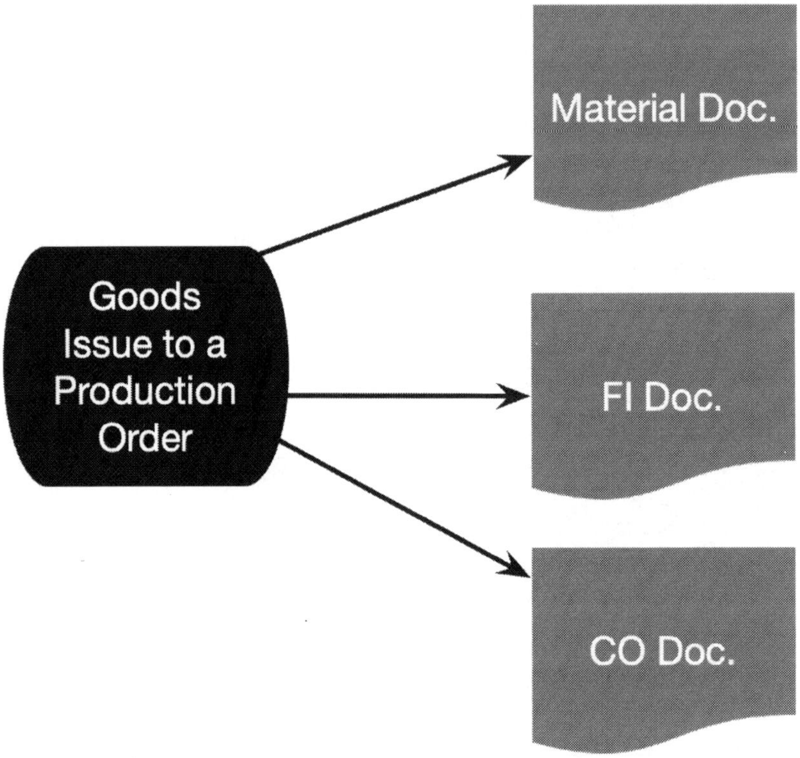

Figure 2.11: Documents for a Goods Issue to a Production Order

In Chapter 1, we described the production process in which one of the steps in that process was a goods issue (transaction) of raw materials to the production order so the work centers could begin assembly. The goods issue transaction for production has several impacts in the SAP S/4HANA system, and an electronic document will be generated for each of these impacts (Figure 2.11). The goods issue is an inventory management transaction initiated in the Materials Management module in SAP S/4HANA. Therefore, the system will create an electronic document within Materials Management that tracks that goods issue describing how many materials were issued, from which storage location(s) and to which production order they were issued. Additionally, we already learned that this goods issue will result in a reduction of the value of those materials in our balance sheet as well as an expense posting in the general ledger because the materials issued are now going to be consumed (used). Therefore, the system will create an electronic document in Financial Accounting to track the legal aspect of this transaction from a financial standpoint. Finally, the production order itself is a cost object. When the expense is posted in Financial Accounting, management will need to track the associated costs within management accounting (Controlling). Again, the SAP S/4HANA system will also generate an electronic document inside the Controlling module to record the cost impact this transaction had on the production order within management accounting.

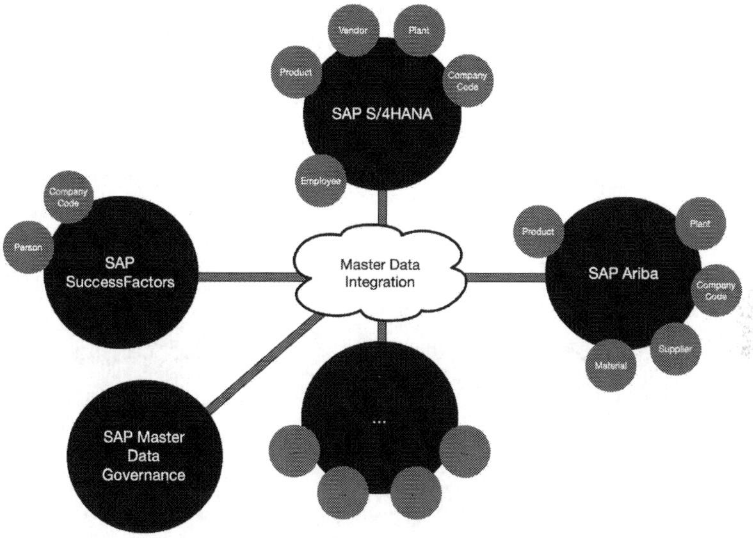

Figure 2.12: SAP Master Data Integration

Why is it so important that we revisit this? Consider what we know about the Intelligent Enterprise. The Intelligent Enterprise gives us the capability to manage steps (transactions) of a business process using a variety of tools beyond SAPS4HANA. Let's look at the purchasing process (Source-to-Pay) as an example. Much of this process can be managed in SAP S/4HANA, however SAP offers some cloud solutions that integrate with SAP S/4HANA to manage aspects of this same process. For example, if we were sourcing using a contractual arrangement with a vendor, then we may consider using SAP Fieldglass in this process. On the other hand, perhaps we are purchasing airfare or hotel accommodations for one of our sales representatives who was traveling to a trade show. In this case, we could enhance the process using SAP Concur. Additionally, we might be looking to purchase a material and may want to scour a network of suppliers to get the best price. Here, SAP Ariba would be most useful. In any one of these scenarios, the Enterprise Structure, Master Data, and Transactional Data needed to support the process must be integrated across these solutions (Figure 2.12). In other words, we need data harmonization across SAP S/4HANA and each of the SAP cloud solutions because there will be an exchange of data flow between these systems. Therefore, we need to establish connections between these solutions. The more solutions we use, the more complex things get, resulting in more connections required. The SAP Business Technology Platform (BTP) offers integration scenarios to help with these connections. In addition to SAP BTP, SAP offers a tool called, Master Data Integration. This tool is used to harmonize master data across various solutions so that master data can be automatically synched across each solution whenever master data is created or modified. SAP also offers SAP Master Data Governance (supported by SAP BTP) to help centralize master data management. Master Data Integration and Master Data Governance allows for harmonization of data with non-SAP system as well as SAP solutions. In combination, these tools ensure master data integrity throughout your Intelligent Enterprise.

Configuring and Customizing an ERP System

SAP provides a packaged solution that a user organization can adapt to its needs. Organizations differ significantly in their internal structures and operational policies and therefore we cannot expect a packaged solution like SAP to work out of the box for its user organizations. Of course, packaged ERP solution vendors like SAP know that organizations differ in many ways and provide features that allow user organizations to configure the ERP system to meet their requirements. In other words, ERP products ship with built-in functionality for several different ways in which companies do business and a particular company can choose the specific variants it needs.

For example, a user organization might not want all the standard steps that SAP provides in its Sales Order Processing module and might choose to turn off some of the steps. People implementing SAP for a user organization expend considerable effort. The process involves extensive discussions with managers in the user organizations to clearly understand their requirements, and to configure SAP accordingly. Configuration does not involve changing any code in the system or adding new code.

Given how businesses differ significantly, organizations often have specific features or practices that none of the built-in configuration settings can capture. In these cases, user organizations must customize the ERP system by adding new code for their specific functionality. Customization calls for significantly more time, resources and effort than configuration.

Given the challenges of customization, organizations try to avoid it as much as possible. In some situations, organizations may choose to change their business processes to suit how the SAP software operates. Although this might sound like cutting your feet to fit the shoes, the approach might not be all that bad. After all, companies that sell packaged ERP offerings do so after extensive experience with numerous client organizations and often incorporate industry best-practices in their software. In most situations, adapting to their product is likely to be a wise choice.

Of course, organizations also try to gain competitive advantages in key areas by doing things differently and perhaps more efficiently than their competitors. In such situations, blindly adapting what an ERP system has to offer might not be in the best interests of a company. To summarize, companies might choose to customize the system in areas of their core competency where they would like to gain a strategic advantage by doing things differently. In other areas, they might just choose to go along with the features that the product has to offer.

There are additional considerations regarding customizations of an SAP system. SAP follows a "Best Practice" methodology. In other words, SAP has leveraged its years of experience across several industries to define best practices for performing business processes. In some regard, these may be considered "out-of-the-box" business scenarios. However, there are sound reasons for following best practices. First, it reduces and optimally eliminates customizations. Doing so reduces total cost and time of implementing the SAP S/4HANA solution. Secondly, the deployment of SAP S/4HANA has a big impact on the scope of customizations an SAP customer might consider. For SAP customers that implement SAP S/4HANA on-premises (on-prem), this means they manage the entire infrastructure as well as the software and data for their company, which can be a huge expense. The alternative is to implement SAP S/4HANA in the cloud. This is something we addressed earlier. When implementing SAP in the cloud, SAP customers rely on hyperscalers. Hyperscalers are cloud providers and provide SAP customers with an infrastructure that easily enables growth of their company using the cloud. As a reminder, some examples of hyperscalers include, but are not limited to: Microsoft Azure, Amazon Web Services, Google Cloud and Alibaba Cloud. These hyperscalers provide ready-to-use SAP solutions that can be immediately implemented for a business. The deployment of SAP S/4HANA on the cloud is an example of Infrastructure as a Service (Iaas).

Despite the ease of implementation in the cloud, there are advantages of doing an on-prem implementation as well as disadvantages of doing a cloud implementation. As noted earlier, that are still many larger SAP customer who are reluctant to move their data to the cloud. Among the reasons is data security. But a growing concern for larger enterprises is a lack of control over the system. Moving to the cloud requires surrendering control of the infrastructure and SAP software to a third party. This means that the enterprise can feel they are at the mercy of SAP and the hyperscaler when updates to the software are released. The enterprise will have no option but to accept the updates and run extensive and frequent testing to make sure the release doesn't negatively impact their business processes. As a result, an enterprise that engages with a significant level of customization will also likely opt for an on-prem implementation to avoid extensive and frequent testing. Similarly, customers who opt to implement SAP S/4HANA in the cloud, will want to reduce and optimally, eliminate such customizations. SAP uses the term, "Clean Core", which means to follow the "Best Practice" scenarios to minimize, and possibly eliminate customizations so update releases can be easily deployed.

This is only a snapshot of what configuration and customization involves. There is also much more to Clean Core. As technology changes, a Clean Core approach reduces challenges associated with technological advancements, making it easier for SAP customers to implement them.

Implementation of Best Practices

When considering the implementation of SAP S/4HANA, engaging in best practices has more advantages. Customers of SAP have access to SAP for Me (me.sap.com). SAP for Me is a single access point for SAP customers, allowing them access to a multitude of resources to support their implementation and support their continuing maintenance needs of their SAP S/4HANA system. Within SAP for Me, customers have access to SAP ALM (Application Lifecyle Manager) and SAP Signavio Process Navigator. Though we won't get into detail regarding SAP Signavio Process Navigator, we briefly explain here the value of this tool for implementation.

During the implementation of SAP S/4HANA, it's important for SAP customers to scope their project and define the business processes required to manage their business effectively. SAP Signavio Process Navigator is modeled after the SAP ACTIVATE implementation methodology and includes best practice scenarios to help standardize end-to-end business processes. The ACTIVATE methodology for implementation is depicted in Figure 2.13. The methodology Includes six phases: Discover, Prepare, Explore, Realize, Deploy, and Run. For more information on SAP Activate Roadmap Viewer see *https://go.support.sap.com/roadmapviewer/*. This is especially important for customers who opt to deploy their SAP S/4HANA system in the cloud. Keep in mind, standardization and maintaining a clean core are essential for cloud customers.

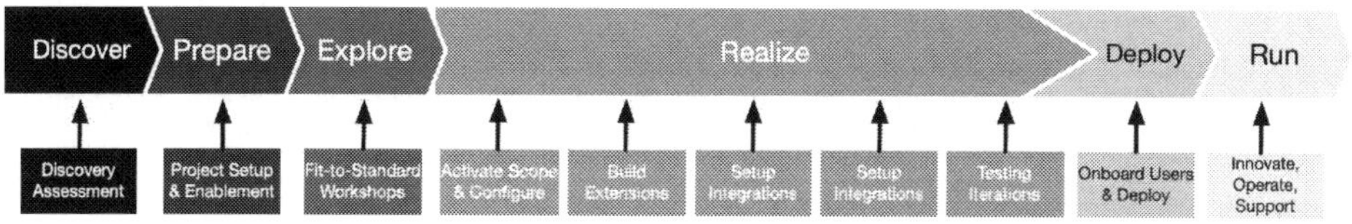

Figure 2.13: Activate Methodology

New User Experience (SAP Fiori UX)

Today's business person is mobile and needs a simpler interface to interact with SAP. With a simplified data model, along comes a simplified user experience, SAP Fiori User Experience (UX). Among the key driving forces behind the development of Fiori was the increase use of mobile devices by end users, management, analysts, and developers. These users don't necessarily interact with the system in the same manner. As a matter of fact, it's most likely they do not.

To support the needs of different users while creating a more simplified experience, SAP altered its way of thinking and redesigned the user experience to one which shifted from a focus on the application/system, to a focus on the role of the user. One of the major advantages of this approach is that the Fiori UX has greatly reduced the navigational pain points as well as the number of clicks necessary to create data, run transactions, and run reports.

Today's users are also composed of a different demographic. We are referring to a demographic who grew up in the age of mobile devices and connectivity. Today's users are accustomed to working with a more contemporary interface. An interface that uses apps which can be downloaded and installed on mobile devices. The main benefit of SAP Fiori is that it will run on any device. It is not exclusive to a desktop or a notebook. Users can work on any device and still use SAP Fiori. The expectation is that the apps serve unique purposes and are streamlined in a manner which makes navigation simpler and the purpose more focused. The design of SAP Fiori takes these measures into account. Users work with apps to perform the necessary transactions required for a unique business purpose. The apps are housed on one screen, which SAP calls the SAP Fiori Launchpad. To simplify navigation, access intelligent technologies from SAP Fiori, and provide for a personalized experience, SAP has introduced the "Spaces Concept" (see Figure 2-14).

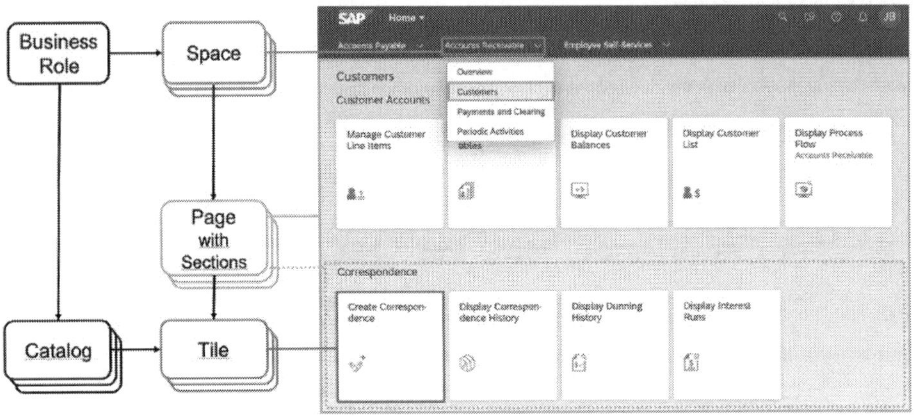

Figure 2.14: An Example of SAP Fiori Launchpad and Spaces[2]

Today's users are also composed of a different demographic. We are referring to a demographic who grew up in the age of mobile devices and connectivity. Today's users are accustomed to working with a more contemporary interface. An interface that uses apps which can be downloaded and installed on mobile devices. The main benefit of SAP Fiori is that it will run on any device. It is not exclusive to a desktop or a notebook. Users can work on any device and still use SAP Fiori. The expectation is that the apps serve unique purposes and are streamlined in a manner which makes navigation simpler and the purpose more focused. The design of SAP Fiori takes these measures into account. Users work with apps to perform the necessary transactions required for a unique business purpose. The apps are housed on one screen, which SAP calls the SAP Fiori Launchpad. To simplify navigation, access intelligent technologies from SAP Fiori, and provide for a personalized experience, SAP has introduced the "Spaces Concept" (see Figure 2-14).

Using the Spaces Concept, Spaces are created for specific user groups to organize how they work. As seen in the example, an accountant in an organization will have their experience organized into different spaces for Accounts Payable, Accounts Receivable, and Employee Self-service. Each of these spaces can then be further divided into Pages. In this example, we see Accounts Receivable space has four Pages, one of which is Customers. The Customers page is further divided into two Sections, Customer Accounts and Correspondence. At the most granular level of the Spaces Concept, users can personalize their Pages by selecting and adding apps into the

[2] Image source: *https://community.sap.com/t5/technology-blogs-by-sap/get-to-know-the-new-spaces-concept-for-sap-fiori-launchpad/bc-p/13457850#:~*

Sections. Using the Spaces Concepts provides 360-degree access to meet the user's needs. It is a personalized approach to enhancing the users' experiences.

There are a few additional things you should know about SAP Fiori. Among them are where to find SAP Fiori Apps. SAP Fiori Apps are publicly available in the SAP Fiori App Library. Anyone can access the App Library at this URL: *https://fioriappslibrary.hana.ondemand.com/sap/fix/externalViewer/#*

Like the design of a physical library, the Apps in the App Library are stored and organized in Catalogs. The Catalogs help organize the Apps based on certain criteria and authorizations. An App may exist in more than one Catalog and users can search for the Apps from within each Catalog. However, not all users have access to all Apps. This makes good business sense as a good practice for companies is to limit access to data, based on a user's level of authorization. This practice is often referred to as Segregation of Duties or Separation of Duties. For a user to be able to use an App, users are assigned Business Roles and their Business Role must be linked to the Catalog where the App resides.

Once users understand this concept, they can then find Apps from the App Library by looking into their assigned Catalogs based on their Business Role. When the user locates the appropriate Catalog, he/she can then access that Catalog from within their profile settings in SAP Fiori and search the Catalog for the desired App. The user can then personalize their experience by selecting the App to add to the SAP Fiori Launchpad using the Spaces Concept discussed above. You can learn more about SAP Fiori by visiting: *https://www.sapfioritrial.com/*.

SAP Fiori Advantages

SAP Fiori provides several advantages for today's user. As noted above, the SAP Fiori Apps are organized on the SAP Fiori Launchpad. The future for the SAP Fiori Launchpad will be based on SAP UI5 technology and will be aligned with the SAP Enterprise Portal and SAP NetWeaver Business Client. This means that the Fiori Launchpad can be run side-by-side with other user interfaces.

Additionally, characteristics of the SAP Fiori experience makes it attractive for current and future SAP users. These characteristics include:

- Role-based
- Delightful
- Coherent

- Simple
- Adaptive

Users

As we discussed above, not all users are the same and thus don't have the same needs when working in SAP S/4HANA. To further simplify things for the user, SAP has grouped users into one of three categories (Figure 2.15). A user can be an Occasional user. This is one who uses the system frequently, but primarily for repetitive tasks. Things such as displaying a purchase order or a business partner master record. They may also be responsible for running simple transactions like creating an invoice in SAP S/4HANA. As such, Occasional users need a simple, easy to use environment with efficient and limited steps. These users are also accustomed to working with a web browser. Because of the ease of navigating a web browser, SAP Fiori is well suited for this type of user.

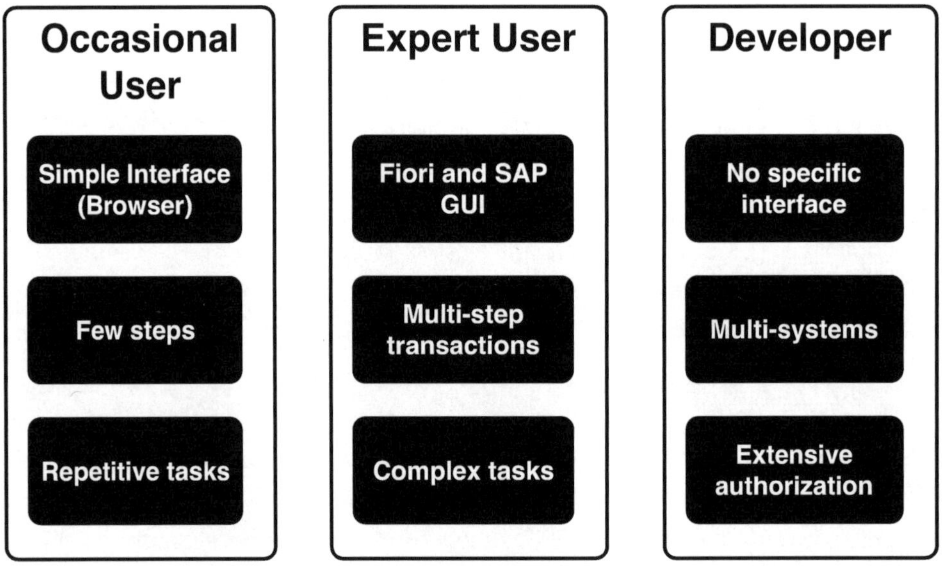

Figure 2.15: User Type in SAP S/4HANA

A second category of user is the Expert user. This type of user may perform some of the tasks which an Occasional user performs but will also engage in more complex tasks, many of them may involve multi-step transactions. Though SAP Fiori does a great job of meeting the needs of the Occasional user, it is not always best suited for the Expert. The Expert user requires access to multiple levels of data because of the added complexity associated with their role. The SAP GUI is still going to be a valid option for this type of user. However, the future may tell a different story as SAP Fiori grows in popularity and functionality.

Finally, the third type of user is the Developer. The Developer may or may not use the SAP GUI. They may use another interface which is more suitable for them. This user is likely to need access to the back-end systems and will need extensive authorization across many systems.

Type of Fiori Apps

Because different users with differing authorizations are going to need access to different Apps, SAP has grouped Apps into three categories. SAP Fiori Apps are either Transactional, Analytical, or Factsheets. It is important to note that ALL Apps will run on SAP HANA. However, Transactional Apps were available prior to SAP HANA. Therefore, Analytical and Factsheets are only available on SAP HANA as seen in Figure 2.16.

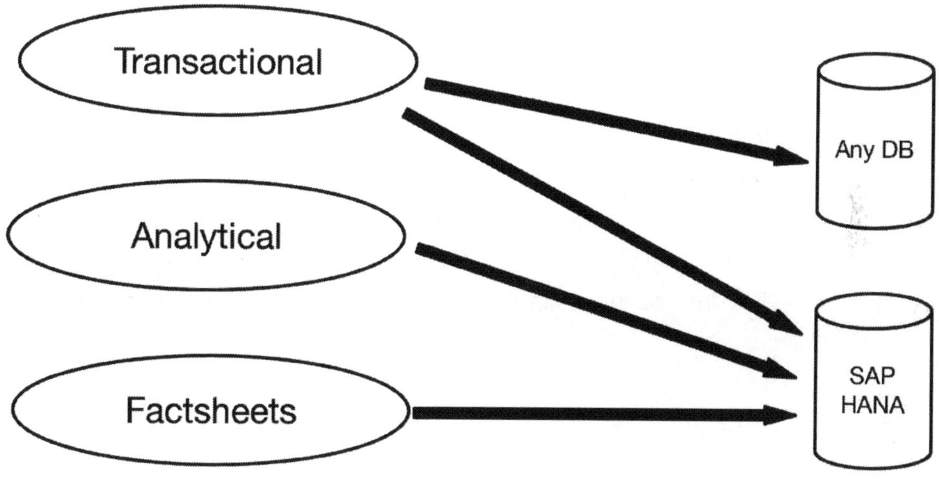

Figure 2.16: SAP Fiori Apps/Database

Figure 2.17 provides more detail on the differences between these three types of Apps in SAP S/4HANA.

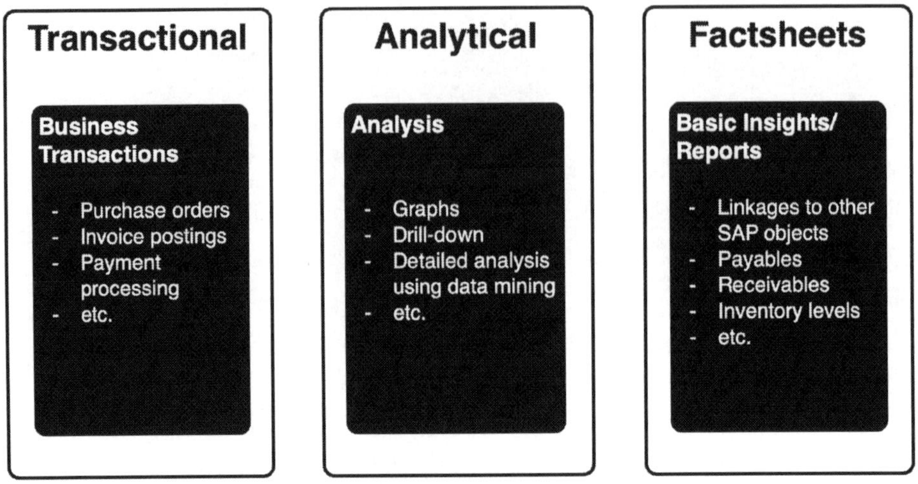

Figure 2.17: Categories of SAP Fiori Apps

SAP Basics Summary

SAP S/4HANA is the next evolution of SAP applications. It brings together the entire SAP Business Suite in a single solution. Inspired by critical mass and convergence of modern technologies, SAP S/4HANA offers SAP customers a variety of deployment options. Based on a foundation of simplicity, SAP has redesigned the data model to offer its customers increased speed, reduction in data footprint, greater throughput and a host of other advantages. Advances in technology and growth of cloud applications has led to a greater demand for integrating SAP S/4HANA with other applications, SAP and non-SAP alike. The SAP Business Technology Platform supports such integrations as well as providing the technological foundation for AI, analytics, app development. With SAP Build, users have the capability of personalizing their experience. With regards to the user experience, SAP has also made SAP Fiori a critical piece of the SAP S/4HANA landscape. SAP Fiori is a new User Experience (UX), designed around the role of the user and not the business function.

Chapter 3: Financial Accounting

The financial accounting function plays a key role in enterprise systems. Much of financial accounting goes on in the background as enterprise systems like SAP S4HANA carry out transactions. Nevertheless, we cannot function effectively in an enterprise system without a full grasp of financial accounting. For this to occur, we must set it up correctly to know which accounts to update at each stage of various business transactions. Setting this up properly requires us to understand basic accounting principles. Without making assumptions that you have a core foundation in financial accounting, we will also take some time to discuss some financial accounting basics.

Introduction

The Financial Accounting process tracks the financial implications of business operations. Examples of business transactions with financial implications include:

- A vendor sends an invoice for products that we ordered
- We send out an invoice to a customer for products that they ordered, and we shipped
- A customer makes a payment against an invoice that we sent out
- We make a payment to a vendor based on an invoice that the vendor sent
- We pay our employees
- A tax payment is coming up

- We collect sales tax from our customers
- We use some material in production
- We receive goods at our warehouse
- A machine depreciates
- Value of land owned by the business appreciates

Businesses carry out numerous such transactions as they execute their operations and need an orderly means of keeping track of their financial implications.

It is imperative to understand the difference between Financial Accounting (FI) and Management Accounting (CO). The above examples provide us with transactions which may impact both FI and CO. However, FI deals primarily with accounting principles which meet legal requirements or specific accounting standards. In a general sense, FI is governed by law and/or accounting standards and there is little flexibility on how business transactions get recorded financially. Table 3.1 provides us with some major differences between FI and CO.

Table 3.1: Financial Accounting versus Management Accounting

Financia Accounting (FI)	Management Accounting (CO)
• Legal accounting • Governed by law and regulations • External audience • Inflexible • Follows accounting standards like USGAAP and IAS • Output: Legal reporting of financial statements - Balance sheet - Income statement - Cash flows	• Internal accounting • Governed internally, not by law • Internal audience • Flexible • Manages costs and revenues • Profitability • Output - Managerial decision making

Organizational Data/Enterprise Structure

In the previous chapter, we discussed SAP S/4HANA basics which included the concept of various types of data in the S/4HANA system, Organizational levels (Enterprise Structure), Master Data, and Transactional Data. As a general rule, our chapters will begin with a brief description of the concepts, followed by a discussion on organizational data. Here, we begin that discussion.

- Client. The client is the highest organizational level in the enterprise. In this sense, the Client organizational level contains all the data in an enterprise.
- Company Code (CoCd). A separate legal entity. This means wherever there is a separate legal reporting requirement, a separate Company Code is required. The General Ledger is maintained in the CoCd.
- Business Segment (Seg). Represents sub-activities of a business for which legal reporting is required.
- Chart of Accounts (CoA). A structured list of all General Ledger Accounts by definition (name, account number, account group, and account type). Chart of Accounts are defined to meet regulatory requirements as well as different accounting standards.

Recall, organizational levels are designed to manage how data is structured in the SAP S/4HANA system. In this chapter we discuss Financial Accounting data. During configuration, enterprises need to review the business requirements (internally and externally) to decide how to define their Enterprise Structure which includes the various organizational levels needed in FI. Though we often view the organizational levels as structured hierarchically, it's more important to view them in terms of how they are related to one another. Configuration consists of two basic steps regarding organizational levels. First, organizational levels are defined, then they are assigned to one another. This assignment is the important step which ensures the data flows correctly between these organizational levels. Figures 1.7-1.10 from Chapter 1 detail the relationships of some of these organizational levels. We will discuss how Charts of Accounts fits into this picture in a bit.

As discussed above, a Chart of Accounts (CoA) is a structured list of all General Ledger Accounts by definition (name, account number, account group, and account type). Chart of Accounts are defined to meet regulatory requirements as well as different accounting standards. Since all financial accounting data flows to the CoCd, it's important to assign a CoCd to a CoA that will satisfy the legal reporting requirements. This assigned CoA is labeled, the Local Chart of Accounts. Local, in this sense means legal reporting specific to that CoCd. As such, the assigned CoA will contain the definitions of the General Ledger (G/L) accounts that satisfy the reporting requirements by law. SAP S/4HANA has many pre-defined CoA in the system to meet the legal requirements of many countries. It is therefore recommended that a CoCd be assigned to the appropriate CoA and to use the pre-defined CoA in the system for this purpose. Figure 3.1 shows an example of assigning Company Codes to Chart of Accounts.

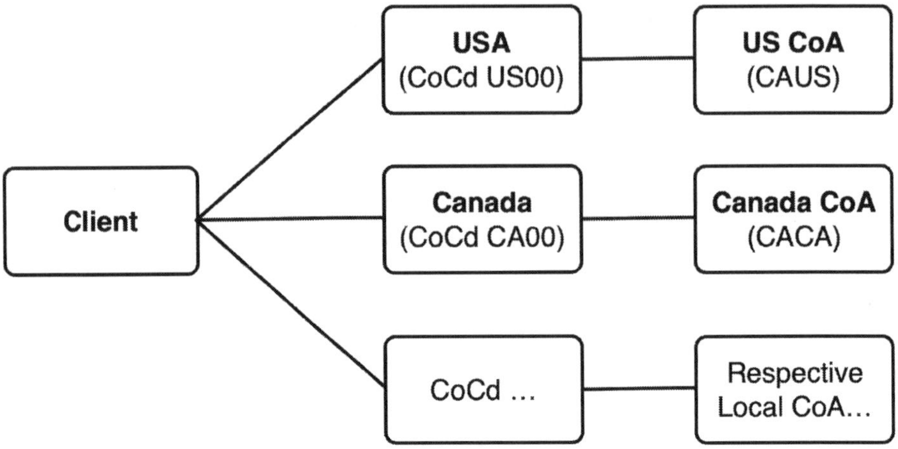

Figure 3.1: Company Code and Local Chart of Account Assignment

Other Charts of Accounts may be necessary. For instance, in the above example it's likely the CEO and other executive officers would like to get a financial picture of the entire enterprise. That is, a single set of financial statements that can be consolidated across all CoCd's. At first glance, this is going to pose a challenge because each CoCd is using a unique CoA. None of them are the same. Therefore, none of the G/L accounts needed to generate a consolidated financial statement for each CoCd are identical to each other and can't simply be added together. In this case, each CoCd may need to use more than one CoA.

Let's take this same example and demonstrate how SAP S/4HANA addresses this challenge. In Figure 3.2, you see the same organizational levels from Figure 3.1 to which we have added some additional CoA organizational levels to support the need to consolidate the financial information from the various general ledgers. First, we have assigned a CoA to the Client. This CoA is called the Leading Ledger (0L). In our example, we have chosen the International Chart of Accounts as the Leading Ledger (INT).

The Leading Ledger (0L) is the CoA used for generating a single consolidated set of financial statements across all company codes. To accomplish this, all CoCd's must also be using the same CoA, that is the INT chart of accounts in our example. In this way, the structure of the G/L in each CoCd will be identical. As you can see, this also means that each CoCd in our example is using more than one CoA. In other words, they are running two G/Ls in parallel. This practice is called Parallel Accounting. By linking the G/L accounts from the Local CoA to corresponding G/L accounts in the INT ledger, both ledgers received updated postings in parallel (simultaneously). The posting from these INT ledgers are then consolidated to the Leading Ledger at the Client level. SAP refers to this as the Ledger Solution. In short, what was described here allows organizations to maintain separate ledgers for different purposes. As a result, a complete set of financial statements can be generated for each of these ledgers. Thus, SAP calls this the Ledger Solution.

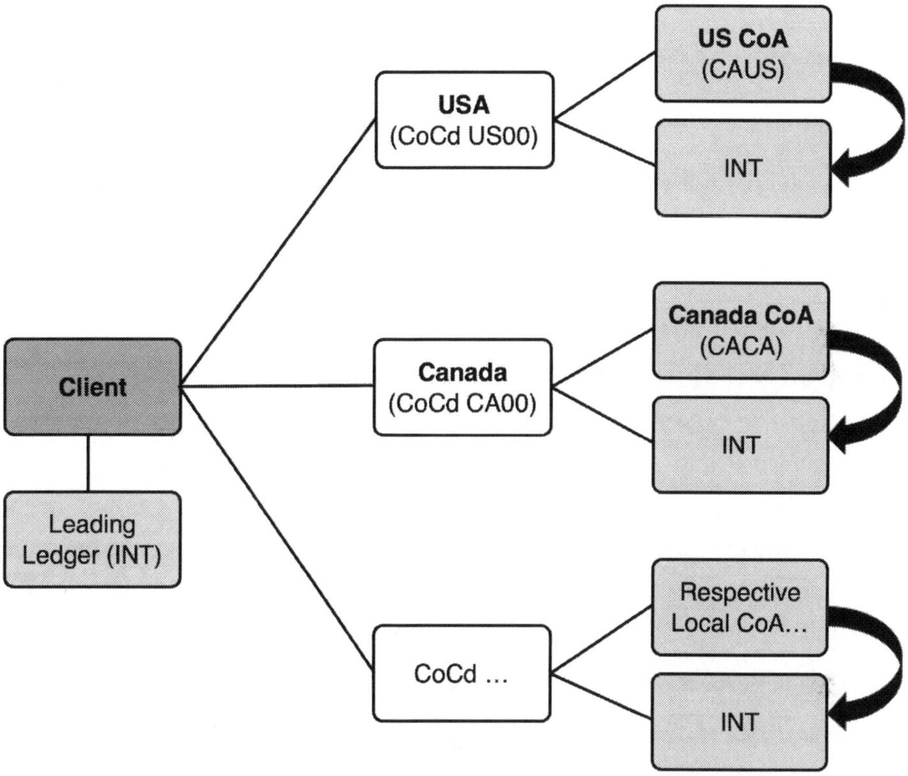

Figure 3.2: Leading Ledger and Parallel Accounting

An Overview of General Ledger Accounting Practices

Again, we don't want to assume every reader has a solid foundation in financial accounting, so we have opted to take a brief moment to showcase some basics in general ledger accounting. It's possible that for many of you, this is unnecessary. However, this will be quite helpful for those who feel they are in need of such insights and it might also serve as a good refresher for others.

The Accounting Equation and the Balance Sheet

At any point in time, a business has things of value or assets – directly as cash, or things it can sell and get cash in exchange. Examples include:

- Cash (direct currency, or money in the bank)
- Land
- Plant and machinery
- Raw materials and finished goods in stock
- Accounts receivable (i.e., money that people owe the business). While this might not appear to have a cash value, it actually does. After all, eventually some or all of the money owed will be paid back. Therefore, accounts receivable can indeed be sold. If you were to sell a business, the buyer of the business would inherit the accounts receivable and hence the rights to receive the payments as and when they are made.
- Investments that are held by the company.

How did the business acquire all these assets? They certainly did not materialize from thin air and the business must have paid money to acquire these assets. Where did the business get the money to buy (or otherwise get) all of these things? The business used the owners' money, and perhaps other borrowings, to fund all these assets. For example, suppose the combined assets of a business are worth $1 million. This might be made up of, for example, cash and bank balances of $ 500,000, material stocks of $ 300,000, accounts receivable of $100,000 and investments worth $100,000. We need to account for how the business obtained assets worth $1 million. That is, how did they fund these assets? Here is one possible scenario:

- The owners started the business with an initial capital of $100,000.
- The company has outstanding bank loans worth $700,00.

- The company has $50,000 worth of raw materials that suppliers have supplied, but the company has yet to pay for (accounts payable).
- Over the years the company has ploughed back profits worth $150,000 into the business (accrued retained earnings).

This accounts for the $1 million in assets. The items: bank loans and accounts payable are called liabilities, and the items: initial capital and accrued retained earnings are together called owners' equity. This exemplifies the basic accounting equation:

Assets = Liabilities + Owners' equity

or, in the current context:

$1m assets = $750,000 liabilities + $250,000 owners' equity

This just reflects the simple fact that whatever the company currently has by way of assets must have been obtained only by using the company's liabilities and owners' equity.

A company's Balance Sheet depicts the basic accounting equation as it applies to the company. However, instead of just showing the assets, liabilities and owners' equity as single numbers, the balance sheet breaks these down further as we show below.

- Various kinds of assets:
  - current assets
  - fixed assets
  - land and buildings
  - raw material inventories
  - finished goods inventories
  - marketable investments
  - accounts receivable
  - ...
- Various kinds of liabilities:
  - short term loans
  - long term loans
  - accounts payable
  - ,,,
- Various kinds of owners' equity:

- preferred stock
- ordinary stock
- retained earnings
- ...

We can also think of the balance sheet as a snapshot of a company at a specific point in time – like a photograph showing the assets, liabilities and owners' equity at that instant. If the company completely stops all its operations and comes to a complete halt (performs no activities that have any financial implications), the snapshot of its assets, liabilities and owners' equity represents its balance sheet. The balance sheet depicts a static view of the company. Of course, things are always happening, and the company seldom comes to a complete halt in all respects. Just like we never come to a complete stop, but people can still take an x-ray image to check on our health. A balance sheet is like an x-ray image to assess some aspects of the health of a company.

Accountants show the assets on the left-hand side and the liabilities and owners' equity on the right-hand side as Table 3.2 shows.

Table 3.2: Sample Balance Sheet

Assets		Liabilities and Owners' Equity	
Cash and Bank	$500,000	Bank Loans	$700,000
Inventories	$300,000	Accounts Payables	$50,000
Accounts Receivable	$100,000	Initial Capital	$100,000
Investments	$100,000	Accrued Retained Earnings	$150,000
	$1,000,000		$1,000,000

The Income Statement or Profit and Loss Statement

If we view the balance sheet as a snapshot of a company at some instant, the income statement summarizes the things a company did over a period of time as it moved from one state to another (or from one Balance Sheet to another). In this sense it presents a dynamic view of what a business did during a time interval; as opposed to the state of a business at some instant which the Balance Sheet shows.

For example, a company had a balance sheet on the start of January 1, 2024 and another at the end of December 31, 2024. These two are almost certain to be quite different. The income statement covering the period January 1, 2024 through

December 31, 2024 will show the financial aspects of what the company did by way of operations during this period. Table 3.3 shows an example.

Table 3.3: Income Statement (Profit and Loss)

Sales Revenue	$200,000
Less: Cost of Goods Sold (cost of raw materials, labor, and other things directly attributable to the product sold)	$100,000
Less: Overhead expenses (selling, general and administrative expenses)	$50,000
Less: Depreciation (to account for wear and tear of plant and machinery)	$10,000
Less: Interest Expenses (on loans)	$10,000
Interest and other Income	-
Profit before taxation	$30,000
Less: Taxes (@40%)	$12,000
Profit after taxation	$18,000
Less: Dividends paid to Shareholders	$5,000
Retained Earnings	$13,000

Chart of Accounts

Though we defined and discussed the use of Chart of Accounts in the beginning of this chapter, we also want to err on the side of caution and provide an overview for those who feel they need a more in-depth understanding. Thus far, we have seen the structure of the balance sheet and of the income statement. Within each, we have seen different broad headings under which financial accounts are aggregated. If we take a closer look, we can see that there are five different account categories:

1. Asset accounts: To track things of value owned by the business
2. Liability accounts: Track money that the business owes to outsiders
3. Owners' equity: Track amounts the business owes its owners
4. Revenue accounts: Track various incomes from business operations
5. Expense accounts: Track payments necessary to run the business

Under each category, we might keep several different sub headings for convenience. For example, under asset accounts we could keep different accounts to track the following things separately:

- Raw material inventories
- Finished goods inventories

- Bank account
- Plant and machinery
- Land
- Investments and marketable securities
- ...

Similarly, under expense accounts, we could have many different accounts to separately track the following:

- Payments for raw materials
- Labor charges
- Rents
- Utility charges
- ...

Each company might choose to maintain a different set of accounts in each category depending on its individual needs and how fine-grained it wants the tracking to be. For example, a company could keep just one single expense account perhaps called rents paid to track all rents that it pays. A different company might keep four different expense accounts to track the rents it pays: office rents, equipment rents, executive residence rents and other rents. What a company actually uses depends on its own needs.

A company that sells several products could keep separate revenue accounts for each product group. A company could also keep separate revenue accounts to track revenues from sale of products and sales of services.

The Chart of Accounts is a complete list of different accounts that a business chooses to maintain to keep track of its financial transactions.

As we already know, with double-entry book-keeping, each transaction affects at least two of these accounts Of course, it is important that a company chooses its accounts judiciously so that it can track finances at the level of granularity and detail that it wants to.

As this relates to SAP, each account in a Chart of Accounts is identified by a unique account number, a name, an account group, and an account type. We will discuss some of these in more detail when we address general ledger master data. But for now, let's focus on the account type because it is the most relevant to this discussion. In SAP each general ledger account belongs to one of 5 account types: Balance Sheet, Cash,

Non-operating expense or revenue, Primary Cost/Revenue, and Secondary cost accounts. Again, we will explain each of these in more detail when we cover general ledger master data. Table 3.4 shows an example of a Chart of Accounts.

Table 3.4: Sample Chart of Accounts

Account Number	Account Name/Purpose
1000	Cash (checking account)
1100	Debtors (accounts receivable)
1200	Stock on hand (inventories)
2000	Creditors (accounts payable)
2100	Bank overdraft
3000	Capital (owners' equity)
3200	Accrued retained earnings
4000	Credit sales
5000	Cost of goods sold
5200	Accounting fees
5300	Bank charges
5400	Rent

A Chart of Accounts is simply a set of account numbers, their types and the purpose for which each account number will be used. The Chart of Accounts is just an empty structure and does not have any actual financial information in it. It has no values included in it. It is merely a design for some company to use as a basis for its actual accounting. For example, many companies can use the Chart of Accounts in Table 3.3 as a basis for their accounting.

As a reminder, in SAP, every Company Code must have a Chart of Accounts associated with it. Several company codes within a Client could adopt the same Chart of Accounts. Each Company Code within a client could also adopt a different Chart of Accounts. Let's also recall that SAP provides several pre-defined charts of accounts. When multiple company codes share a common Chart of Accounts, they all have a similar accounting structure. This facilitates easy account consolidations across company codes.

General Ledger

Companies keep the details of accounting transactions in their General Ledger (GL). The G/L is a collection of all accounts in the company along with the details of all transactions posted in these accounts. When we said earlier that a company code must have a Chart of Accounts, what we meant is that the G/L of every company code must be based on a Chart of Accounts.

If a company chooses to base its G/L on the Chart of Accounts shown in Table 3.3, then the G/L will have all the accounts shown there and each transaction that occurred in those accounts will be listed in the G/L.

The General ledger is a report showing for each account (in the Chart of Accounts being used), the transactions that occurred for that account over a certain period of time. For example, the general ledger account for the bank account would keep track of all withdrawals from and deposits into the account. Likewise, the material stock account will keep track each instance where materials were received into stock and each instance where materials were issued from stock. The sum total of debits and credits (discussed below) in the overall general ledger must always match because of the practice of double-entry book-keeping. If not, we know that something is wrong.

Accounting Transactions

When companies maintain their General Ledger in paper form, they actually record transactions into the G/L as they carry out business. With automated business transaction processing and with ERP systems like SAP, accounting entries mostly occur seamlessly in the background as we carry out other business transactions like buying, selling and manufacturing. Of course, this is possible only if someone has properly configured things so that SAP has enough information to determine which accounts to update for each stage of a business process.

Despite accounting entries mostly being posted automatically, you might still find it useful to understand the logic of double-entry accounting postings.

Logic of double-entry book-keeping

In single-entry book-keeping we enter each transaction in only one place. In double-entry book-keeping, every transaction affects at least two different accounts, and sometimes more. In double-entry book-keeping, every account has two sides: debit and credit. The amount of each transaction is recorded equally on the debit and credit sides of different accounts. This redundancy helps to avoid some types of errors.

For an accounting transaction worth $1,000, there will be a total debit of $1,000 entered into one or more accounts and an equal amount entered as credits into one or more other accounts. The rules for debits and credits can sometimes seem quite confusing, but they need not be. We now turn our attention to these rules.

Whenever there is a financial transaction, there is a shift of value from one entity to another. For example, if Adam gives Janice $1,000, then $1,000 have changed hands from Adam to Janice. Although some value has changed hands, the total value between their two accounts is still constant.

You might have already come across some rules like "debit what comes in" and "credit what goes out" and found them to be quite confusing. The main culprit in this confusion is our (mis)interpretation of the terms debit and credit in terms of their normal day-to-day usage. We tend to erroneously think of debit as a decrease, or as an outflow, and credit as an increase, or as an inflow.

The key to financial accounting heaven, if ever there can be such a thing, lies in banishing these evil misunderstandings. So, for now, simply forget any association of increase or decrease with the terms debit and credit. You have to remember just one single rule for correctly understanding debit and credit accounting postings!

The original creator of the double-entry system of bookkeeping quite arbitrarily decided that when an asset increases, we should debit the corresponding asset account. You need to remember just that single rule. You can derive all the other rules from it. Consider these examples:

- We buy a machine our fixed assets increase by the value of the machine. Applying the above rule, we debit the fixed asset account.
- Our material stocks increase (because a vendor shipped items that we ordered), then we debit the stock account.

So, the only rule, or axiom is: "When an asset account increases in value, debit it."

What did we mean when we said that we can infer all other rules from this one axiom? Let us see.

What would you do when an asset account decreases in value?

Suppose we sell a machine (a fixed asset) and therefore the fixed assets decrease.Should we not do the reverse of what we did when an asset increased? Yes, of course! In this case, we credit the fixed assets account.

What about revenue and expense accounts? Think a bit about the relationship of these to assets and liabilities. If we can figure out where these would eventually end up on the balance sheet, as everything must (why?), then we can finagle the rules we already have to arrive at the posting rules for these as well.

So how does sales revenue affect the balance sheet? The answer lies in understanding the income statement. Note that the last line of the income statement says that the money left over after taking away all costs, interest, taxes and dividends is transferred to retained earnings on the balance sheet, which is part of owners' equity. It therefore behaves like a liability. Sales revenue will tend to increase this figure and expenses will tend to decrease this. Thus, revenue accounts can be treated similar to owners' equity and liabilities, and expense accounts can be treated the opposite; that is, like assets. That is all there is to it! Table 3.5 summarizes the logic of account postings.

Table 3.5: General Ledger Accounting Posting Logic

Account Type	Increase/ Decrease	Action	Logic
Asset	Increase	Debit	Axiom
Asset	Decrease	Credit	Converse of the axiom
Liability/Owners' Equity	Increase	Credit	Converse of the axiom since Liabilities and Owners' Equity represent sources of funds whereas Assets represent the use of funds
Liability/Owners' Equity	Decrease	Debit	Converse of the row above
Revenue - Gain	Increase	Credit	Source of funds - treat like a Liability
Expense - Loss	Increase	Debit	Use of funds - treat like Asset

Let us consider a few examples of manual posting of transactions:

Example 1: The business owner gives the business $2,000 as capital by transferring it to the company's bank account. Which accounts are involved here? Owners' equity and Cash are the accounts affected by this. Let us look at it from two viewpoints. Consider owners' equity. It is increasing by $2,000. By our rules, it should be credited and hence cash should be debited. Alternately, look at cash. It is an asset and is increasing. So, it should be debited according to the rule. So, Owners' equity should be credited. Both ways of reasoning lead to the same result.

We credit Owner's equity account for $2,000 and debit the Checking account by the same amount. Table 3.6 shows the entries.

Table 3.6: Account Postings for Owner Giving $2,000 to the Business

Account Type	Debit	Credit
Checking account	$2,000	
Owners' Equity		$2,000

Example 2: The Company buys raw materials worth $300 from a vendor, and the terms of payment are 40% up-front (from our checking account) and 60% due in 15 days. Assume that the vendor has delivered the material. Look at the state after we have paid the 40% and are yet to pay the 60%. Which accounts does this affect?

Checking account, since we pay 40% or $120 up-front. Material stock, since the vendor has delivered, causing the material stock to increase. And Accounts Payable, since we still owe 60% or $180 to the vendor. What happened to each of these accounts? Cash, an asset, went down – so it (the checking account) should be credited for the $120 that it decreased by. Accounts payable, a liability, went up, so it should be credited by the $180 it increased by. Material stock, an asset has gone up and hence should be debited for the entire $300. Table 3.7 shows the full picture.

Table 3.7: Account Postings for Material Purchase in Example 2

Account Type	Debit	Credit
Checking account		$120
Accounts Payable		$180
Material Stock	$300	

Example 3: The company spends $1,500 on advertising.

The affects cash (or checking account), and an expense account (advertising). The balance in the checking account went down and so we credit it. The expense account went up and so we debit it. Table 3.8 shows this example.

Table 3.8: Account Postings for $1,500 Advertising Expense

Account Type	Debit	Credit
Checking account		$1,500
Advertising	$1,500	

Example 4: The Company sells goods worth $500. The customer pays $300 upfront and will pay the balance in 30 days. The cost of goods sold (the cost of making the goods) is $400.

This affects cash (asset), sales revenue (revenue) and accounts receivable (asset). Cash has increased – debit. Revenue has increased – credit. Accounts receivable has increased – debit. Table 3.9 shows these.

Table 3.9: Initial Account Postings for Material Sales in Example 4

Account Type	Debit	Credit
Sales Revenue		$500
Checking account	$300	
Accounts Receivable	$200	

However, we are still not done here. After all, the materials the company sold were in the material stock account. After the sale, these materials are gone from there, but our earlier postings have not reflected this change. This part of the transaction affects the material stock account (asset) and the cost of goods sold account (expense). Table 3.10 shows this posting.

Table 3.10: More Postings for Material Stock in Example 4

Account Type	Debit	Credit
Material Stock		$400
Cost of Goods Sold	$400	

It's our hope that this discussion and these examples helps put financial accounting into better perspective. This foundational knowledge will help make better sense of subsequent discussion related to how SAP supports these accounting practices.

Master Data

Earlier in this book we have seen the relationship between master data and organizational levels. Keep in mind, master data are entities needed to carry out various business transactions. By their very definition, master data is DATA. Therefore, it must be organized by assigning it to one or more organizational levels. By assigning the master data to the proper organizational levels, the data can be easily found, used for transactions, and the resulting data stored correctly in the system.

General Leader Accounts

Each General Ledger Account is considered master data. For every G/L account, we must maintain data which defines that account as well as how that account will be used by the CoCd.As you can see from Figure 3.3, the Chart of Account Data provides the definition for the G/L account, while the Company Code data tells the system how the CoCd will use that account.

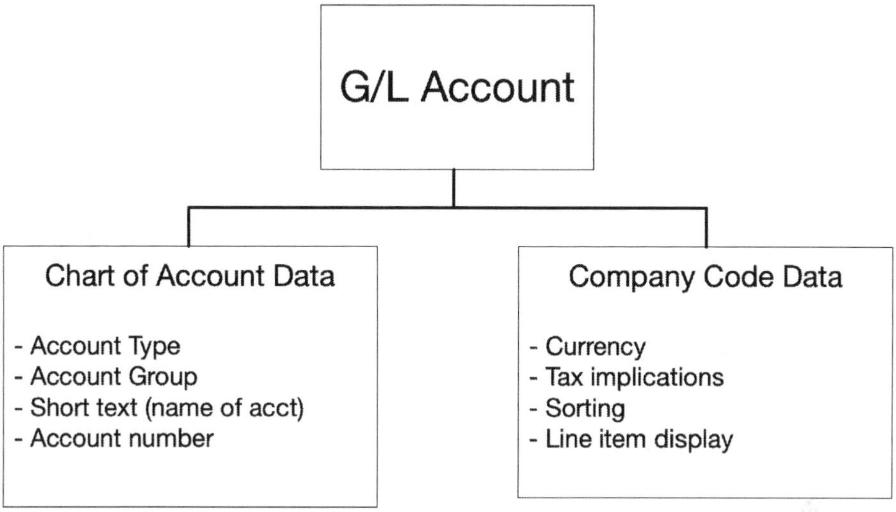

Figure 3.3: General Ledger Account Master Data

The Chart of Account definition includes the Account Group, Account Type, Name of the Account, and Account number. The Account Group is used to organize the G/L accounts. Thus, account numbers are determined by the Account Group. Each Account Group has a predefined number range from which the Account numbers can be derived. The Chart of Account definition also includes the Account Type. As a result of the simplified data model approach, SAP S/4HANA, has four (5) account types. This is a major difference from previous versions of SAP ERP.

The five account types in the G/L are as follows:

X – Balance Sheet accounts

C – Cash accounts

P – Primary Cost/Revenue accounts

N – Non-operating expense/revenue accounts

S – Secondary Cost accounts

Balance sheet accounts manage assets and liabilities from an accounting perspective. Examples of these types of accounts include Inventory Valuation, Accounts Payable, Accounts Receivable, Loans, Cash accounts and many others.

Cash accounts is the newest addition to account types. It allows customers to consolidate multiple banks into a single account, called a Cash account. This account is considered a “monetary” account and is primarily used to generate cash flow statements.

Non-operating expense/revenue accounts include expenses and revenues that will not be tracked in management accounting (CO). These may include Gains or Losses from small price differences. But may include many other things as determined by the enterprise. Remember, CO is governed internally and not by law.

Primary cost/revenue accounts manage expenses (primary costs) and revenues. These accounts are what we described earlier as typical income statement accounts. Examples of these accounts include Labor expense, Supplies expense, Utilities expense, Sales revenue and many more. It’s important to note that this account type has direct integration with Controlling. Therefore, we not only include data in the Chart of Account and the Company Code, we must also include data in the Controlling Area organizational level. More to come on that.

Traditionally, these four account types are included in the legal financial statements for each company code. All four account types must be reported legally. However, that is not the case with Secondary Cost accounts. These accounts exist to simply track movements of costs and revenues within CO. We refer to these as cost allocations. Along with Primary Cost/Revenue accounts, this account type also requires that data be entered into the Controlling Area organizational level.

Primary costs/revenues and secondary costs were exclusive to CO in previous versions of SAP ERP. These were managed in CO as Cost Element master data (Primary and Secondary respectively). Cost Element master data are still required in Controlling. However, they are now automatically created in parallel when a Primary cost/revenue account or Secondary cost account are created as General Ledger master data. Therefore, cost element master data are now maintained in the General Ledger in SAP S/4HANA. It is for this reason that we must include data in the Controlling Area for these two account types. For general ledger accounts that are created as Primary cost/revenue accounts and Secondary cost accounts, we must define the Cost Element Category in the Controlling Area data so a cost element master record can be created in parallel. We will discuss more related to CO in the next chapter.

Business Partner Master Data (Vendors/Customers) and Reconciliation Accounts

In the previous chapter we discussed the Business Partner Approach and the use of Roles for the Business Partner. As you can see in Figure 3.4, there is a FI Vendor Role and a FI Customer Role. These roles are necessary because both vendors and customers are considered subledger accounts in SAP FI.

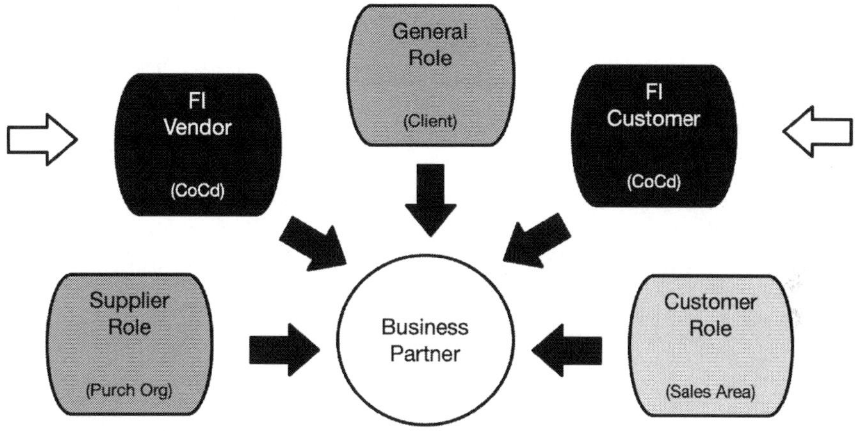

Figure 3.4: Business Partner Roles

Subledger accounts allow for the management of individual assets and liabilities. Imagine a company just billed two different customers for two separate sales orders which belonged to the same CoCd. Billing both customers resulted in total Receivables in the amount of $250. However, that amount doesn't give us any information regarding how much each of those two customers owes. To be able to see that information, we need to treat each customer as a subledger account. The individual receivable from each customer needs to be associated with a Reconciliation Account for Receivables so it can be posted to the General Ledger. This is accomplished by entering the appropriate Reconciliation Account number in a field in the FI Customer Role of the Business Partner. In addition to the Reconciliation Account, the FI Role also contains payment data, tax information, and correspondence information.

Likewise, when vendors invoice a company, the company needs subledger accounts for each vendor so it can manage these liabilities individually. The company also needs to ensure these individual liabilities are properly recorded in the General Ledger. Thus, the FI Vendor role contains the link to the corresponding Reconciliation Account for Payables in the General Ledger.

Reconciliation Accounts are defined as a Balance Sheet Account in the General Ledger, while customers are considered subledger accounts. See the example in Figure 3.5 where Customer X is billed $100 and Customer Y is billed $150 and these debit (asset) postings flow into the reconciliation account in the general ledger from the individual subledger accounts.

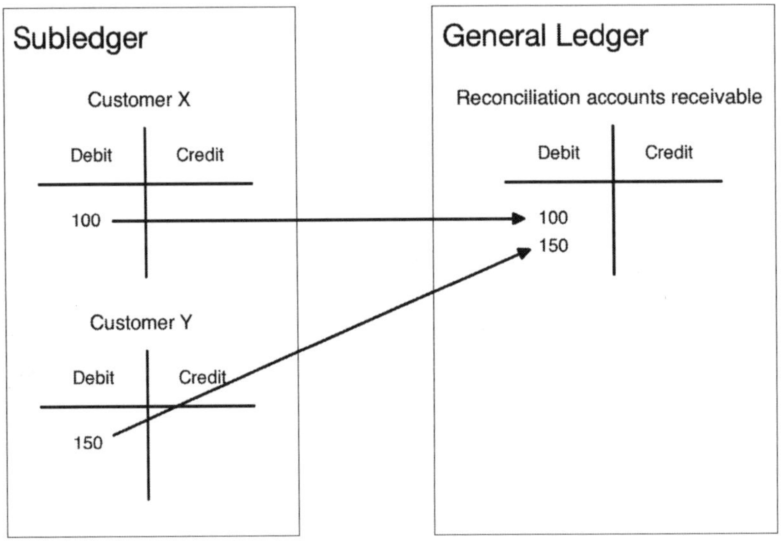

Figure 3.5: Customer Subledger/Reconciliation Account Postings

The relationship between subledger accounts and the Reconciliation Accounts is not unique to vendors and customers. It is also used to manage other assets and liabilities such as banks, loans, and fixed assets.

Asset Master Data

Master Data must also be maintained for fixed assets in SAP S/4HANA. Fixed assets include such things as machinery, computers, buildings, vehicles and others. The Asset master record contains all the necessary information for managing the asset. All assets must be linked to the following:

- Asset Class
- Company Code
- Business Segment
- Cost Center

The Asset Class is perhaps the most important characteristic of an asset. It determines how that asset will be managed. The asset class provides the system with information needed for depreciating that asset as well as the account number assigned to the asset. Because assets are master data in FI, each asset is also assigned to a CoCd and Business Segment so it can be managed financially. Finally, each asset is assigned to a responsible cost center. We will discuss cost centers in more detail in the next chapter. But for now, cost centers are responsible for the associated depreciation costs of the fixed asset.

When assigned to an Asset Class, each asset master record will contain information related to depreciation. A company may depreciate an asset differently for different accounting purposes. At the very least, there is legal depreciation that each fixed asset must undergo but other depreciation methods exist. These different methods of depreciation are known as Depreciation Areas. Each asset can be assigned one or more Depreciation Areas, dependent on the Asset Class. Figure 3.6 demonstrates the characteristics that define a Depreciation Area. These characteristics are referred to as Depreciation Parameters.

Useful Life

- How long will the asset be placed in use?
- The useful life of an asset is dependent on the asset class

Usage

- Has the asset already been in service?
- For how long?

Depreciation Key

- Holds information regarding the values to be calculated during depreciation
  - Example: straight line depreciation

Depreciation Start Date

- When was the asset put into service?

Figure 3.6: Depreciation Parameters (Characteristics of Depreciation Areas)

Transactions

There are many transactions in the SAP S/4HANA system which have indirect financial accounting impacts. We won't address those transactions in this section. We will learn more about those types of transactions in later chapters. For now, we will focus on some direct financial accounting transactions and their impacts.

Remember: ALL transactions in SAP S/4HANA result in the creation of at least one electronic document in the system. Any transaction that results in an impact in FI, will generate a FI accounting document.

General Ledger Journal Entries

The most basic transaction in financial accounting is a General Ledger (G/L) journal entry. Below is an example of a G/L journal entry in SAP in Figure 3.7. There are a few main areas to be concerned with during this entry: The Document Header, Information Area, and Line Items. The Document Header contains all the information relevant to the entire document. This includes the Document Date, Posting Date, Document Currency, and any relevant notes regarding the journal entry.

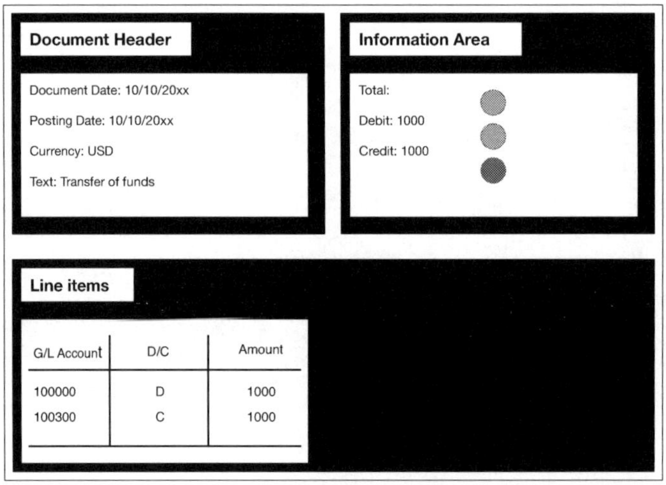

Figure 3.7: G/L Journal Entry

The Information Area provides the user with information regarding the G/L balance for the document. All G/L postings must be balanced and the total amount of Debit and Credit postings from the Line Items are tabulated here. SAP uses a Red, Yellow, Green traffic light indicator to let the user know if the document is in balance. In our example above, you see the Green light is illuminated.

Finally, the Line Items of the G/L Journal entry include the exact G/L accounts receiving the postings, whether that line item is receiving a debit or credit posting, and the amount for each line item. When the document is properly prepared for posting, the user will select the option to Post it to the G/L. The system will verify this posting with the accompanying FI Document number displayed on the screen.

Document Types

SAP uses Document Types (Figure 3.8) to distinguish between the various accounting documents that are generated during transactions. The document type can be found in the header of each document. Below are some examples of document types.

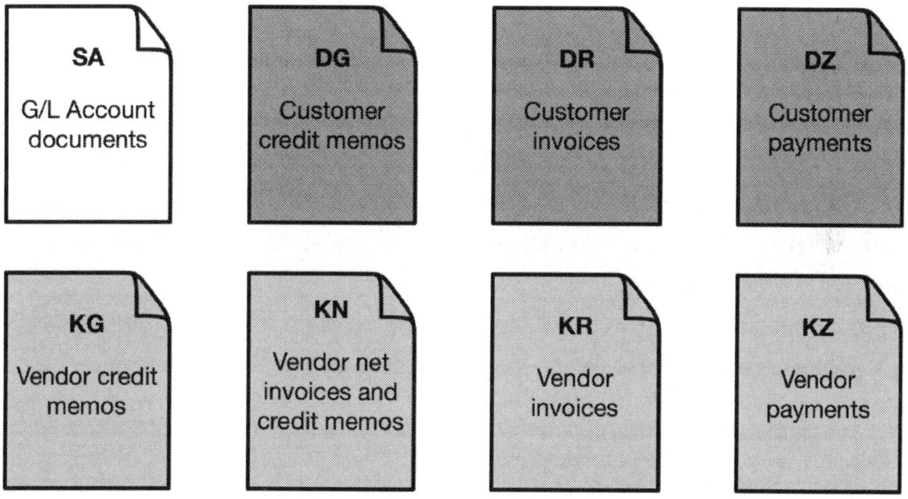

Figure 3.8: Examples of Document Types

Posting Keys

While Document Types are in the Header of the FI document, the resulting FI document from a G/L journal entry will also provide details at the line-item level. This includes the postings to the G/L accounts associated with each line item. Each line items will appear in this document along with a 2-digit numeric Posting Key. The Posting Key is automatically derived for manual G/L journal entries, such as the one in the above example (Figure 3.7). This is NOT the case for transactions involving fixed assets, which we will discuss a little later. But for now, Figure 3.9 shows the controls associated with the Posting Key for each line item in the FI Document.

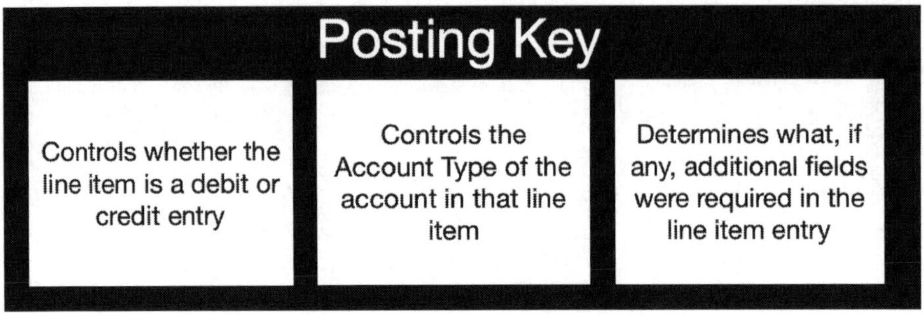

Figure 3.9: Posting Key

The Universal Journal

As we discussed in the previous chapter, SAP developed the Universal Journal (ACDOCA table) as part of the simplified data model in SAP S/4HANA. Figure 3.10 demonstrates how various accounting impacts are written to the Universal Journal. The Universal Journal provides a single source of truth from an accounting standpoint. There is no longer a need for reconciliation between different SAP modules. As you can see, the results of the earlier example of the G/L Journal entry will be recorded in this table.

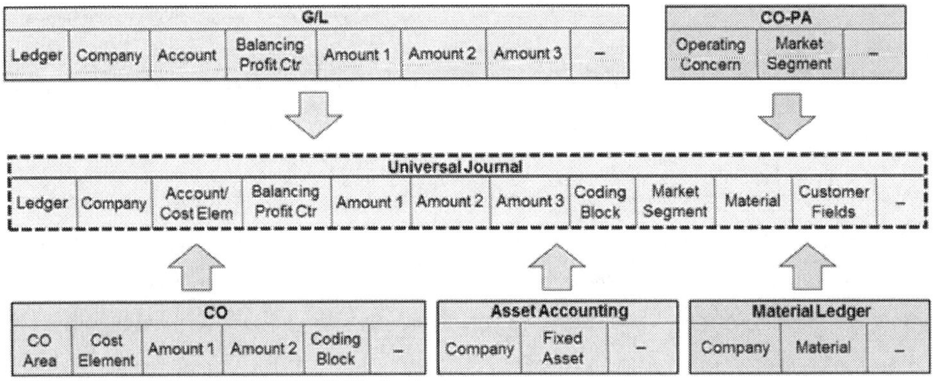

Figure 3.10: Universal Journal (replica of Figure 2.9)

Other areas within SAP S/4HANA are also recorded to this table. They include postings from Profitability, Management Accounting, Fixed Asset Accounting, and the Material Ledger. The next section in this book deals with postings related to Fixed Assets. The Material Ledger (ML), though optional in previous versions of SAP ERP, is mandatory in SAP S/4HANA. The ML allows for the maintaining of valuations for materials using multiple currencies, supports Actual Costing of materials during an accounting period by statistically recording the actual values at the time of posting, and supports parallel accounting by capturing values which adhere to different accounting standards.

Asset Transactions

Asset transactions are numerous and vary considerably. It's not possible to go into every possible example involving asset transactions, but we will look at a few of them. To begin our discussion, let's identify some broad categories of asset transactions. These are found in Figure 3.11. We will then go into some criteria regarding some of the transactions by looking at a few examples.

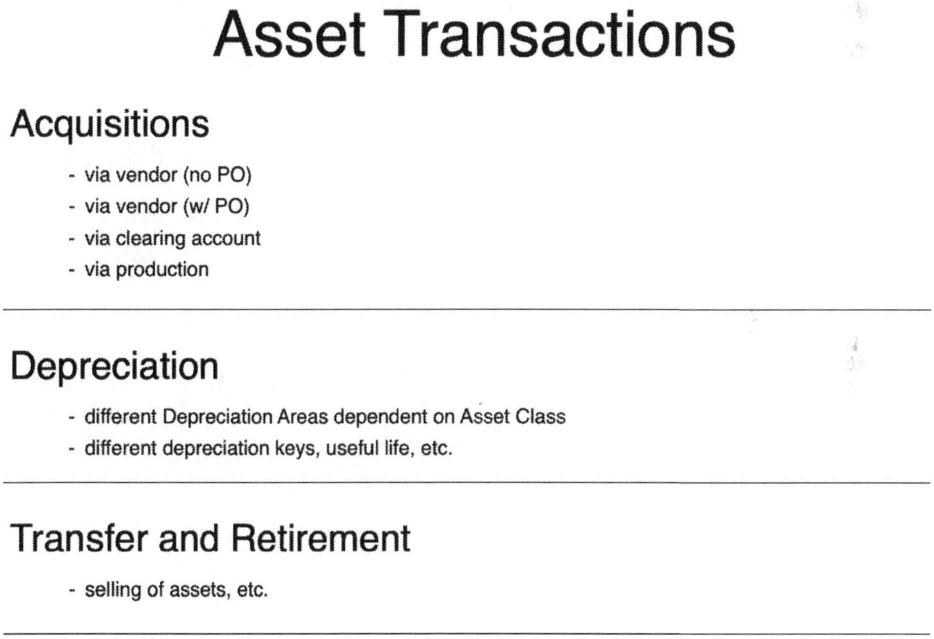

Figure 3.11: Asset Transactions

Asset Acquisition

Let's take an example of an asset acquisition via a vendor without a purchase order. In this example, the company would simply enter an invoice for the asset from the vendor into the system. Figure 3.12 shows the entry for this transaction. The Document Header contains the information about the vendor as well as the amount in the invoice. This entry results in the credit posting to the vendor subledger account, creating the liability to the vendor for acquiring the asset. The Line Item section includes the Asset account. This amount will result in the debit posting to that asset, resulting in the acquisition value. Once again, the Information Area indicates the document is balanced.

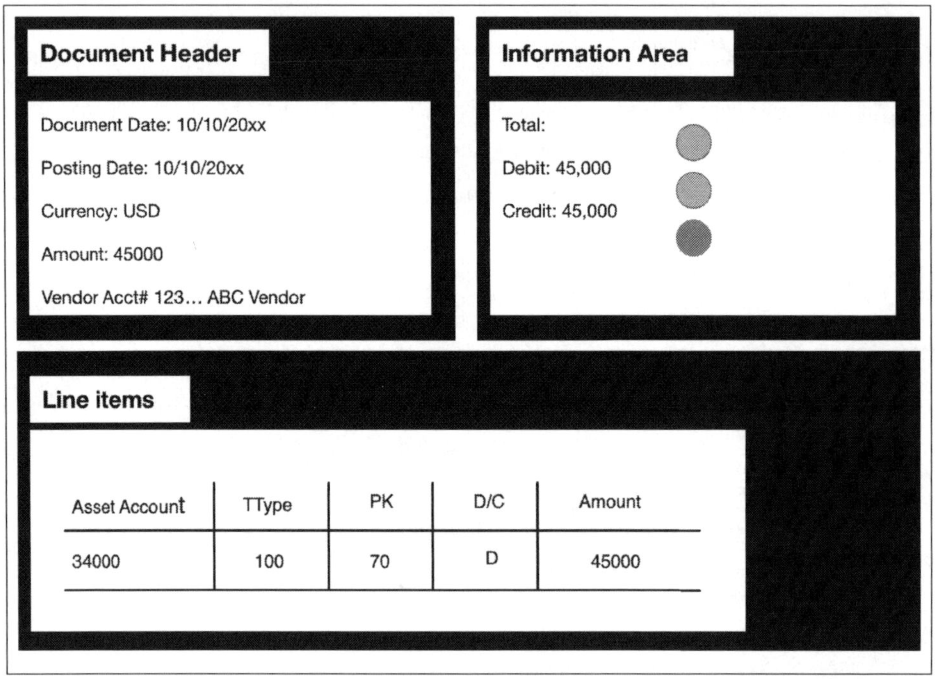

Figure 3.12: Asset Acquisition via Vendor w/o PO (*this image is just an example and actual entries may be different)

It is important to note two additional characteristics, found in the Line Item section of this transaction. You will see the Transaction Type (TTpye) and the Posting Key (PK). Asset transactions, such as this acquisition, require a manual entry of these two characteristics. Without these entries, the system will be unable to determine the correct postings to the G/L. Keep in mind, the vendor and the asset are both subledger accounts.

Integrated Asset Acquisition

As of SAP S/4HANA 2020, Integrated Asset Acquisition postings divide the transaction into two parts. First, an operational document followed by valuating documents. To understand what this means, we need to reflect back to the concept of parallel accounting. Recall, parallel accounting is when a company code is using multiple ledgers simultaneously. In our earlier example, we demonstrated that a company code would use a local Chart of Accounts (CoA) for legal reporting, but would also use the Leading Ledger CoA (0L) for consolidating data at the client level. Company codes may use other CoAs for more than just consolidating financial data. They may also use multiple CoAs to satisfy different accounting standards, such as USGAAP (US Generally Accepted Accounting Principles) and IFRS (International Financial Accounting Reporting Standards).

To enable simultaneous postings in all of these ledgers, SAP employs the Ledger Solution. The Ledger Solution is simply the tool which manages each of these ledgers in ledger groups. In Integrated Asset Acquisition, multiple ledgers will be impacted. The operational document displays the transaction against a technical clearing account that will apply to all ledger groups (see top part of Figure 3.13). The valuation documents display the posting against the technical clearing account for each applicable accounting principle, meaning only specific ledger groups (see the bottom part of Figure 3.13). This ensures a balance of zero for each accounting principle that applies.

Operational Document

D/C	PK	Name	Account #	Amount
D	70	Technical Clearing Acct	100100	45000
C	31	Accounts Payable	210000	45000

Valuation Documents

USGAAP

D/C	PK	Name	Account #	Amount
D	70	Vehicles	190000	45000
C	75	Technical Clearing Acct	210000	45000

IAS

D/C	PK	Name	Account #	Amount
D	70	Vehicles	190000	45000
C	75	Technical Clearing Acct	210000	45000

Figure 3.13: Integrated Asset Acquisition Postings

Depreciation Run

Depreciation is also another form of an asset transaction. As we have discussed previously, there are several methods for depreciating a single asset. These methods are known as Depreciation Areas. When a Depreciation Run is initiated, it can run actual depreciation using planned depreciation values or unplanned depreciation values as defined in the transaction in the system. The result of the depreciation run is a posting of depreciation in FI (as well as CO for posting the depreciation costs). As is the case with all transactions, SAP S/4HANA will generate document for this transaction in each module impacted. In the case of depreciation postings, the system will generate a FI document and a CO document.

The results of all asset transactions, including depreciation, can be found by pulling up a tool called the Asset Explorer. The Asset Explorer is a sort of one-stop shop for all the information needed regarding a single asset. It provides information regarding the depreciation areas and their parameters, planned depreciation, posted depreciation and other values such as acquisition, and comparisons of values from period to period. Figure 3.14 demonstrates the views of the Asset Explorer.

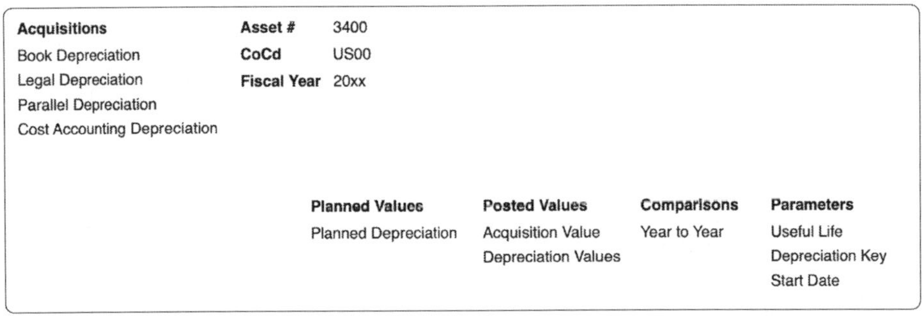

Figure 3.14: Asset Explorer

By selecting a Depreciation Area, the Asset Explorer will present the Depreciation Parameters specific to that Depreciation Area. The user can then view the methods of depreciation from within the Asset Explorer.

Document Splitting with Vendor Invoicing

One of the organizational levels discussed in this chapter is the Business Segment. Because there are laws in some countries that require companies submit financial statements per Business Segment, SAP S/4HANA uses the Document Splitting functionality as a means for breaking out balance sheet postings by Business Segments. In this way, companies can generate complete sets of accurate financial statements by Business Segment.)

In this next example, we'll look at a vendor invoice for Rent Expense. Suppose Company A rents warehouse space and each month the landlord sends an invoice in the amount of $10,000 for this rent expense. The warehouse is used to store materials for two different areas of the business. One area of the business is Appliances, while the other is Computers. Appliances utilizes approximately 60% of the warehouse space, while Computers utilizes 40%. For legal purposes, the government has mandated Company A to report separate financial statements for each of these areas.

To successfully do this in SAP S/4HANA, Company A has created to separate Business Segments (Segment A for Appliances and Segment C for Computers). Figure 3.15 shows the vendor invoice (note: the 10% tax rate).

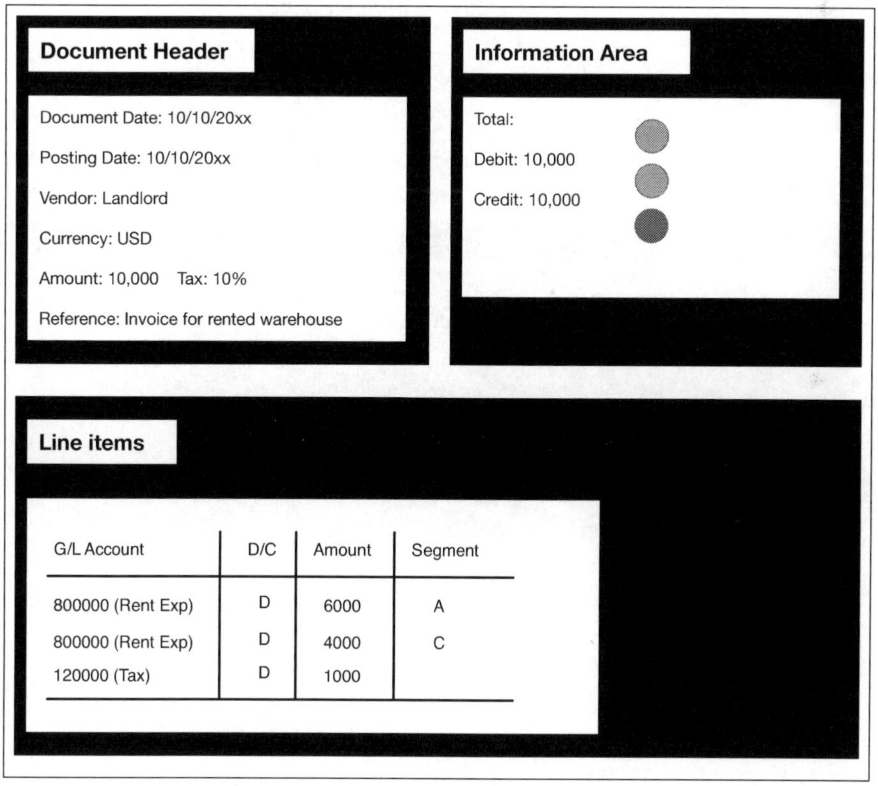

Figure 3.15: Vendor Invoice by Segment

When the invoice is Posted, a Financial Accounting document will be created by the SAP S/4HANA system. Recall, a vendor is a subledger account and is linked to a

Reconciliation Account for Payables. However, it is not possible to post directly to a Reconciliation Account, so the direct entry as shown in Figure 3.15, is to the subledger account. The Financial Accounting document will be presented in the "Entry View", which means we will see the postings to the subledger account, not the Reconciliation G/L account. Figure 3.16 depicts what this document will look like.

Financial Accounting Document Entry View

Document #: 190000001		CoCd:	US00	Fiscal Year:	20xx
Doc. Date:	MM/DD/20xx	Posting date:	MM/DD/20xx	Period:	Month

CoCd.	PK	Account	Name	Amount	Currency	Segment
US00	31	#####	Landlord	11000	USD	
	40	800000	Rent Exp	6000	USD	A
	40	800000	Rent Exp	4000	USD	C
	40	120000	Tax	1000	USD	

Figure 3.16: Document Splitting Entry View

By switching to the General Ledger View, the SAP S/4HANA automatically splits the tax by Business Segment, allowing for separate reporting. This is shown in Figure 3.17. Also notice that because of the split, additional line items appear in this view.

Financial Accounting General Ledger View

Document #: 190000001		CoCd:	US00	Fiscal Year:	20xx
Doc. Date:	MM/DD/20xx	Posting date:	MM/DD/20xx	Period:	Month

CoCd.	PK	Account	Name	Amount	Currency	Segment
US00	31	210000	Reconciliation A/P	11000	USD	
	40	800000	Rent Exp	6000	USD	A
	40	120000	Tax	600	USD	
	40	800000	Rent Exp	4000	USD	C
	40	120000	Tax	400	USD	

Figure 3.17: Document Splitting General Ledger View

Financial Accounting Summary

Successful Financial Accounting (FI) results in the creation of accurate Financial Statements. Because there are different legal requirements for a global company, each Company Code will need to generate unique Financial Statements for the respective countries. Because of this need, SAP has included predefined Financial Statement

Versions. The different versions are used to satisfy different reporting requirements. Financial Statements include Balance Sheet, Income Statement, and Cash Flow reports. It is possible to customize these reports for external and internal purposes.

In this chapter we addressed the organizational levels, master data, and transactions associated with Financial Accounting. There is much more to this, so keep in mind what we covered is not an exhaustive list. You'll see many more transactions having FI impacts in subsequent chapters.

Chapter 4: Management Accounting

The financial accounting function keeps track of monetary flows in an organization with the goal of external reporting according to established laws. The management accounting function also aims at tracking monetary flows but aims to use such information internally for making sound managerial decisions. This chapter introduces the broad ideas related to management accounting, and specifically explains some important SAP S/4HANA concepts and terms involved. For purposes of understanding, SAP refers to Management Accounting as Controlling. It is for this reason, that "CO" is often used to abbreviate management accounting.

As a reminder, it's important to understand the major differences between Financial Accounting and Management Accounting. For convenience, Table 4.1 revisits a figure we saw in the previous chapter. Again, financial accounting is governed by law, accounting standards, and very structured. Its goal is to be able to generate accurate financial statements that satisfy the legal requirements.

On the other hand, management accounting is less structured and allows a company the flexibility to manage costs and revenues in a manner best suited to make decisions. It is management accounting which helps inform the enterprise about who is responsible for generating costs and in many cases, revenue. We will see that financial accounting and management accounting are tightly integrated.

The primary source of information in management accounting is financial accounting and many business transactions will involve integration between both.

Table 4.1: Financial Accounting versus Management Accounting (replica of Table 3.1)

Financia Accounting (FI)	Management Accounting (CO)

• Legal accounting
• Governed by law and regulations
• External audience
• Inflexible
• Follows accounting standards like USGAAP and IAS
• Output: Legal reporting of financial statements
  - Balance sheet
  - Income statement
  - Cash flows
	• Internal accounting
	• Governed internally, not by law
	• Internal audience
	• Flexible
	• Manages costs and revenues
	• Profitability
	• Output
	  - Managerial decision making

Management Accounting Organizational Levels/ Enterprise Structure

Again, we begin our discussion with a focus on the organizational levels which represent the Enterprise Structure. In Management Accounting (CO), there are only two (2) organizational levels directly associated with it. They are the Operating Concern and the Controlling Area. Because of the tight integration between Financial Accounting and Management Accounting, the Company Code and Chart of Accounts also have implications in CO.

To better understand this, we need to acknowledge the fact that CO manages costs and revenues, while FI deals with expenses and revenues, but a whole lot more, like assets and liabilities. Assets and liabilities have no integration between FI and CO. They remain as postings in FI only. However, postings to expense and revenue accounts are likely to have integration between FI and CO. The characteristic which defines whether a G/L account is a balance sheet account, or expense or revenue account is the Account Type. Recall from the previous chapter, there are five (5) Account Types in SAP S/4HANA. Below are these Account Types.

The five account types in the G/L are as follows:

X – Balance Sheet accounts

C – Cash accounts

P – Primary Cost/Revenue accounts

N – Non-operating expense/revenue accounts

S – Secondary Cost accounts

Only Primary Cost/Revenue and Secondary Cost accounts in the General Ledger have relevance to CO. Balance Sheet, Cash accounts, and Non-operating expense/ revenue accounts have no integration with CO. We will discuss Primary Cost/Revenue and Secondary Cost accounts in more detail a little later, but for now it is very important to understand which Account Types are CO relevant and which are not CO relevant. Let us also not forget, it is the Chart of Accounts(CoA) segment of the G/L account which defines the Account Type. For this reason, the CoA plays an important role in CO.

Figure 4.1: ERPI - Controlling Areas and Their Mapping to Company Codes (replica of Figure 1.12)

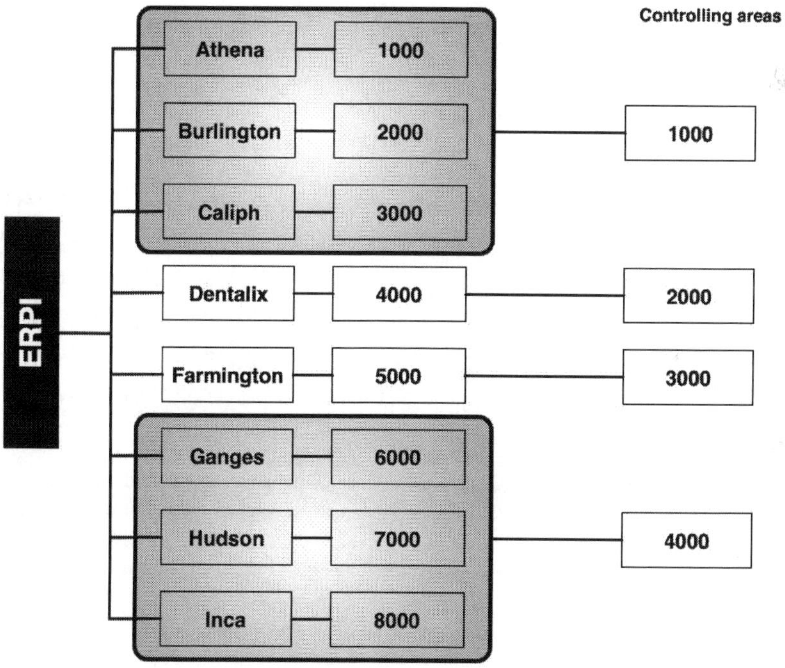

We mentioned above, the Company Code(CoCd) also plays a role in CO. And that is because the information in CO originates from postings in Financial Accounting. As an example, if there is a FI posting to a Primary Cost/Revenue account, it must also be recorded in CO. For this to occur, the CoCd needs to be integrated with an organizational level in CO. That integration occurs when a CoCd is assigned to a Controlling Area (COAr). Figure 4.1, which we have already discussed in the first chapter, reminds us of the relationship between Company Codes and Controlling Areas.

In Figure 4.2 you get a more well-rounded view of how all these organizational levels relate to one another. Though the figure is drawn hierarchically, it would be more beneficial to understand the relationships (assignments) of the organizational levels to one another. To simplify things, Figure 4.2 depicts two CoCds (US and Canada) and a single COAr (North American). In this example, you will see that a COAr may have one or more CoCds assigned to it. However, a CoCd can be assigned to only one COAr. Creating the relationship between the CoCds and COAr allows for the integration of information between them. You will also notice the COAr has been assigned to the Operating Concern. The Operating Concern is used to perform Profitability Analysis (also known as Margin Analysis) or CO-PA for short. CO-PA is the only function of the Operating Concern. All other management accounting activities occur within a COAr. Hence, the COAr is the most important organizational level in CO.

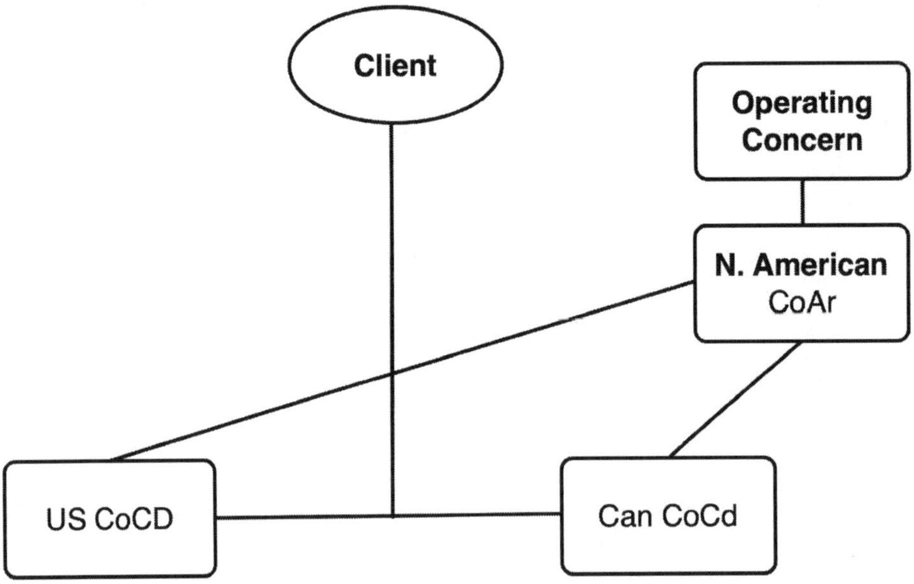

Figure 4.2: Relationship Between Operating Concern, Controlling Area and Company Codes

Taking the same example from Figure 4.2, we are going to add the Chart of Accounts into Figure 4.3. We have already established the principle of Parallel Accounting in the previous chapter. Parallel Accounting occurs when a CoCd needs to use more than one CoA for accounting purposes. In the previous chapter, we discussed a CoCd needing a Local CoA for legal reporting, but possibly a second CoA to consolidate to the Leading Ledger at the Client level. We now add another CoA. This CoA is used to consolidate postings to the COAr. It is referred to as the Operative Chart of Accounts (sometimes referred to as the Operational Chart of Accounts). By definition, the Operative CoA is actually the ledger used for daily postings for each CoCd. Since accounting information is now being consolidated at the COAr, both CoCds in our example must also use the same Operative CoA to be able to perform this consolidation. In other words, the definition of the Primary Cost/Revenue accounts and the Secondary Cost accounts must be identical since these two Account Types are the ones effecting the COAr.

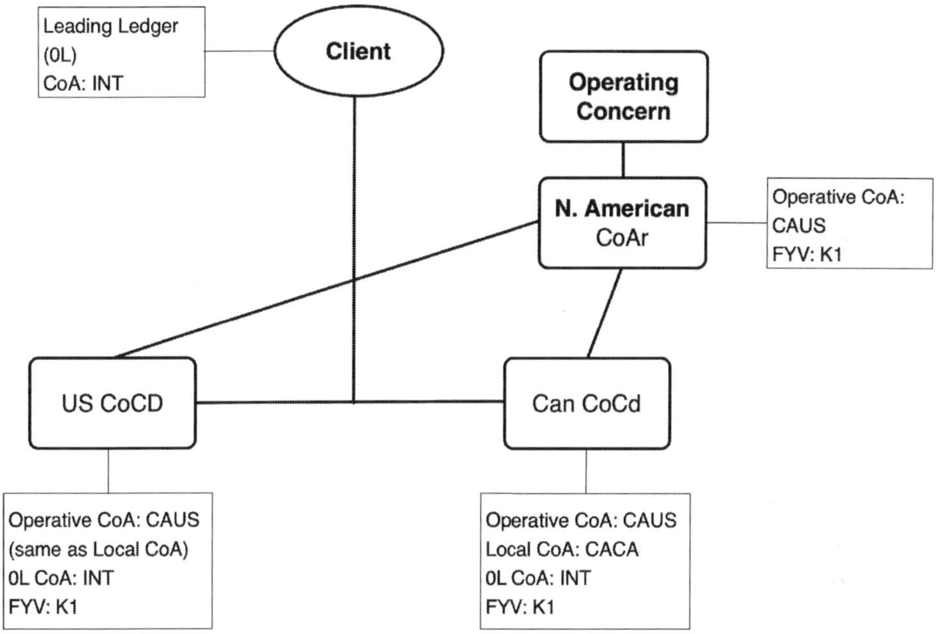

Figure 4.3: Chart of Accounts and Fiscal Year Variants in CO

There are two (2) rules for assigning CoCds to a COAr:

1. The CoCds must be using the same Operative CoA
2. The CoCds and COAr must use the same Fiscal Year Variant (FYV)

Figure 4.3 demonstrates these relationships, including the CoA and FYV.

Notice from this example the Operative CoA is the same as the Local CoA for the US CoCd. Because of this, the US CoCd would not need an additional CoA. However, when looking at the Canadian CoCd, their Local CoA and Operative CoA are not the same, so the Canadian CoCd must use three CoA in parallel. Finally, all CoCds assigned to the COAr are also using the same FYV as well as the same Operative CoA.

Management Accounting Master Data

There are several master data in CO that we will discuss in this section. Examples of some of the master data we will see includes, but are not limited to, Cost Centers, Profit Centers, Statistical Key Figures, Activity Types, and Activity Prices. All the master data we cover in this chapter are created in the Controlling Area. As an example, when a Cost Center is created, it is created for a specific Controlling Area. Figure 4.4 represents the areas within CO and the organizational levels in which they exist. Each of these areas has its own set of master data which are used to carry out one or several management accounting transactions.

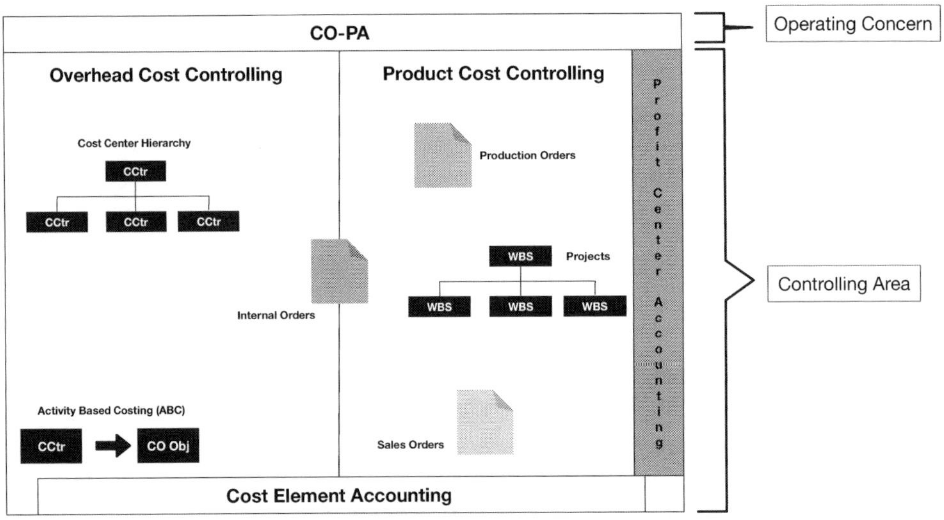

Figure 4.4: Areas Within CO

The areas within CO include CO-PA (Profitability Analysis), CO-OM (Overhead Cost Controlling), CO-PC (Product Cost Controlling), CO-OM-CEL (Cost Element Accounting), and EC-PCA (Profit Center Accounting)[1]. A little later in this chapter we will get into more detail regarding the transactions that result in value flows within and between some of the objects in Figure 4.4. For now, we will focus on the master data associated with these areas as well as the relevant organizational levels.

---

[1] EC-PCA is part of Enterprise Controlling in SAP S/4HANA

Cost Element Accounting

Again, we want to highlight Primary Cost/Revenue and Secondary Cost accounts because these two Account Types have relevance in CO. In the previous chapter on Financial Accounting, we addressed General Ledger master data. In that chapter we addressed the fact that in SAP S/4HANA, any G/L account, regardless of Account Type is created in the Financial Accounting-General Ledger Accounting.

Prior to SAP S/4HANA, there were only two Account Types (Profit and Loss accounts, and Balance Sheet Accounts). As a result of the simplified data model in SAP S/4HANA, Primary Cost Elements and Secondary Cost Elements are no longer created as separate master data in Controlling. When a Primary Cost/Revenue account is created in the G/L in FI, it simultaneously creates a Primary Cost Element master record in CO. Likewise, when a Secondary Cost account is created in the G/L in FI, a Secondary Cost Element master record is created in CO. It is for this reason that when these two account types are created in the G/L, they require additional data in the Controlling Area to include the Cost Element Category.

Cost elements are used to post costs in the SAP S/4HANA system. Primary Cost Elements manage the posting of costs between FI and CO, while Secondary Cost Elements manage the posting of costs strictly within CO. When postings of costs occur only within CO, we can define these postings as Allocations. Later in this chapter we will discuss different types of allocations with Secondary Cost Elements. We will also see examples of the use of Primary Cost Elements to track expenses (and in some cases, revenue) that originate in FI.

Overhead Cost Controlling

Cost Centers/Cost Center Groups

Cost centers and cost center groups are structured hierarchically in CO. The hierarchy is labeled, the Standard Hierarchy and there is only one Standard Hierarchy per Controlling Area. When a cost center is created, there are some required and optional entries that are included in the master record. Figure 4.5 lists the items contained in a cost center master record.

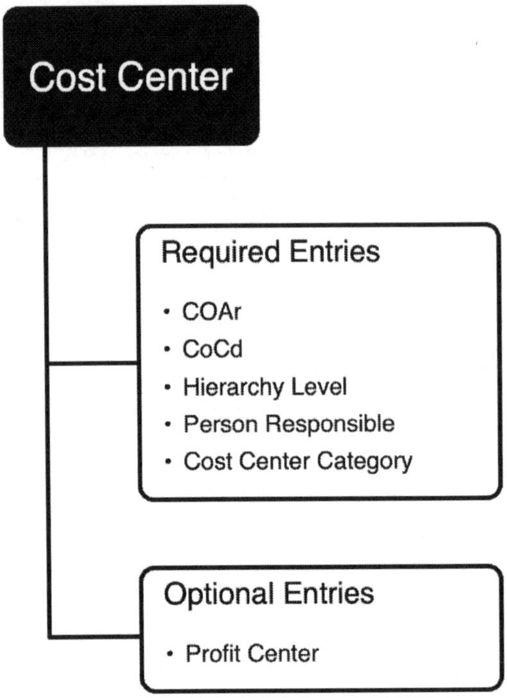

Figure 4.5: Cost Center Master Data

A Cost Center (CCtr) represents an area within the enterprise where costs are incurred. Many of these costs are considered overhead costs such as insurance, utilities, and supplies costs. Since CO is not governed by law, it is up to the enterprise to determine how to structure its cost centers. It could be a functional department within an enterprise, such as the Billing department or the HR office. It could also be broader, like an entire office building. If we use a department as a cost center, such as the finance department, we can get a clearer view on how costs are managed. For example, the finance department directly incurs costs (e.g., salaries paid to employees in the department and the cost of stationery that the department uses). Other costs, although not directly incurred by the finance department, might still be allocated to it (e.g., a portions of rent paid for the part of the office building the finance department occupies). Since these types of costs are the responsibility of the finance department, creating a cost center is the ideal way to track them.

Often, it makes sense for an enterprise to track costs across multiple cost centers. Let's suppose the enterprise has also created cost centers for the billing department, accounts payable department, and general accounting office. We now have four cost centers that can be grouped together to manage costs collectively. There are many reasons for doing this, but for now it's important to understand that cost centers can be grouped together by creating Cost Center Group master data. In this case, a Cost Center Group for Financial Management can be created. Figure 4.6 depicts the example described above.

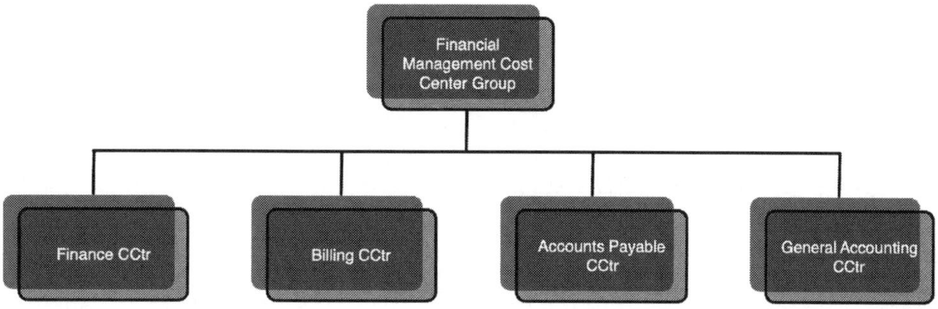

Figure 4.6: Cost Centers and Cost Center Groups

One of the main benefits of structuring cost centers hierarchically, is to facilitate cost planning for cost centers. Using the same example above, let's suppose we successfully planned costs at each of these four lower level cost centers: Finance, Billing, Accounts Payable, and General Accounting. In doing so, we would have the planned costs we need at the cost center group for Financial Management. If other cost center groups exist at the same level in the hierarchy as the Financial Management group, they can be used to plan costs at the next level up the hierarchy, and so on. In short, costs are planned from the bottom-up to generate what is needed for a budget request. When a budget is approved, it is then distributed from the top-down. The use of hierarchies is not unique to cost centers in CO. We will see this again later in Chapter 10 when we address Projects in SAP S/4HANA.

Finally, cost centers can never be used for purposes of capturing statistical costs. That is, costs for information purposes only. Costs centers can only receive and send actual costs. Thus, cost centers are considered "true" cost objects.

Activity Based Costing

Overhead Cost Controlling (CO-OC) also consists of a process known as Activity Based Costing (ABC). Since this is a process, by itself, ABC is not considered master data. However, very specific master data is required to perform ABC. For now, a brief overview of ABC will be important to understand what it is about.

ABC is a form of an allocation. That is, it is a process by which costs are transferred within CO. However, it is a unique type of an allocation. It is an allocation whereby costs are allocated to one or more objects based on work performed. An object may be a Cost Center, an Order (like a production order), a Project, along with several other possibilities. A typical example is the allocation of labor costs to a production order. The work being performed on a production order typically originates from a cost center. When the work is completed, the cost center will want to allocate the appropriate labor costs to the production order so it can be included in the total costs of production.

In order to perform Activity Based Costing, four master data are required. They are as follows:

1. Secondary Cost Element
2. Sending Cost Center
3. Activity Type
4. Activity Price

As well as each of these having a function in ABC, they are also linked to one another in the master data creation. To begin our discussion, we'll address the first type of master data required, the Secondary Cost Element.

The Secondary Cost Element is required because ABC is a form of an allocation. A Secondary Cost Element is required to manage these costs so they can be tracked in the system. All Secondary Cost Elements are associated with a Cost Element Category (assigned when creating this as an account in the G/L), which defines the function of the Cost Element. Examples of Cost Element Categories include Activity Allocation, Assessments, and Settlement. Obviously, when a Secondary Cost Element is created for use in ABC, it would receive the Cost Element Category – Activity Allocation.

The second form of master data required in ABC is the Sending Cost Center. We define this Cost Center as a "Sending" cost center because a cost center is the ONLY object in CO that can allocate costs using ABC. In other words, it is the only object in CO that can "send" costs to other objects using ABC. However, as mentioned above, it is not uncommon for a cost center to also be the receiver of costs as a result of ABC.

Earlier in this chapter we identified the required data for creating cost centers. One of those pieces of data is the Cost Center Category. Like Cost Element Categories, the Cost Center Categories define the type or purpose of the cost center. Some examples of Cost Center Categories include Administrative, Service, Production. For instance, a company may create a cost center for IT Services (Figure 4.7). This cost center will perform IT support for several other cost centers and will need to allocate the costs of work they perform. This cost center would be assigned the Cost Center Category, "Service".

1. Secondary Cost Element for "Support" (Cost Element Category - Activity Allocation)
2. Sending Cost Center for "IT Services" (Cost Center Category - Services)
3. Activity Type "IT Support" (assigned to the Secondary Cost Element "Support" and assigned to the Cost Center Category - Services form the Sending Cost Center "IT Services")
4. Activity Price (assigned to the combination Cost Center and Activity Type)

Figure 4.7: Master Data Example for Activity Based Costing

The third form of master data in ABC is the Activity Type. The Activity Type is master data used to describe the work being performed by a cost center. Using the previous example, an Activity Type master record would be created to describe the work performed by the IT Services cost center. Perhaps it is given the name, "IT Support". When the cost center, "IT Services" provides support for another cost center, the Activity Type, "IT Support" would be used to describe that work.

The Activity Type master record has two key fields of entry that establish the integration necessary for ABC. First, the Activity Type master record must be linked to a Secondary Cost Element. Continuing with the example of IT Services, a Secondary Cost Element for posting and tracking cost allocations for "Support" would first be created in FI as a G/L account with the Cost Element Category for Activity Allocation (Figure 4.7).

The Activity Type must also be associated with one or more Cost Center Categories as shown above. This link between the Cost Center Categories and the Activity Type defines which cost centers can perform which activities. Not all cost centers can perform all activities. However, some activities can be performed by more than one cost center, and some cost centers can perform more than one activity.

Finally, the last master data needed for ABC is the Activity Price. The Activity Price places a value on every unique combination of Cost Center/Activity Type. It is important to note that this price is for every unique combination of Cost Center/Activity Type (Figure 4.8) because more than one cost center can perform the same activity. For instance, suppose there was a second cost center who can also provide IT Support. Each of these two cost centers likely have different rates of pay for their employees. So, it is very possible the value of IT Support performed by one cost center is different than the value performed by the other. The Activity Price can include fixed and/or variable rates and is often planned with the use of many criteria in the SAP S/4HANA system, such as rates of pay as in our example.

HINT: Every time you encounter a combination of Cost Center/Activity Type combination in any business process, you should immediately be thinking the system will automatically derive the associated Activity Price.

Figure 4.8: Activity Type/Cost Centers - > Activity Price

Internal Orders

Internal Orders are temporary cost collectors, usually for a specific purpose. They are considered temporary cost collectors because one or more cost objects (e.g., costs centers) are ultimately responsible for the actual costs. We often refer to internal orders as examples of Order-Related Cost Objects. There are four basic types of internal orders:

1. Overhead Orders
2. Investment Orders
3. Accrual Orders
4. Orders with Revenue

Overhead orders are generally used to capture different types of overhead costs (e.g., utilities, insurance) that will later be settled to one or more receivers of those costs. As an example, an Overhead Order can be used to centralize and track the costs of electric usage for a given month. When the monthly electric bill arrives, the cost can be sent directly to the overheard order for this purpose. This order will hold these costs until the end of the month when the costs need to be settled to the cost centers responsible for generating the electric costs. This type of an internal order is often settled to costs centers.[2]

---

[2] This is only a single example and isn't intended to be exhaustive for the functions on Overhead Orders.

The term, “settle” will be discussed later in this chapter when we get into more detail about the various transactions for Order-Related Cost Object Controlling. For now, “settle” in terms of an internal order simply means sending the costs from an order to responsible receivers of those costs.

Investment orders are typically settled to Asset accounts. An example of using an investment order may be to track the costs of renovation of a building. Assuming the completion of the renovation will add value to the building (i.e, fixed asset), the costs of the renovation can be used to calculate the added value. Hence, the renovation is an investment in that fixed asset. All costs associated with the renovation can be posted directly to the investment order, then settled later to the asset to show the increase in value of that asset.

Accrual orders are often settled to various receivers. Like other types of internal orders, an accrual order can be used to track costs for a specific purpose. As costs are incurred, they can be posted directly to the accrual order. In the end, one or more parties are going to be responsible for the actual costs and the internal order will then be settled to the responsible parties. How the costs are settled will also be addressed later in this chapter.

An Order with Revenue is generally used when the company is using a third-party software solution for sales. The sales process is generally where revenue is generated. If a company is not using an SAP solution to do this, there is limited capacity in the system to generate revenue. When revenue is generated using a third-party software solution, an order with revenue can be created to track the revenue. Using this type of internal order for this purpose allows the revenue to be recorded in the SAP system and further managed in CO.

Finally, internal order can also be statistical. Statistical simply means the order is being used to track information about costs and/or revenues and DOES NOT collect any actual costs or revenues. A statistical order CAN NOT be settled. An order can only be settled if there are actual values in the order. Suppose we create a statistical internal order for a company picnic to record information regarding the costs of the picnic. Doing so will allow the company to still be able to manage the sum of the costs in one place. However, if a statistical order is used for the company picnic, the order can not be settled because there are no real or true costs to settle. Instead, these costs MUST be posted directly to the responsible party immediately as they are incurred. Figure 4.9 shows several Statistical Objects.

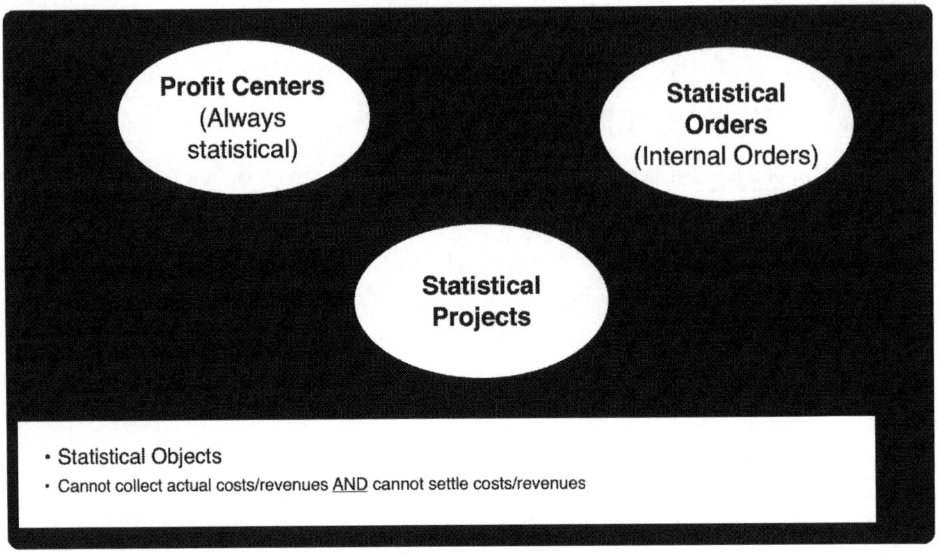

Figure 4.9: Statistical Objects

Statistical Key Figures

Statistical Key Figures (SKF) are an example of Tracing Factors, which are metrics used to perform allocations within CO in SAP S/4HANA. More specifically, SKFs are master data used to measure periodic allocations. A periodic allocation can be either a Distribution or an Assessment and is performed at the end of the accounting period (typically at month's end). Again, we will discuss the transactional aspects of management accounting a little later in this chapter. But for now, let's use an example to further explain the use of SKFs. In Figure 4.10, you see a cost in the amount of $500 associated with an incoming invoice from the local utility company for water usage. The company has decided to post the cost directly to one of its cost centers (CCtr A) rather than creating an internal order to manage the cost.

Since Cost Center A, as well as two additional cost centers (CCtr B & CCtr C) consume water, the cost of $500 needs to be distributed accordingly by the end of the accounting period. The question becomes, how much of the $500 is allocated to each of the three cost centers?

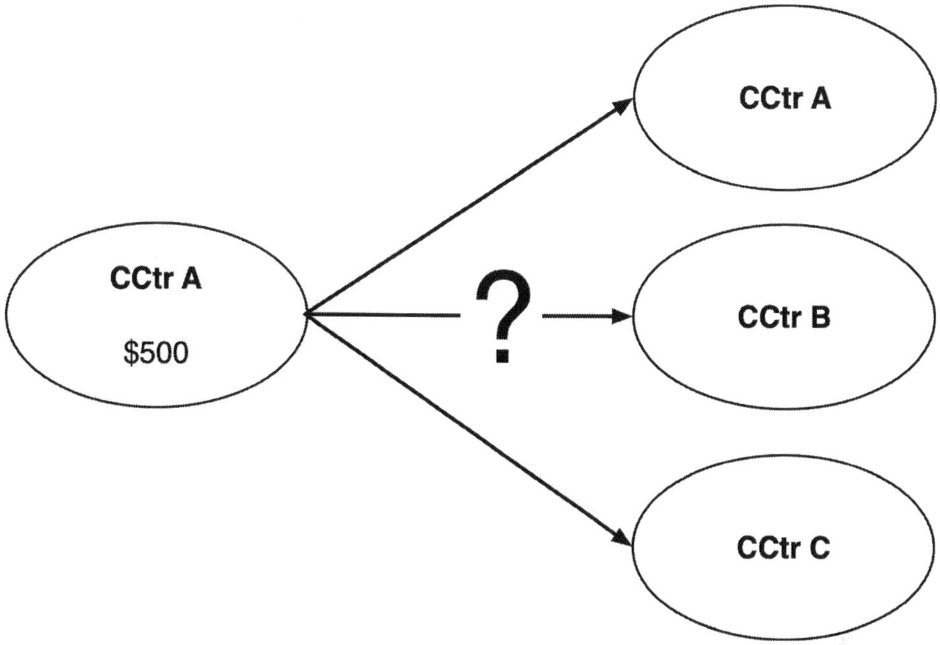

Figure 4.10: $500 Utility Costs Posted to Cost Center A

To answer this question, we can use Statistical Key Figures. There are two types of SKFs: Fixed and Totals. In short, a Fixed SKF is used when you perform the allocation based on some fixed values that don't typically change each period. These are things like number of employees, square footage of space. A Totals SKF is essentially based on actual consumption statistics. In the above example, the use of a Totals SKF would require each cost center have a means for recording the actual use of water each month. If these cost centers represent offices within a building, this would be an impractical approach for allocating the $500. Instead, a Fixed SKF would be more appropriate. Let's assume the number of employees is used as the Fixed SKF and the number of employees in each costs center are as follows: CCtr A – 50, CCtr B – 30, CCtr C- 20. Knowing the number of employees in each cost center can then be used to perform the allocation. Figure 4.11 shows the results of the allocation using the Fixed SKF of number of employees.

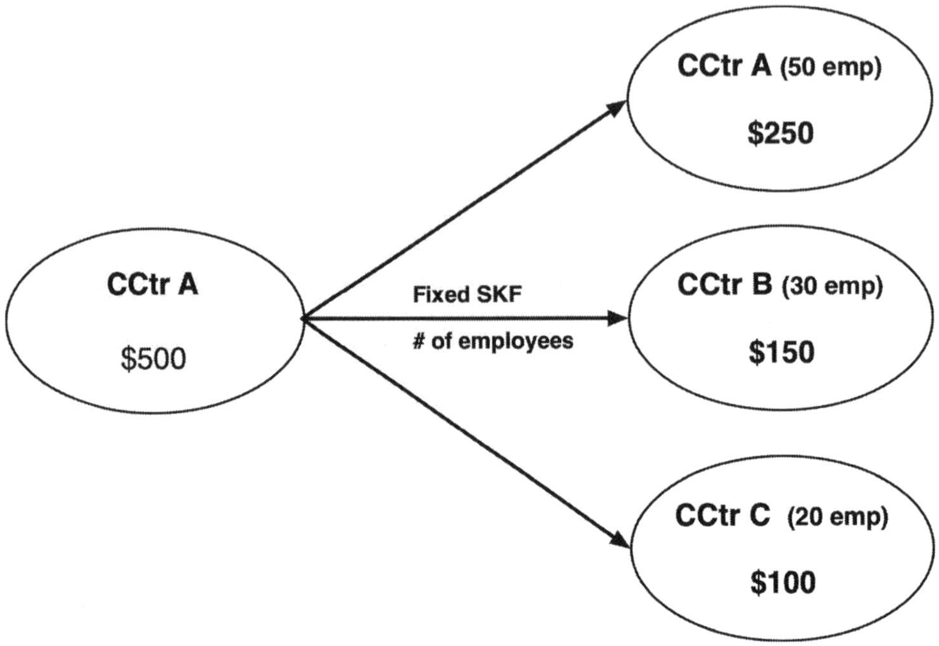

Figure 4.11: Periodic Allocation of $500 Utility Costs Using a Fixed Statistical Key Figure

A few years back, a hurricane stormed through the neighborhood where one of the author's lives. There was significant damage to some of the common areas in the neighborhood including damage to the pool, clubhouse, and roads that were littered with downed trees. Because the homeowners in the neighborhood belong to a Homeowner's Association (HOA), the HOA paid for the repairs out of the its cash account. The cost of repairs was not budgeted in the homeowners' dues, so the sum of these costs was allocated to the homeowners. In other words, each homeowner was assessed a share of these costs. An assessment is performed in the same manner as described in our previous example. An assessment combines costs that need to be allocated using a SKF. Thus an assessment requires a Secondary Cost Element.

Profit Center Accounting

As you can see from Figure 4.9, Profit Centers are ALWAYS statistical. Profit Centers are used to manage costs and revenues for internal areas of responsibility. They can also be used to manage things like return on investment (ROI). Because they are statistical, profit centers receive only information about costs and revenues for which it is responsible. Let's suppose a company has decided to open and manage a cafeteria in one of their office buildings so employees have an option for lunch without having to leave their place of work. A profit center can be created to calculate ROI for the cafeteria as well as looking at the impacts the cafeteria has on the business. As we saw from our discussion on cost centers, the company could also create a cost center for the cafeteria and link it to the profit center. Because cost centers are not statistical, any costs incurred at the cafeteria (e.g., labor, supplies) would be posted directly to the cost center, then statistically recorded in the profit center. As revenue is generated, the revenue from items sold can also be recorded in the profit center. This provides the company with the necessary information to calculate ROI as well as the profitability of the cafeteria. (See Figure 4.12)

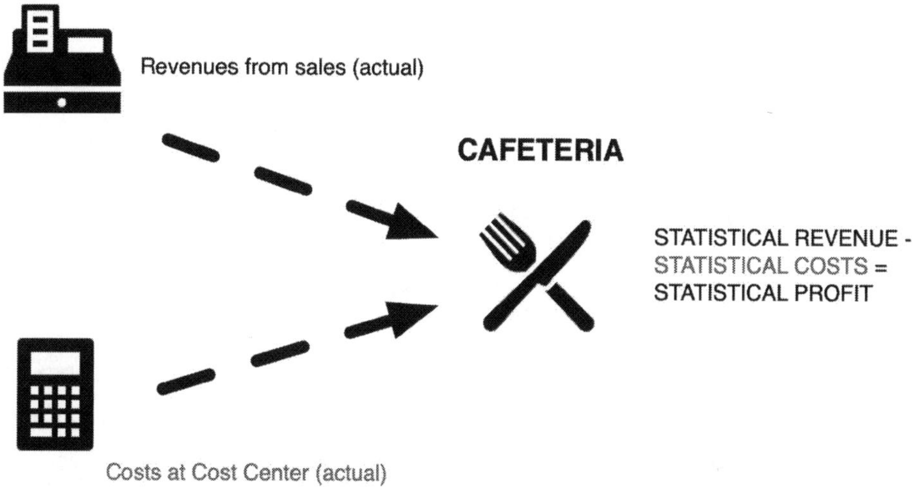

Figure 4.12: Profit Center Example

Several objects can be assigned to a Profit Center to ensure the Profit Center receives statistical postings. These objects include, but are not limited to, cost centers, profitability segments, materials, line items in a sales order, internal orders, and production orders.

Profitability Analysis (Margin Analysis)

Profitability Segment

While Profit Centers measure profitability of internal areas of responsibility, Profitability Analysis (CO-PA) measures profitability of external market segments, also known as profitability segments. This is information often used by market analysts, strategists, and planners in the enterprise. CO-PA is performed in the Operating Concern organizational level.

Profitability segments are composed of two or more characteristics. Examples of such characteristics include Product, Customer, Country, Sales Organization, Sales Rep. While characteristics make up a profitability segment, key figures are used as measures for profitability. Key figures include such things as: Revenue, Material Costs, and Quantities.

A typical CO-PA scenario would be to analyze the profit of products by customer and country. In this scenario, products, customers, and country define the profitability segment. Key figures such as revenue and cost are used to calculate profit margin.

Product Cost Controlling

Product Cost Controlling Object

The category of Product Cost Controlling consists of several types of cost objects. Of course, Production Orders fall into this category. However, some forms of Internal Orders, Projects, and Maintenance Orders can also be categorized under Product Cost Controlling. We have already had a brief discussion above on Internal Orders and we will discuss Projects and Maintenance Orders a bit later in this book. So, for the time being, we will focus on Production Orders here.

Product Cost Controlling

There are three phases associated with Product Cost Controlling. They are listed below:

- Product Cost Planning
- Cost Object Controlling
- Actual Costing and Material Ledger

Product Cost Planning

The objective of Product Cost Planning is to generate a Product Cost Estimate (sometimes referred to as the Standard Cost Estimate) for a product. Because our focus here is on integration, we don't take a deep dive into the methodologies for calculating some of the planned costs. What is important is understanding how specific master data factor into the planned costs. For now, we will only provide a brief description of the master data involved. More detail about these master data will be covered in the chapter related to production.

Let's suppose you were asked to define what it costs to assemble an office chair. You would likely begin by suggesting we consider the costs of the parts that go into the office chair. In Figure 4.13, you see an example of the parts that make up an office chair.

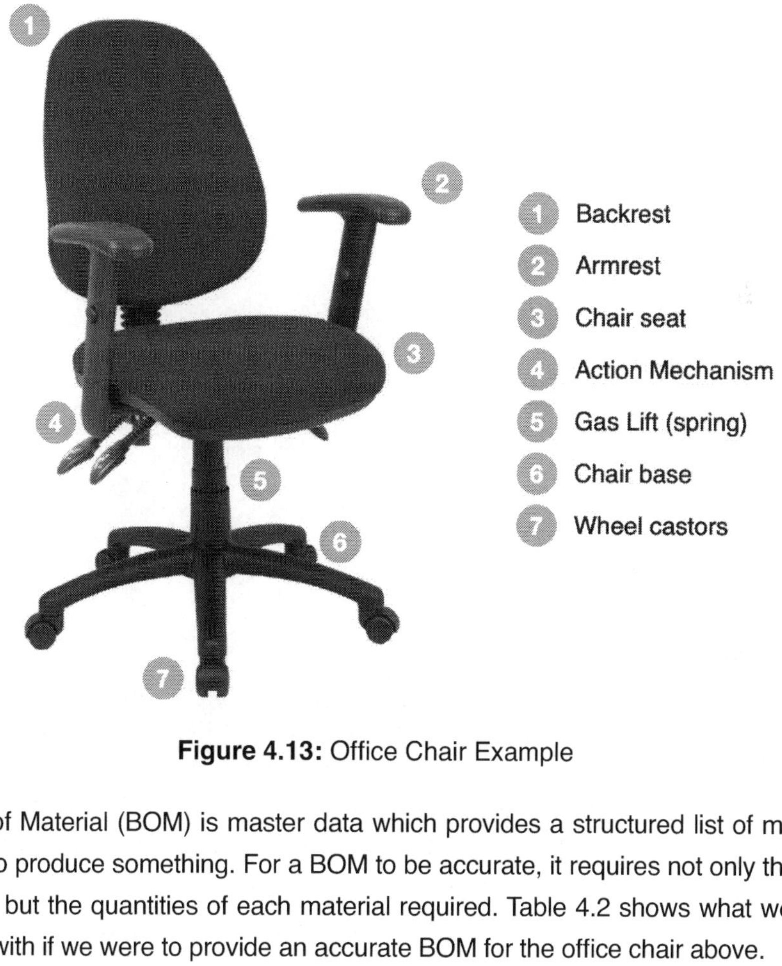

Figure 4.13: Office Chair Example

A Bill of Material (BOM) is master data which provides a structured list of materials required to produce something. For a BOM to be accurate, it requires not only the list of materials, but the quantities of each material required. Table 4.2 shows what we might come up with if we were to provide an accurate BOM for the office chair above.

To capture the costs of producing the office chair we would also need to know the value of each of the materials listed above. SAP refers to this value as the Material Price. The Material Price depends on the type of material used in production. As a rule, materials purchased for use in manufacturing use a Moving Average valuation method. This means the material valuation could change each time we purchase that material.

Materials that are produced internally (i.e., not purchased from a supplier), use a Standard Price valuation method. This means the value of the material will remain constant. We will address the Standard Price in a little while when we cover the last phase of Product Cost Controlling: Actual Costing and Material Ledger. For purposes of simplicity, let's use the information in Table 4.3 to derive the costs of producing the office chair.

Table 4.2: Office Chair Parts (BOM)

Material	Quantity
Backrest	1ea
Armrest	2ea
Chair seat	1ea
Action mechanism	1ea
Gas lift (spring)	1ea
Chair base	1ea
Wheel castors	5ea

Table 4.3: Material Costs of Office Chair

Material	Quantity	Price Per Unit	Total Costs
Backrest	1ea	$7	$7
Armrest	2ea	$2	$4
Chair Seat	1ea	$7	$7
Action Mechanism	1ea	$10	$10
Gas Lift (spring)	1ea	$10	$10
Chair Base	1ea	$5	$5
Wheel Castors	5ea	$1	$5
			Total: $48

The information from this table provides us with a good estimate of the material costs of producing the office chair. Keep in mind, this is simply an estimate because some of the costs were likely derived by using the Moving Average Price, which means the costs shown above are time dependent. If we were to repeat this process at a later date, it's very possible the value of some of the materials listed would have changed.

Referring to the original task of defining the costs to produce this office chair, you would also suggest considering labor costs required to assemble the office chair. The Master Data which defines the assembly of the office chair is called a Routing. Routing master data contains operations, or more simply, the steps required to produce something. Table 4.4 shows the Routing to produce the office chair.

Table 4.4: Routing Master Data: Operations to Produce Office Chair

Operation	Activity Type	Work Center/ Cost Center	Time (min)
Attach Chair seat to Backrest	Assembly	Production	5
Attach Armrest	Assembly	Production	5
Attach Action mechanism	Assembly	Production	3
Attach Gas lift (spring) and Wheel castors to Chair base	Assembly	Production	7
Attach Chair seat to Gas lift (spring)	Assembly	Production	5

If you recall from our discussion on Activity Based Costing (ABC), activity types and cost centers are used perform the allocation of costs based on work performed. Our example above includes both the activity type and cost center information. The combination of activity type/cost center provides us with the activity price (Figure 4.8).

Let's assume the Activity Price for Assembly Activity Type/Production Cost Center combination is $1/min. Our Routing example now contains the information regarding labor costs associated with producing the office chair (Table 4.5).

Table 4.5: Routing: Labor Costs for Office Chair

Operation	Activity Type	Work Center/ Cost Center	Time (min)	Activity Price	Costs
Attach Chair seat to Backrest	Assembly	Production	5	$1/min.	$5
Attach Armrest	Assembly	Production	5	$1/min.	$5
Attach Action mechanism	Assembly	Production	3	$1/min.	$3
Attach Gas lift (spring) and Wheel castors to Chair base	Assembly	Production	7	$1/min.	$7
Attach Chair seat to Gas lift (spring)	Assembly	Production	5	$1/min.	$5
					Total: $25

We now have the material costs ($48) and labor costs ($25) associated with producing the office chair. Two master data were used to assist with deriving these costs: The Bill of Material and Routing. Thus, the Product Cost Estimate is derived by analyzing the BOMs and Routings on both a Quantity and Value structure (Figure 4.14).

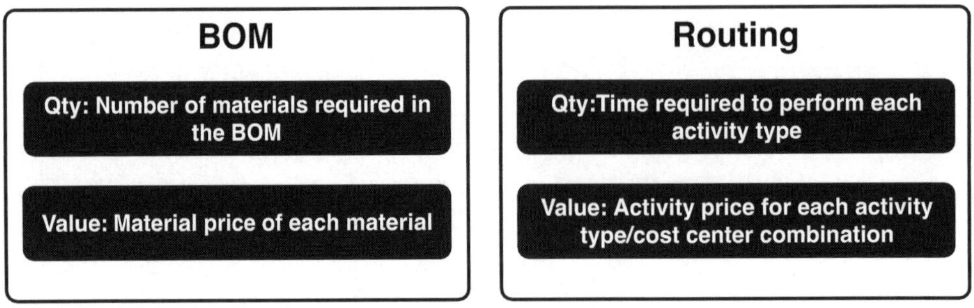

Figure 4.14: BOM and Routing on a Qty and Value Structure

If you were thinking that there are other costs associated with producing the office chair, you would be correct. However, we mentioned above that we will not be taking a deep dive into how some of these other costs are derived. These additional costs can be categorized as Overhead and Process costs. From an integration perspective, it's most important for you to know that costs for the Product Cost Estimate come from the BOM and Routing by looking at their respective quantity and value structures.

What is so important about the Product Cost Estimate? Why does it matter? There are four main uses of the Product Cost Estimate and they are not mutually exclusive (Figure 4.15).

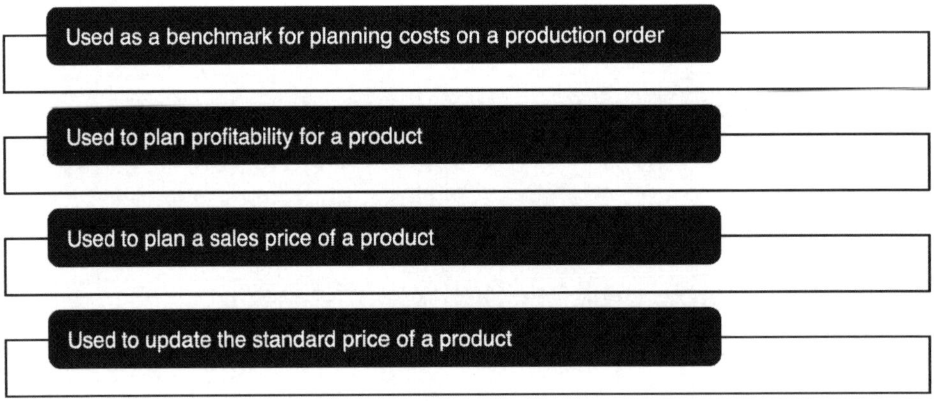

Figure 4.15: Uses for Product Cost Estimate

<u>Cost Object Controlling</u>

The objective of Cost Object Controlling is to capture actual costs during the production process. In this section, we introduce you to Order-Related Cost Object Controlling.

We have seen earlier that cost centers can collect costs for possible reallocation. In SAP, cost centers are not the only objects that can collect costs. In the Cost Object Controlling phase of Product Cost Controlling, we consider the production order as the cost object. Let's take an example of a production order with a requirement of 100 units of some product. In order to compute the unit cost of that batch of material, we would need to accumulate all costs that go towards completing that production order. Similar to the way in which we planned costs to produce something we look at the BOM and Routing to find the material and labor costs for actual production. In Cost Object Controlling, we need to capture the actual costs, so we use the production order to collect these costs as production progresses. For example, when materials are issued, the materials costs are added to the production order. Later some labor time might be incurred on the production order and those costs are also added to the production order, and so on. Thus, the production order acts as a cost collector and is an example of an Order-Related Cost Object.

As we noted earlier, in addition to production orders, other orders like maintenance orders, internal orders (also called CO orders), and projects can collect costs. These are also Order- Related Cost Objects. Though each of these orders is used for different processes, there are great similarities in the management accounting process that each goes through.

They all follow a standard sequence of steps from a management accounting viewpoint. Figure 4.16 shows the steps in the standard process that applies to all order-related costs objects.[3]

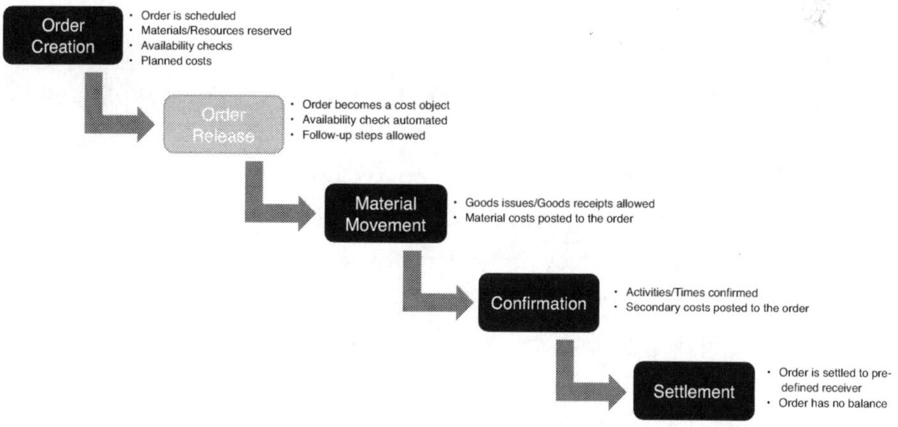

Figure 4.16: Order-Related Cost Object Controlling

[3] Order-related cost objects are managed using order types. Some of these order types may have additional steps required that are unique to its own process.

During order creation, the order has not yet become a cost object. At this stage, this simply means costs cannot yet be posted to the order. However, the order is scheduled (as in the case of a production order) when resources necessary to perform work on the order become available. Thus, resources become reserved for this order. Materials from the BOM will also be required for the production order. Like resources, materials are placed on reservation for the order. In addition, the Product Cost Estimate is referenced to plan costs for this production order.

The next step in order-related cost object controlling is the order release (highlighted in Figure 4.16). This is the most important step. If the order is not released, none of the follow-on steps can be completed. It is this step in which the order officially becomes a cost object. Actual costs can now be posted to this order and can be compared to the planned costs that were calculated using the Product Cost Estimate. If the user did not check material availability when the order was created, SAP S/4HANA automatically checks to see if materials are available. If they are not available, depending on the system settings, the system can block the order release until materials become available.

The step after the release of the order is generally a goods movement. The goods movement could be a goods issue from inventory to the order, or a goods receipt from a purchase order to the order. When these goods movements are posted, they are posted to a primary cost account in financial accounting. Recall, the primary cost account is now the account type used for primary cost elements which are required to post the costs to the order in management accounting. These are actual costs which again can be compared to the planned costs in the order.

Material costs are not the only costs associated with order-related cost object controlling. There are additional costs resulting from work completed on the order by one or more work centers.[4] These costs are posted to the order when work centers confirm the work they performed. They could confirm this work in various ways, but the most common methods are to confirm the amount of time they spent working on the order as well as which activities they performed. These costs are considered secondary costs because they are not a result of direct expenses posted from financial accounting. Instead, they are costs that are allocated to the order from a cost center in management accounting. Recall that secondary cost elements are now a G/L account type used to allocate such costs. Like the planning of labor costs, the Routings contain the operations used to record the labor costs on the production order.

---

[4] A work center is associated with a specific cost center.

Finally, the order will go through the settlement step. Here, the costs collected in the order are normally settled to a predefined receiver. A receiver is an object that is ultimately responsible for the costs in the order. In management accounting, an order-related cost object can settle its costs to financial accounting general ledger accounts. Other receivers might be cost centers, projects, other orders, or profitability segments. In the end, the order is settled so there are no remaining costs. In other words, the order has no balance on the debit or credit sides. Its debit and credit entries balance out.

Actual Costing and Material Ledger

Actual costing is a process supported by SAP S/4HANA, in which the system tracks actual costs of a material during an accounting period and uses these actual costs to value materials. Some refer to this as the "actual price" because actual costs are used to determine its value. It is also referred to as a "per unit price". All goods movements are valued based on the material price found in the Accounting view in the material master record. Raw materials are valued using a moving average price, while semi-finished and finished goods use a standard price. The Material Ledger allows these material prices to be maintained in various currencies. Because Actual Costing is used to keep track of actual value of a material, it can be used as a basis for updating the standard price of the material. The Material Ledger is also part of this process. The Material Ledger keeps track of values of all goods movements that had an impact on the balance sheet and records that value at the time of each goods movement. Because SAP uses moving average prices to value materials, it does not natively support LIFO/FIFO (Last In, First Out/First In, Last Out) accounting. The Material Ledger can be used for this purpose when specific accounting principles require LIFO/FIFO accounting practices. Keep in mind, the standard price can only be updated once per accounting period. Thus, its price remains constant throughout the entire period.

Updating the Standard Price is a three-step process (Figure 4.17). First, the business must analyze the cost results. The cost results could be from Actual Costing, Material Ledger, and/or from the Product Cost Estimate. If the analysis provides substantial evidence for updating the value of the material in the general ledger, then the costs are marked. Marking the costs results in a "Future Price". This is an indication that the price needs to be updated before the next accounting period. The last step is to release the costs. Releasing the costs results in the updating of the standard price and a change in valuation in the general ledger. What was previously the "Future Price" now becomes the "Current Price".

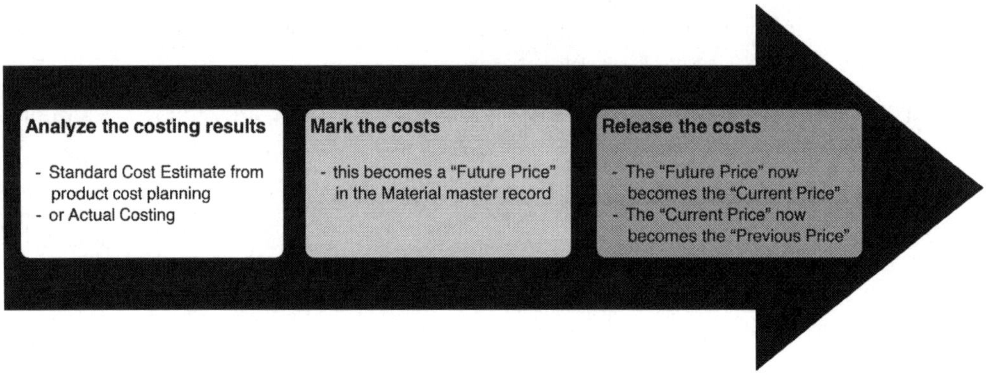

Figure 4.17: Updating Standard Price of a Material

Management Accounting: Other Transactions

Posting Logic

One of the more important transactions that occur in Management Accounting are the postings that originate in Financial Accounting. These transactions follow a very specific posting logic and the process remains constant in each situation.

As a rule, when a posting occurs that impacts a Primary Cost Account, it must be recorded to a cost object (account assignment object) in Controlling. As a result, the transaction gets recorded in both FI and CO. To gain a better understanding, let's use the following example. Suppose the HR department processed payroll for one of the existing cost centers. For purposes of demonstration, let's use the cost center "Marketing". The payroll run will result in an impact in financial accounting because it will be recorded as a payroll expense and the funds will come out of a cash account. (Figure 4.18).

The Payroll Expense account above is the Account Type "Primary Cost or Revenue Account". Recall from our earlier discussions, a Primary Cost Element in CO was created simultaneously with this G/L account in FI. The Cash account is of Account Type "Balance Sheet", and that account type is not relevant to Controlling. However, postings to Primary Cost or Revenue Accounts will also need to be recorded in Controlling.

Figure 4.18: FI Impact of Payroll

Because the posting to the Payroll Expense Account must be recorded in Controlling, the S/4HANA system will need to know the account assignment object responsible for this cost. It is mandatory to enter the account assignment object in EVERY transaction that will post to a Primary Cost or Revenue Account in the general ledger. An account assignment object is the cost object in Controlling responsible for the cost. In our example, the account assignment object is the Marketing cost center. As we can see in Figure 4.19, as soon as the transaction is posted in FI, the primary cost element recognizes the expense posting and records it as a cost to the cost object.

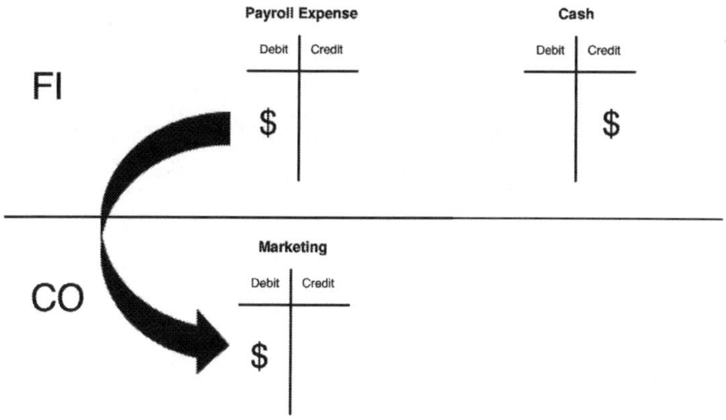

Figure 4.19: FI and CO Impact on Payroll

The posting logic (Figure 4.20) doesn't change because the business transaction does. In every instance where a posting impacts a Primary Cost or Revenue account, the primary cost element will record that as a cost to the assigned cost object.

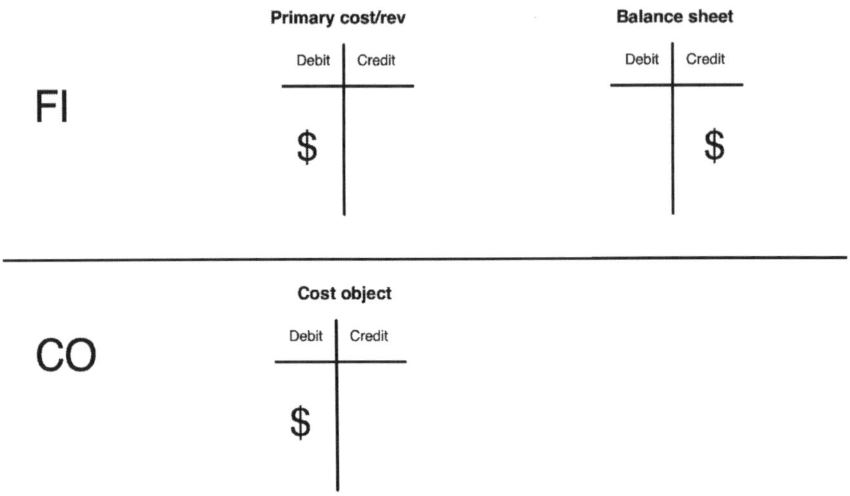

Figure 4.20: Posting Logic

Activity Allocations

Activity Allocations are the result of Activity-Based Costing (ABC). There are two types of activity allocations, Direct and Indirect. In Direct Activity Allocation, a transaction is performed to specifically allocate costs from one cost center to another using an activity type. Indirect Activity Allocation can be seen in the confirmation step in Order Related Cost Object Controlling. During confirmation, the work center confirms actual time worked on operations in the order. As a result, the associated cost center automatically allocates costs to the order. This is considered an indirect allocation because the allocation occurs as a result of the confirmation transaction. It might be easiest to think of "Direct" as a manual transaction, while "Indirect" is an automated response to another transaction, such as confirming times on an operation of an order.

Assessments

Assessments are an example of Periodic Allocations which use Statistical Key Figures SKF). Earlier in this chapter we discussed Statistical Key Figures and provided an example of an assessment. Statistical Key Figures fall into one of two categories: Fixed or Totals. SKFs are used to measure allocations of costs during periodic allocations. In an assessment, multiple primary costs (and possibly some secondary costs) are collected in a cost center and are later allocated to other cost centers using an SKF at the end of the accounting period. A secondary cost element is used to perform an assessment.

Management Accounting Summary

Management accounting is a complex topic. There are many areas which make up management accounting, but only two organizational levels which make up the Enterprise Structure: Operating Concern and Controlling Area. The Operating Concern is used for Profitability Analysis. All other areas of Controlling (Overhead Cost Controlling, Product Cost Controlling, and Cost Element Accounting) reside in the Controlling Area.

In Cost Element Accounting, primary cost elements are used to post expenses from FI as costs in CO. And, secondary cost elements are used to perform allocations within CO.

Overhead Cost Controlling includes Cost Center Accounting, Internal Orders, and Activity Based Costing.

Product Cost Controlling involves Production Orders, Maintenance Orders, and Projects. Regarding production, there are three phases of Product Cost Accounting: Product Cost Planning, Cost Object Controlling, and Actual Costing and Material Ledger.

Chapter 5: Procurement

The procurement function entails the acquisitions of goods and services required by the business. Our focus in this chapter regarding this function will be the Source-to-Pay process. The Source-to-Pay process is a logistics process in the SAP S4HANA system. You will find that we will take a similar approach in each chapter of this book by addressing the various organizational levels in the Enterprise Structure, master data, and transactions involved. Where applicable, we will also address the process in the context of the Intelligent Enterprise. This chapter marks the first logistics module in SAP S/4HANA that we cover in this book. With that said, you will find some consistencies across all logistics modules.

Best-Practice Scenario for the Source-to-Pay Process

Before we dive into some specifics related to data and transactions, we will take a look at items that are included in a "best-practice" scenario related to the Source-to-Pay process. A little background on "best-practice" scenarios is necessary to gain an understanding of what this entails.

Prior to June 2023, SAP maintained a repository of "best-practice" scenarios in the SAP Best Practices Explorer. The SAP Best Practices Explorer was a tool which provided SAP customers with scenarios for various business processes that were pre-defined and built on years of experience for various industries. After June 2023, the SAP Best Practices Explorer was replaced with the SAP Signavio Process Navigator, which essentially serves a similar purpose. All of the business processes we cover in this book are based on these "best-practice" scenarios. To do this, we present you with the "best-practice" scenario for the Source-to-Pay process in the Intelligent Enterprise in Figure 5.1.

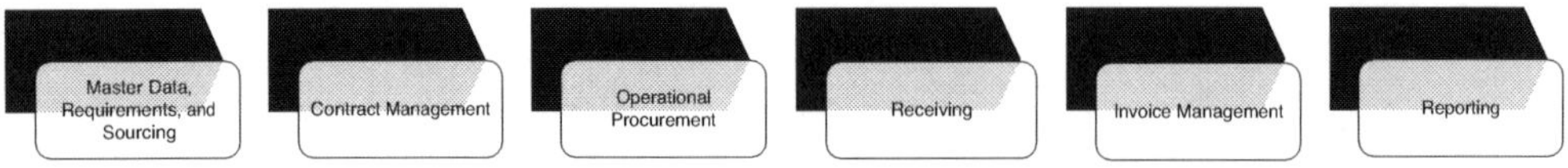

Figure 5.1: Best-Practice Scenario for the Source-to-Pay Process

Master Data, Requirement, and Sourcing

The first item in the "best-practice" scenario for this process, "Master Data, Requirement, and Sourcing" is quite inclusive. It addresses several items which we will address in more detail later in this chapter. But for now, let's get a broad understanding of what this item entails. First, the Source-to-Pay process is going to require specific Master Data. This should come as no surprise to us, since we are already aware that business transactions always require some elements of master data.

Second, we need an understanding of what is meant by "Requirement". To better understand this, think of "Requirement" as being synonymous with "demand". In this sense, "Requirement" simply means that there is a "demand" to procure something. This is what triggers the process. On a personal level, we typically don't make a decision to purchase something without having a need or desire. The need or desire represents some demand that drives us to purchase items. In SAP, the "Requirement" is documented with the creation of a Purchase Requisition.

Third, we address the inclusion of "Sourcing" as part of the first step of this process. Sourcing answers the question: Who do we buy from? The answer to this question can be resolved in numerous ways that range from simple to complex. Later in this chapter, you'll see that master data can also serve a role in helping answer this question.

As we continue discussing this part of the process, let's reflect on a discussion we had in Chapter 2. In Chapter 2, we described the Intelligent Enterprise as the bringing together of Intelligent Technologies, Intelligent Processes, Collaborative Networks, Cloud capabilities, and a Technology Platform in a manner that supports innovation. The Intelligent Enterprise is on full display in the first step of the Source-to-Pay process. SAP offers several cloud technologies that integrate with procurement, however one in particular is of exceptional value in this step: SAP Ariba.

SAP Ariba is a cloud-based product that digitizes the entire Source-to-Pay process. Digitization of the process reduces errors, creates efficiencies, and leads to cost savings. SAP Ariba includes the SAP Ariba Business Network (formerly the Ariba Network). The Business Network includes thousands of sellers (vendors) from which companies can explore to help find the best products, at the right prices, from the most suitable vendor.

There are several components of SAP Ariba which enhance the first step in the Source-to-Pay process, the first of which is SAP Ariba Procurement. SAP Ariba Procurement can be leveraged to manage the entire procurement process, including the creation of purchase requisitions. This means an SAP customer can take advantage of SAP Ariba Procurement to create a purchase requisition and integrate it with the SAP S/4HANA solution using the integration capabilities available in the SAP Business Technology Platform. In addition to SAP Ariba Procurement, SAP Ariba Sourcing, SAP Ariba Business Network Discovery, SAP Ariba Supplier Management, and SAP Ariba Strategic Sourcing are available solutions within SAP Ariba to support sourcing.

Contract Management

"Contract Management" is the second item in the "best-practice" scenario for the Source-to-Pay process in the Intelligent Enterprise. Contract Management can result from sourcing where the buyer finds a valid supplier for materials, but can take it a step further by creating long-term agreements with that specific supplier. It is equally likely that Contract Management can be used to assist with a sourcing decision. In such cases, SAP S/4HANA can be configured in such a way that when a requirement for a material is identified, the system will look to see if a contract exists and can then assign the source of supply automatically.

In SAP S/4HANA, Outline Agreements is the term used to represent two different forms of long-term purchasing agreements: Contracts and Scheduling Agreements. Let's start with Contracts since this one is probably more familiar to you than Scheduling Agreements. There are two basic types of contracts in SAP. The first is labeled a "Quantity Contract". In a Quantity Contract, an agreement is made with the supplier to include specific quantities of one or more materials to be purchased over a specific period of time. The other type of contract is a "Value Contract". A Value Contract is an agreement with a supplier to include a monetary value that the buyer will spend over a specified period of time. In both cases, the contracts are used as references for creating Purchase Orders.

Scheduling Agreements is the other form of an Outline Agreement. The differentiating factor between Contracts and Scheduling Agreements is that Scheduling Agreements are used to manage shipments/deliveries of materials from the supplier. In these cases, the supplier agrees to specific quantities to be delivered to the buyer over an agreed upon period of time. Shipments/deliveries from the supplier are planned using "Schedule Lines". Scheduling Agreements can be managed two different ways based on the document type assigned to the scheduling agreement. First, it can be managed "Without Release Documentation". This means the agreements includes schedule lines with a fixed delivery schedule from the supplier. The other type is "With Release Documentation". In this scenario, a forecast for deliveries from the supplier is generated so the supplier has a general sense of when materials may be needed. However, in this scenario the schedule lines for delivery are not necessarily communicated in advance to the supplier.

Like the first step in the Source-to-Pay process in the Intelligent Enterprise, this step can be managed with intelligent technologies and does not have to be managed within SAP S/4HANA. Again, SAP Ariba can help support this part of the process through SAP Ariba Contract Management. But SAP Ariba is not the only cloud solution that can be employed here. If a company is interested in procuring services or external skillsets, SAP Fieldglass is a cloud-based vendor management solution. It can be used to procure services, temporary help, or long-term contract arrangements with a service provider (supplier).

Operational Procurement

"Operational Procurement" is simply Purchase Order processing. As mentioned above, we will get into more specifics regarding the Source-to-Pay process in more details a little later in this chapter. With that said, an introduction to Purchase Orders is necessary. In the first step of this process, we were introduced to Purchase Requisitions. A Purchase Requisition documents the "requirement" to purchase something. However it is not a binding document. It is a document internal to the company with the intent to letting the buyers know that there is a demand to purchase something. Unlike a Purchase Requisition, a Purchase Order (PO) is a formal document, legally binding between buyer (the company) and seller (supplier). The PO becomes the document of record for the process and manages all the subsequent steps in the process.

There are again implications here for how PO processing is managed in the Intelligent Enterprise. As noted earlier, SAP Ariba Procurement can be used to manage all or part of this entire process. PO processing can be managed with SAP S/4HANA, but as is the case with other steps involving the Intelligent Enterprise, SAP customers have more tools at their disposal than just SAP S4HANA to execute these steps.

Receiving

The "Receiving" step is the part of the Source-to-Pay process when the supplier has fulfilled the PO and delivered the materials to us. It's at this step where we take receipt of these materials to be placed into inventory (stock items) or to be received for immediate use (consumption) for parts of the business. For materials received into inventory, there is also possible integration with Warehouse Management (LE-WM) or Extended Warehouse Management (SCM-EWM). More information regarding the future of LE-WM and SCM-EWM is provided in Chapter 7. We will cover the impacts of the Receiving step later in this chapter where we explore this in much more detail. For now, it's important to take note that this step results in a great deal of integration across the business. It is also the first step in this process that will integrate with Financial Accounting (Chapter 3). From an Intelligent Enterprise perspective, this step can also be managed within SAP Ariba Procurement.

Invoice Management

If you have some industry experience, you're probably very much aware that this process can be managed using different sequencing for the steps in the Source-to-Pay process. However, this book is based on SAP's Best Practice process scenarios and thus "Invoice Management" follows the "Receiving" step. "Invoice Management" involves two parts, managing vendor invoices and managing payments to vendors. Again, details of this step will be addressed later in this chapter where we will refer to this as "Logistics Invoice Verification" and "Payment". But for now, we will discuss this step at a macro level.

In this step, we receive a bill from the supplier for goods that were delivered and received in the previous step. We refer to this bill from the supplier as a vendor or supplier invoice. An accurate invoice will reflect what was order and received based on the information included in the Purchase Order (PO). Recall, the PO is a legally binding document, therefore it's essential that the invoice accurately reflects what is contained in the PO. The receipt of this invoice results in a financial liability to supplier. In Chapter 3, we discussed the implications of receiving an invoice from a vendor. It creates a liability to the vendor (sub ledger account), which we will refer to as an "open item", and simultaneously posts the liability to our Reconciliation for Accounts Payable in the General Ledger. Recognizing this liability is important for the second part of this step, which is managing payments to vendors.

WIthout a liability to the vendor, we won't have a basis (open item) for submitting a payment to them. Once that liability is recorded via receipt of the vendor invoice, we can now process payment and clear the open item (i.e., liability to the sub ledger account).

As we have already seen regarding the Intelligent Enterprise, SAP Ariba Procurement can support every step along the way in this process. It can manage everything from the creation of the purchase requisition through payment.

Reporting

Although standard reports are available within SAP S/4HANA, this step in the Source-to-Pay process is best managed using cloud solutions. SAP Ariba Spend Management can help SAP customers identify areas where opportunities exist to reduce costs during the process. Likewise, SAP Ariba and SAP S/4HANA Procurement can take advantage of the analytic capabilities of SAP Analytics Cloud.

Procurement Organizational Levels/ Enterprise Structure

Now that we have covered procurement at a macro level, it's time to dig into some of the details which support the Source-to-Pay process. As is the case with each module in SAP S/4HANA that we include in this book, we begin evaluating the necessary data to support the processes by looking at the Enterprise Structure. Every logistics module in SAP S/4HANA (Materials Management (MM), Sales and Distribution (SD), Production (PP) and for our purposes, Enterprise Asset Management (EAM)) involve the same four organizational levels. These are Client, Company Code, Plant, and Storage Location (Figure 5.2). Some logistics modules, like Materials Management Procurement (MM Procurement), will require additional organizational levels. We are already familiar with the Client and Company Code organizational levels. So, let's take a look at the others.

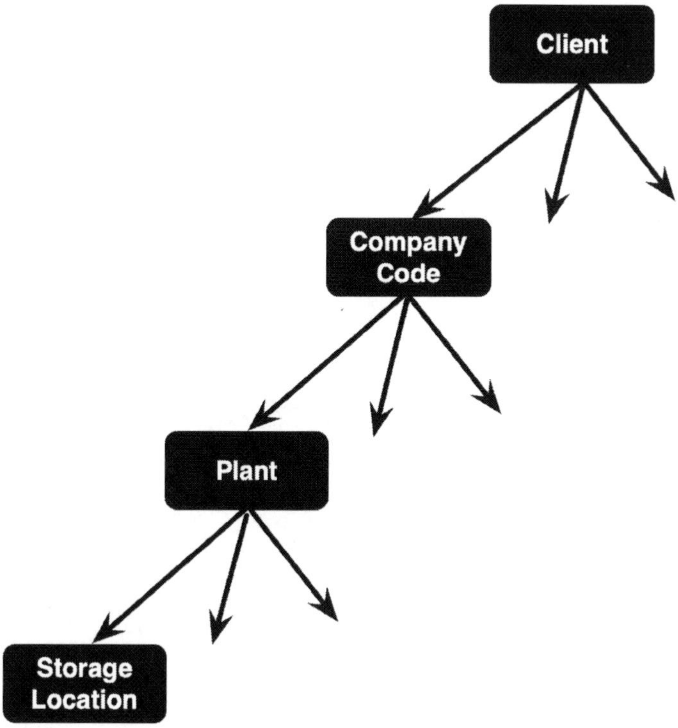

Figure 5.2: Logistics Organizational Levels

A company code may have one or several plants assigned to it. It is important to note that plants in SAP are not always production plants. Plants could also be locations from which services are provided. A plant is where logistics activities occur.

In SAP S/4HANA, materials are managed at the plant level. A plant can also have one or several storage locations assigned to it. A storage location is a location where inventory data is maintained. Thus, we might have 10,000 units of a material in a company code, but this inventory might be kept in several different storage locations across different plants, all of which belong to the same company code.

In MM Procurement, there is one additional organizational level within the Enterprise Structure that is required. That is the Purchasing Organization.

Purchasing Organizations in SAP S/4HANA allow a company to strategically manage the purchase process. A purchasing organization is the organizational level where data regarding terms and conditions are stored. The terms and conditions may be negotiated by many different individuals in the company. It's important to note that purchasing organizations do not represent the "people" who necessarily perform the negotiations. Purchasing activities such as sourcing and buying, are performed by Purchasing Groups. Purchasing Groups could be an individual or a group of individuals tasked with these activities. Purchasing organizations are the organization levels where data related to negotiated terms and conditions are stored. A purchasing organization can thus serve all plants in every company code, only plants within a specific company code, or only a specific plant.

- **Cross-Company Code Purchasing**

  If a company would like every Plant in every Company Code to share the same terms and conditions for purchasing, it would be considered a centralized purchasing strategy. This is also known as "Cross-Company Code Purchasing". In such cases, the negotiated terms and conditions stored in that Purchasing Organization are valid for all of these organizational levels. In other words, this data is "Client-level" data.

- **Cross-Plant Purchasing**

  If a company would like all Plants within a single Company Code to share the same terms and conditions for purchasing, it is considered "Cross-Plant Purchasing". In such cases, the negotiated terms and conditions are stored in a Purchasing Organization that is assigned to a Company Code.

- **Plant SpecificPurchasing**

  Perhaps a company would like for the Plants to be responsible for negotiating their own terms and conditions for purchasing. In such cases, this is considered a decentralized purchasing strategy. This is also known as "Plant Specific Purchasing". In "Plant Specific Purchasing", the negotiated terms and conditions are stored in a Purchasing Organization which is assigned uniquely to one Plant. In this scenario, each Plant would have its own Purchasing Organization assigned.

Figure 5.3 shows the assignment of the Purchasing Organization for the three purchasing strategies.

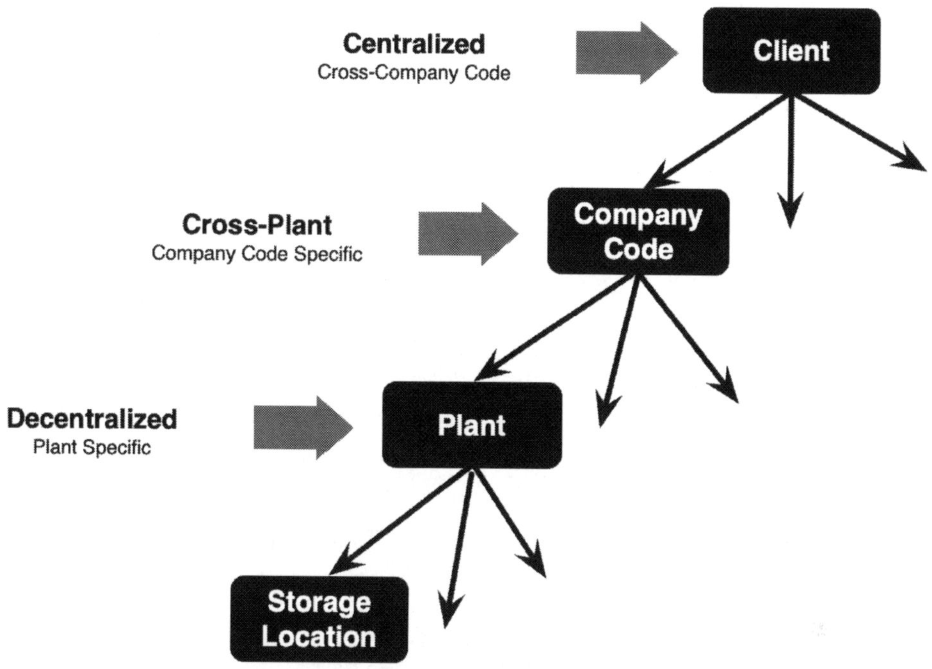

Figure 5.3: Purchasing Strategies/Assignment of Purchasing Organizations

Materials Management: Procurement Master Data

Material (Product) Master Data

Materials account for a significant proportion of purchasing needs in a company. As such, material master data is required to support the purchasing process. As we have discussed in earlier chapters, all master data must be associated with one or more organizational levels. To mitigate the risk of master data redundancy, basic data for a material master record is maintained one time and is stored at the Client level. The basic data would include things like the material name, material number, and other characteristics which describe dimensions of the material (e.g.,weight, and size). The basic data is considered one of the "views" of the material master record. Other views exist which represent the various touchpoints the material will have on the business.

The other views are dependent upon the Material Type assigned to each material. When creating a material master record, every material is assigned a Material Type. Examples of Material Types include, but not limited to, Raw Materials, Semi-finished Products, Finished Products, and Trading Goods. If we take a quick look at some of the material types, you will see how the material master views are dependent on them.

Let's consider a raw material. A raw material is something that is purchased from an external vendor and is used in the manufacturing process to produce something. A raw material will need views for purchasing and production, but it would not be normal to maintain views for sales of a raw material since these materials are not typically used in the sales process. Likewise, a finished product is manufactured and sold, but it is generally not purchased from an external vendor. Thus, views for production and sales are needed, but not views for procurement.

Earlier in this chapter, we mentioned that a Plant is the organization level where logistics activities occur. Materials are widely used in logistics processes and because of this, relevant data for each material is maintained at the plant level to support the business activities, such as those mentioned above for raw materials and finished products. If more than one plant uses the same material, each plant must maintain its own data. Figure 5.4 is an example of how material master data must be maintained when more than one plant uses that material.

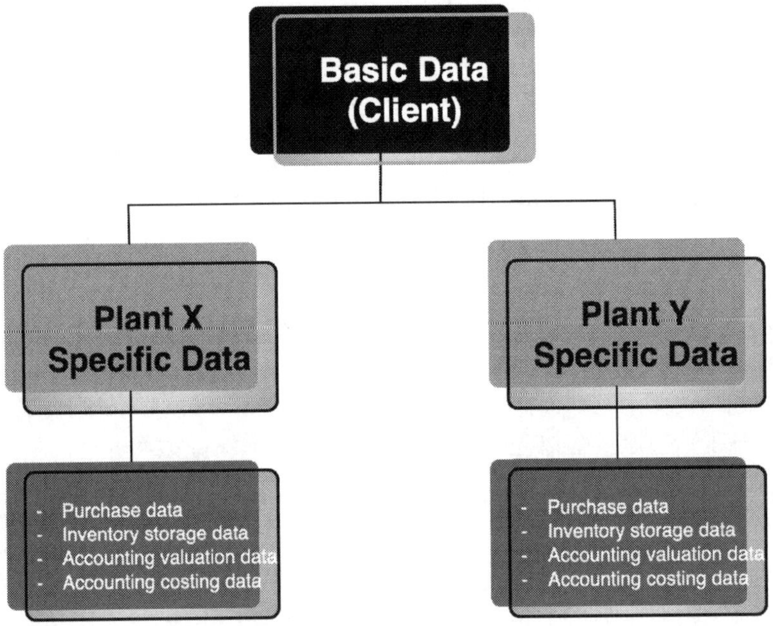

Figure 5.4: Material (Product) Master Data

Within a plant, it is also possible to maintain data specific to other organizational levels. As an example, it is possible to store data specific to a Storage Location. In such cases, we create the data not only at the plant level, but at the storage location level as well.

Vendor Master Data

In Chapter 2, we introduced you to the Business Partner Approach for managing vendors and customers (see Figure 2.11). Master data for vendors in SAP S/4HANA are now maintained as Business Partners. When creating a Business Partner, the first step is to define the Business Partner Category. The Business Partner Categories are listed below:

- Person
- Group
- Organization

The category, Person is generally used in a Business to Consumer relationship. A group category is a bit more challenging to grasp. A group is a group of people, not necessarily a business. An example might be a student organization on a college campus which consists of several student officers. This would qualify as a group for a Business Partner Category. Finally, a business partner can be categorized as an organization. This is usually a business to business relationship.

To support the procurement activities, a vendor master record is required. To create a vendor using the business partner approach, three partner roles are needed. First, the General Business Partner role is required. Like material master data, it is important to mitigate the risk of master data redundancy. Therefore, this role is created at the client organizational level. In this role we maintain data such as the business partner name, business partner number, address (multiple addresses may be stored), and language.

Next, we need the role of FI Vendor. This role is needed to link the vendor subledger account to the reconciliation account in the General Ledger. For vendors, we link the business partner to the reconciliation account for payables. This role is maintained at the company code organizational level because that is where we perform all G/L account entries.

Finally, to support the purchasing process in MM Procurement, it is required to maintain the Supplier Role (sometimes referred to as the Vendor Role). This role is stored in the purchasing organization level. In here we can keep information regarding terms that have been negotiated with the business partner. These include such things as payment terms and currencies. Figure 5.5 shows the business partner roles required for a vendor.

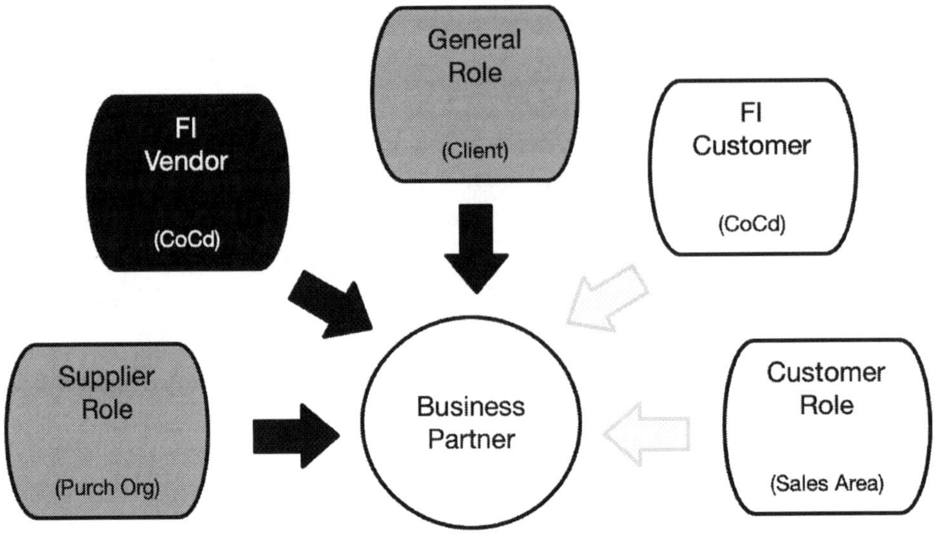

Figure 5.5: Business Partner Roles for Vendors (Replica of Figure 2.11)

Purchasing Info-Record

Purchasing Info-Records (Figure 5.6) are master data that serve various functions in the procurement process. But one of its primary objectives is to support the buyers when making sourcing decisions. The Purchasing Info-Record links a material to a vendor. It is a one-to-one relationship, which means it contains information for only one material and one vendor. Because this master record supports the sourcing decision, it's important to include terms and conditions data. Terms and conditions are stored in a purchasing organization. Therefore, a Purchasing Info-Record is maintained at the purchasing organization level.

From the example in Figure 5.6, we see conditions and terms or purchasing as described earlier. But other data can also be included in a Purchasing Info-Record. It is possible to keep text/notes regarding the relationship of this material and vendor. Such things as the quality of materials, defect rates, and other notes to support the buyer in their decision for sourcing. It is also possible to keep information specific to the vendor. For instance, the vendor is likely to use a different material number than our material number. And finally, the buyer has access to the last purchase order created for this material/vendor combination. This provides the buyer with the most recent purchasing history for this material/vendor combination.

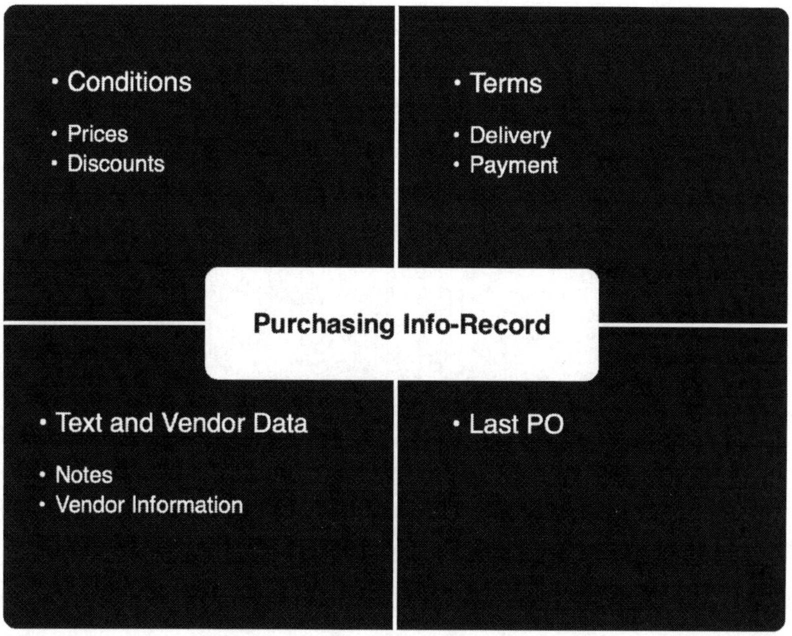

Figure 5.6: Purchasing Info-Record

Conditions

Conditions are another master data in the MM procurement process. Conditions include the following:

- Prices
- Discounts
- Surcharges
- Taxes
- Freight

Conditions appear in many purchasing documents as well as the Purchasing Info-Record discussed above. Figure 5.7 identifies the use of conditions in the MM procurement process.

The Purchasing Info-Record has been separated from the other objects in the above example because Purchasing Info-Records are master data, while the other objects represent documents in the MM Procurement process.

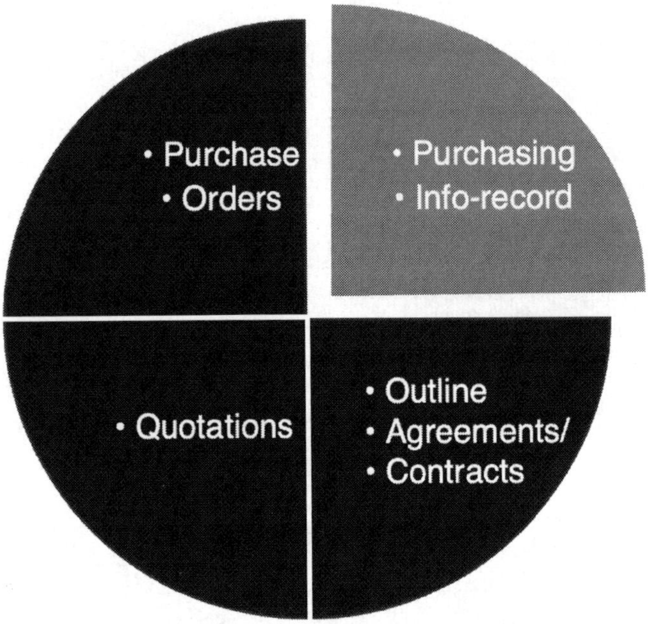

Figure 5.7: Conditions in Purchasing

Output

Output is master data used to communicate and transmit documents during the MM Procurement process. For example, once a purchase order (PO) is created in the SAP S/4HANA system, it needs to be sent to the vendor. If the vendor doesn't receive the PO, the process will not proceed. One method of transmitting the PO to the vendor is to simply send the PO document to a printer and mail it to the vendor. Of course, this is not consistent with working in a digital world, so SAP S/4HANA also offers other medium for transmitting the PO document. Other forms of output might be to email the PO document to the vendor or use some type of electronic data interchange. Sending the PO document to the vendor is not the only example of using output master data in this process. Naturally, after we receive an invoice from the vendor, we need to submit a payment to them. During the payment step there are also various options for output master data. For instance, a check could be printed and mailed to the vendor, or a form of electronic funds transfer can be used to send funds directly to the vendor's bank account.

Output in SAP S/4HANA now supports formats such as Adobe and SmartForms. This will not be the last we see of output master data. We will also address this concept again when we discuss the sales order fulfillment process.

Materials Management: Detailed Procurement Process

Figure 5.8 represents the complete Source-to-Pay process at a micro level. Many of the process steps can be considered "transactional", which is important in SAP S/4HANA. Every transaction in SAP S/4HANA results in the creation of one or more documents. These documents are electronic records of that transaction and they are functionally specific. In other words, a transaction that has a financial accounting impact will create a financial accounting document (FI Doc). If that transaction or another transaction has an impact in Materials Management, the system will generate a type of a materials management document (MM Doc). As we move into this section on MM Procurement, we will address each of the steps separately and include information regarding the types of documents generated during each step. Later, we will also get introduced to some additional concepts: Stock Types, Consumption, and Movement Types.

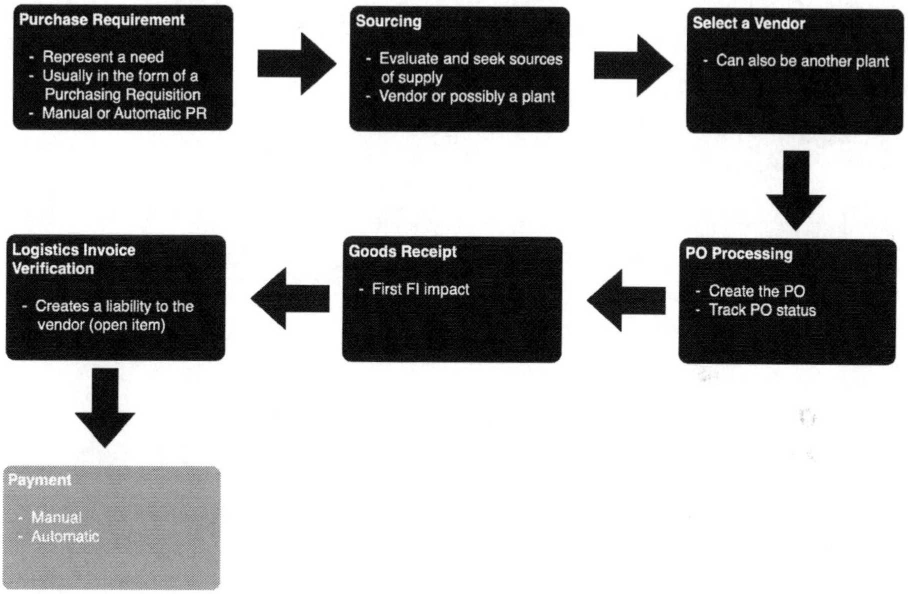

Figure 5.8: Source-to-Pay Process

Purchase Requirements

To initiate the purchase to pay process, there must be a need (requirement). The requirement could be as simple as someone wanting to buy pens for an office. Regardless of the nature of the need, a requirement exists. The document associated with this requirement is a Purchase Requisition (PR). The PR can be created manually in SAP S/4HANA, automatically from other business processes, or via other applications such as Supply Chain Management (SCM) or as noted earlier, SAP Ariba. The PR is a form of MM Doc and a document number will be generated when the PR is created and saved. This document is an electronic record validating that this transaction occurred in the system.

The structure of the PR document shown in Figure 5.9 contains three main sections: Header, Item Overview, and Item Detail. The Header includes the Document number and the Document Date. The Item Overview section includes the materials, their quantities, required delivery date and the Plant requesting the material. When data is entered in the Item Overview section, it becomes available in the Item Detail section for more detailed management of that item. We will address the Item Detail section a little later in this chapter.

Purchase Requisition

Header

Doc#	10000223
Doc date	mm/dd/20xx

Item Overview

Item	Acct assign. Cat	Matl	Desc	Qty	UoM	Date	Plant	SLoc
10		X	Widget	10	Ea.	mm/dd/20xx	1010	

Item Details

Item	Matl	Desc	Qty	UoM
10	X	Widget	10	Ea.

Figure 5.9: Structure of the PR Document

Sourcing and Selecting a Vendor

The step which follows the purchase requirement is sourcing. In this step, the buyer is evaluating options for suppliers. This could mean evaluating known sources of supply and unknown sources of supply. A known source of supply is a supplier from whom the buyer has purchased in the past or a supplier with a vendor master record. Unknown sources of supply represent situations where the buyer is not certain as to who will supply the materials needed.

The sourcing decision is represented in Figure 5.10. As we discussed earlier, outline agreements represent contracts or scheduling agreements with a specific vendor. If the materials in the PR are supplied by a vendor with a contract or scheduling agreement this would constitute a known source of supply. If there is no outline agreement, the supplier can look to see if a Purchasing Info-Record exists for this material. Again, if one does, that would also constitute a known source of supply. However, if none of the above are available OR the buyer would like to reevaluate sources of supply, then the source of supply would be unknown. In such cases, the buyers can choose to convert the PR to a Request for Quotation (RFQ). The RFQ would be sent to selected vendors and quotations would be returned from the vendors to assist the buyer in making a sourcing decision. As a result of the sourcing decision, the buyer will select a vendor.

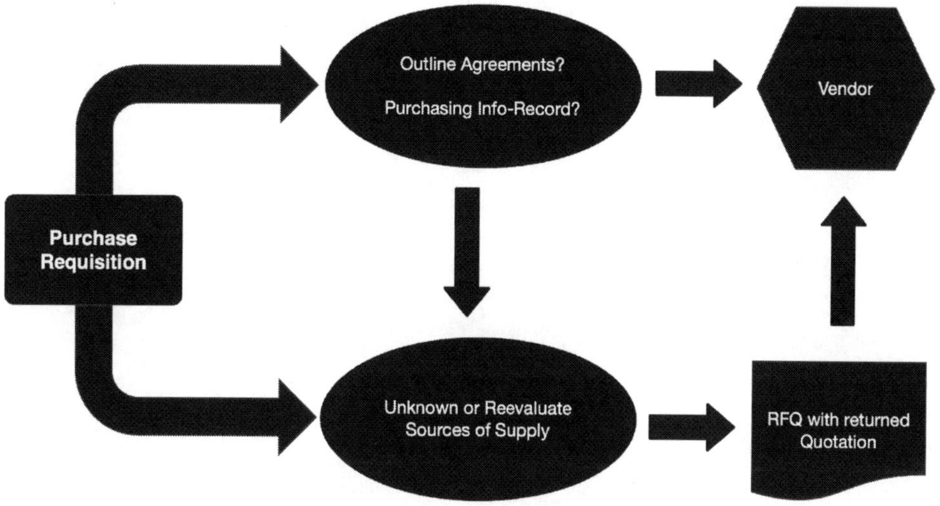

Figure 5.10: Sourcing Decision

As a reminder, all of this functionality related to sourcing is available within SAP Ariba. Keep in mind, as part of the Intelligent Enterprise, the business could leverage the SAP Ariba Business Network to locate potential sources of supply and use SAP Ariba to issue RFQs. The Intelligent Enterprise equips SAP customers with a myriad of options for managing the sourcing decision.

Purchase Order Processing

Once the buyer has determined the source of supply, the PO can be created. There are various methods for PO creation. Though we have described the Purchase Requirement as a step in this process, it is not necessary to have a PR created for the purchase requirement. It is possible to create a PO directly without the existence of a PR or other purchasing documents. We often refer to this as creating a PO without reference because there is no pre-existing document used as a reference for the PO. Other options also exist for creating purchase orders. Figure 5.11 depicts some of those options. These other options involve creating a PO with reference because other documents are used as a reference for the creation of the PO. As you can see, a PO can be created from a PR, Quotation, Contract, or even an old PO.

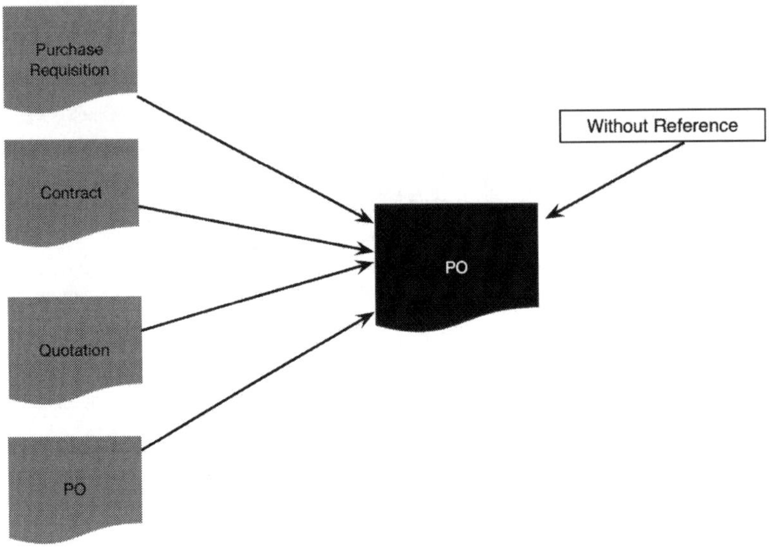

Figure 5.11: PO Creation

Additionally, SAP S/4HANA provides the capability of automatically creating a PO from a PR. Below is a list of requirements to allow for the automatic creation of a PO from a PR:

- The Automatic Purchase Order indicator must be turned on within the Material master record for the relevant items in the PR.
- The Automatic Purchase Order indicator must be turned on within the Vendor master record. This is located in the Supplier/Vendor Role at the Purchasing Organization level.
- The item(s) in the PR must have a pre-existing valid source of supply. It is important to note here that the source of supply does not have to be the same for each item. If different valid sources of supply exist for different items, this will result in more than one PO being generated.
- The document must be free of any additional required entries, such as tax codes, and automatic goods receipt indicators.

The structure of a Purchase Order is almost identical to that of a Purchase Requisition. Purchase Orders also have three main sections: Header, Item Overview, and Item Detail. In a PO, there is required master data and organizational levels in the

Header. As you can see in Figure 5.12, the Vendor master record is required in the Header of the PO. It is also required to include the organizational data of Purchasing Organization, Purchasing Group, and Company Code. You will also see there is data in the Item Overview of a PO that did not exist in the Purchase Requisition. This data includes the condition price and currency. The Item Detail data remains the same as a PR.

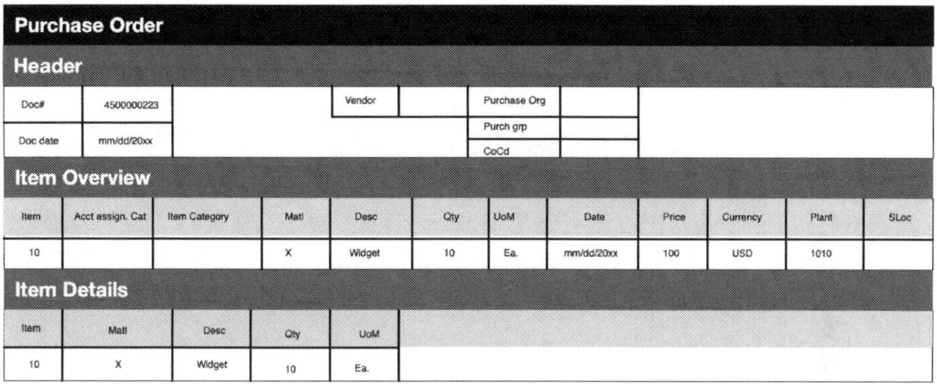

Figure 5.12: Structure of the Purchase Order

Item Categories

Item Categories are also available in the purchasing document. While creating the purchase order (or a purchase requisition), an Item Category is used to differentiate between different ways each item is processed for subsequent steps. As an example, a company may subcontract work to a supplier. In these cases, options exist for either the supplier to be responsible for procuring necessary materials or for the company to provide the materials for the supplier. If the company is responsible to providing the materials, then the business process for purchasing such items differs from the standard approach. The item category "L" for subcontracting would be used in this scenario to inform the business that the purchased items will need to be shipped to the supplier (Figure 5.13). The business process would then require a goods issue of the purchased items to the supplier followed by a goods receipt of the material the supplier assembled as part of the subcontracting process. Other Item Categories exist and are outlined below.

- Normal (standard) (the Item Category field is left blank)
- Subcontracting
- Consignment (we will see more related to this Item Category in Chapter 7)

- Stock Transfer (we will see more related to this Item Category in Chapter 7)
- Service

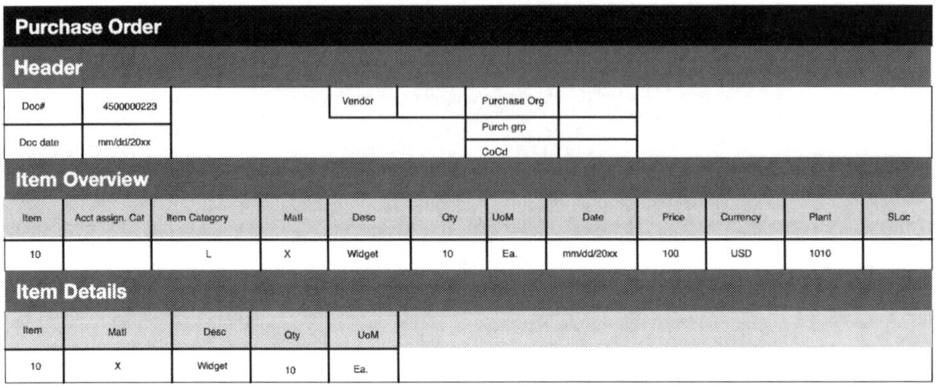

Figure 5.13:Item Category for Subcontracting

Commitments/Consumables

Commitments represent future costs and they occur either during the creation of a purchase requisition or a purchase order that contains a consumable item. A consumable item in a purchasing document is a line item that will be expensed upon receipt of that item from the supplier. To get a better understanding of what this means, we need to refer to the Account Types discussed in Financial Accounting.

The four account types in the G/L are as follows:

X – Balance Sheet accounts

C - Cash accounts

P – Primary Cost/Revenue accounts

N – Non-operating expense/revenue accounts

S – Secondary Cost accounts

To understand consumables, we also need an understanding of inventory. Inventory is managed on a quantity and/or value base. Quantity-based inventory is managed in Storage Locations. This means we can keep track of quantities of materials stored in inventory. Value-based inventory is managed in the Balance Sheet. This means we can keep track of the value of items in inventory. When a consumable appears as an item in a purchasing document (PR and/or PO), upon receipt it will always post to a Primary Cost/Revenue account in the general ledger. It will not impact the Balance Sheet from an inventory standpoint. Therefore, consumables are NEVER managed in inventory on a value base. However, it is possible to manage consumables in inventory on a quantity base.

In general, there are two categories of materials, Stock and Non-stock. A stock item is a material that can be managed in inventory on both a quantity and value base. A non-stock item is NEVER managed in inventory on a value base (does not post to an inventory balance sheet account). This means that a non-stock item is ALWAYS considered a consumable. However, it is possible for a stock item to be treated as a consumable. Figure 5.14 summarizes these ideas.

Stock items

- Require material master record
- Post to inventory balance sheet upon receipt
- Can be treated as a consumable

Non-stock items

- Only requires a material master record if managed as quantity based inventory
- ALWAYS treated as a consumable
- Never value-based inventory (balance sheet)

Figure 5.14: Stock/Non-Stock Items

When purchasing a consumable, there are mandatory entries in the PR and/or PO. These entries are necessary for the SAP S/4HANA system to know how to process the item upon receipt of the materials. It is also important for the SAP S4HANA system to designate the commitment (future cost) to the proper cost object. We looked at the structure of the PR and the PO earlier in this chapter. We're now going to revisit the PO, but we will add a consumable item in that document.[1]

Let's assume we are again purchasing Material "X" as we did in the previous PO example in Figure 5.12. This time the R& D cost center has requested 1ea of this material to be used for testing. To do this, we are going to add a second line item to the PO for Material "X", with a quantity of 1ea to be purchased specifically for the R&D cost center. Upon the receipt of this material, we want the first line item with the quantity of 10ea to be received into inventory and the second line item with the quantity of 1ea to

[1] Since the same procedures apply for the PR as the PO, we only need to address consumables in the PO.

be sent directly to R&D (Figure 5.15). Since 10 ea. are being received into inventory, it will impact the inventory balance sheet account. This means Material “X” is a stock item and requires a material master record. Although it is a stock item, you can see that in the second line item, we are still able to purchase it as a consumable.

Purchase Order

Header

Doc#	4500000223	Vendor		Purchase Org	
Doc date	mm/dd/20xx			Purch grp	
				CoCd	

Item Overview

Item	Acct assign. Cat	Matl	Desc	Qty	UoM	Date	Price	Currency	Plant	SLoc
10		X	Widget	10	Ea.	mm/dd/20xx	100	USD	1010	
10	K	X	Widget	1	Ea.	mm/dd/20xx	100	USD	1010	

Item Details

Item	Matl	Desc	Qty	UoM	Act assign
10	X	Widget	10	Ea.	R&D

Figure 5.15: Purchase Order with a Consumable

As noted above and can be seen in Figure 5.16, there are required entries in the PO for the second line item (consumable). The first required entry is in the Item Overview section. It is mandatory to enter the Account Assignment Category for this item. The Account Assignment Category informs the system of the type of cost object responsible for the consumable. Recall from the previous chapter in Management Accounting, there are several types of cost objects, such as: Cost Centers, Orders (production, maintenance, internal orders), and Projects. For this example, we will enter “K”, which is the key for a Cost Center category.When the Account Assignment Category is entered in the Item Overview section for that line item, a new tab appears in the Item Detail section with the label, “Account Assignment”. This is the second required entry for that item. If you notice in our example, since we entered the key for Cost Center as the Account Assignment category for the consumable in Line Item 20, we are now required to enter the specific Cost Center in the Item Detail section of the PO document for that line item. Here you see we have assigned this item to the R&D cost center.

The purchase price for the material is $100 ea. As a result of creating this PO, a commitment in the amount of $100 is recorded to the R&D cost center. This is a future cost because it hasn't yet been realized as an expense posting to the general ledger. Commitments are important because they are counted against the cost center's budget. Even though the cost center has not yet realized the actual cost of $100, it knows that it is responsible for $100 of costs as soon as the materials are received. The commitment tracks these future costs to help ensure cost objects don't exceed their budgets.

Goods Receipt

The Goods Receipt step is the first step in this process that has a financial accounting impact. As you will soon see, it is also a very integrated step in this process as it can impact several areas of the business. To begin our discussion on the good receipt, let's expand on how the system manages stock and non-stock items. Figure 5.16 shows the general guidelines for stock and non-stock items.

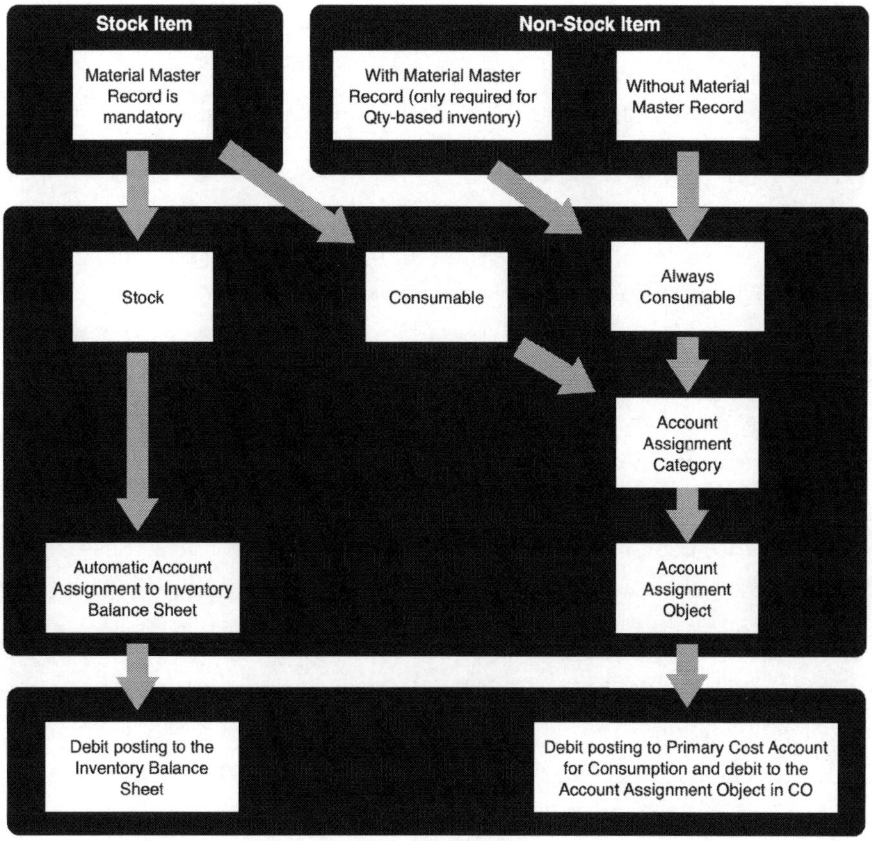

Figure 5.16: Goods Receipt for Stock and Non-Stock Items

As you see, this image has been broken up into three separate segments. The top segment describes the situations in which a material master record is required. For stock items, a material master record is mandatory. While for non-stock items, it is possible to purchase this type of item with or without a material master record. A material master record is only required for a non-stock item if there is a plan to manage inventory for that item on a quantity base. Otherwise it is not required.

The second segment of the above image details how the item is handled in the purchasing documents (PR and PO). A non-stock item is always treated as a consumable and requires an account assignment category (Item Overview) and account assignment object (Item Detail). Again, it is clear to us that a stock item may be purchased as a consumable. If this is the case, it must meet the same requirements as the non-stock item. If a stock item is not treated as a consumable, the SAP S/4HANA system will derive the assigned inventory balance sheet account to that item.

Finally, the third segment depicts how the system processes each item at the time of Goods Receipt. For a stock item, the system will post directly to the inventory balance sheet account. While items which are consumed will post directly to a primary cost account for consumption and the primary cost element will assign the cost to the cost object in Controlling.

Every transaction in the SAP S/4HANA system generates at least one document as an electronic record of that transaction. In each of these scenarios, a financial accounting document is generated showing the goods receipt on a value base. The Header of the financial accounting document contains the document number and document date. The items section of this document shows the postings to the general ledger accounts. As we saw above, an inventory balance sheet account is debited for a stock item and a consumption primary cost account is debited for a consumable. The credit posting for all goods receipts from a PO is the GR/IR account. This is a balance sheet account that posts the temporary liability until the vendor submits an invoice. Because a consumable item results in a cost posting to the responsible cost object in Controlling, a Controlling document is also generated depicting this posting.

Now that we understand the accounting impacts of the goods receipt, we need to address other integration. The goods receipt is an example of a goods movement and all goods movements result in the creation of a Material Document. The Material Document validates that the transaction occurred and records the good movement on a quantity base. This document includes a Header with a document number and document date. It also includes line items which provides information on what was received, the quantities received, a movement type, and information on where the materials were received. A Movement Type is required for every goods movement. It is a key which differentiates between the differing goods movements supported in the system.

Other integration occurs if there is a material master record for an item at the time of goods receipt. For stock items received into inventory, the material master record updates with quantity ad value in the Accounting view of the material. For consumables with a material master record, consumption statistics are updated in the Additional Data section of the material master record.

If a stock item is received into a Storage Location of a Plant that is associated with a Warehouse Management number, the SAP S/4HANA system will automatically create a Transfer Requirement document in the warehouse for the materials to be put away. Additionally, any materials that are subject to the Quality Management (QM) module in SAP S/4HANA, will result in an inspection lot at the time of goods receipt.

It is possible at the time of goods receipt to identify into which stock type the material will be received. Below is a list of the Stock Types:

Stock Types:

1. Unrestricted Use
2. Quality Inspection
3. Blocked Stock

Setting for these stock types can be predefined in the material master record and/or the PO.

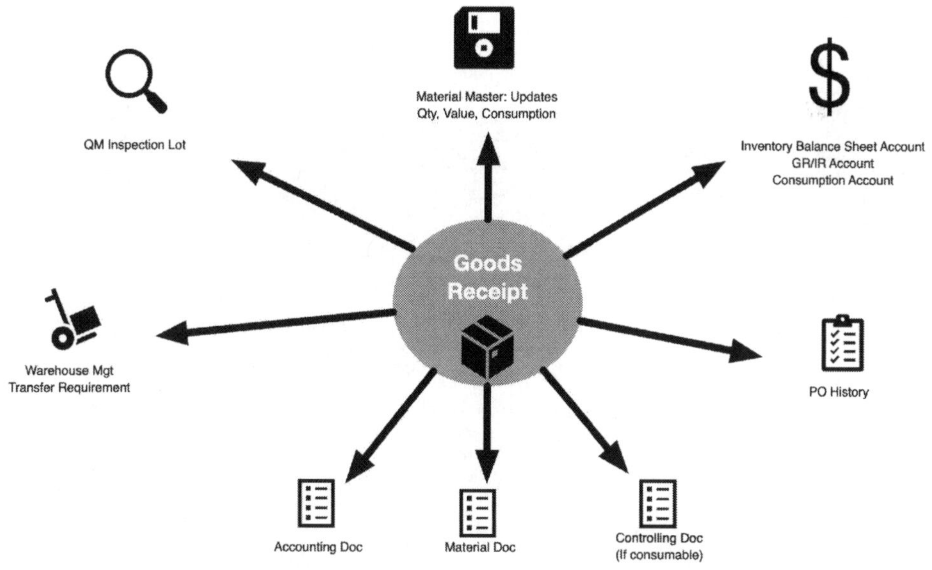

Figure 5.17: Goods Receipt Integration

Finally, the PO is updated. In the Item Detail section of the PO a new tab appears labeled, Purchase Order History. In the Purchase Order History tab, the Material Document number is present which allows the user to access the impacts of the Goods Receipt step. The status in the Header of the PO is also updated with the Material Document number, showing the materials have been delivered. Figure 5.17 recaps the impacts of the Goods Receipt step in this process.

Logistics Invoice Verification

The Logistics Invoice Verification step is initiated with the receipt of an invoice from the vendor. When the vendor invoice arrives, it is entered into the SAP S4HANA system and checked against the PO and Material Document resulting from the goods receipt. This check is also referred to as the 3-way match. The three documents in the 3-way match are the vendor invoice, PO, and Material document. The PO document includes data regarding quantities ordered as well as terms and conditions. Recall, the Material document now appears in the PO History tab of the PO document. The Material Document is important because it verifies the quantities received with the quantities invoiced. The 3-way match can therefore be easily accomplished by simply referencing the PO document number when entering the information from the vendor invoice.

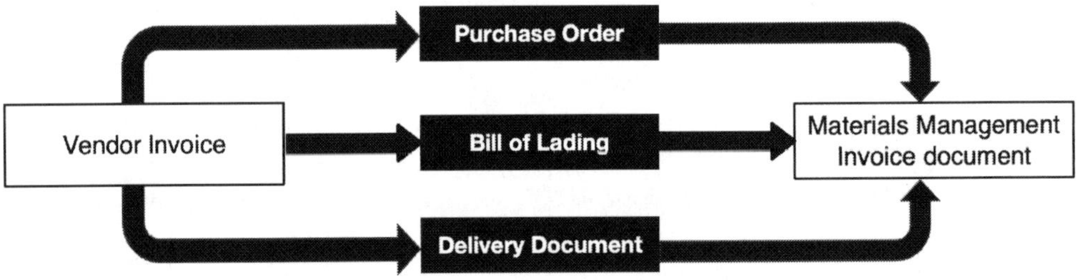

Figure 5.18: Logistics Invoice Verification

It's possible to reference other documents during the invoice verification step (Figure 5.18). One option is to verify the vendor invoice against a Bill of Lading. A Bill of Lading is a packing slip provided by the vendor and is entered into the SAP S/4HANA system when the goods receipt takes place. In doing so, the Bill of Lading is linked to the PO. Another option is to verify the vendor invoice against a Delivery Document. A Delivery Document is used in a variety of ways in the SAP S/4HANA system, but simply put, it is a document linked to shipping. In the case of a Scheduling Agreement with a supplier, a Delivery Document is used to manage the shipment, including the goods receipt. In other cases, the Delivery Document could be linked to a standard PO to manage the shipping of the materials from the vendor. Again, at the time of goods receipt the Delivery Document is updated with the quantities received and can now be used as a reference document for invoice verification.

Upon verifying the vendor invoice, the SAP S/4HANA system will generate an Invoice document in Materials Management. Additional documents and integration occur with this step.

Because the invoice posting creates a liability to the vendor, there is a financial accounting impact. The result of all financial accounting impacts is a financial accounting document. As we discussed in the chapter in financial accounting, the posting in FI is directly to the vendor subledger account. The financial accounting document generated is presented in the Entry View, which shows the credit to the vendor subledger account and the clearing of the GR/IR account (Figure 5.19).

Financial Accounting Document Entry View

Document #: 190000001 CoCd: US00 Fiscal Year: 20xx

Doc. Date: MM/DD/20xx Posting date: MM/DD/20xx Period: Month

CoCd.	PK	Account	Name	Amount	Currency	Segment
US00	31	12501	Vendor	10000	USD	
	86	310000	GR/IR	11000	USD	
	40	120000	Tax	1000	USD	

Figure 5.19: FI Accounting Document - Entry View

The general ledger view of this financial accounting document reflects the impact to the Reconciliation account for payables (Figure 5.20).

Financial Accounting General Ledger View

Document #: 190000001 CoCd: US00 Fiscal Year: 20xx

Doc. Date: MM/DD/20xx Posting date: MM/DD/20xx Period: Month

CoCd.	PK	Account	Name	Amount	Currency	Segment
US00	31	210000	Reconciliation A/P	10000	USD	
	86	310000	GR/IR	11000	USD	
	40	120000	Tax	1000	USD	

Figure 5.20: FI Accounting Document - General Ledger View

Figure 5.21 depicts the integration that occurs as a result of Logistics Invoice Verification.

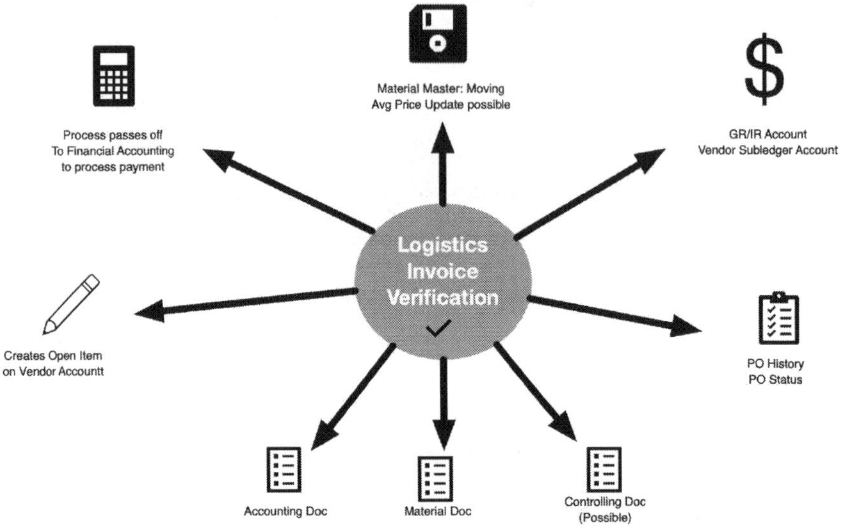

Figure 5.21: Logistics Invoice Verification Integration

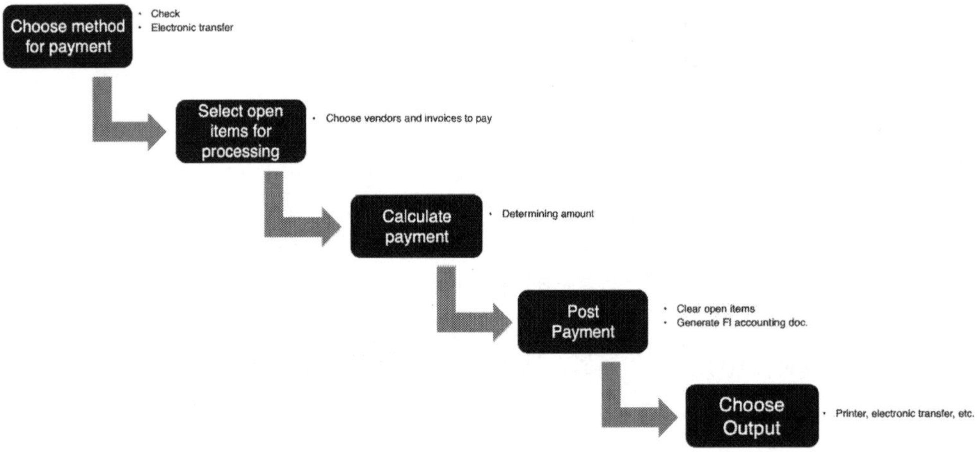

Figure 5.22: Payment Process

Payment

The Payment step in the Purchase to Pay process occurs in the Financial Accounting module. After Logistics Invoice Verification, the process hands off to Financial Accounting where two options exist for processing payment. The payment can be handled either manually or automatically. In either case, there are some basic steps that apply to this payment process (Figure 5.22).

The automatic payment process follows the same basic steps as those listed above. However, the automatic payment process is managed by generating a payment run. Figure 5.23 shows the steps in the automatic payment run process.

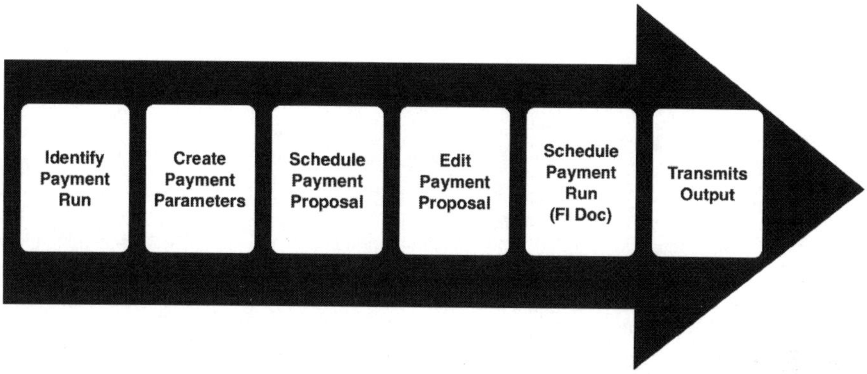

Figure 5.23: Automatic Payment Run

Procurement Summary

The purchase to pay process in the Materials Management module represents the first logistics process we cover in this course. As with all chapters in this book, we address the organizational levels, master data, and transactions involved in this process. We also incorporated the Intelligent Enterprise into our discussions, showing that all or parts of the process can be managed using intelligent technologies as well as with SAP S/4HANA.

From an organizational level perspective, all logistics modules involve the following: Client, Company code, Plant, and Storage Location. In the MM Source-to-Pay process, we also include the Purchasing Organization as part of the Enterprise Structure. The assignment of the purchasing organizations allows for flexible purchasing strategies: Plant Specific, Cross-Plant, and Cross-Company Code.

Master data in the purchase to pay process includes materials, vendors (business partner approach), purchasing info-records, conditions, and output.

The Source-to-Pay process involves many steps. It is very important to understand the standard sequence of steps in this process, the use of intelligent technologies, as well as the integration which occurs throughout.

Chapter 6: Human Resource Management

Human Resource Management is the business function that is essentially responsible for ensuring the optimal staffing levels in an enterprise. At the highest level, this means having the right people in the right place, at the right time, at the best possible price/ cost. Human capital management (HCM) is the module in SAP S/4HANA that provides SAP customers with the tools to manage all their Human Resource needs. As we have pointed out, SAP S/4HANA can be deployed on-premise, full cloud, or a hybrid option. But please note, HCM is not SAP's cloud solution for human resources. SAP SuccessFactors is SAP's cloud solution for human resources. For purposes of differentiating between HCM and SuccessFactors, one should be aware that HCM is part of SAP S/4HANA ERP solution, while SuccessFactors is not. SuccessFactors is a cloud-based solution that can integrate with the ERP solution and can therefore be deployed alongside SAP HCM in a hybrid fashion or as a standalone tool. More on SuccessFactors a little later.

Human Experience Management (HXM) represents a shift in focus and approach as it relates to the management of human resources (HR). In a general sense, HXM shifts attention from operational to the more human-centric aspects of HR. Things that provide employees with a better work experience. Such as taking advantage of intelligent technologies to enhance an employee's work experience. Doing this in ways which make them more productive and gain a sense of individualism, while still feeling like a team member and contributor to the organization. Three key components that are essential to HXM are mentioned here, and they include Teams, Organizations, and Individuals.

We will delve deeper into SAP SuccessFactors and its HXM Suite a little later in this chapter. For now, we will focus our attention on the HCM (on-premise) solution.

Human Capital Management (HCM): Organizational Levels

Enterprise Structure

In Human Capital Management (HCM), the organizational levels are defined in the Enterprise Structure (Figure 6.1).

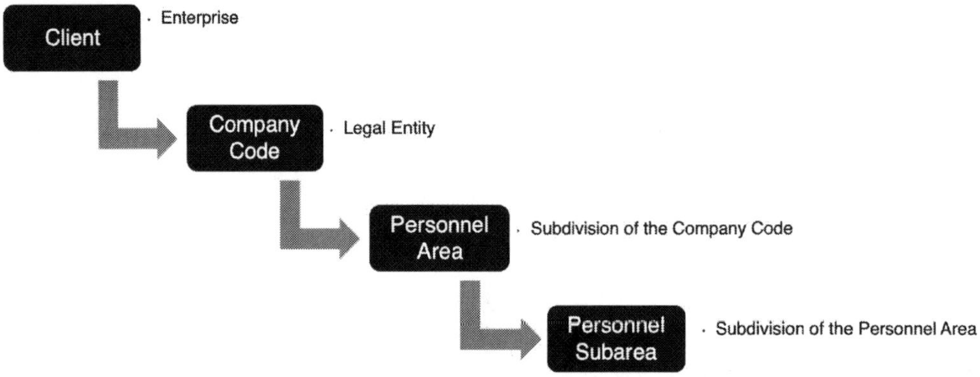

Figure 6.1: HCM Enterprise Structure

The client represents the entire enterprise. All organizational levels exist within the client. From a financial accounting standpoint, the company code represents a legal entity for reporting purposes. In HCM, people are defined as a legal person in the enterprise. The personnel area is a subdivision of the company code. Though there are many ways to describe a personnel area, we could do it geographically. For instance, if the company code is the United States (US), a personnel area may be a geographic region within the US, such as a state. The personnel subarea is where the tasks associated with personnel administration occur. For instance, compensation rates would be addressed in the personnel subarea. To put this in perspective, two people whose work responsibilities are the same may work in different personnel subareas. One may work in New York City, while the other in Topeka, Kansas. Though both have the same responsibilities, they're likely to be compensated much differently because of where they work.

Organizational Structure

In Human Capital Management (HCM), the term "organizational" appears quite often and can have a much different meaning depending on the context of that term. In this section, we are discussing the organizational structure. The organizational structure is a hierarchical structure in HCM which contains the following elements: Organizational Units, Positions, Jobs, People, and Cost Centers.

To begin our discussion on the organizational structure, we need an understanding of organizational units. An organization unit is what an employee might refer to as a "department" in which they work.

From an operational management perspective, there have been different philosophies on how enterprises should be structured organizationally. In SAP S4HANA, an organization's structure is organized in an organizational chart depicting the various departments in the company hierarchically. The hierarchy defines the reporting structure amongst these departments (i.e., organizational units). Included in this structure are the various positions that exist in each organizational unit. People are hired into positions within the organizational structure. An organizational unit may have several positions which belong to it and an organizational unit is assigned a responsible cost center. Figure 6.2 shows organizational units and positions.

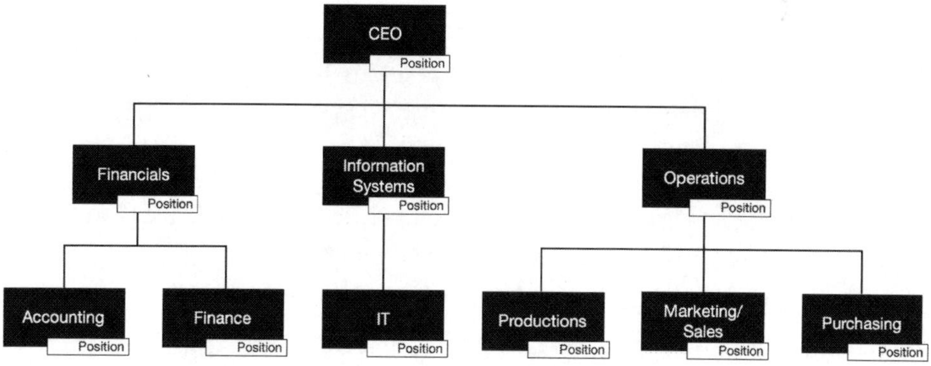

Figure 6.2: HCM Organizational Units and Positions

The next element in the organizational structure is jobs. Jobs are broad descriptions for positions. Jobs provide the default characteristics for positions, including position requirement. Jobs are designed to be used to describe several positions. In this way, it is easier to maintain the required information for the various positions. Though jobs can describe many positions, a position can only be described by one job. Figure 6.3 shows an example of a job, "Department Chair" at a university. Since there are many department chairs within a university, the job, "Department Chair" can be used to describe each of those positions and provide default values for the position requirements. Each position can in turn, add other requirements specific to that position if needed.

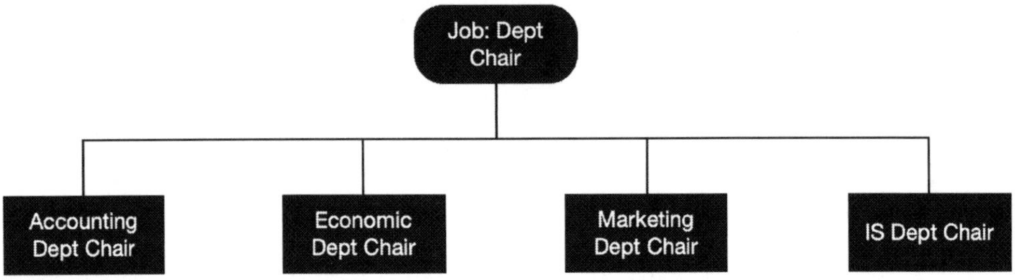

Figure 6.3: HCM Jobs and Positions

The positions represent where people are hired. A position can be vacant (no one hired into that position), completely filled (the positions is 100% occupied), or partially filled (the position is less than 100% occupied, but not vacant). A position is generally held by one person, though it is possible for a position to be held my more than one person. In SAP S/4HANA HCM, a person can only hold ONE position.

Additionally, each position is associated with only one cost center. The position will either inherit the cost center from the organizational unit to which it belongs, or it can be assigned to a different cost center depending on the business requirements. In Figure 6.4 we have added people and cost centers to the positions.

Try repeating the following to get an understanding of how the organizational structure is designed: "A person holds a position that is described by a job and belongs to an organizational unit. That position either inherits the cost center from the organizational unit or is assigned to a different cost center."

Organizational Management

Simply put, Organizational Management is the component within SAP HCM which is used to manage the organizational structure. Any changes to the organizational structure are handled within Organizational Management. As an example, if a department needs to add a new position this is accomplished by accessing the Organizational Management component in the SAP S/4HANA system. Within Organizational Management, the user would search for the organizational unit in which the position will be added, then simply add the position.

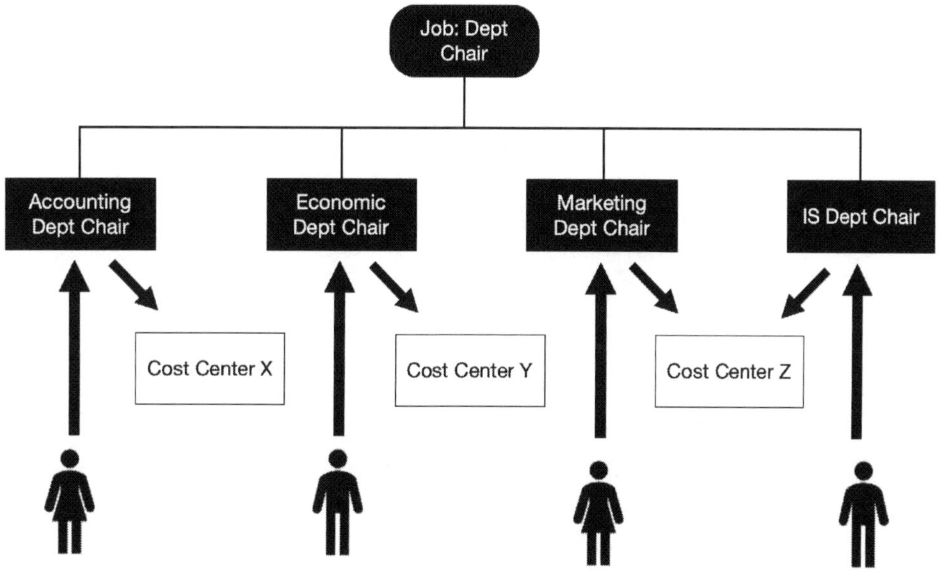

Figure 6.4: HCM Positions, People, and Cost Centers

Personnel Administration

Personnel administration is the component in HCM that manages employees from hiring through termination and retirement. Before a person can be hired, there is a recruitment process. The recruitment process (Figure 6.5) begins with the posting of an open position. The opening can be posted internally, so only employees can see the posting, or externally so the public has access to the posting. Candidates submit applications via E-Recruiting, which means this process is handled electronically via the intranet (internally) or internet (externally). Once applications are received, they are reviewed to see if the candidate's qualification meet the position's requirements. This is accomplished using a Profile Matchup in the HCM system (Figure 6.6). Candidates who meet the requirements are given further consideration and eventually a candidate is hired into the position using personnel management.

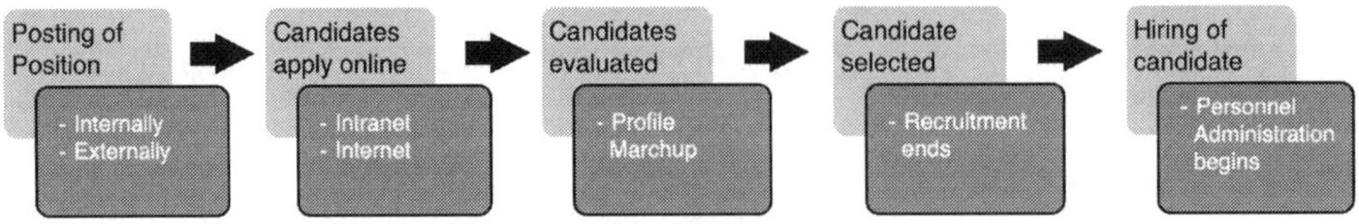

Figure 6.5: E-Recruitment to Hiring (Personnel Administration)

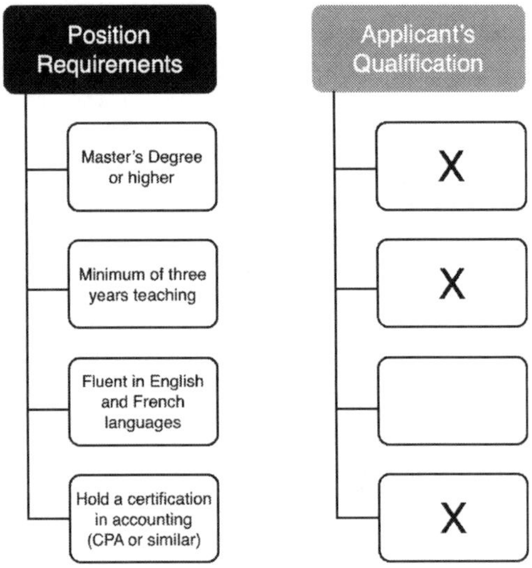

Figure 6.6: Profile Matchup for Accounting Faculty Position

The integration between Organizational Management and Personnel Administration is the Position (Figure 6.7). When a person is hired into a position, it's critical to define where this person belongs in the organizational structure. Again, "A person holds a position that is described by a job and belongs to an organizational unit. That position either inherits or is assigned a cost center."

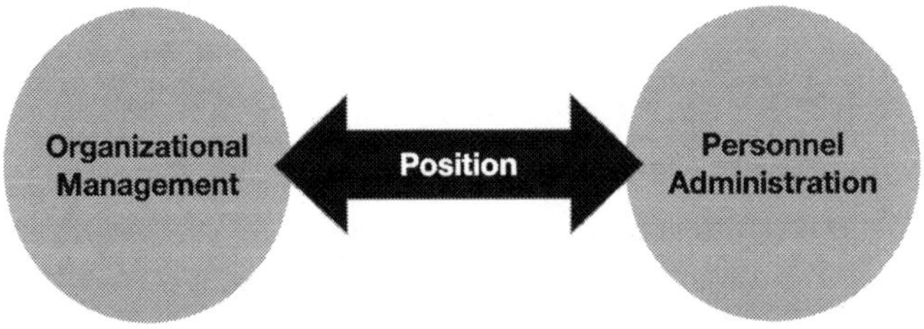

Figure 6.7: Integration Between Personnel Administration and Organizational Management

Human Capital Management (HCM): Master Data

Info-Types

Info-types are master data in HCM. This is master data maintained about the employees in the company. SAP describes an info-type as a logical collection of data fields. If you think about it, before the computer era new employees filled out many paper forms in person at the Human Resource Department. Each form was a logical collection of data fields. As an example, there was a form for address and personal information. Another form was information regarding the position the employee was hired into and yet another for the employee to sign and confirm their pay rate. SAP has taken this concept and digitized these forms as info-types.

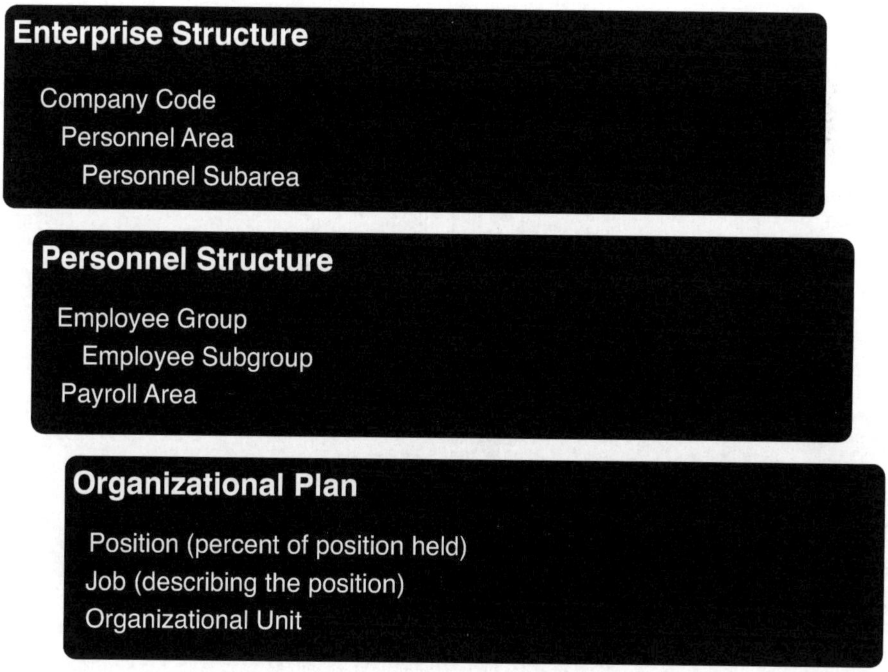

Figure 6.8: Organizational Assignment Info-Type

An employee will have many info-type master records maintained. Each info-type serves a specific purpose and is defined by a name and a four-digit number. For example, the first info-type maintained is info-type 0000, "Actions". An Action is something that must be processed on an employee. There are many Actions in the SAP HCM module. Hiring, transfer, termination, and retirement are a few examples of Actions. Another info-type, 0001 is the Organizational Assignment info-type

(Figure 6.8). This info-type details information regarding the Enterprise Structure, Personnel Structure, and Organizational Plan for an employee. We've already been exposed to the Enterprise Structure. The Organizational Plan is simply where the employee exists in the organizational structure.

In Figure 6.8, we also see that the Personnel Structure includes several important pieces of information. Two of these are the Employee Group (Figure 6.9) and the Employee Subgroup (Figure 6.10). It's important to distinguish between various types of employees, and for this reason SAP HCM makes use of the Employee Group. The most common Employee Group is an Active Employee. But not all data about employees in HCM are for Active Employees. Some employees are hired as Contractors, others as Volunteers. Some are employees who are Pensioners. These are people for whom the company is making pension payments. The Employee Subgroup is a bit confusing, because the Employee Subgroups are not seemingly subdivisions of the Employee Group. The Employee Subgroup is used to determine the method of compensation for employees. Figure 6.10 provides examples of Employee Subgroups.

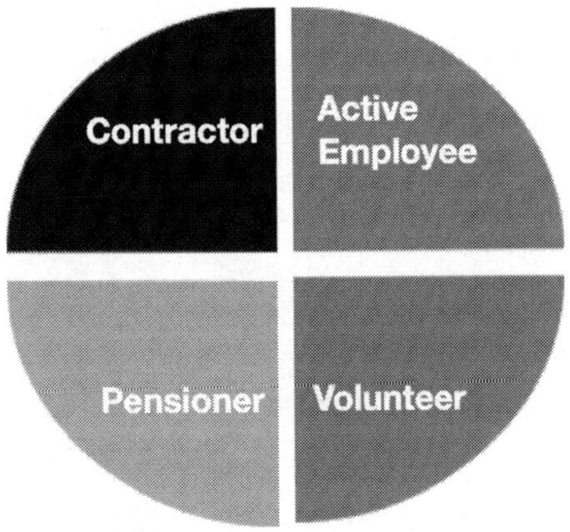

Figure 6.9: Employee Groups

The Personnel Structure also includes the Payroll Area. A Payroll Area defines when payroll is run for an employee. Examples of payroll areas include, amongst others, every Friday, every other Friday, 1st and 15th day of the month, and last day of the month.

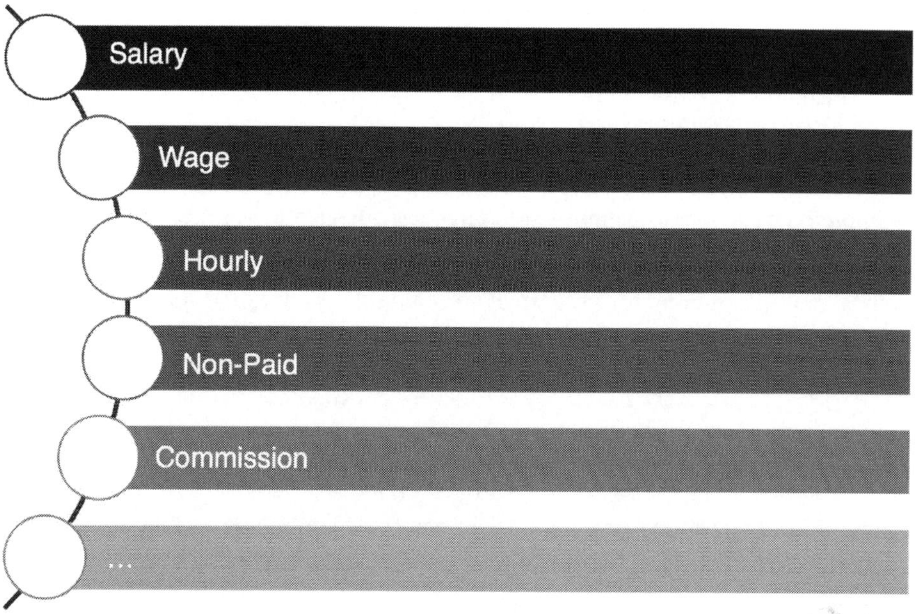

Figure 6.10: Employee Subgroups

Although we spent some time on the Organizational Assignment Info-type, it is just one of many. We aren't going to address any additional info-types at this time, but we will discuss the various methods for maintaining info-type master data. There are three options for maintaining info-types (Figure 6.11). Each one is listed below, with some detail surrounding their uses.

Single Screen One Info-Type/One Employee

- This is the simplest form of maintaining info-types, but only when maintaining a single info-type for a single employee

Fast Entry One Info-Type/Many Employees

- This option is best used when several employees require maintenance for the same info-type

Personnel Actions Sequence of info-types for one employee

- This is the preferred when an Action (e.g., hiring, transfer and termination) is performed for an employee
- The system takes the user through a sequence of info-types that must be maintained to complete the Action

Figure 6.11: Info-Type Maintenance

Once info-types have been maintained, they are easily found using various search methods. To determine if an info-type exists the user can call up the info-type maintenance screen and search for the info-type by entering all or part of the info-type name. If the user enters part of the name, the system will suggest names of all info-types containing the partial entry. If the user knows the info-type number, that can also be used to find the desired info-type. When info-types are maintained, they have key dates associated with them. For example, an employee may have held more than one position during their tenure with the company. It's possible to search for an info-type by selecting key dates during their employment. If the user desired to search for the Organizational Assignment for an employee during the year 2001, the user can enter a start date of 1/1/2001 and an end date of 12/31/2001. If any Organizational Assignment info-type(s) exist during that period, they will appear.

Finally, from within the info-type maintenance screen, the user can look to see if there are green check marks next to an info-type. The green check marks are an indication that the info-type has been maintained. Any info-types which do not display the green check are info-type for which no data has been maintained.

Personnel File

Upon hiring an employee, the employee is assigned a unique identifier called the personnel number. Every info-type that has ever been maintained for a single personnel number is considered the employee's Personnel File. The personnel file is a collection of all info-types maintained for a single personnel number and the info-types are displayed in ascending numerical order. Figure 6.12 shows the Personnel File. Remember, info-types have a four-digit identifier. Should more than one info-type exist for a personnel number, those info-types are displayed chronologically until no more of the same info-type remain. The next info-type in ascending numerical order will again follow.

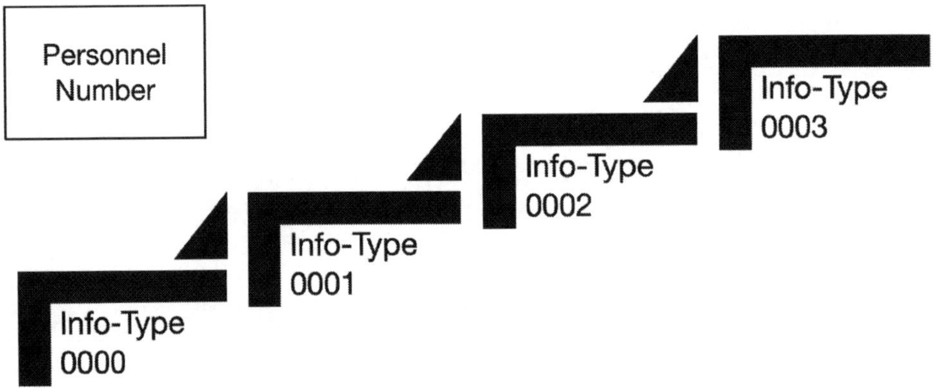

Figure 6.12: Personnel File

Human Capital Management (HCM): Transaction Data

Employee Self-Service (ESS)

Employee self-services (ESS) allows employees to maintain and manage some of their own data in HCM. Employees are also able to view information and make decisions about their benefits that in the past required the assistance of an HR administrator. Table 6.1 shows some examples of ESS available in SAP S4HANA HCM.

Table 6.1: Employee Self-Service (ESS)

View working schedules	Book into training events
Benefits selection	Update personnel information
View payroll information	Enter working times
Search directories	Submit expenses
Update banking information	Update qualifications

Manager Self-Service (MSS)

In SAP S/4HANA HCM, there is also Manager self-services (MSS). MSS includes tools that managers need to manage their employees in their workplace. Be careful not to confuse MSS with ESS. Yes, managers are also employees and have access to ESS, but the functionality of MSS is much different. Table 6.2 shows some examples of MSS in SAP S/4HANA HCM.

Table 6.2: ManagerSelf-Service (MSS)

Lookup employee data	Recruitment tools
Reporting tools	Evaluating employees
Cost allocations	Evaluating candidates
Cost planning	Approval of times
Budgeting	Personnel levels

SAP Success Factors

Best-Practice Scenario for the Recruit-to-Retire Process

As we begin our discussion on SAP SuccessFactors, let's remind ourselves of "best-practice" scenarios. In Chapter 5, we discussed that we will only be covering "best-practice" scenarios as outlined by SAP in their SAP Signavio Process Navigator. With that in mind, Figure 6.13 presents the "best-practice" items in the Recruit-to-Retire process.

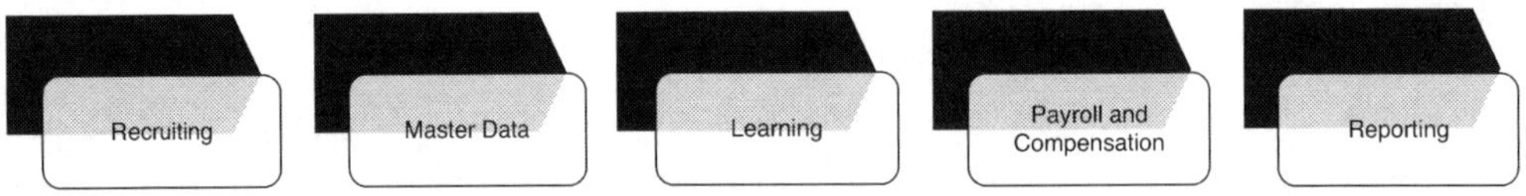

Figure 6.13: Best-Practice Scenario for the Recruit-to-Retire Process

Recruiting

SAP SuccessFactors offers a variety of tools to support the complex process of recruitment. There are four components within SAP SuccessFactors Recruiting. They are:

- Job Requisition and Application Management
- Self-service Career Site
- Candidate Relationship Management
- Sourcing Analytics

Job Requisition and Application Management are combined to support the recruiting process. As positions become available within the company, it's the responsibility of the recruiter to create a job requisition. The job requisition includes all the details about the job opening, such as the job description, job title, location, hiring manager, potential compensation and benefit information, as well as any additional pieces of information that is appropriate for advertising the job. The recruiter can also use this tool to help advertise the job. Once this has been put in place, applicants can now begin submitting their application data for the job. At this point, the application management function is used to collect applicant data, help screen candidates, and support the selection of the best candidate. As candidates submit applications, a Candidate Profile is created along with their application data. It's also possible to include pre-screening questions during the application process to help filter out candidates who may not be qualified. As candidates apply, recruiters can leverage the Candidate Workbench within SAP SuccessFactors to ensure the process is being followed correctly for each candidate. This is accomplished using the Talent Pipeline tool within the Candidate Workbench. It provides recruiters with information on each candidate to see where they are in the selection process. Once a candidate is selected and approved, recruiters have the ability to create an offer letter to be sent to the candidate. The offer can be made verbally, using the Career Site (see below), or via email.

The Self-service Career Site is a tool within SAP SuccessFactors Recruiting that is easily customizable to assist users in building a company career website without a lot of support from the technical team. Career websites are beneficial in that they offer an easily accessible site for applicants to visit to explore career opportunities and submit applications.

Candidate Relationship Management is a tool that allows recruiters to retain applicant data, and organize that data into talent pools that support current and future recruiting efforts. This tool also supports email marketing campaigns to help locate and recruit the best talent.

Like other analytic tools we will see in this book, Sourcing Analytics can be used to help manage investments/spending as it relates to recruiting efforts. It provides drilldown capabilities that provide the business with in-depth knowledge as it relates to recruiting.

Master Data

Master data is the next item in the Recruit-to-Hire process. This occurs once a candidate accepts the job offer. There are essentially two components within Master Data: Onboarding and Employee Central.

The goal of onboarding is to bring new hires into the company, preparing them to become productive employees in an effective and efficient manner. The Onboarding component in SAP SuccessFactors is used for more than just new hires. It is also the component used for bringing employees back into the company after a leave. Onboarding can be initiated either manually or via integration with SAP SuccessFactors Recruiting. Integration with Recruiting is exceptionally beneficial since a lot of the new employee data was captured during the application process. From within Recruiting, onboarding can be done by selecting the job requisition, choosing the selected candidate, and initiating the onboarding steps.

Alternatively, onboarding can be manually initiated. In fact, there are two scenarios in which manual onboarding is required. Manual onboarding is required for an employee returning from a sabbatical or when hiring a high-level employee. A high-level employee is for someone whose recruitment doesn't follow the normal recruiting steps. An example might be the recruiting and hiring of a new provost at a university. The steps for manually onboarding are below:

1. Hiring Manager receives notification of the new hire and that onboarding is ready to begin. The hiring manager sends a request for additional information to the new hire.
2. New Hire receives the notification to complete tasks and is given credentials to access SAP SuccessFactors to complete the required tasks.
3. SAP SuccessFactors creates required documents to be reviewed and signed by the new hire and the hiring manager.
4. The new hire appears under the "Manage Pending Hires" within SAP SuccessFactors. Hiring data is entered into SAP SuccessFactors Employee Central. (More on Employee Central a little later.)
5. SAP SuccessFactors activates the new hire's data and status on their start date.

In addition to onboarding, SAP SuccessFactors has an Offboarding solution. This is used to process someone exiting the company. Offboarding can be implemented alongside Onboarding or as a separate solution.

Employee Central is part of SAP SuccessFactors that manages core data and processes within the Recruit-to-Retire process (Figure 6.14). There are similarities between what is available in SAP HCM and what is contained in SAP SuccessFactors Employee Central. For instance, HCM Info-type is master data about the employee. One of the Info-types was the Organizational Assignment Info-type which contained information about the Enterprise Structure, Personnel Structure, and Organizational Plan. Objects stored in this Info-type included the legal entity (company code), personnel area and personnel subareas to support compensation decisions, employee group and employee subgroups as well as the organizational unit, job key and position. These are all objects representing data that is fairly stable as it relates to the employee. In SAP SuccessFactors Employee Central there are Foundation Objects. Foundation Objects represent entities in SuccessFactors about an employee that are fairly stable and include similar objects, like the legal entity and organizational structure representing where the employee works and what job they hold. Additional examples of Foundation Objects are as follows: Business Unit, Division, Department, Location, Job Classification, Job Code, Position, Pay Grade, Pay and Range.

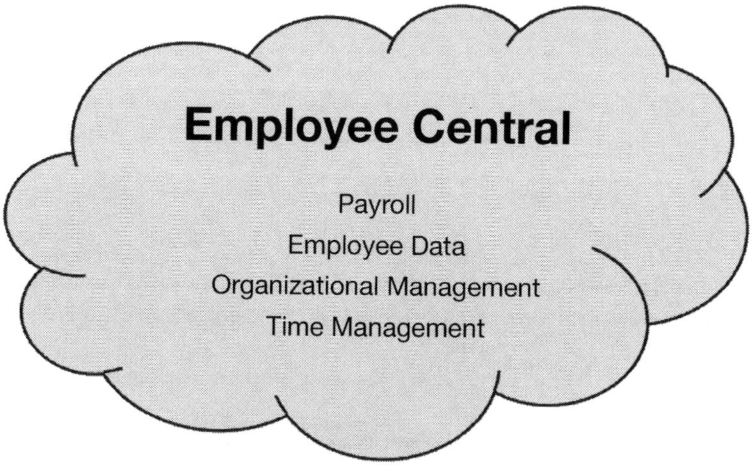

Figure 6.14: SAP SuccessFactors - Employee Central

Other aspects of Employee Central also include self-services. Like HCM, Employee Central provides the capability for both employee and manager self-service. Providing self-service capabilities eases the burden on the HR department and creates efficiencies. Role-based permissions are critical in determining what access users have to HR data.

Finally, Employee Central includes workflows, event reasons, and business rules associated with various transaction in HR. Workflows provide the structure for HR processes and the approval steps associated with it. Events are changes that are applied to an employee. Event reasons provide the reason behind the event that took place. Business rules include the logic associated with a transaction.

Learning

Learning is the third item in the Recruit-to-Retire process. SAP SuccessFactors Learning is more than simply training. It is a cloud-based solution that includes a Learning Management System (LMS) to provide employees with the a tool that delivers training and professional development content. Learning can be personalized and integrated with analytics to evaluate the progress of employees. Additionally, companies can take advantage of Learning to deliver compliance training to employees.

Payroll and Compensation

Payroll and Compensation are actually separate components in SAP SuccessFactors, yet they are closely aligned. Compensation is a critical factor for recruiting, retention, and business planning. From a business planning standpoint, compensation plays an important role in cost planning and budgeting.

Payroll is part of SAP SuccessFactors Employee Central and is designed to ensure accuracy and timeliness for paying employees. The payroll process requires info-type master data as well as time data. Once that data is collected and validated, the steps in the payroll process can proceed (Figure 6.15).

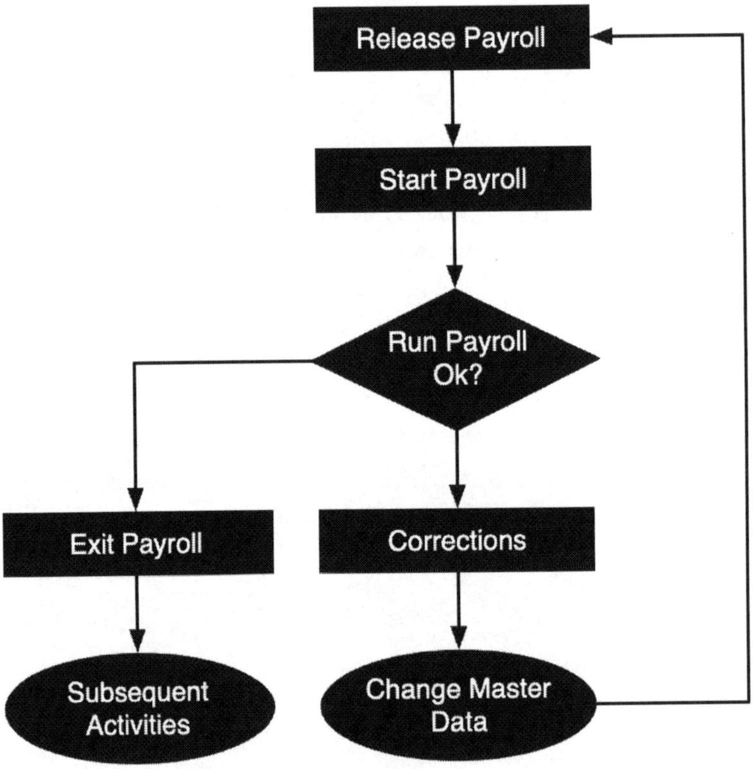

Figure 6.15: Payroll Process

The payroll process is initiated with a payroll release. After payroll is released, the payroll run is started. The results of the payroll run are analyzed to ensure accuracy. If everything is correct, payroll is exited and follow-on activities occur (e.g., checks printed, direct deposit, integration with accounting, etc.). Should there be any problems with the payroll run, changes to the necessary master data are implemented and the process begins over with the payroll release.

Reporting

Reporting involves People Analytics which includes a broad combination of analytic capabilities. Workforce analytics, stories, and other transaction analytics are integrated with SAP Analytics Cloud to provide management with better decision making capabilities and users with easy to use reporting tools. Reporting provides the business with key insights into planning and performance.

SAP SuccessFactors and the Human Experience Management (HXM) Suite

SAP SuccessFactors includes extensive functionality in a cloud-based HR solution. We've touched on some of its functionality above (e.g., People Analytics, Learning, Recruiting, Onboarding, Payroll and Compensation, and Employee Central), but there are other aspects of SuccessFactors that we should also mention.

- Performance and Goals
    - Management and employees can collaboratively develop plans to enhance employee performance providing benchmarks and measurements for assessment.
- Succession and Development
    - Succession and development work in unison to ensure vacancies are filled quickly with qualified internal candidates. Developing employees to be ready to fill vacancies in advance is an effective way to maintain a qualified workforce and reduce costs.

The SAP SuccessFactors Human Experience Management Suite leverages intelligent technologies to enhance the working experience for employees. Examples of intelligent technologies include Robotic Process Automation (RPA), Machine Learning (ML), and Artificial Intelligence (AI). Implementing RPA as part of the HXM suite frees up employees from repetitive tasks, giving them more time to focus on core competencies, which in turn increases employee productivity. ML predictions and nudges can be used to remind employees about responding to email on a timely manner as well as to follow up on tasks to improve readiness. And, things such as conversational AI enable employees to use voice recognition and commands to simplify tasks, making their work environment easier and more enjoyable.

Human Resource Management Summary

SAP Human Capital Management and SAP SuccessFactors provide SAP customers with all the tools to meet their human resource needs. HCM is part of the ERP solution in SAP S/4HANA and for our purposes is considered an on-premise HR solution, while SuccessFactors is a cloud-based solution.

It's important to understand the organizational levels which make up the Enterprise Structure in SAP HCM. There are other aspects within HCM which are also important. These include the Organizational Structure and the management of that structure (Organizational Management). Personnel Administration is the component in HCM for hiring and maintaining master data about employees in SAP HCM, which SAP refers to as Info-types. It's important to understand the options for maintaining info-types as well as being able to describe the personnel file.

In addition to the organizational levels and master data, there was a brief discussion of some transactional aspect in SAP HCM. These included Employ Self-service (ESS) and Manager Self-service. You should be able to identify activities belonging to each of these.

Finally, SAP SuccessFactors is a cloud-based HR solution with greater capabilities than the on-premise HCM solution. It integrates with intelligent technologies to support Human Experience Management (HXM). SAP SuccessFactors includes an HXM Suite designed to improve the work environment for employees by providing them with tools and capabilities that offer them a greater sense of accomplishment and belonging. It focuses on three key areas: Individuals, Teams, and Organizations.

SAP SuccessFactors offers SAP customers with a myriad of tools to enable to e Recruit-to-Retire process. It's a good idea to familiarize yourself with these tools, such as Job Requisitioning, Career Sites, Onboarding, and Master Data that support this process.

Chapter 7: Warehouse and Inventory Management

The warehouse and inventory management functions entail managing and tracking the physical movements of materials to support the business. With SAP S/4HANA, customers have flexibility for managing warehouse activities. Because SAP S4HANA is not a single product, customers can opt for a warehouse management solution that meets their warehouse needs. Managing warehouse activities is scalable in SAP S/4HANA, so customers with large, complex warehouse management requirements do not have to look outside of SAP S4HANA for a solution to meet their needs. Likewise, customers with minimal warehouse requirements, and customers somewhere in between, can also find what they are looking for in SAP S/4HANA. In addition to discussing warehouse management, we are also going to look at various options available for performing stock transfers and transfer postings. Stock transfers and transfer postings are examples of goods movements and are part of Inventory Management activities. We will learn that not all goods movement transactions consist of a physical movement of materials.

Warehouse Management: Organizational Levels and Master Data

Organizational Levels

As noted in the introduction to this chapter, in SAP S/4HANA customers have flexibility because the warehouse management solutions can meet the requirements regardless of their warehouse management needs. This is true because SAP S/4HANA offers two main solutions for warehouse management. Warehouse Management (WM) and Extended Warehouse Management (EWM). For purposes of discussion in this book, we will continue to refer to SAP WM as their warehouse management system for small to medium sized warehouse requirements. There are plans for SAP WM to be retired at the end of 2025 and for it to be replaced with SAP Stock Room Management (STRM). A little later in this chapter, we will talk in more detail regarding the differences between SAP WM and SAP EWM. But for now, let's get an understanding of the organizational levels for both.

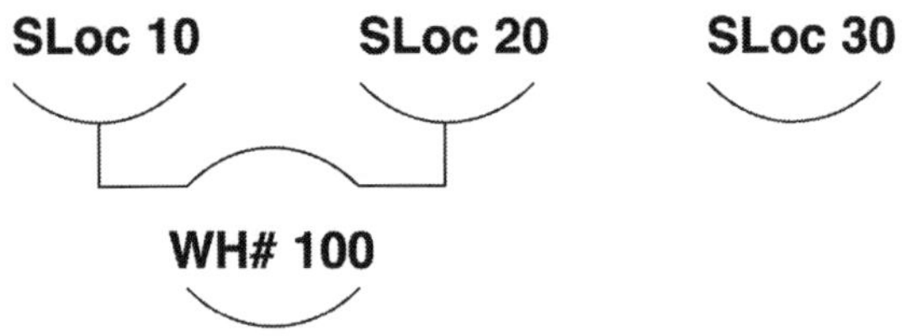

Figure 7.1: Warehouse Management Organizational Levels

As a reminder, when discussing organizational levels, we are also referring to the Enterprise Stricture. In WM, the main organizational level is the Warehouse Number. It is identified with a 3-digit character and is assigned to one or more plant/storage location combinations. It is essential to assign a WM number to a combination of plant/ storage location because storage location numbers are not unique at the Client level. They are unique at the Plant level. This means a storage location number can be repeated in the SAP S/4HANA system as storage locations in different plants can have the same storage location number. Figure 7.1 depicts a typical structure for assigning a warehouse number. In this figure, we can see that Warehouse Number 100 is assigned to more than one plant/storage location combinations. In this example, Storage Location 30 in Plant 1000 is not assigned a WM number. Therefore, that storage location is not managed using warehouse management functionality. It is managed using only inventory management functions.

Extended Warehouse Management (EWM) is as described in its name, an extension of Warehouse Management (WM). EWM has its own number and it is a 4-digit character. To enable EWM, the WM number is assigned to an EWM number as seen in Figure 7.2. You can see from this example that the same plant/storage location combinations are now being managed in EWM because WM number 100 has been assigned to the EWM number 1000.

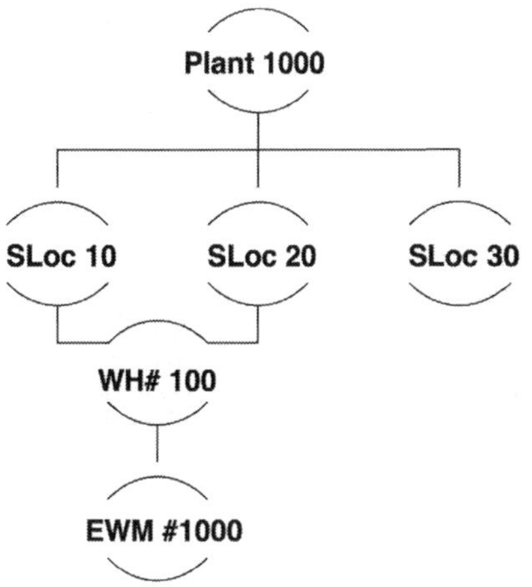

Figure 7.2: Extended Warehouse Management Organizational Levels

Structure of the Warehouse Number and Bin Master Data

The warehouse number has its own structure. To understand the structure of the warehouse number, we need to understand the differences between warehouse management and inventory management.

Warehouse management deals with the physical logistics of placing materials into the warehouse (putaway) and removing them from the warehouse (picking). You must pay careful attention to the difference between inventory management and warehouse management. The former is concerned only with tracking the quantity and value of material stock at various storage locations and with periodic reconciliation of physical inventory with book inventory

As mentioned above, the two are closely linked and SAP achieves the linkage by allowing us to enable warehouse management for storage locations. Not all storage locations are managed using putaway and picking strategies. Some may and others may not, based on how a company wants to handle this. Some storage locations might be small and not require the use of any warehouse management at all. For example, a storage location could be just a room for storing a few hundred items and hence not need any warehouse management at all. Other storage locations might be huge facilities with several square kilometers of space which could need extensive warehouse management capabilities to function efficiently. We could also have special storage needs like refrigerated/freezer storage which have special requirements, thus a need for warehouse management processes. Figure 7.3 clarifies the structure of a warehouse number.

The structure of the warehouse number supports the picking and putaway strategies of WM. Within the warehouse number, there are Storage Types. Some examples of storage types we recently mentioned above, refrigeration and freezer. Materials that require these special forms of storage are managed in a storage type. Other examples may include things such as rack storage, cantilever storage, hazardous materials, shelf storage, and many more.

Within each storage type are Storage Sections. These have also been referred to as "Storage Areas" and/or "Picking Sections". A storage section would be a sub-division of a storage type. For instance, if materials needed to be stored on a rack in the warehouse, the next logical set of questions would be, where on that rack? Top? Middle? Bottom? Strategies in the warehouse are often defined by the materials themselves. Heavier materials for rack storage would logically belong on the bottom part of the rack, while lighter materials would be stored at the top. If the storage type was freezer storage, items used most frequently would be stored in a section closest to the freezer door for purposes of efficiency and to ensure the warehouse workers aren't spending more time than necessary in the freezer.

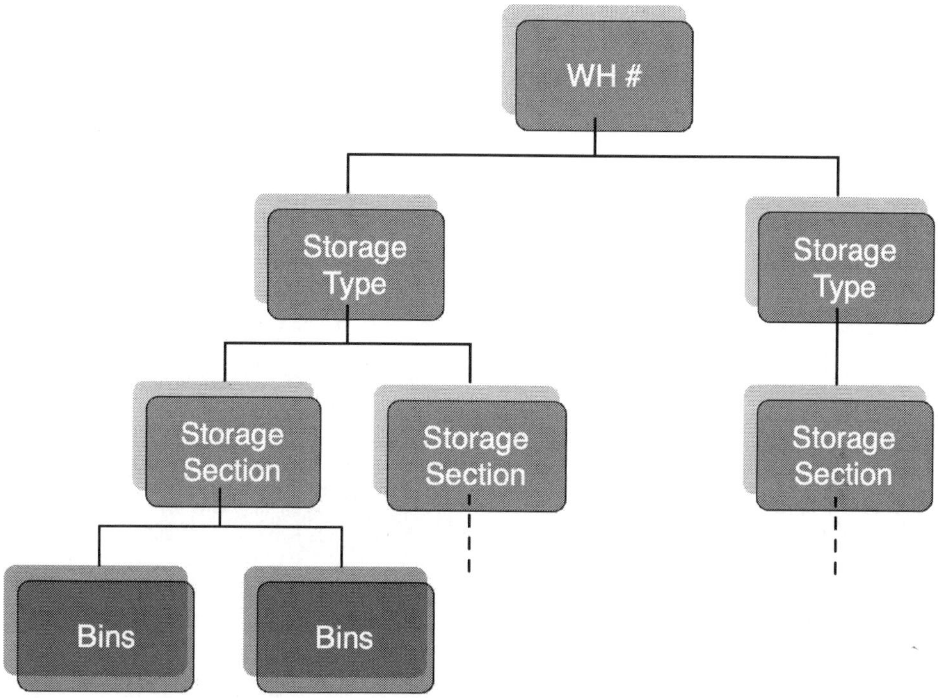

Figure 7.3: Structure of the Warehouse Number

The exact location within the warehouse number where the materials are putaway or from which they are picked, is called the Bin. Bins are further sub-divisions of storage sections and they have specific dimensions because the bins are generally associated with specific materials. Bins are considered master data. When materials are placed into a bin, this is referred to as a putaway. When materials are removed from a bin, this is called picking.

In the warehouse number, materials are putaway into a bin, within a storage section of a storage type. In a similar manner, materials are picked from a bin, within a storage section of a storage type. In this way, the SAP S/4HANA system provides customers with detailed information on materials stored in the warehouse.

Other Master Data

EWM is part of the Supply Chain Management (SCM) system in SAP S4HANA (Figure 7.4). Recall, in SAP S/4HANA, SCM is now natively integrated, but that was not always the case. Pervious to SAP S/4HANA, SCM was a separate system with its own terminology. Now that SCM is embedded in SAP S/4HANA, we will focus on that scenario as the sole deployment option for EWM.

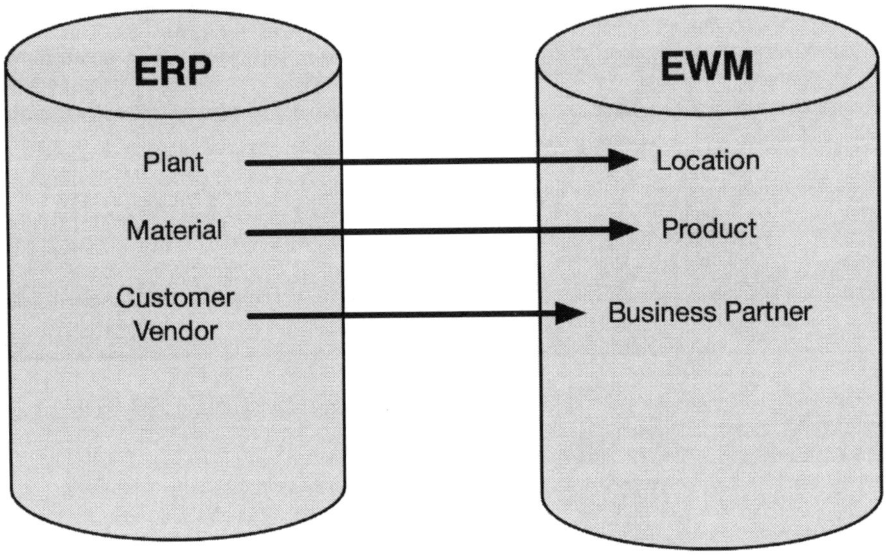

Figure 7.4: EWM Terminology

Warehouse Management and Extended Warehouse Management

Warehouse Management Options

As we previously discussed, not every customer has the same warehouse requirements. Because of this, there are varying levels of warehouse management options (Figure 7.5). Of course, one option is to not use warehouse management at all. But for very small warehouse needs, customers can opt to use Lean WM. In Lean WM, a fixed bin strategy is used. This means that each material has a specific bin for putaway and the bin is assigned in the material master record. There is less flexibility with this warehouse option, but the normal warehouse activities of putaway and picking still occur and these are managed with a Transfer Order as is the case with standard WM.

The next level up from Lean WM is WM. WM is used to satisfy small to medium sized warehouse needs. This is not necessarily an optimal solution for complex warehouse management needs and the focus of WM is on internal warehouse activities. (Reminder: SAP WM will be replaced by SAP Stock Room Management at the end of 2025.) Putaway and picking in WM is handled with Transfer Orders. However, a fixed bin strategy is not mandatory, allowing SAP customers flexible placement of materials in the warehouse. While customers can manage materials at the bin level, inventory goods movements (goods receipts/goods issues) and shipping activities still occur outside of WM.

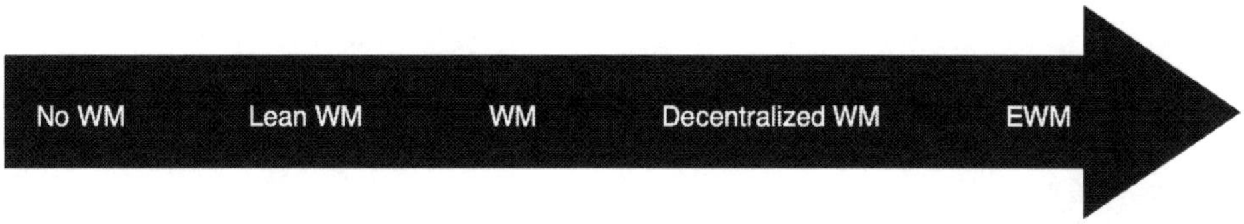

Figure 7.5: Warehouse Management Options.

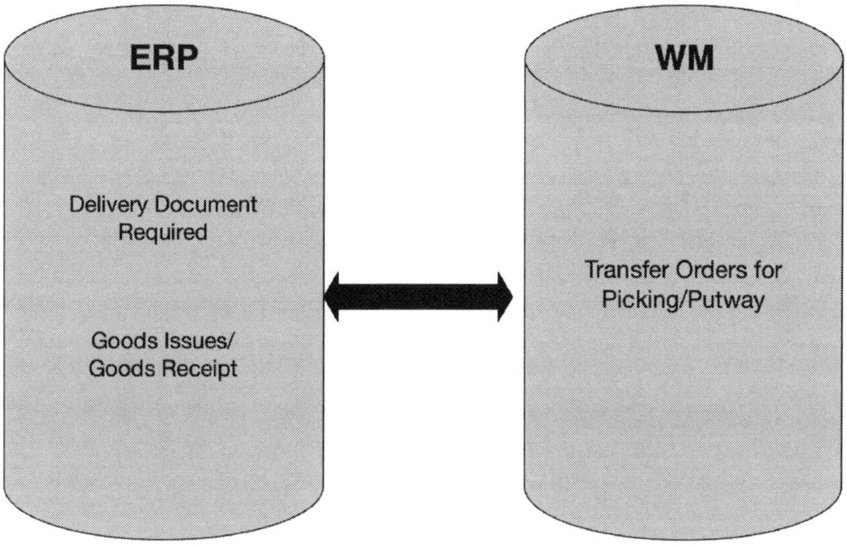

Figure 7.6: Decentralized Warehouse Management

Because many warehouses operate 24/7, WM solutions can be very demanding on a system. For load balancing purposes, many WM systems are housed on a separate server. This is known as a Decentralize WM environment (Figure 7.6). In such cases, the WM activities are physically separated from the other ERP activities. For instance, sales order processing with outbound deliveries is still managed in ERP, but the picking of the materials at the bin level with the Transfer Order are managed on a different server. Physically separating WM from ERP also allows customers the option to connect their WM system to more than one ERP system. In any decentralized WM environment, it is required to generate a Delivery Document on the ERP side in order to process a Transfer Order in WM. When WM is running on the same system as ERP, it is considered a centralized WM (Figure 7.7).

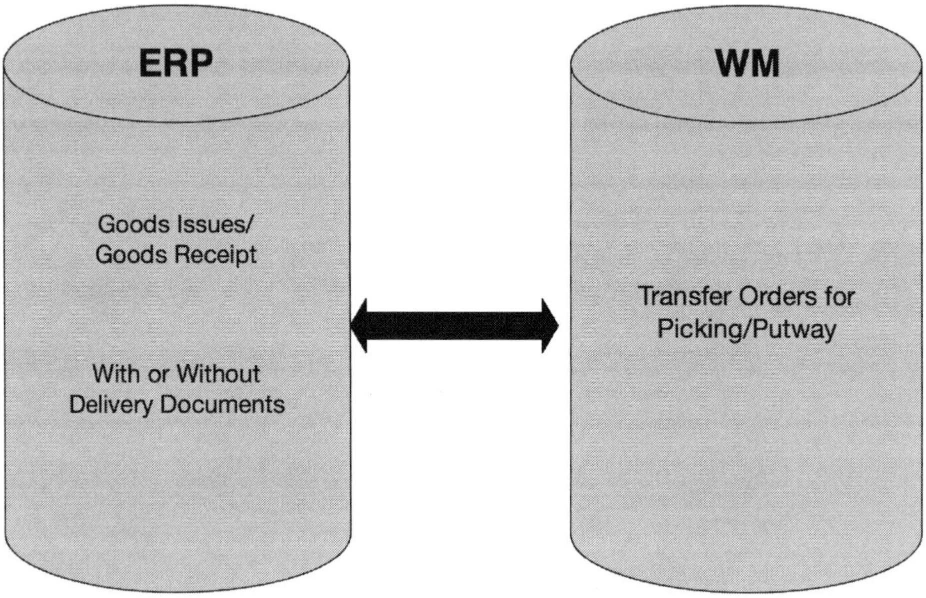

Figure 7.7: Centralized Warehouse Management

Extended Warehouse Management (EWM) is considered best-in-class regarding warehouse systems and offers the most extensive warehouse capabilities, designed for warehouses that are complex and high volume. EWM is for mid-size to large warehouse needs and offers flexible automation that focuses on activities that are both internal and external to the warehouse. EWM is natively available in the SAP S/4HANA system and therefore can be deployed on the same server as the ERP. Prior to SAP HANA, EWM was for too complex and demanding to run on the same system as ERP, therefore it was always physically separated.

Since EWM historically was physically separated (typically on a SCM server), delivery documents were required in ERP (as they are in a decentralized WM). With the increased throughput capabilities of SAP HANA, it is now possible to run EWM on the same server as SAP S/4HANA system (embedded). However, it is still required to use delivery documents on the ERP side. From this perspective, EWM is always considered a decentralized warehouse management system (Figure 7.8).

In EWM, Delivery Orders (not Transfer Orders) are used to manage the warehouse tasks of picking and putaway. Thus, Delivery Documents in ERP are required to create Delivery Orders in EWM. Figure 7.8 also shows another significant difference between WM and EWM. You'll notice that the goods movements (goods issues/goods receipts) take place at the Bin level within the EWM system. The goods movement from within EWM then updates the delivery document on the ERP side.

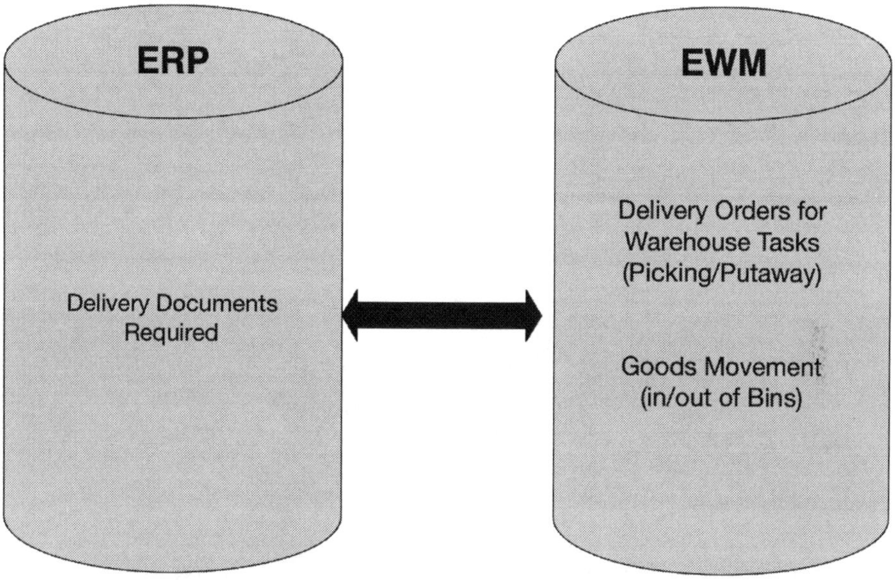

Figure 7.8: Extended Warehouse Management (Same System or Separate)

Differences Between WM and EWM

Some of the differences between WM and EWM can be seen in the processes we discussed in the previous section. In review, WM can be centralized or decentralized depending on whether it is running on the same system as ERP or not. If it is decentralized, delivery documents are required on the ERP side. Delivery documents may still be used in ERP regardless of it being a centralized WM environment. However, they are for other logistics purposes and not a requirement for WM. In either situation, transfer orders are used in WM to process the picking and putaway activities. The goods movements (goods issues/goods receipts) take place in ERP.

On the other hand, EWM is always considered decentralized because delivery documents are always required in ERP. However, the picking and putaway are called warehouse tasks, and are performed with delivery orders within EWM. The goods movements also occur at the bin level in EWM and the result of the goods movement is an update to the delivery document in ERP. Because the goods movements are inventory management transactions, and in EWM these take place at the bin level, it can be stated that EWM allows for inventory management at the bin level.

For customers using EWM, it is important to establish whether the EWM activities are for inbound logistics processing (materials going into the warehouse) or outbound logistics processing (materials leaving the warehouse). This is very important because delivery documents in ERP and delivery orders in EWM are NOT generic. There are both inbound delivery documents and outbound delivery documents in ERP. For inbound logistics processing in EWM, it is required to create an inbound delivery document in ERP. The inbound delivery document in ERP is then used to create an inbound delivery order in EWM. Likewise, for outbound logistics processing in EWM, an outbound delivery document is required in ERP to create an outbound delivery order in EWM.

In EWM, the delivery orders are used to complete the warehouse tasks. For an inbound delivery order in EWM, the warehouse task is putaway. For an outbound delivery order in EWM, the warehouse task is picking. Figure 7.9 and Figure 7.10 depict both processes.

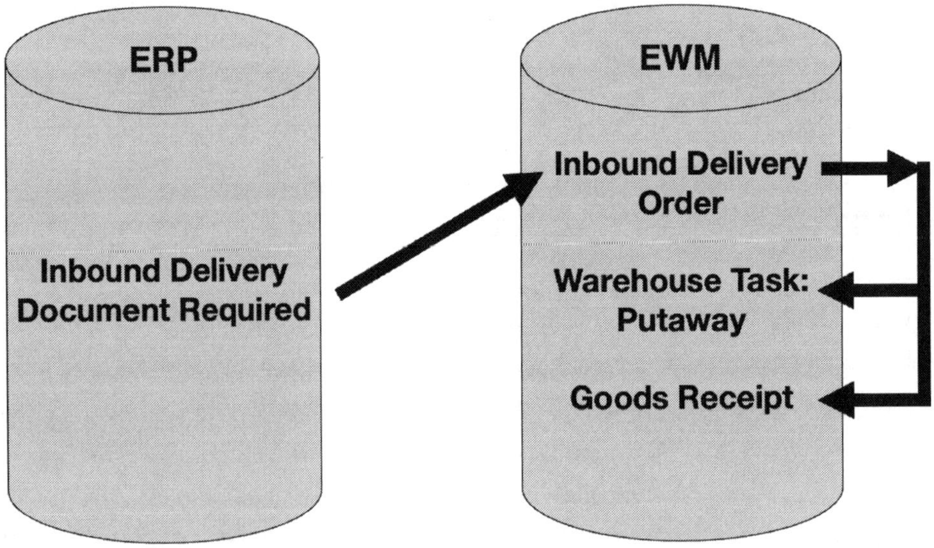

Figure 7.9: Extended Warehouse Management - Inbound Processing

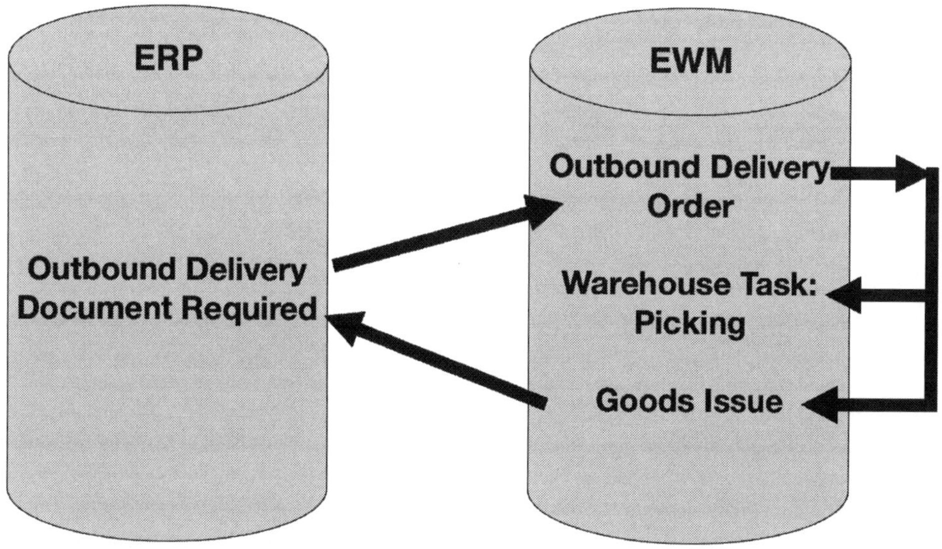

Figure 7.10: Extended Warehouse Management - Outbound Processing

Other than process-oriented differences, there are functional difference as well. As noted above, EWM allows for inventory management at the bin level. Some additional functions also exist and though WM may offer aspects of the following functions, they are fully supported in EWM.

- Putaway and picking strategies
- Planning of receipts
- Warehouse automation
- Yard management
- Cross-docking
- Labor management
- Slotting and Rearrangement
- Wave Management

Slotting and Rearrangement in EWM

The goal of slotting and rearrangement is to ensure the materials are in an optimal bin location within the warehouse. Since receipts can be planned in EWM, slotting ensures the materials are placed in bins that optimize use of the materials under various criteria, such as how quickly materials are used. Once materials are in the warehouse, they can also be rearranged for further optimization. Keep in mind, much of this can be automated in the EWM system.

Wave Management in EWM

Wave management is an automated process in EWM used to create efficiencies and reduce costs in processing orders and shipments. With high volume warehouses, several items in the warehouse may need to be delivered at one time. When this happens, the items are grouped into waves so they can be picked collectively and prepared for further outbound processing. The groupings are based on predefined criteria which allows the EWM system to determine which items belong in which groups. The idea is to collectively process as many items as meet the criteria and stage them until they are ready to be delivered from the warehouse.

Technologies

There are many new technologies available to assist with warehouse activities for both WM and EWM scenarios. The following are examples of some of these technologies and this certainly is not an exhaustive list by any means.

- Infrared technologies (IR readers and scanners)
- Smart glass technologies (i.e. Google glasses)
- Handheld scanning devices
- Voice activated

EWM Warehouse Monitor

The EWM Warehouse Monitor is the tool in EWM that manages the warehouse. Within the Warehouse Monitor, users select the warehouse activity from a navigational tree and then manage the activity in a work area. The Warehouse Monitor is used for tracking quantities, bin situations, capacities for inbound and outbound processing, and alerts. The Warehouse Monitor alerts can inform warehouse personnel of any issues in the warehouse, such as bottlenecks. The alerts could be for current issues, but also potential issues that need attention. This allows the warehouse managers to be proactive and prepare to remedy situations that are or may occur.

It is within the Warehouse Monitor that Inbound and Outbound Delivery Orders are processed. Warehouse tasks and goods movements are also processed in the

Warehouse Monitor. Figure 7.11 shows a typical warehouse layout with both inbound and outbound processing areas. You can see from this figure that there are many considerations in EWM that not only includes activities internal to the warehouse, but also external to the warehouse, such as Yard Management. In a later chapter we will see there is integration between EWM and SAP Transportation Management (TM).

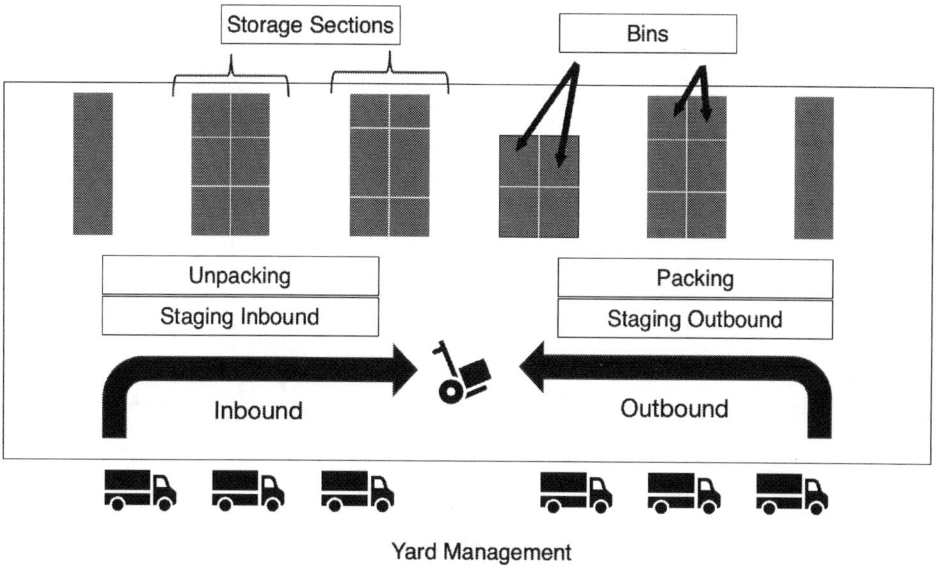

Figure 7.11: Typical Warehouse Layout

Transfer Postings and Stock Transfers

Transfer Postings and Stock Transfers are examples of goods movements in SAP S/4HANA. These are inventory management transactions and may require additional warehouse management activities, but warehouse management is not the focus of this discussion. We will begin our discussion with transfer postings and then tackle stock transfers.

Transfer Postings

Transfer postings are a form of goods movement that do not include a physical movement. All goods movements, regardless of being a physical movement or not, will result in the creation of a Material Document (a quantity-based electronic record of the goods movement). All goods movements are also managed with a Movement Type. A movement type is a key assigned to a goods movement that defines the purpose of the goods movement and differentiates it from all other goods movements. There are three basic categories of transfer postings as shown in Figure 7.12. Further examples of Stock to Stock transfer postings and their movement types are seen in Figure 7.13.

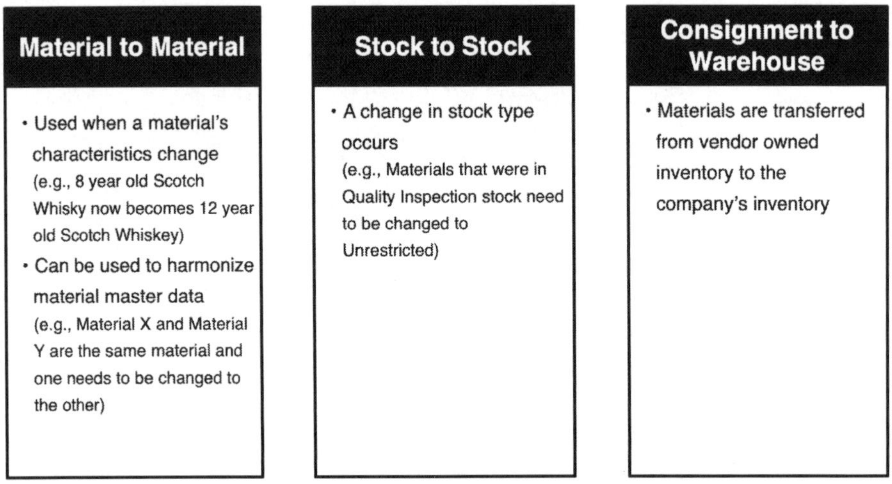

Figure 7.12: Transfer Postings

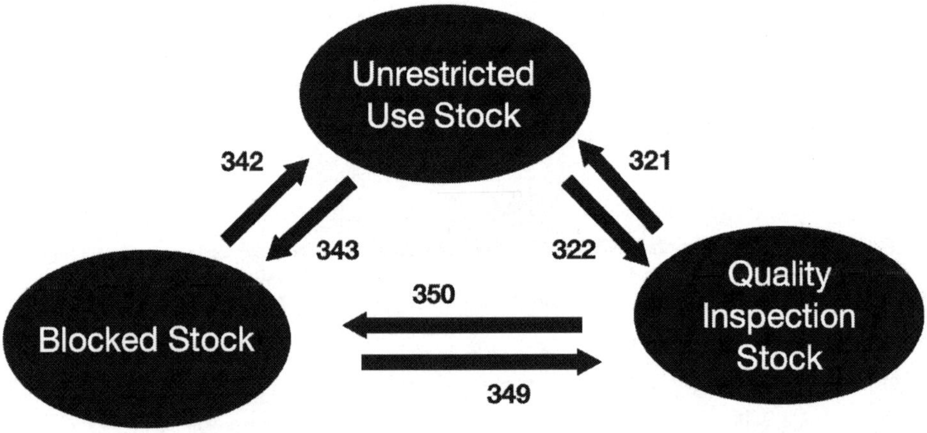

Figure 7.13: Stock to Stock Transfer Postings with Movement Types

While transfer postings are not physical, it's also important to note that additional physical movements are possible.

Stock Transfers

Unlike transfer postings, stock transfers are a physical movement of materials. There are three basic forms of stock transfers described below in Figure 7.14.

Storage Location to Storage Location

- Materials are physically removed from one storage location to a different storage location within the same plant

Plant to Plant

- Materials are physically removed from a storage location in one plant to a storage location in a different plant

Company Code to Company Code

- Materials are physically removed from a storage location in a plant of one company code to a storage location in a plant in a different company code

Figure 7.14: Stock Transfers

Stock transfers can be performed in either a one-step procedure or a two-step procedure. The difference between the two is quite simple. In a one-step procedure, the stock transfer occurs in a single transaction. A two-step procedure requires two transactions. Because the stock transfer requires the removal of materials from inventory as well as a placement of materials in inventory, a goods issue and goods receipt are required. In a one-step procedure, both the goods issue and goods receipt occur in the same transaction. Because it is only one transaction, only one material document will be generated. However, that material document will be composed of two separate line items. The first line item will display the goods issue while the second line item displays the goods receipt. In a two-step procedure, a material document is created for each step (transaction). Since the first step is always the goods issue, the goods issue appears in the first material document. The second material document generated from the second step will therefore show the goods receipt.

In a one-step procedure, the materials are considered issued out of the issuing location and received into the receiving location simultaneously. From a practical standpoint, this is an impossibility. So, the decision to perform a one-step stock transfer requires some consideration because the materials can't be tracked when they are physically being transferred. Because of this, some customers may opt to use a two-step procedure. In a two-step procedure, the first step is the goods issue. At the time of the goods issue, the materials are considered removed from the issuing location physically and systematically. The materials are systematically (not physically) considered part of the receiving location's inventory. However, because the materials are not physically received until the goods receipt is performed, the system will display the materials as part of the receiving location's inventory as "In Transfer". Once the second step (goods receipt) is performed, the materials are removed from "In Transfer" and will appear in the storage location at the receiver.

There are also financial accounting (FI) considerations for stock transfers. From what we have learned regarding material master data, the valuation level for a material is the Plant. If materials move within the same plant, there will be no financial accounting impacts.[1] Therefore, Storage Location to Storage Location stock transfers will not have any financial accounting impacts and will not result in the creation of any accounting documents (FI docs). If materials are moved between plants, regardless of whether they are in the same company code or not, there will be a financial accounting impact. It is of critical importance to note that valuation (balance sheet impact) of the goods movement ALWAYS occurs at the time of goods issue. Therefore, any accounting documents (FI docs) created are created at the time of the goods issue. It is equally important to note, the financial impact of the goods issue is valued at the material price of the issuing location. Whether a stock transfer is performed using a one-step or two-step procedure, the accounting document(s) are generated at the time of goods issue.

As you can surmise from our discussion, it is possible to get more than one FI document for a stock transfer. This will be true when there is a Company Code to Company Code stock transfer. Two FI documents are created at the time of goods issue because two company codes are impacted financially. Therefore, each company code will get its own FI document as an electronic record of the financial impacts resulting from the stock transfer.

To simplify this, Table 7.1 is a grid depicting the impacts of the various stock transfers. The one-step Storage Location to Storage Location stock transfer is unique. For every other type of stock transfer, the materials must be issued out of unrestricted use stock and received into unrestricted use stock. The one-step Storage Location to Storage Location stock transfer allows for materials to be issued out of and received into any stock type. A two-step procedure is required if the user does not have authorization in both the issuing and receiving locations.

---

[1] Though there are exceptions to this, we won't be covering them in this book.

Table 7.1: Stock Transfers and Document

Stock Transfert	One Step	Two Step (In-Transfer at Receiver after the first step)
Storage Loc to Storage Loc	1 Material document 0 FI document	2 Material documents 0 FI document
Plant to Plant	1 Material document 1 FI document	2 Material documents 1 FI document
CoCd to CoCd	1 Material document 2 FI documents	2 Material documents 2 FI documents

Alternative Stock Transfer: Stock Transport Orders

In addition to the traditional forms of stock transfers discussed above, SAP S/4HANA offers an alternative, the Stock Transport Order (STO). A STO is a stock transfer performed using a Purchase Order. A Stock Transport Order is a type of Purchase Order where the supplier is another Plant instead of a Vendor. Using the same example from Chapter 5, you can see a PO containing a stock item and a consumable in Figure 7.15.

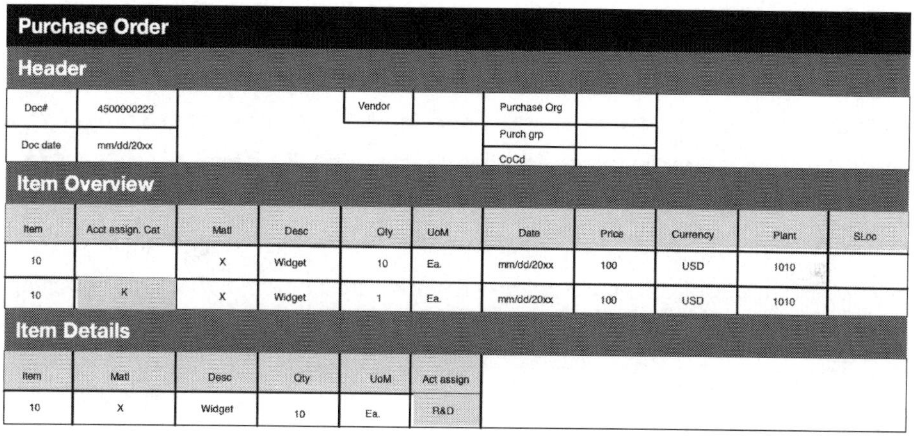

Purchase Order

Header

Doc#	4500000223	Vendor		Purchase Org	
Doc date	mm/dd/20xx			Purch grp	
				CoCd	

Item Overview

Item	Acct assign. Cat	Matl	Desc	Qty	UoM	Date	Price	Currency	Plant	SLoc
10		X	Widget	10	Ea.	mm/dd/20xx	100	USD	1010	
10	K	X	Widget	1	Ea.	mm/dd/20xx	100	USD	1010	

Item Details

Item	Matl	Desc	Qty	UoM	Act assign
10	X	Widget	10	Ea.	R&D

Figure 7.15: Purchase Order for Stock and Consumable (Replica of Figure 5.15)

Suppose during the sourcing decision, the receiving/requesting plant was able to locate the needed materials in another plant instead of buying them from an external vendor. A Plant to Plant or Company Code to Company Code stock transfer can be used for the stock item, but not for the consumable item. In such a case, the receiving/requesting plant can use a STO. Because a STO is just another form of a PO, the receiving/requesting plant can include the stock item as well as the consumable item in the STO. This is a major advantage of the STO over stock transfers. Figure 7.16 shows what the

STO would look like. Notice, the order type is no longer a Purchase Order, it is now a Stock Transport Order. Also, the Vendor field has been replaced with Supplying Plant. Everything else essentially remains the same.

Stock Transport Order

Header

Doc#	4500000223	Supplying Plant	Purchase Org	
Doc date	mm/dd/20xx		Purch grp	
			CoCd	

Item Overview

Item	Acct assign. Cat	Matl	Desc	Qty	UoM	Date	Price	Currency	Plant	SLoc
10		X	Widget	10	Ea.	mm/dd/20xx	100	USD	1010	
10	K	X	Widget	1	Ea.	mm/dd/20xx	100	USD	1010	

Item Details

Item	Matl	Desc	Qty	UoM	Act assign
10	X	Widget	10	Ea.	R&D

Figure 7.16: Stock Transport Order for Stock and Consumable

A STO has other advantages besides being able to plan a consumable. Recall from Chapter 5, terms and conditions are part of a PO. Therefore, terms and conditions for this form of stock transfer can be negotiated between plants and included in the STO. (Remember, valuation of materials in a normal stock transfer are based on the material value at the issuing location and can't be negotiated.) It is also possible to receive materials into any stock type using a STO. However, the materials must still be issued form unrestricted use stock at the issuing plant. For normal stock transfers, both the goods issue and goods receipt must be of stock type unrestricted use. The exception being a one-step storage location to storage location stock transfer. But STOs are not needed for such cases. They are used for cross-plant scenarios (Plant to Plant or Company Code to Company Code). Finally, STO's can be managed with or without delivery documents and they are MRP relevant. This means MRP can include STO's when preforming supply and demand calculations.

Figure 7.17 shows the STO process. As you can see the STO is created at the receiving/requesting plant. When the STO is created, the receiving/requesting plant can view the Stock Overview report to see the materials were placed on order. Once the issuing plant posts the goods issue, the Stock Overview will still show the materials on order but will show the materials "In Transit" and as part of the receiving/requesting plant's inventory. This is different than "In Transfer", which is where materials display after the first step of a two-step procedure. This way, the user can tell which materials originate from a STO and which originate from a stock transfer. When the goods receipt is posted, the materials can be received into any stock type and placed in a storage location.

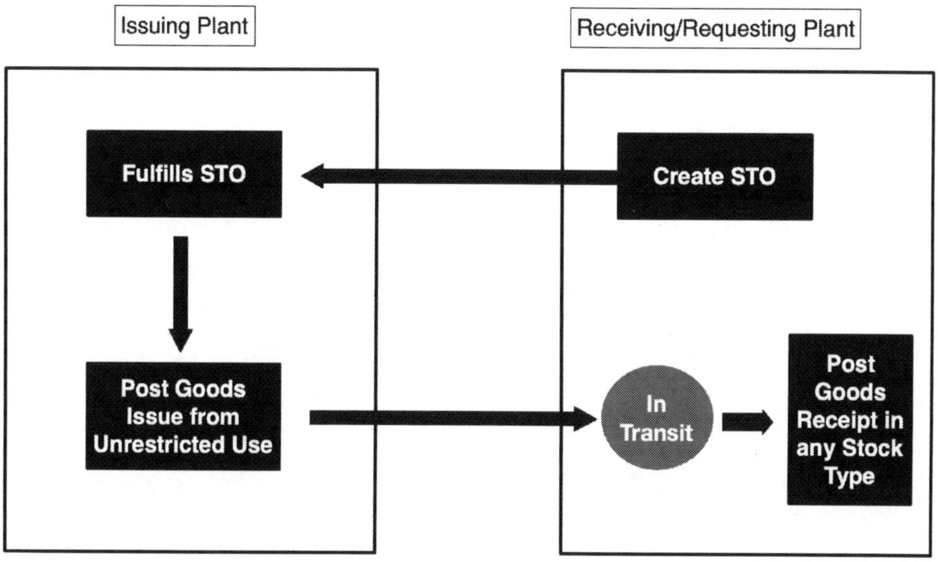

Figure 7.17: Stock Transport Order Process

Warehouse Management Summary

In this chapter we made a distinction between warehouse management and inventory management. Regarding warehouse management, SAP S/4HANA offers flexibility from using no warehouse management to using EWM. For small to medium warehouse needs, WM is most appropriate. While medium to large warehouse are better suited for EWM.

From an organizational level perspective, the warehouse number is the essential organizational level in WM, while the Extended Warehouse number is needed for EWM. The warehouse number also has a structure, with materials being putaway and picked from Bins. Bins are considered master data.

WM can be run in a centralized or decentralized environment. A decentralized environment means it is running on a separate server and requires the use of delivery documents in ERP. EWM always requites delivery documents in ERP and therefore is always considered a decentralized warehouse management system. However, with

SAP S/4HANA, EWM can be embedded in S/4HANA, which means it can be run on the same server.

There are additional distinctions between WM and EWM. WM uses Transfer Orders for putaway and picking, while EWM utilizes Delivery Orders. Be sure to familiarize yourself with other differences, including the ability to plan receipts in EWM, inventory management at the Bin level (goods movements), managing activities internal and external to the warehouse (Yard Management and integration with Transportation Management), Slotting and Rearrangement, and Wave Management.

We also explored Transfer Postings and Stock Transfers. The three different Transfer Postings are Material to Material, Stock to Stock, and Consignment to Warehouse. Transfer Postings do not necessarily include physical movement of materials. Stock Transfers are physical goods movements and can be performed in a one-step or two-step procedure. Different types of Stock Transfers included Storage Location to Storage Location, Plant to Plant, and Company Code to Company Code. We also looked at Stock Transport Orders as an alternative to the other forms of stock transfers. A STO has several advantages over traditional stock transfers.

Chapter 8: Manufacturing Planning and Execution

This chapter is extensive in terms of content. The Manufacturing Planning and Execution function involves the complex planning of materials and capacities to support the manufacturing of products in an enterprise. For clarity, in this book manufacturing execution involves the processing of production orders. Both planning and the execution of manufacturing are managed in the Design-to-Operate business process. The Design-to-Operate process has integration across many business functions and involves several SAP solutions. We will see how Production Planning (PP) module in SAP S/4HANA integrates with other modules within S/4HANA ERP to include Controlling, Financial Accounting, Sales, and Inventory Management. We will also see integration with other SAP products, such as Integrated Business Planning (IBP) and Advanced Planning (AP). There is talk about IBP replacing AP, but for now we will continue to discuss both solutions as both are still currently available to SAP customers. Though we have not yet been introduced to IBP and AP, we have already seen integration with Controlling when we covered Product Cost Planning in Chapter 4. We will revisit that because it is an important part of manufacturing and has implications not only on the planning side, but also on the manufacturing execution side. As we have done in pervious chapters, we will begin our discussion with the organizational levels (Enterprise Structure) associated with Production Planning (PP). We will then take a look at an overview of the "best-practice" scenario for the Design-to-Operate process, which will include master data elements as well as detailed views of the transactional/process-oriented content.

It's important to note that we are not covering all aspects of PP. The goal of this book is to learn how integration occurs across the intelligent enterprise. There are many different forms of manufacturing which will not be covered. For the most part, our discussions will focus primarily on discrete manufacturing with a make-to-stock strategy. To put this in context, discrete manufacturing means that all productions orders will have discrete quantities associated with them. In other words, the yield quantity for a production order can be pre-defined. Make-to-stock simply means that sales orders will be satisfied from inventory. Therefore, when planning production, it is important to forecast sales so production can meet the inventory needs to satisfy future sales orders.

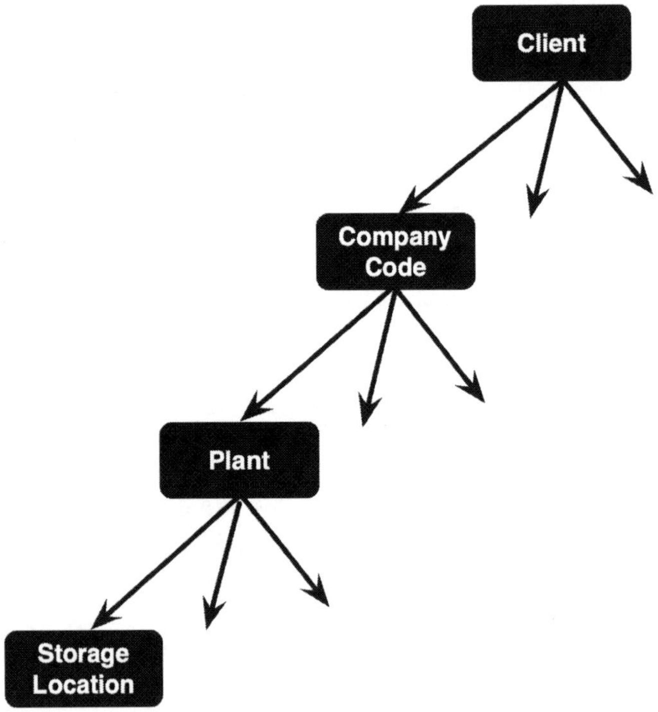

Figure 8.1: Logistics Organizational Levels (Replica of Figure 5.1)

Organizational Levels (Enterprise Structure)

As a reminder, organizational levels provide us with the data structure in the SAP S/4HANA system. The Production Planning (PP) module in SAP S/4HANA is a logistics module. Recalling from previous chapters, all logistics modules require the same four organizational levels. These can be seen in Figure 8.1 and include the Client, Company Code, Plant, and Storage Locations. The Plant is the key organizational level in PP because that is where data regarding operational activities reside. Therefore, all master data in the PP module will be created at the Plant organizational level. And, for the most part, all transactions will also occur at the Plant level.

Unlike the Source-to-Pay Process in the Materials Management module, there are no additional organizational levels required in Production Planning. The only required organizational levels are the four mentioned above.

Best-Practice Scenario for the Design-to-Operate Process

Keeping in line with our approach to this book, we will look at the Design-to-Operate process using SAP's "best-practice" scenario. This can be seen in Figure 8.2.

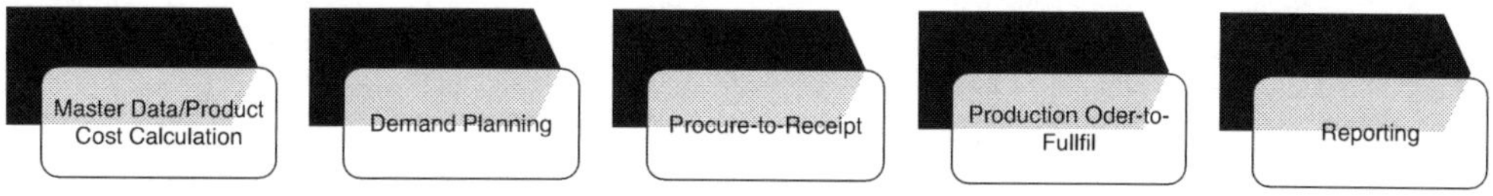

Figure 8.2: Best-Practice Scenario for the Design-to-Operate Process

Master Data/Product Cost Calculation

The first item in the "best-practice" scenario contains two components. First, there is the master data requirements for Design-to-Operate, followed by the transactional process of performing a product cost calculation. There are several master data in the PP module. All the master data we will see are created at the Plant organizational level. We are going to begin by looking into each of the master data in PP as well as gaining some insight into how each of these master data are related to support the process. We will then evaluate how this master data is leveraged to perform product cost calculations.

Material/Product Master Data

For our discussions, we will speak primarily about Material Master data. However, Material and Product master data are generally viewed as synonymous. For the PP module it is important to understand the Material Types involved before we can start discussing the data that is to be maintained in the Material Views. For PP, there are three material types that are important: Finished Goods (Products), Semi-finished, and Raw Materials. For clarification, finished goods are materials that are produced (procured internally) and sold. Semi-finished materials are produced (procured internally) and used as components to produce another product. And, raw materials are procured externally and used as components to produce other products. All three material types must be planned and therefore require data in the MRP Views of the material master records. Finished goods and semi-finished goods are manufactured and require data be maintained in the Work Scheduling Views of the material master record. The MRP and Work Scheduling views are plant specific.

The MRP views of the material master record are essentially the instructions that the MRP transaction will use to plan that material. There are several MRP views and it is most important to understand the data in each of these views. Figure 8.3 shows the data maintained in the MRP views.

- MRP Type
  - Standard MRP or Consumption Based
- MRP Controller
  - Person responsible for MRP runs
- Lot Size Rule
  - Fixed/Lot-for-Lot
- Procurement Type
  - Internal/External
- Goods Receipt Processing Time
- Schedule Margin Key
  - Defines Openings Periods (Floats)
- Production Strategies
  - Make-to-Stock, Make-to-Order, etc.
- Availability Checks
  - How system checks availability for MRP

Figure 8.3: Material Master Data: MRP Views

For materials that are procured internally (produced in-house), the Work Scheduling view is required. The Work Scheduling view contains data regarding the scheduling profile and capacity requirements (times) for in-house production which are derived from the routings (more on routings shortly). The capacity requirements could be lot-size dependent. In addition to this data, it's also important to identify the production supervisor in charge of the production of that product.

Bill of Material

Regarding Bill of Material (BOM) master data, we will revisit our discussion from Chapter 4. Figure 8.4 is the same example of the office chair from that chapter. As we noted, the bill of material is a structured list of all the components required to produce a product. It is also important to identify a base quantity of the product and component quantities (quantity of components required to make the base quantity).

For simplicity, let us assume that all the components from Figure 8.4 are raw materials. This means we do not produce any of the components. All of them are procured externally using the MM Source-to-Pay process. In this case, the office chair would be a finished good, while all the components would be raw materials.

Figure 8.4: Office Chair Example (Replica of Figure 4.13)

A more accurate depiction of what the BOM master record would look like in SAP S/4HANA can be seen in Figure 8.5. There are two main sections of the BOM master record, the Header and Component Items.

Header

Material:	Chair
Plant:	1000
BOM Usage:	1 (Production)
Alternative BOM:	1
Validity from Date:	1/1/2019

Base Qty:	1 ea

Item Categories

L: Stock Item
N: Non-Stock Item
F: Document Item
R: Variable-Size Item

Components Items		**ItC**	**Qty**
10	Backrest	L	1ea
20	Armrest	L	2ea
30	Chair seat	L	1ea
40	Action Mechanism	L	1ea
50	Gas Lift (spring)	L	1ea
60	Chair Base	L	1ea
70	Wheel Castors	L	5ea

Figure 8.5: Office Chair BOM

The header of the BOM contains the material of the BOM item and the Plant where the BOM master record is created. The BOM Usage defines the business function for which the BOM is being used. In this case, the BOM is used for production.[1] The Header of the BOM also contains information as to whether or not there are alternative BOMs for this product, the validity dates for the BOM, and the base quantity which we described above.

The Component Item section of the BOM contains the components and the quantities of those components required to produce the base quantity in the Header. You also see each component item is associated with an Item Category. The item category tells the system how to process that component. There are four basic item categories which you see described in the figure above: stock items, non-stock items, document items (assembly diagrams), and variable-size items. The item categories are very important during the planning process. Let's look at two item categories in particular, stock and non-stock. A stock item implies that this component is normally stored in inventory. During the planning steps, the system will check inventory levels to see whether or not enough of that material is available for the planned production quantities. For a non-stock item, the system will immediately trigger the MM Source-to-

[1] This implies there are other BOM Usages for other business functions.

Pay process by creating a purchase requisition for that component because the system will know that a non-stock item will never be available in inventory.

In our example, we worked under the assumption that all the components were raw materials. However, if we produce one or more of the component items, then the items would be considered semi-finished products. In SAP S/4HANA, all BOMs are single-level. This means there is only one level of component items for the header item. If a component in a BOM is a semi-finished product it would then require its own BOM master record. Therefore, a component in a BOM can itself, have a BOM master record.

Let's assume that the component, "Gas Lift (spring)" is a semi-finished product. That is, we also produce that item. In this case, the "Gas Lift (spring)" component would require a BOM master record. In SAP S/4HANA, when a component of a BOM has its own BOM master record, the system will automatically place a check mark in the "Assembly" column for that component. Figure 8.6 shows the BOM for the Office Chair, but with the semi-finished product, "Gas Lift (spring)".

Header

Material:	Chair
Plant:	1000
BOM Usage:	1 (Production)
Alternative BOM:	1
Validity from Date:	1/1/2019

Base Qty:	1 ea

Item Categories

L: Stock Item
N: Non-Stock Item
F: Document Item
R: Variable-Size Item

Components Items		ItC	Qty	Assembly
10	Backrest	L	1ea	
20	Armrest	L	2ea	
30	Chair seat	L	1ea	
40	Action Mechanism	L	1ea	
50	Gas Lift (spring)	L	1ea	✓
60	Chair Base	L	1ea	
70	Wheel Castors	L	5ea	

Figure 8.6: Office Chair BOM w/ Semi-Finished Component

Routing Master Data

Routing master data contains the operations required to produce a product. The operations are hubs of information as so much is linked to each operation. For starters, each operation is linked to a Control Key. The Control Key defines whether that operation is performed internally by a work center, or externally by a vendor. Given this information, an internal operation is also assigned to a work center (master data which we will discuss in more detail in the following section). External operations are performed by a vendor and will integrate with the MM Source-to-Pay process and trigger the creation of a purchase requisition. This is similar to what we saw with item categories. If it helps, think of it logically. Stock items and internal operations represent what is available within the company. Non-stock items and external operations are not available, therefore we need to procure them. If it's not available, the system will create a purchase requisition to buy it.

To help plan the scheduling of the operations, each operation is also assigned a time component (i.e., how long it takes to perform the operation). For internal operations that are assigned to work centers, the business will need to plan the capacity requirements for each work center based on the time associated with the operation. This time component is also used to assist with the planning and calculation of costs. All operations are linked to one or more activity types, which in combination with a cost center will return an activity price (refer to Activity Based Costing in Chapter 4). Finally, components from the BOM are also assigned to operations where they are needed. This is done to ensure that the required materials will be available to perform the operations.

The Routing master data has a Header. The header of the routing has information about the product associated with the Routing and the Plant where the master record is stored. The header also has a usage which explains the business function for which this routing applies (in this case it is production). From the header, the user can link to other areas of the routing. For our purposes this includes the Operations, Components Allocation, and Operations Sequencing. Continuing with our example of the Office Chair, Figure 8.7 shows the Header of the Routing for producing the office chair.

Header

Material:	Office Chair
Plant:	1000
Usage:	1 (Production)

Operations | Sequences | Component Allocation

Figure 8.7: Office Chair Routing: Header

By selecting the Operations button, the Routing master record provides information about each operation. Notice each operation in Figure 8.8 is linked to a Control Key, Work Center, Time, and Activity Type.

Header | Sequences | Component Allocation

Operations

Operation	Description	Work Center	Ctrl Key	Time (min)	Act Type
10	Attach Chair Seat to Backrest	Production	Int	5	Assembly
20	Attach Armrests	Production	Int	5	Assembly
30	Attach Action Mechanism	Production	Int	3	Assembly
40	Attach Gas Lift (spring) and Wheel Casters to Chair Base	Production	Int	7	Assembly
50	Attach Chair Seat to Gas Lift	Production	Int	5	Assembly

Figure 8.8: Office Chair Routing: Operations.

Components are assigned to operations. An operation can have more than one component assigned to it and the default assignment is the first operation. So, if the user does not manually assign a component to an operation, it must be available at the start of the first operation and it will be consumed (cost posted) at the start of the first operation. From a practical standpoint, it makes sense to assign the components to the operations where they are needed. Doing so ensures the materials be available and costed as needed and not sooner than necessary. By selecting the Component Allocation button, the user can opt to make or change a component assignment. Figure 8.9 shows what this may look like for the Office Chair

Header | Sequences | Operations

Component Items		ItC	Qty	Activity/Op
10	Backrest	L	1ea	10
20	Armrests	L	2ea	20
30	Chair Seat	L	1ea	10
40	Action Mechanism	L	1ea	30
50	Gas Lift (spring)	L	1ea	40
60	Chair Base	L	1ea	40
70	Wheel Castors	L	5ea	40

Figure 8.9: Office Chair Routing: Component Allocation

Regarding sequencing in the routing, there are only two that you should be aware of. The first is a Standard sequence. In a standard sequence, the operations in the routing are performed in order, one after the other. However, there are times when more than one operation can be performed at the same time. For instance, it may be possible in our example for the Gas Lift and the Wheel Casters to be attached to the base while the Backrest is being attached to the seat. In such cases, this type of sequencing is called a Parallel sequence.

Work Center Master Data

Work centers are master data which are also plant specific. They are assigned to operations in the routing because it is the work centers where the operations are performed. Work centers have three main functions in PP. Work centers provide the data required for scheduling, available capacities, and costing for production planning (Figure 8.10).

Work Center		
Scheduling	Capacities	Costing
• Formulas for scheduling production based on operations requirements in maintenance orders	• Capacity category (Labor/Machine) • Formulas for calculating available capacity • Capacity usually measured in time contingent on hours of operation available, utilisation, breaks, and number of people/ machines	• Assigned to a cost center • Assigned valid activity types

Figure 8.10: Work Center Master Data

Work centers are also tightly integrated with the Human Capital Management module. Because people work in work centers, the capacity available is contingent, not only on how many people work there, but also their working hours. Let's suppose a work center has only two employees working there. One of the two employee has requested a day off from work. If the day off is approved, it will reduce the available labor capacity by fifty percent which is a significant reduction that will impact production. Likewise, when an employee is on vacation, that will also reduce capacity at the work center. Knowing an employee's work schedule is critical to meeting the demands of production and scheduling. For these (and other factors), work centers must have integration with HCM.

Other data is stored in work centers beyond the three types identified in Figure 8.10. It might be worth noting that work centers also contain Basic Data and Default Values. Basic data is information about whether or not the times at the work center is strictly based on labor, machines, or possibly both. Default values can be used to identify default units of measure for times as well as printing options.

Production Version Master Data

Production versions represent different methods for producing the same thing. A valid combination of BOM and Routing define a Production Version. As we discussed earlier in this chapter, there is the potential to have alternative BOMs for a product. The same is true for routings. Let's take an example of producing an umbrella. The umbrella in the example below has two BOM's (A & B) and two Routings (X & Y). The umbrella can be produced using BOM "A" and Routing "X". If BOM "B" is used, Routing "Y" would be required (Figure 8.11).

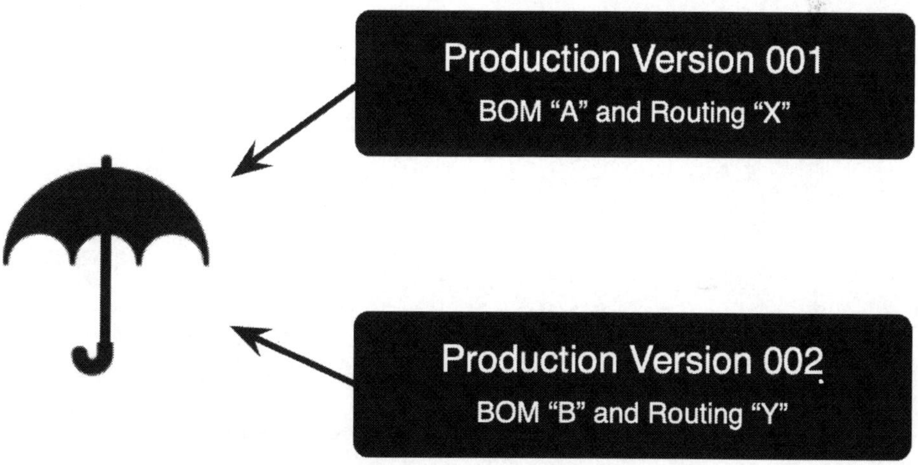

Figure 8.11: Production Version Master Data

As we can see, there are two methods for producing the same umbrella. Each method requires a valid combination of BOM and Routing and is considered a Production Version.

Production Resource Tools (PRTs) Master Data

A Production Resource Tool (PRT) is a tool needed during the manufacturing execution process, but is not included in the finished product, therefore is not a component in the

BOM. Examples of PRTs include, but are not limited to such things as blades, drill bits, and others. PRTs are included in the production order for a product.

Master Data in Advanced Planning

Though we haven't discussed the functionality of Advanced Planning, Advanced Planning (AP) is part of Supply Chain Management and there is a need to discuss the master data requirements. During our discussion on Extended Warehouse Management (EWM), we were introduced to master data terminology in Supply Chain Management (SCM). Because AP is part of SCM, there are similarities with master data. Like EWM, Advanced Planning is now embedded in SAP S/4HANA. Figure 8.12 shows the difference in terminology between S/4HANA ERP and Advanced Planning in SCM.

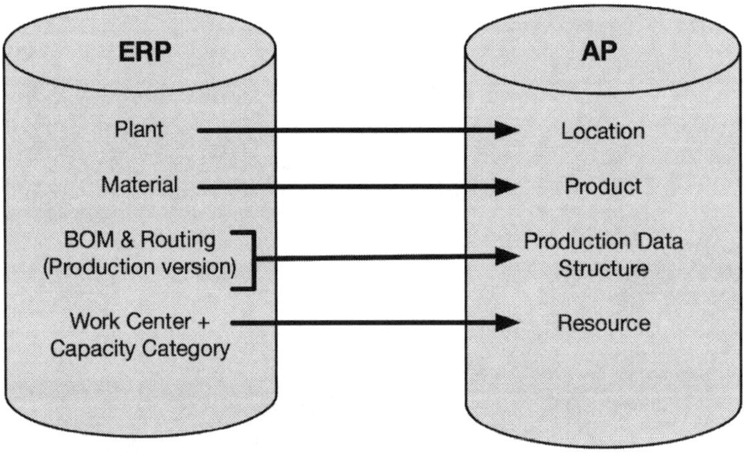

Figure 8.12: Master Data in Advanced Planning

Master Data Integration

As promised, before we move on from our discussion on master data, it's worth looking at how the master data in SAP S/4HANA integrate with one another. Figure 8.13 is a depiction of how many of the master data in PP flow together. As you can see, material master data is needed for the Header item and Component items in the BOM. The components from the BOM are assigned to operations in the Routing. And, the operations in the Routing are assigned to Work Centers.

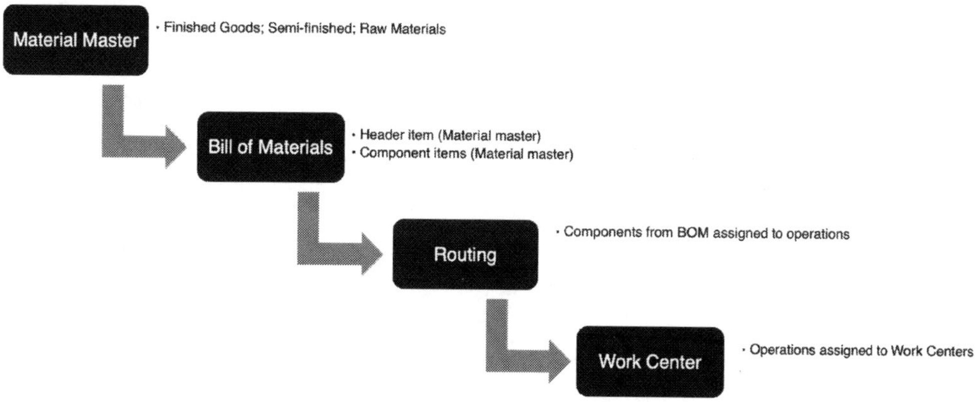

Figure 8.13: Master Data Integration in Production Planning

Product Cost Calculation

Beside master data, the other aspect of the first item in the "best-practice" scenario for the Design-to-Operate process is Product Cost Calculation. In essence, this is the same as Product Cost Controlling which we were initially introduced to in Chapter 4 on Management Accounting. But it is so integral to Production Planning that it bears repeating.

There are three phases associated with Product Cost Controlling. They are listed below:

- Product Cost Planning
- Cost Object Controlling
- Actual Costing and Material Ledger

A key objective of Product Cost Planning is to generate a Standard Cost Estimate for a product. This is foundational in the Product Cost Calculation. Product Cost Planning benefits the business in many ways. Though our focus will be primarily on generating a Standard Cost Estimate, it's also good to realize the other benefits. Some of those benefits are listed below:

- Determine cost of goods manufactured (COGM)
- Determine cost of goods sold (COGS)
- Determine break even price for a product
- Identify production costs at the plant level
- Identify primary and secondary costs for production

- Evaluate production costs at an itemized level
- View costs based on different lot sizes

Let's bring our focus now back to the Standard Cost Estimate. It's important to gain an understanding of how specific master data factor into the cost calculation. Now that we have a clearer understanding of master data such as the BOM and Routings, this may make more sense to you.

We continue to look at the office chair as the product. In Figure 8.4, you see an example of the parts that make up an office chair. As we now know, Bill of Material (BOM) is master data which provides a structured list of materials required to produce something. For a BOM to be accurate, it requires not only the list of materials, but the quantities of each material required. If we were to provide an accurate BOM for the office chair above, we would identify what is shown in Table 8.1.

Table 8.1: Office Chair Parts (BOM) (Replica of Table 4.2)

Material	Quantity
Backrest	1ea
Armrest	2ea
Chair seat	1ea
Action mechanism	1ea
Gas lift (spring)	1ea
Chair base	1ea
Wheel castors	5ea

To capture the costs of producing the office chair we would also need to know the value of each of the materials listed above. SAP refers to this value as the Material Price. The setting of the Material Price is maintained in the material master record, using the Price Control. The Material Price depends on the type of material used in production. As a rule, purchased materials use a Moving Average valuation method. This means the material valuation could change each time we purchase that material. Materials that are produced internally (not purchased from a supplier), use a Standard Price valuation method. This means the value of the material will remain constant. The Standard Price is covered in the last phase of Product Cost Controlling: Actual Costing and Material Ledger. For purposes of simplicity, let's use the information in Table 8.2 to derive the costs of producing the office chair.

Table 8.2: Material Costs of Office Chair (Replica of Table 4.3)

Material	Quantity	Material Price per Unit	Total Costs
Backrest	1ea	$7	$7
Armrest	2ea	$2	$4
Chair Seat	1ea	$7	$7
Action Mechanism	1ea	$10	$10
Gas Lift (spring)	1ea	$10	$10
Chair Base	1ea	$5	$5
Wheel Castors	5ea	$1	$5
			Total: $48

The example above provides us with a good estimate of the material costs of producing the office chair. Keep in mind, this is simply an estimate because some of the costs were likely derived by using the Moving Average Price, which means the costs shown above are time dependent. If we were to repeat this process at a later time, it's very possible the value of some of the materials listed would have changed.

Referring to the original task of defining the costs to produce this office chair, you would also suggest we consider labor costs required to assemble the office chair. The Master Data which defines the assembly of the office chair is called a Routing. Routing master data contains operations, or more simply, the steps required to produce something. Again, we provide an example of what this might look like to produce the office chair (Table 8.3).

Table 8.3: Routing Master Data: Operations to Produce Office Chair (Replica of Table 4.4)

Operation	Activity Type	Work Center/ Cost Center	Time (min)
Attach Chair seat to Backrest	Assembly	Production	5
Attach Armrest	Assembly	Production	5
Attach Action mechanism	Assembly	Production	3
Attach Gas lift (spring) and Wheel castors to Chair base	Assembly	Production	7
Attach Chair seat to Gas lift (spring)	Assembly	Production	5

If you recall from our discussion on Activity Based Costing (ABC) in Chapter 4, activity types and cost center master data are required to perform the allocation of costs based on work performed. Our example above includes both the activity type and work center information from the routing. We learned earlier in this chapter, that the work center has several functions, one being costing. A work center is linked to a cost center in the work center master record. Because of this, the cost center can be derived when a work center is assigned to an operation. The combination of activity type/cost center provides us with the activity price (Figure 8.14).

Figure 8.14: Activity Type/Cost Center - > Activity Price (Replica of Figure 4.8)

Let's assume the Activity Price for Assembly Activity Type/Production Cost Center combination is $1/min. Our Routing example now contains the information regarding labor costs associated with producing the office chair (Table 8.4).

Table 8.4: Routing: Labor Costs for Office Chair (Replica of Table 4.5)

Operation	Activity Type	Work Center/ Cost Center	Time (min)	Activity Price	Costs
Attach Chair seat to Backrest	Assembly	Production	5	$1/min.	$5
Attach Armrest	Assembly	Production	5	$1/min.	$5
Attach Action mechanism	Assembly	Production	3	$1/min.	$3
Attach Gas lift (spring) and Wheel castors to Chair base	Assembly	Production		$1/min.	$7
Attach Chair seat to Gas lift (spring)	Assembly	Production	5	$1/min.	$5
					Total: $25

We now have the material costs ($48) and labor costs ($25) associated with producing the office chair. Two master data were used to assist with deriving these costs: The Bill of Material and the Routing. Thus, the Product Cost Estimate is derived by analyzing the BOMs and Routings on both a Quantity and Value structure. See Figure 8.15.

If you were thinking that there are other costs associated with producing the office chair, you would be correct. However, we mentioned above that we will not be taking a deep dive into how some of these other costs are derived. These additional costs can be categorized as Overhead and Process costs. From an integration perspective, it's most important for you to know that costs for the Product Cost Estimate come from the BOM and Routing by looking at their respective quantity and value structures.

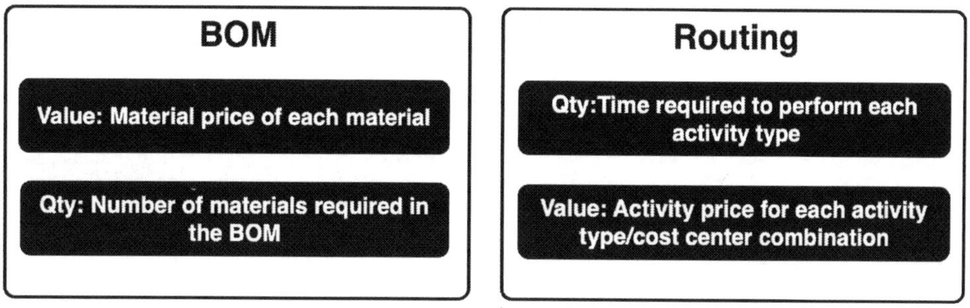

Figure 8.15: BOM and Routing on a Qty Value Structure (Replica of Figure 4.14)

What is so important about the Standard (Product) Cost Estimate? Why does it matter? There are four main uses of the Standard Cost Estimate and they are not mutually exclusive (Figure 8.16).

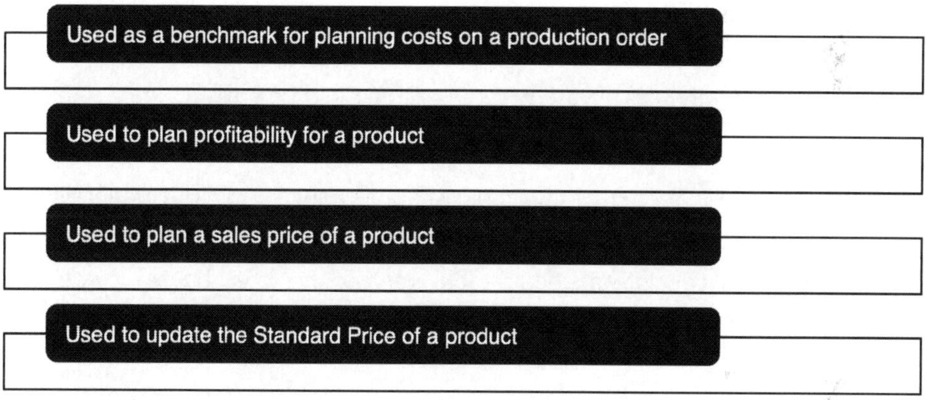

Figure 8.16: Use of Product Cost Estimate (Replica of Figure 4.15)

Let's now talk about other methods and reasons for calculating a standard cost estimate. The method for calculating the cost estimate depends on the Product Lifecycle. The Product Lifecycle begins with a Product Idea. At this stage, it's very difficult to get a accurate picture of costs associated with the production of this product, however it's necessary to get a cost estimate in order to determine whether or not it's wise to move forward. SAP offers a solution that coincides with the Product Lifecycle called, Product Lifecycle Costing (PLC). One of the main views of PLC is the PLC Cockpit. The phases of PLC are seen in Figure 8.17. As you scan through the phases in PLC, the PLC Cockpit can manage the various cost calculations for each phase and store them for evaluation.

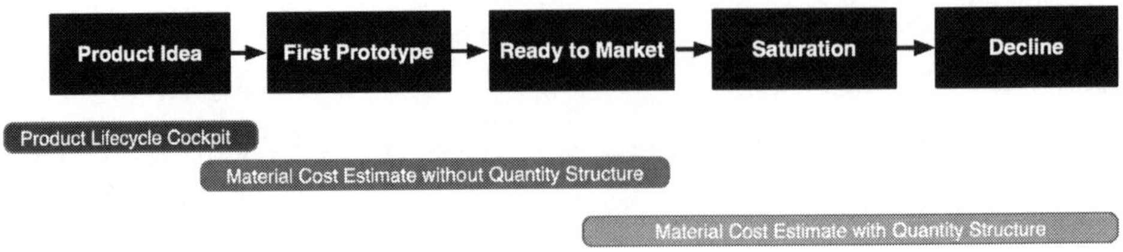

Figure 8.17: Phases of the PLC

In the previous section, we learned how to perform a cost calculation with a quantity structure. Cost calculations can also be performed without a quantity structure. Differentiating between the two is not overly complex. When we performed the cost calculation using the quantity structure, it involved master data (BOMs and Routings) which provided a foundation for calculating costs. Costs that are calculated without a quantity structure do not use BOMs and Routings. Instead, users manually enter information about costs for materials and activities required for production. The costs can come from different prices. It's possible to use material prices for raw and semi-finished materials if they exist. Otherwise, users can use commercial prices based on market value.

With regards to PLC, cost calculations without quantity structure generally occur early in PLC, while cost calculations using a quantity structure are performed later in PLC. This is a logical conclusion since the business will not likely have accurate BOMs and Routings established until well after the product idea and prototype phases

The second phase of Product Cost Controlling is Cost Object Controlling. The objective of Cost Object Controlling is to capture actual costs during the production process. In this section, we introduce you to Order-Related Cost Object Controlling.

We have seen earlier that cost centers can collect costs for possible reallocation. In SAP, cost centers are not the only objects that can collect costs. In the Cost Object Controlling phase of Product Cost Controlling, we consider the production order as the cost object. Let's take an example of a production order with a requirement of 100 units of some product. In order to compute the unit cost of that batch of material, we would need to accumulate all costs that go towards completing that production order. Like the way we planned costs to produce something, we look at the BOM and Routing to find the actual material and labor costs for production. In Cost Object Controlling, we need to capture the actual costs, so we use the production order to collect these costs as production progresses. For example, when materials are issued, the materials costs are added to the production order. Later some labor time might be incurred on the production order and those costs are also added to the production order, and so on.

Thus, the production order acts as a cost collector and is an example of an Order-Related Cost Object.

As we noted earlier, in addition to production orders, other orders like maintenance orders, internal orders (CO orders), and projects can collect costs. These are also Order- Related Cost Objects. Though each of these orders is used for different business purposes, there are great similarities in the process that each goes through.

They all follow a standard sequence of steps from a management accounting and logistics viewpoint. Figure 8.18 shows the steps in the standard process that applies to all order-related costs objects. Order-related cost objects are managed using order types. Some of these order types may have additional steps required that are unique to its respective process.

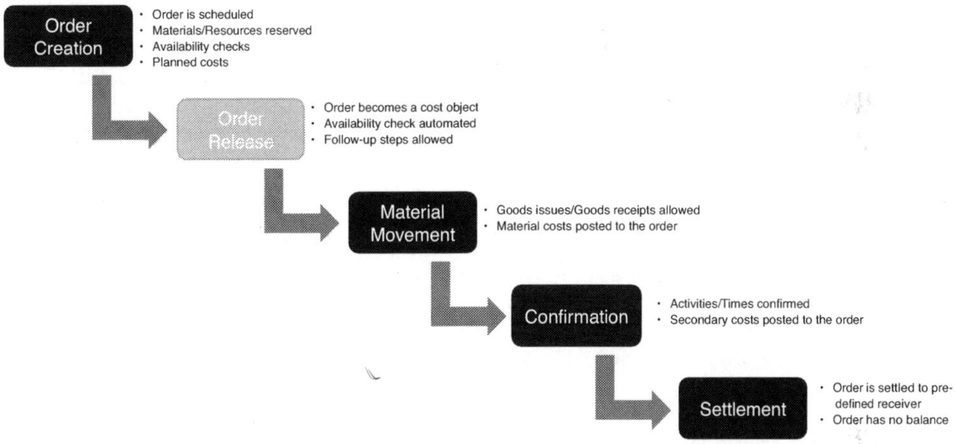

Figure 8.18: Order-Related Cost Object Controlling (Replica of Figure 4.16)

During order creation, the order has not yet become a cost object. At this stage, this simply means that no processing can take place and costs cannot yet be posted to the order. However, the order is scheduled (as in the case of a production order) based on the availability of resources required to perform work. Thus, resources are reserved for this order. Materials from the BOM will also be required for the production order. Like resources, materials are placed on reservation for the order. Keep in mind, this process applies to more than production.

The next step in order-related cost object controlling is the order release (highlighted in Figure 8.18). This is the most important step. If the order is not released, none of the follow-on steps can be completed. It is this step in which the order officially becomes a cost object. Actual costs can now be posted to this order and can be compared to the planned costs that were calculated using the Standard Cost Estimate. At the time of release, SAP S/4HANA will always perform an automatic availability check for materials, regardless of whether or not one was performed manually. If they are not available, depending on the system settings, the system can block the order release until materials become available.

The step after the release of the order is generally a goods movement. The goods movement could be a goods issue (stock items) from inventory to the order, or a goods receipt (non-stock items) from a purchase order to the order. When these goods movements are posted, they are posted to a primary cost account in financial accounting. Recall, the primary cost account is now the account type used for primary cost elements which are required to post the costs to the order in management accounting. These are actual costs which again can be compared to the planned costs in the order.

Material costs are not the only costs associated with order-related cost object controlling. There are additional costs resulting from work completed on the order by one or more work centers. These costs are posted to the order when work centers confirm the work they performed. They could confirm this work in various ways, but the most common methods are to confirm the amount of time they spent working on the order as well as which activities they performed. These costs are considered secondary costs because they are not a result of direct expenses posted from financial accounting. Instead, they are costs that are allocated to the order from a cost center in management accounting. Recall that secondary cost elements are now a G/L account type used to allocate such costs. Like the planning of labor costs, the Routings contain the operations used to record the labor costs on the production order.

Finally, the order will go through the settlement step. Here, the costs collected in the order are normally settled to a predefined receiver(s). A receiver is an object that is ultimately responsible for the costs in the order. In management accounting, an order-related cost object can also settle its costs to financial accounting general ledger accounts. Other receivers might be cost centers, projects, other orders, or profitability analysis. In the end, the order is settled so there are no remaining costs. In other words, the order has no balance on the debit or credit sides; its debit and credit entries balance out.

The final phase on Product Cost Controlling is Actual Costing with the Material Ledger. Actual costing is a process supported by SAP S/4HANA, in which the system tracks actual costs of a material during an accounting period and uses these actual costs to value materials. Some refer to this as the "actual price" because actual costs are used to determine its value. It is also referred to as a "per unit price". All goods movements are valued based on the material price found in the Accounting view in the material master record. Raw materials are valued using a moving average price, while semi-finished and finished goods use a standard price. The Material Ledger allows these material prices to be maintained in various currencies. In addition to this, the Material Ledger serves as a sub-ledger account keeping track of costs as they are incurred (during goods movements) and can be used to track the actual value of a material. These can be used as a basis for updating the standard price of the material. Keep in mind, the standard price can only be updated once per accounting period. Thus, its price remains constant throughout the entire period.

It is a common practice to use the Standard Cost Estimate generated during Product Cost Planning as the foundation for updating the standard price. This is considered a "best-practice". Figure 8.19 shows the process for updating the standard price.

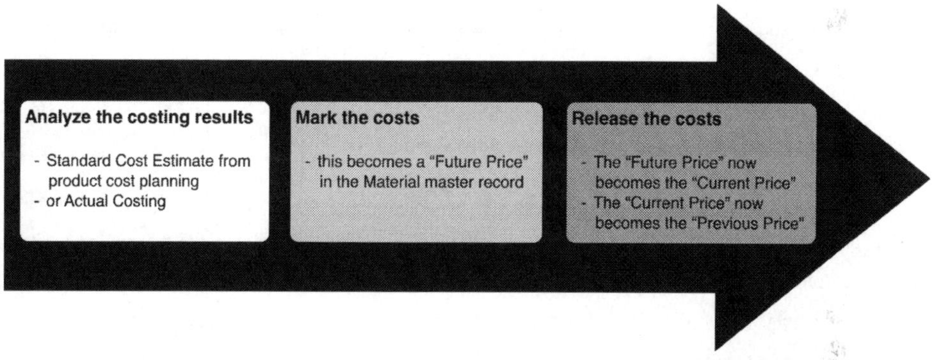

Figure 8.19: Updating Standard Price of a Material (Replica of Figure 4.17)

Demand Planning

This next items in our "best-practice" scenario covers the initial planning steps (i.e., Demand Planning) in the Design-to-Operate process. In this section we will get introduced to SAP Integrated Business Planning (IBP).

Integrated Business Planning (IBP) is complex planning tool to manage and plan materials throughout the entire supply chain. It has analytic capabilities and monitoring capabilities, allowing SAP customers to predict and receive alerts regarding material availability and planning of materials across the supply chain. Figure 8.20 depicts the various modules and their functionality that make up the IBP Landscape.

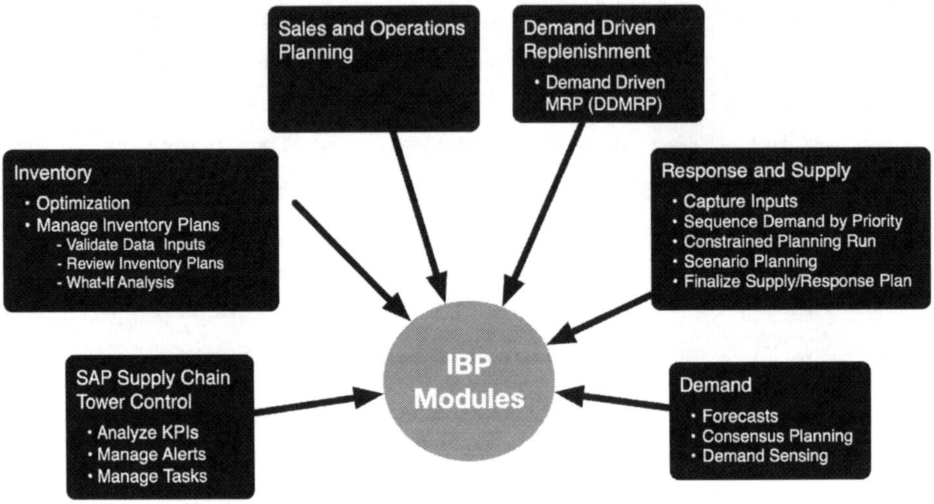

Figure 8.20: SAP Integrated Business Planning (IBP)

Our focus will be on the Demand Planning aspects of IBP and how the results of IBP are used to provide clear and accurate information for further materials planning. Prior to IBP, Sales and Operations Planning (SOP) in ERP was the primary tool for planning demand. With the introduction of SAP S/4HANA, SOP in ERP is no longer recommended as the tool for demand planning. SAP customers can now merge their Sales and Operations Planning activities within IBP. Because IBP is a cloud-based supply chain management tool, its integrated capabilities extend beyond simple demand planning. IBP with SOP provides SAP customers with a tool that can plan materials across the entire supply chain, taking into account historical data to provide accurate forecasts for material demand. It integrates tightly with the needs and demands of the sales and marketing team, the profitability and spend concerns of the finance group, as well as the logistics personnel who are involved in the process of trying to ensure adequate supplies while dealing with potential supply chain disruptions.

Using IBP for SOP involves a sequence of formal steps before planning data can be transferred to S/4HANA. These steps with a high-level overview are as follows:

1. Perform a Product Review
    A. Evaluate the Product Life Cycle for new and existing products
2. Demand Review
    A. Define a plan to be the starting point for Demand Planning in IBP
    B. Define different scenarios based on best-case to worse-case for demand

3. Supply Review
    A. Compare the plans against available resources for capacity constraints
4. Demand-Supply Balancing
    A. Determine a supply plan and analyze it based on what-if scenarios
    B. Compare the plan to assess its financial impact and make recommendation
5. Executive Decision
    A. Decide on a Sales and Operations Plan to be implemented

Let's develop an example and put some of this into practice. Assume we are in the business of producing pepperoni pizza. Our first step is to perform a Product Review to determine where this product is in the Product Lifecycle. As pepperoni pizza is still a popular product and not a new product, we don't have much uncertainty about its demand. Therefore we will move on to perform a Demand Review. After analyzing historical sales for pepperoni pizza, we can comfortably develop an initial forecast for demand. We may opt to create different forecasts based on the expected demand as well as forecasts for situations where sales may not meet expectation or for situations when demand might exceed expectations.

Our next step is to perform a Supply Review to compare these plans in terms of feasibility based on available resources followed by Demand-Supply Balancing. Since IBP is integrated across several business functions, we can analyze our plans against financial considerations (cost/revenue potential), resource availability, and sales demands. Based on all of these factors we can develop a supply plan to meet our forecasted demand and run what-if analysis to see the impacts should there be a mismatch between our demand and supply plans. Ultimately, a plan is decided upon and a recommendation is passed on to an executive committee. This is the final step, where an Executive Decision is made on a plan. In the end, we will have a plan for demand (forecast) as well as a plan for supply to meet that demand.

Continuing with our example of pepperoni pizza, let's assume a forecast for demand has been approved. Table 8.5 shows the result of our plan. At this point the data from our forecast is transferred to SAP S/4HANA where we will perform Demand Management based on this forecast. The result of Demand Management is Planned Independent Requirements.

Table 8.5: Integrated Business Planning Table - Forecast of Sales

Week	Forecast Qty (each)
W1	
W2	
W3	500
W4	800
W5	600
W6	800
W7	500
W8	500
W9	600
W10	700

Procure to Receipt

The next item in the "best-practice" scenario for the Design-to-Operate process is Procure to Receipt. The primary tool in this step is Materials Requirement Planning (MRP). But before we get into the details of MRP, we need to revisit some things we have already discussed. For starters, we need to revisit master data, specifically the BOM. In an effort to continue to provide relevance for these concepts, we will still use our pepperoni pizza example. Figure 8.21 shows two separate BOM master records. We have shaded the two BOM master records differently. The first is for the finished good (pepperoni pizza) and the second BOM is for the pizza dough (semi-finished product). For simplicity sake, we are going to assume all other components in the BOMs are raw material.

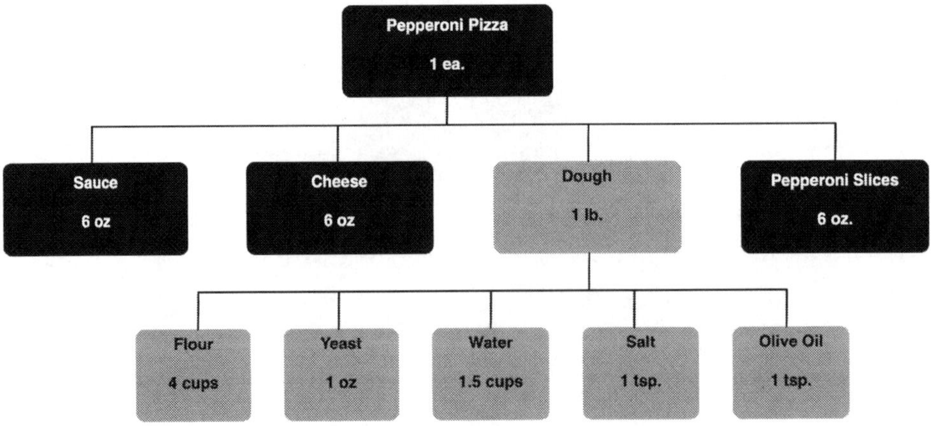

Figure 8.21: Sample Multi-Level BOM View for Pepperoni Pizza

As a reminder when the planning information (forecast) from IBP was transferred to S/4HANA, Demand Management provided us with Planned Independent Requirements for the Pepperoni Pizza.

SAP S/4HANA includes a reporting tool that helps us view and manage this demand. This reporting tool is called the Stock/Requirements List (SRL).

This report provides users with quick view into supply as well as demand information for a single material or group of materials. We have been using the phrase, "Requirements" quite a bit. You may recall from an earlier discussion that the term "requirement" is synonymous with "demand". PIRs therefore represent demand of the finished goods. The SRL will show requirements of a material, including the PIRs created from the planning table. The SRL will display each requirement as well as the weeks in which the requirement occur. The SRL also includes a column, "Available Qty" which will show the current stock level based on the supply and demand. Figure 8.22 shows what the SRL would look like after saving the PIRs.

Detail	Date	Stock/Requirement Type	Qty	Available Qty
🔍	Week 1			0
🔍	Week 2			0
🔍	Week 3	Plan Ind Rqt	500	-500
🔍	Week 4	Plan Ind Rqt	800	-1300
🔍	Week 5	Plan Ind Rqt	600	-1900
🔍	Week 6	Plan Ind Rqt	800	-2700
🔍	Week 7	Plan Ind Rqt	500	-3200
🔍	Week 8	Plan Ind Rqt	500	-3700
🔍	Week 9	Plan Ind Rqt	600	-4300
🔍	Week 10	Plan Ind Rqt	700	-5000

Figure 8.22: Stock/Requirements List

As you can see from the SRL, demand exceeds supply (negative values in the Available Qty column). There are currently no plans to meet these requirements. In order to do that, we need to proceed to the next topic, which is Materials Requirements Planning (MRP).

Material Requirements Planning

Material Requirements Planning (MRP) is quite simple in terms of its objectives, but very complex in terms of processing. Objectively, MRP looks at demand and checks to see if there is enough supply to meet the demand. If there is, MRP doesn't process any further. However, if there isn't enough supply, then MRP will suggest ways to generate enough supply to satisfy demand. MRP provides two main outcomes:

1. Generate Dependent Requirements
2. Generate Procurement Proposals

Dependent Requirements are significantly different than Independent Requirements. In order to generate Dependent Requirements, MRP must explode the BOM(s). It begins by looking at the finished good (in our example, the Pepperoni Pizza). Starting with the forecast from IBP that was passed through Demand Management, MRP can see there is a PIR for 500 each of Pepperoni Pizzas in Week 3. MRP then explodes the BOM for the Pepperoni Pizza to view the components. It sees that for each Pepperoni Pizza, 6 ounces of sauce is required. Therefore, it creates a Dependent Requirement of 3000 ounces of sauce (6oz X 500). It continues to do this for every component in the Pepperoni Pizza BOM. The additional Dependent Requirements are: 3000 ounces of cheese, 500 pounds of dough, and 3000 ounces of pepperoni slices.

An SAP customer can opt to plan at this level and not proceed any further. But there are also options to plan to other levels in other BOMs. From our example, we see the Dough material also has its own BOM. From our previous discussion on BOM master data, MRP will know this because there will be a check box in the Assembly column for the Dough component in the BOM for the Pepperoni Pizza. Should the user decide to plan further, MRP will see this and explode the BOM for the Dough. Recognizing the Dough has a newly created Dependent Requirement for 500 pounds, this becomes the basis for planning the components for the Dough. In our example, the results of MRP would generate Dependent Requirements of 2000 cups of flour, 500 ounces of yeast, 750 cups of water, 500 teaspoons of salt, and 500 teaspoons of olive oil. The dependent requirements can be further viewed by calling up the Stock/Requirements List for each of these materials.

The second result of MRP is Procurement Proposals. We refer to these as procurement proposals because MRP doesn't order, it plans. The procurement proposals are plans to procure materials either in-house or externally. If they are procured in-house, the materials are produced using production. Externally procured materials follow the Materials Management Source-to-Pay process.

For MRP to know how to plan each material, it refers to the MRP views of each materials master record. And like it does with the planning of dependent requirements, MRP starts by exploding the BOM for the finished product and then explodes through as many levels of BOMs as the user chooses. But before MRP can generate a procurement proposal, it must first check stock levels to see if demand exceeds supply. Remember, if demand does not exceed supply, MRP will not suggest any procurement.

Material Requirements Planning: Net Requirements Calculation

The Net Requirements Calculation considers the supply and demand situation for each material MRP will plan. It's important to understand the various items that make up supply and demand (Figure 8.23).

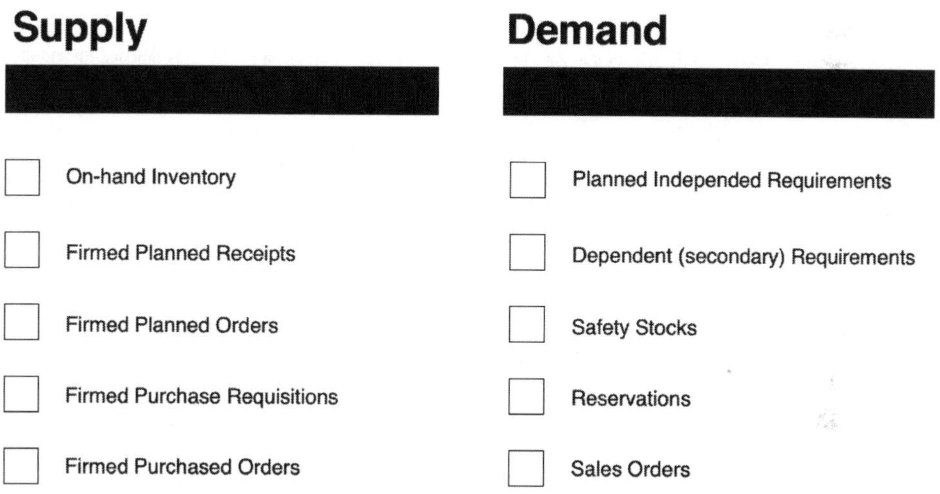

Figure 8.23: Net Requirements Calculation

From the perspective of Supply, notice the term, "Firmed". This is important because such things as planned orders, and purchase requisitions are not physically in inventory. They are things expected to be part of supply. However, MRP needs to know when they are going be part of available supply. The term, "Firmed" refers to items that will be available as supply by the time they are needed. Because of that, they are considered part of the supply side during the Net Requirements Calculation.

On the Demand side, there are also a couple of interesting items. We are already familiar with PIRs and Dependent Requirements being part of demand, but sales orders also make up demand. Although the plan from IBP served as the basis for the PIR's, the PIRs are in part based on a forecast of sales. If actual sales orders arrive, then these become additional demand. It is possible to set the system to allow such sales orders to consume the PIRs (replaces PIR quantities with sales order quantities). When that happens, re-planning is sometimes needed. We also see reservations on the demand side. When a material in inventory is reserved, that means it must be held and can't be used for whatever MRP is planning. To offset the supply side on-hand inventory quantity, the reservations are added to the demand side of the equation. Finally, we see safety stock as part of the demand side in the Net Requirements Calculation. This is one that often confuses people, so let's describe this as clearly as possible. Safety stock is an additional level of stock required. This means it is an additional need, above and beyond normal demand. Therefore, it is part of demand during the Net Requirements Calculation.

Let's look at this in the context of our Pepperoni Pizza example to demonstrate how MRP uses the Net Requirements Calculation for purposes of generating procurement proposals. MRP always begins planning with the finished good. If we look at the SRL from Figure 8.22 for Pepperoni Pizza, we notice an on-hand inventory of zero. But we see a PIR in Week 3 of 500 each. Using what we know regarding the Net Requirements Calculation, the total quantity on the supply side is zero, while the total quantity on the demand side (for Week 3) is 500 each. In this case, demand exceeds supply and a shortage exists. When a shortage exists, MRP will refer to the Material Master record for the Pepperoni Pizza and review information stored in the MRP views. First, it will look to the Procurement Type field. In our discussion about Material Master data, we learned that the Procurement Type field informs MRP whether that material is procured in-house or procured externally. Since Pepperoni Pizza is a finished good, the value for in-house procurement would be used because it is something that is produced, not procured from a vendor externally. MRP will **ALWAYS** generate a procurement proposal in the form of a **Planned Order** whenever the Procurement Type is in-house. Please note that MRP does not generate a production order because it only generates procurement proposals and does not order production.

The next order of business for MRP is to determine the quantity that is proposed in the Planned Order. To do this, MRP once again refers to the MRP views of the Material Master record to locate the Lot-size Rule. Again, this was previously discussed in the section on Material Master data in this chapter. The lot-size rule informs MRP whether the quantity proposed is a fixed quantity or a lot-for-lot quantity. A fixed quantity means MRP can only propose the quantity defined in the Material Master record. A lot-for-lot quantity means MRP will propose the exact quantity needed to meet the shortage. Assuming the lot-size rule for Pepperoni Pizzas is lot-for-lot, the shortage is 500 each.

Therefore, MRP will generate a procurement proposal in the form of a Planned Order, with a quantity of 500 each.

To further our demonstration, let's look at the raw material, Sauce and see how MRP treats this material during the planning phase. To help make this easier to understand, we've provided a Stock/Requirements List for the Sauce (Figure 8.24). Note: Qty is in ounces.

Detail	Date	Stock/Requirement Type	Qty	Available Qty
🔍	Week 1			1000
🔍	Week 3	Purch Ord	1000	2000

Figure 8.24: Stock/Requirements List: Sauce

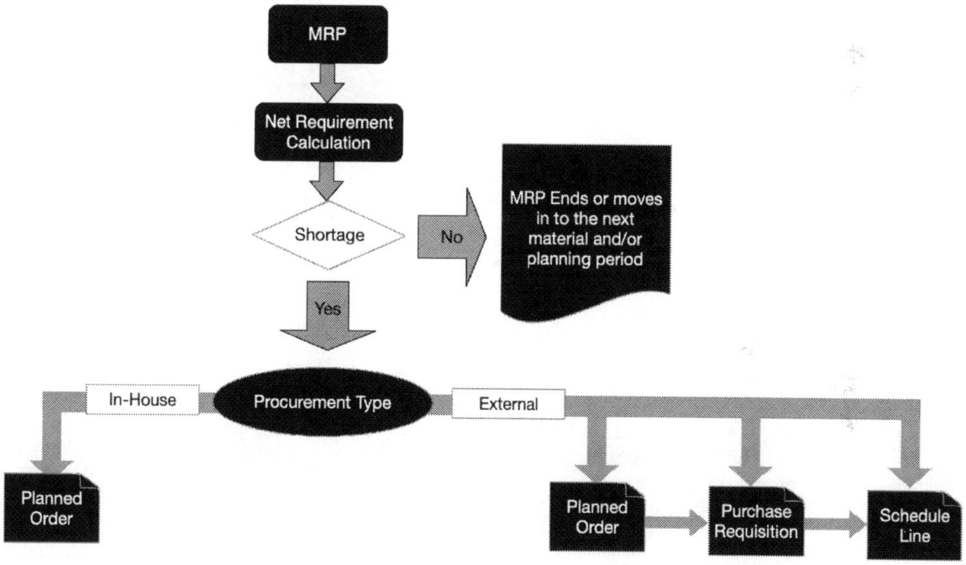

Figure 8.25: MRP Decisions

To reinforce our discussion, notice for this material there is already an on-hand inventory level of 1000 ounces in the first week. We also see an existing Purchase Order in the amount of 1000 ounces in Week 3. This means there is a total supply of 2000 ounces. As a reminder, when MRP runs, it will create Dependent Requirements. Therefore, a Dependent Requirement in the amount of 3000 ounces will be created for Week 3. This cannot be shown in the Stock/Requirements List, because it won't display in the SRL until after MRP is completed. Given a supply of 2000 ounces and a new demand of 3000 ounces, there is one again a shortage. Now MRP refers to the MRP views of the Material Master record of the Sauce to determine how it should proceed. Since the Sauce is a raw material, the Procurement Type would be external because we do not produce the sauce, we procure it from an external vendor. Figure 8.25 demonstrates the MRP decisions that occur during the MRP run. Notice for In-House procurement, the resulting procurement proposal is ALWAYS a Planned Order. However, for External procurement, MRP can generate one of three procurement proposals.

For external procurement, MRP can generate a Planned Order, Purchase Requisition, or a Schedule Line. For the Sauce, let's assume MRP is set to generate a Purchase Requisition. Now that MRP has generated that procurement proposal, and it must now determine the quantity for that proposal. Once again, it looks to the MRP views of the Material Master record to check the settings in the Lot-size Rule field. Suppose for Sauce, we must purchase it in a fixed lot size of 500 ounces. With a shortage of 1000 ounces, MRP will generate two Purchase Requisitions in the amount of 500 ounces each (Figure 8.26). We will discuss the other external procurement proposal options a little later.

Detail	Date	Stock/Requirement Type	Qty	Available Qty
	Week 1			1000
	Week 3	Dept Rqt	3000	-2000
	Week 3	Pur Ord	1000	-1000
	Week 3	Pur Req	500	-500
	Week 3	Pur Req	500	0

Figure 8.26: Stock/Requirements List: Sauce After MRP Run

Referring back to the MRP Decision in Figure 8.25 you can see a Planned Order is a flexible procurement proposal because it can be converted to a Production Order, as is the case for In-House procurement, or it can be converted to a Purchase Requisition for External procurement. This allows planners flexibility, specifically with production.

As far as planning the rest of the materials, this process is repeated by MRP until all the material components are planned. Once that occurs, MRP will then move on to plan the next planning period (Week 4). And it will continue to repeat the process until everything, for every planning period has been planned.

Material Requirements Planning: MRP Run and Control Parameters

The MRP Run is the transaction that initiates the steps described above. When users elect to run MRP, there are several options available to them. The options are considered Planning Modes and are listed below:

1. Single-item, Single-level
2. Single-item, Multi-level
3. Interactive Planning
4. MRP Live

Single-item, Single-level MRP planning restricts the MRP planning to only a single BOM. In other words, MRP will not explode any additional BOMs even if a component in the BOM has its own BOM.

Single-item, Multi-level MRP planning informs MRP to explode all BOMs, including component BOMs.

Interactive MRP is single-item MRP. When running this version of MRP, it will simulate the MRP run and allow users to review the plan and modify it as necessary.

The first three Planning Modes discussed above are part of Classic MRP. "Classic" in this sense refers to an older version of MRP. The future of MRP in S4HANA is MRP Live. This is also considered a Planning Mode and it is the recommended Planning Mode for SAP customers. Since MRP Live is recommended, it bears more discussion.

In short, MRP Live is MRP running on SAP HANA. Since SAP HANA provides speed and increased performance as well as better processing capabilities, MRP Live is more robust and preferred over Classic MRP. In SAP S/4HANA, MRP Live can plan one or more materials across one or more plants online and interactively. There are additional advantages of using MRP Live:

- Integration with IBP with SOP
- Support Demand Driven MRP (DDMRP)
- Analyzes and Manages Material Bottleneck using the MRP Cockpit
- Optimization using Constraint-based Planning (PPDS - more on this later)
- Predictive MRP (pMRP) using simulations for planning
- Mitigates the risk of planning with obsolete data

Additional settings are also made at the time of the MRP run. These settings are

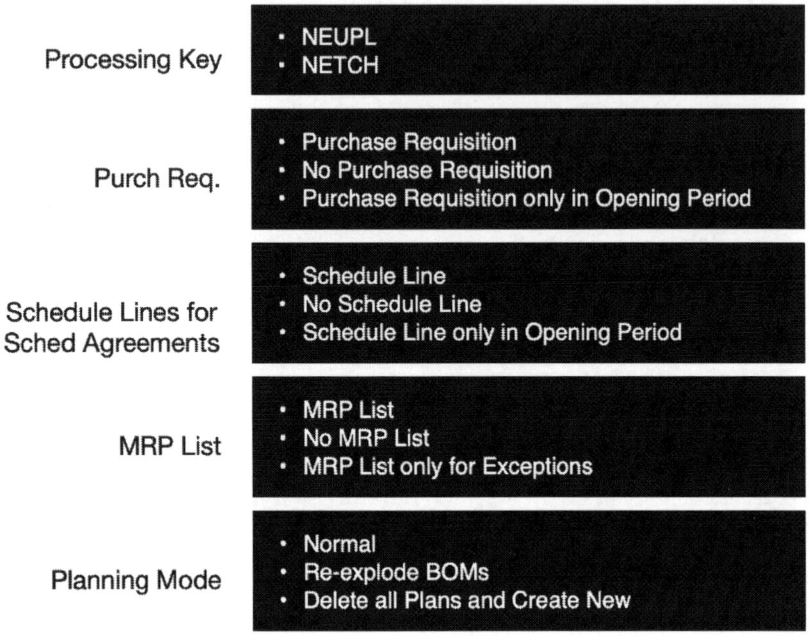

referred to as the Control Parameters. Figure 8.27 provides us with the Control Parameters and their settings.

Figure 8.27: MRP Control Parameters

The first Control Parameter we encounter is the Processing Key (Figure 8.28). The Processing Key is very important because it determines the scope of the MRP run. Because MRP can be very detailed and complex, the Processing Key helps manage the impact the MRP run will have on the system performance. The Processing Key with the largest scope is NEUPL (Regenerative Planning). If the user opts to run Regenerative Planning, any previous MRP runs will become invalid and MRP will generate all new procurement proposals. Essentially it is an entirely new plan.

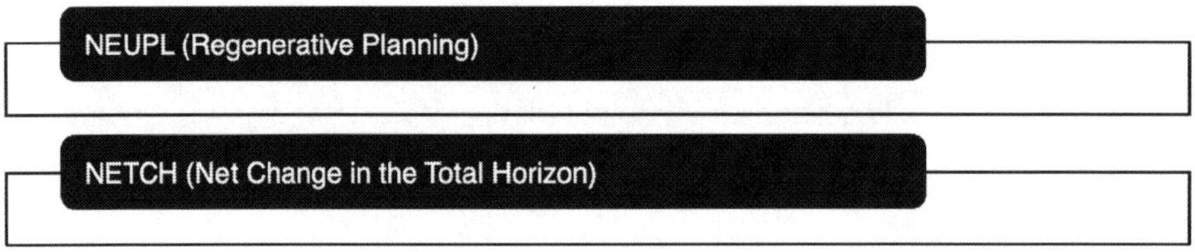

Figure 8.28: Scope of the MRP Run (Processing Keys)

The smaller scope is NETCH (Net Change for Total Horizon). In this scenario, MRP will only re-plan materials that have changed since the last MRP run. It will not re-plan everything, thus it is a smaller scope than Regenerative Planning. Suppose we already ran MRP for the Pepperoni Pizza and dependent requirement and procurement proposals were created. After that MRP run we make a slight change to the BOM, adding an extra ounce of Pepperoni to the BOM. If we use Regenerative Planning, it will re-plan all the components, delete original procurement proposals, and create new procurement proposals. However, if we select NETCH as the Processing Key, the only procurement proposal that would be deleted and recreated is the procurement proposal for Pepperoni. This is because that is the only item that changed since the prior MRP run.

The next Control Parameter provides us with setting for Purchase Requisition creation. In the previous section, we demonstrated how MRP responds when the Procurement Type is external. Recalling from that discussion, MRP can generate the procurement proposal in the form of a Planned Order, Purchase Requisition, or Schedule Line. This Control Parameter determines whether a Planned Order or Purchase Requisition is generated. Figure 8.27 provides information detailing three possible options: Purchase Requisition, No Purchase Requisition, or Purchase Requisition only in the Opening Period. If the user opts for Purchase Requisition, then MRP will create a Purchase Requisition for external procurement. If the user opts for No Purchase Requisition, then MRP will generate a Planned Order instead. The last option, Purchase Requisition only in the Opening Period, refers to the Schedule Margin Key set in the MRP views of the Material Master record. The Scheduling Margin Key defines the Opening Period as a timeframe serving as a float or buffer just prior to production. If we are in the Opening Period, this means we are very close to production and selecting this option will result in the creation of a Purchase Requisition.

The Control Parameter for Schedule Lines operates like the Control Parameter for Purchase Requisitions. First the S/4HANA system will check to see if there are any Scheduling Agreements for the material it is planning. If there are, MRP will look to this Control Parameter to see if a Schedule Line should be generated.

The next Control Parameter relates to an MRP List. The MRP List is a report that MRP generates based on the other Control Parameter settings. It is very important to know that any MRP List that is generated is ONLY valid for the MRP run that is taking place. Should the user re-run MRP, the initial MRP List becomes obsolete. The MRP List looks very similar to the Stock/Requirements List. Figure 8.29 compares the two. It provides information regarding stock on-hand, requirements, and procurement of that material. However, the MRP List will have no data in it unless MRP is run. Recall from earlier that a Stock/Requirements List (SRL) can be generated at any time. We reviewed the SRL for the Pepperoni Pizza after demand planning using Integrated Business Planning (before the MRP run). The SRL also differs from the MRP List because the SRL can remain current by simply refreshing the report. This is not possible with an MRP List. The user can elect to have an MRP List generated or not have one generated. Additionally, the user can choose to have one generated on the existence of Exception messages. An Exception message is an indication of potential issues with the planning run.

MRP List	Stock/Requirements List
• Valid for a single MRP run • Cannot be refreshed • Obsolete if MRP is re-rum • Has no content until after MRP run • Can be used to further process procurement proposals	• Can be made current by refreshing • Can see information prior to MRP run • Can be used to further process procurement proposals

Figure 8.29: MRP List Versus Stock/Requirements List

Advanced Planning: PPDS

Advanced Planning is now natively integrated with SAP S/4HANA. Prior to S4HANA, Advanced Planning existed in the Supply Chain Management (SCM) application in the Business Suite and resided on a separate server. Recall our earlier discussion on MRP Live. One of the advantages was optimization using constraint-based planning (CBP). Production Planning/Detailed Scheduling (PPDS) is the functionality in Advance Planning that allows SAP customers to plan materials in an optimized fashion by planning materials and capacities simultaneously. We will spend some time on PPDS as we go through this section of this book.

Since Advanced Planning is formerly part of SCM, we should revisit the master data for Advanced Planning. You'll recall from earlier in this chapter we looked at the differences in terminology between ERP and SCM and provided an image showing the relationships between them. This can be seen in Figure 8.12. Customers and Suppliers are also considered Location data in Advanced Planning.

When master data is replicated in Advanced Planning, the basic characteristics of the master data in ERP are transferred to Advanced Planning. However, the way they are displayed differs. Figure 8.30 shows how work centers in ERP are displayed as resources in Advanced Planning. Notice each capacity category becomes its own resource in Advanced Planning.

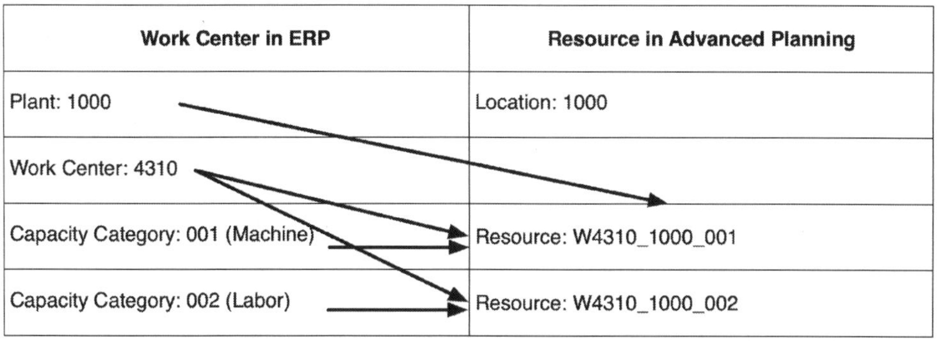

Figure 8.30: Work Centers/Resources

It's important to understand SAP customers have flexibility in how they utilize Advance Planning. It is not ideal for every material or product that gets planned. But for some of the more important materials, it is likely a good option. Customers can also make decisions about the scope of planning in Advanced Planning. For instance, it is possible to run MRP in ERP to generate all the Dependent Requirements and Procurement Proposals and then transfer these to Advanced Planning for optimization. Likewise, customers may opt to use Advanced Planning to generate Dependent Requirements and Procurement Proposals.

When Advanced Planning is used to create dependent requirements and procurement proposals, it explodes the Production Data Structures (like BOM explosions in ERP) to determine the requirements. It also uses backwards scheduling to determine availability of materials to plan procurement when there are shortages. Lot sizes are determined from the corresponding master data and are used as the basis for proposed quantities in the procurement proposals. In PPDS, SAP customers also have the flexibility to interactively plan. In doing so, the user can modify the results of the original plan and perform additional functions like adjustments in procurement proposal quantities (Figure 8.31).

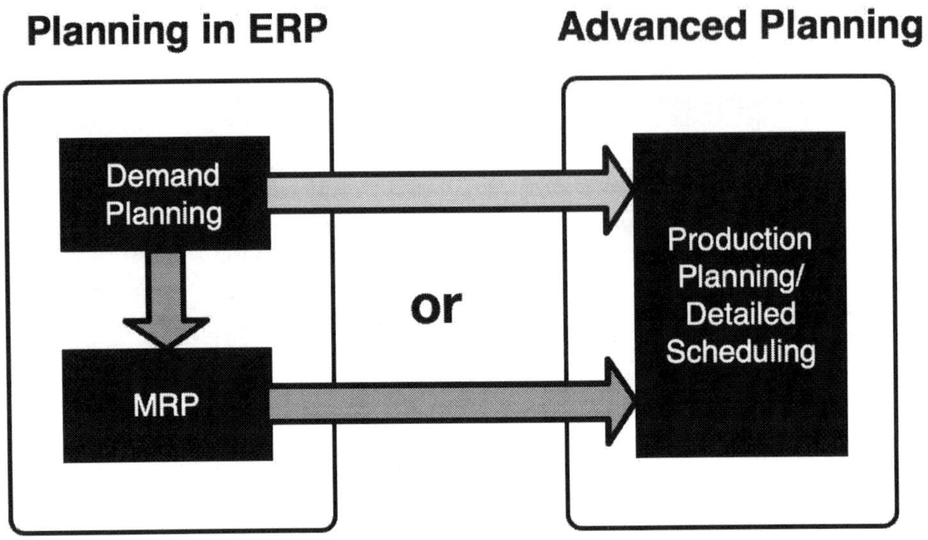

Figure 8.31: Planning in ERP and PP/DS

When procurement proposals from MRP are transferred to Advanced Planning, the quantities are transferred without taking capacities into consideration. This is considered infinite planning. One of the advantages of Advanced Planning is finite planning, which means the exact times for production and procurement are defined as a result of PPDS. During finite planning, capacity constraints are taken into consideration and scheduled times for the procurement proposals are optimized based on these constraints.

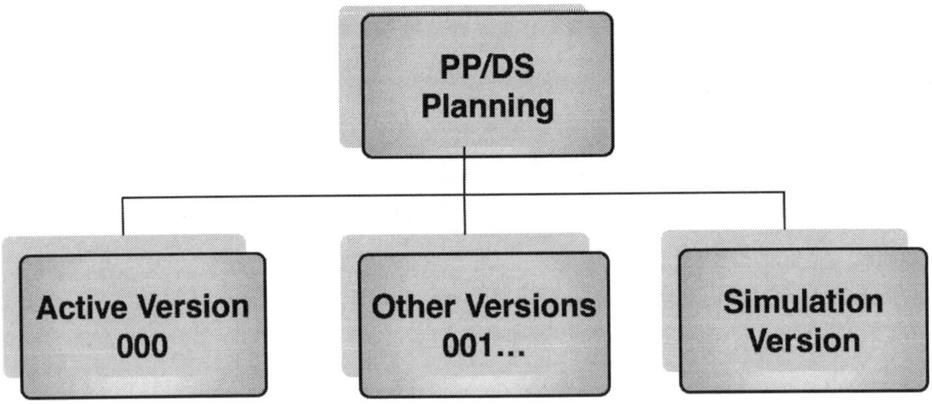

Figure 8.32: Planning Versions in PP/DS

Again, SAP customers can interactively modify the results of any original plans. When plans are transferred, they are transferred as versions. An Active Version always exists as Version 000. This version is based on the transactional and master data transferred from ERP. Additional planning versions may also be created as well as simulated planning versions in PPDS (Figure 8.32).

In PPDS, SAP customers navigate the plans for a product (material in ERP) using the Product View. The Product View (Figure 8.33) has some essential information and functionality. It is the Product View where customers can interactively work with products in PPDS and view any plans for that product. The Product View is specific to a Product and Location (Material and Plant). It has some visual and dynamic similarities to the Stock/Requirements List in ERP. Requirements and procurement proposals appear as line items in the Product View. Customers can modify results of planning by running additional heuristics for PPDS, such as reducing lots sizes and increasing the number of planned orders. Scheduling heuristics are used to optimize scheduling of the plans using capacity constraints for finite planning.

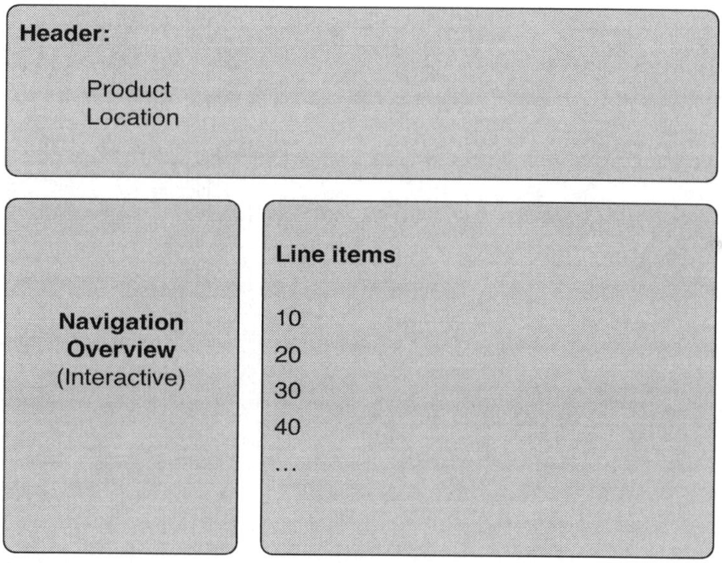

Figure 8.33: Product View in PP/DS

Like other SCM based solutions, Advanced Planning also offers an Alert Monitor (Figure 8.34). We were exposed to similar functionality with EWM using the Warehouse Monitor. The Alert Monitor in Advanced Planning gives SAP customers visibility into potential issues (exceptions) during the planning in PP/DS so they can respond to them by making appropriate adjustments to the plan.

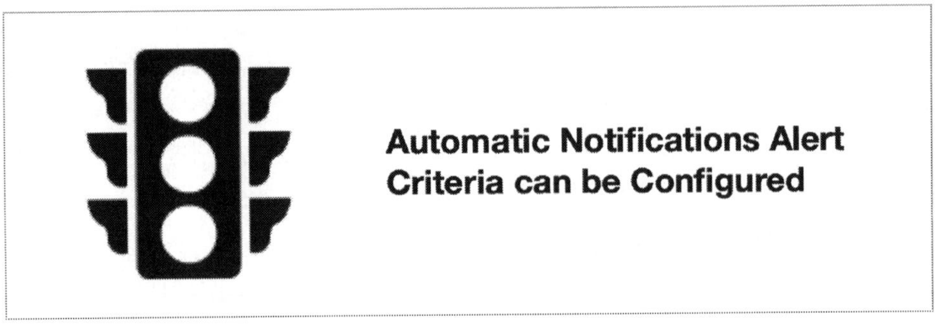

Figure 8.34: Alert Monitor in PP/DS

Another functionality of PPDS is the ability to create Production Orders in PPDS from a PPDS Planned Order. From within the Product View, SAP customers can select a Planned Order and check the indicator for "Conversion". In doing so, a Production Order is created in PP/DS and is immediately transferred to SAP S4HANA ERP.

Flexibility has been a common theme in this section on Advanced Planning and again, customers have the flexibility to create production orders on the ERP side in the classic manner. As planned orders are created in PPDS integration with ERP results in the automatic transfer of these planned orders in ERP. Like other requirements and procurement proposals, they can be viewed in the Stock/Requirements List. Figure 8.35 demonstrates the flexible options for creating production orders.

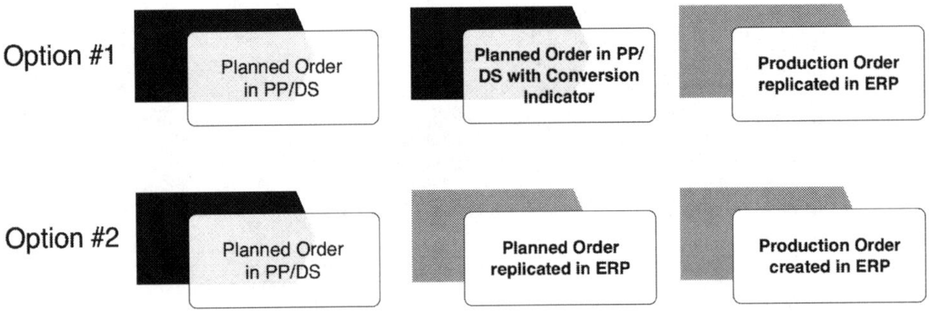

Figure 8.35: Production Order

When planned orders in PPDS are transferred to ERP, only basic dates for production are transferred. Operations times are not created until the creation of production orders. We will embark on that topic in the next section where we address Production Order Processing.

Production Order to Fulfill

The planning aspects in Production Planning are many and included things such as planning of costs, material prices, requirements, and procurement proposals. Once all the planning has been completed and accepted, it's time to move on to the next phase of the Design-to-Operate process.

Production Order Processing

We will use the Order-Related Cost Object Controlling example as a basis for understanding the production order processing, which is often referred to as the manufacturing execution process. The Order-Related Cost Object Controlling process provides a perfect framework for this. Since it is only a framework, we will expand on it somewhat to ensure we get a well-rounded view of the necessary steps in the process. To begin our discussion, let's review Order-Related Cost Object Controlling. We were introduced to it in Controlling and more specifically as it is related to production, we saw it as part of Product Cost Controlling. The three phases of Product Cost Controlling are Product Cost Planning, Cost Object Controlling, and Actual Costing/Material Ledger. Order-Related Cost Object Controlling is the second of the three phases listed above. This represents when actual costs are posted to the production order. The actual costs during the production process can then be compared to the planned costs that resulted from Product Cost Planning. Figure 8.18 depicts the Order-Related Cost Object Controlling steps.

As mentioned above, for manufacturing execution we will need to expand on the framework provided to us in Figure 8.18. There are a couple of additional steps in manufacturing execution not listed in the example above. As we approach those additional steps, we will discuss them in more detail.

Keep in mind, we are focusing on limited aspects of manufacturing. For the most part, our discussions reflect the production process for discrete manufacturing and make-to-stock production. Again, our objective and focus are on the basic process steps based on best practices, and the integration that occurs during the process steps.

Order Creation

The process is initiated with the creation of the production order. In the previous section, we noted that the production order can be created from planned orders within PPDS or from within ERP.

In SAP S/4HANA ERP, there are three methods for converting Planned Orders to Production Orders.

Options for Converting Planned Orders to Production Orders:

1. Collective Processing
   A. With collective processing, multiple Planned Orders can be converted into multiple production orders. This can be done as a background process (this means it can be done automatically without manual interaction). Each Planned Order that is converted is deleted once the Production Order is created.
2. Individual Processing
   A. Individual Processing involves converting one Planned Order to one Production Order. This is usually accomplished from within the Stock/Requirements List (not required). When the conversation takes place, the Planned Order is deleted.
3. Partial Processing
   A. In partial processing, a common practice is to convert only a portion of the Planned Order to a Production Order. In this instance, additional Production Order(s) will be necessary for the remaining quantity in the Planned Order. After the initial partial conversion, the Planned Order still remains in effect.

Regardless of how the production order is created, the same things occur (Figure 8.36). It's important to note the impacts of the order creation.

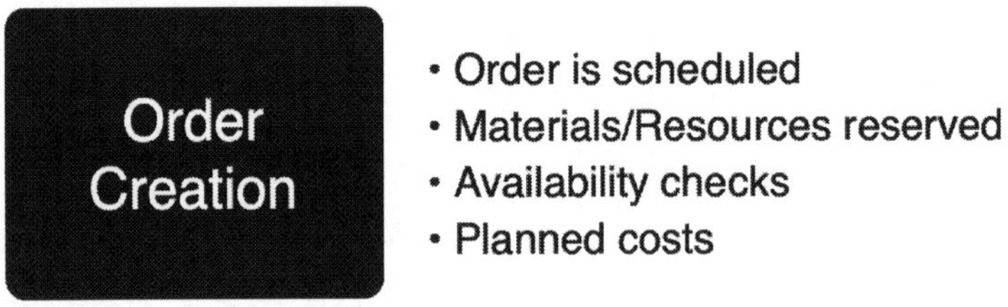

Figure 8.36: Production Order Creation

When a production order is created the operations in the order will be scheduled and the capacities at the assigned work centers will be reserved. Stock items from the BOM(s) will also be placed on reservation for the production order. It's possible for the system to be configured to automatically perform availability checks for materials and resources, though these checks can be called up manually. Finally, the standard cost estimate for the product is used to provide planned costs for the production order. This is all that can occur upon creation of the order. No materials movements can be posted, and no documents can be printed yet.

The production order itself, contains all the relevant information for managing the production process (Figure 8.37).

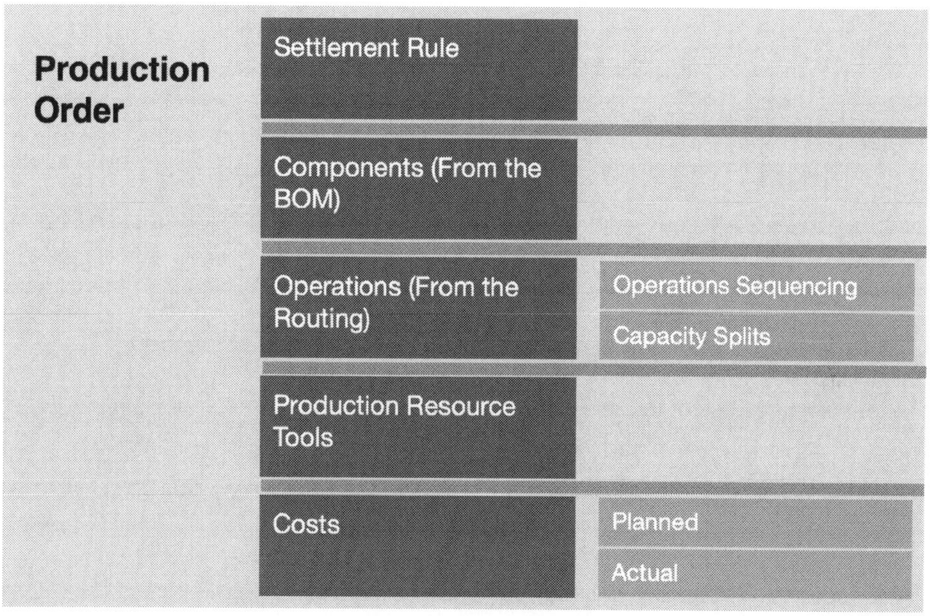

Figure 8.37: Elements of a Production Order

The settlement rule can be found in the Header of the production order. For our purposes, the settlement rule for production orders is for production variances to be settled to the Material Ledger and to a Profitability Segment in CO-PA. Users can also access material components from the BOM in the production order as well as operations from the Routing. Regarding the operations, the operation sequences and capacity splits (assignment to work centers) can also be viewed. Production Resource Tools (PRTs) assigned to the production order are also accessible. Finally, the production order will contain cost information for the order. In there users can see planned costs from order creation as well as any actual costs posted during the production process.

Production Order Release

The order release is perhaps the most important step in the process. Nothing can be executed on the production order until it has been released (Figure 8.38).

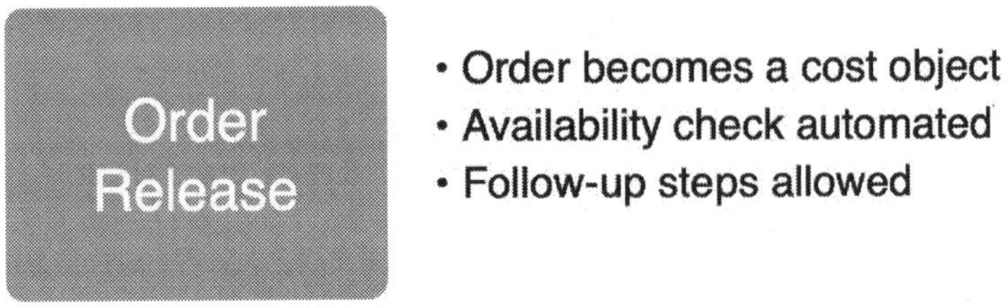

Figure 8.38: Production Order Release

When the production order is released, it receives the status, "REL" (Released). One of the impacts of the order release will always be an automated availability check. Though an availability check can be performed at the time of order creation, time can pass between then and the release of the order. During that time, it's possible that inventory levels may have changed due to any number of possible circumstances. Thus, this automated availability check is critical to the release of the order.

In released status, costs can now be posted to the order. Since this is a unique step in the process, the release must either be performed manually or configured to release automatically. The order will not be considered a cost object without being in release status.

We can now expand and add some steps to the Order-Related Cost Object Controlling process. The release is like an action notice for production. It informs the rest of the system as well as those involved in the process that action on the order can now take place. Any machines or robotics in the work centers can be programmed for the operations and the schedule of operations can be sent to time data collection systems on the shop floor to track and collect times on the order. In addition to this, any documents used in the order can now be printed (e.g., engineering drawings, and withdrawal slips for warehouse). The printing of these documents can also be an automated step in the process.

Goods Movement

The Goods Movement step could involve several goods movements (Figure 8.39). In the production process, a goods movement could be a Goods Receipt from a Purchase Order or a Goods Issue from inventory. To simplify our discussions, we will focus only on goods issues for production

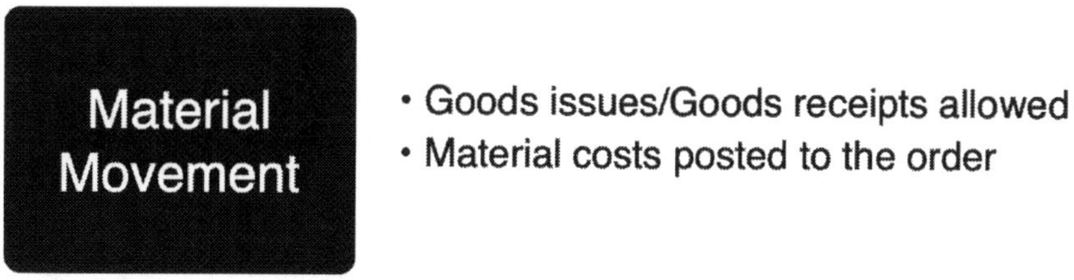

Figure 8.39: Goods Movements

Goods movement always result in the creation of a Material Document, which we know to be an electronic record of the goods movement and records the transaction on a quantity base. When materials are issued from inventory, there will also be a credit posting the stock/inventory account and a debit posting to a consumption expense account. Postings to G/L accounts also result in the creation of a Financial Accounting Document. Furthermore, the consumption expense account is a Primary Cost/Revenue Account. The posting logic in the Controlling module requires an account assignment object for this goods issue transaction. For the costs to be accurately recorded as a debit to the production order, the goods issue is ALWAYS posted to the production order. The result of the cost posting to the order is the creation of a Controlling Document. Finally, since S/4HANA requires the use of the Material Ledger, a Material Ledger (ML) document is also created at the time of this goods movement. This document tracks the value of the material as posted in the material ledger. To recap, four documents are generated at the time of goods issue (Material Document, FI Document, CO document, and ML document).

When the production order was created, stock items needed for the order were reserved. When the goods issue is posted, the reservation quantity is reduced by the quantity issued. Additionally, the material master records for the materials issued are also updated. Stock quantity and value in the Accounting view of the material master are reduced and consumption statistics are appropriately updated in the Additional Data section of the material master record. It's also possible to have the S/4HANA system print goods issue slips at the warehouse.

Figure 8.40 displays the impacts of the goods issue.

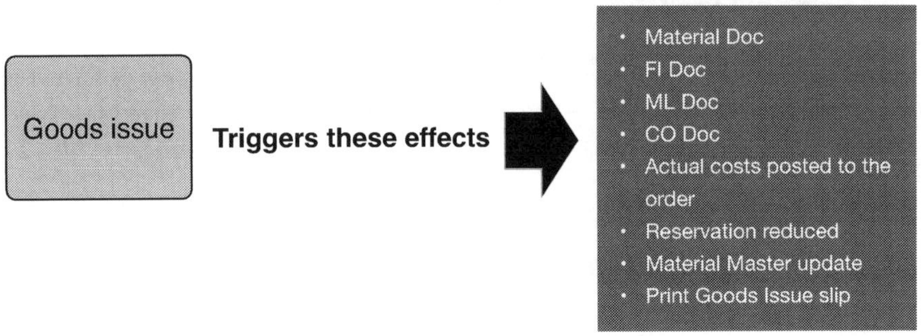

Figure 8.40: Goods Issue Integration

Production Processing

Production Processing is another additional step in the process. Production processing is simply the workers at the work center/shop floor performing the operations on the production order. From a practical sense, this can take a considerable amount of time. But once again we are not focusing on the minute details of these steps. We are more interested in the impacts these steps have on the process. For this reason, we are going to assume all of the processing is completed before we proceed with the next step in the process, Confirmation.

Confirmation

Confirmation occurs when operations on the production order are completed. As mentioned above, from a practical standpoint, it's common practice to confirm each operation as they are completed. But SAP offers the flexibility to confirm the entire production order at one time at the completion of all operations. During the confirmation step, the work centers record actual working times for completing the operations on the order. The actual times can be manually entered or collected at the plant data collection systems installed on shop floors. The importance of the confirmation is that actual costs are once again posted directly to the production order. The confirmation costs are secondary costs because they are a result of indirect activity allocation. The work centers performing the operations are associated with costs centers, and the operations are associated with activity types. That combination allows the system to derive the activity price and factor that price with the actual times to allocate the labor costs on the production order.

The confirmation also has several impacts on the production order (Figures 8.41 and 8.42).

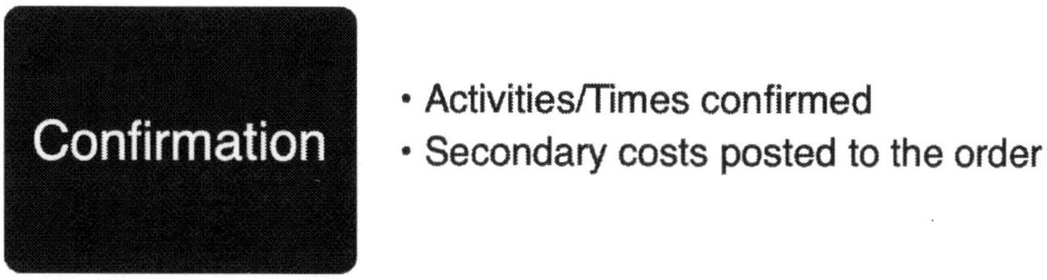

Figure 8.41: Order Confirmation

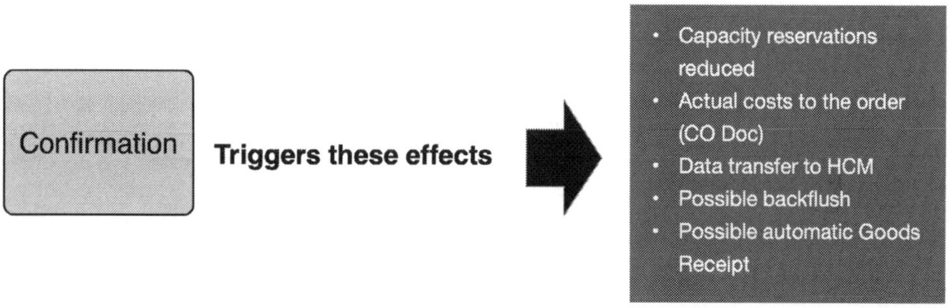

Figure 8.42: Impacts of Confirmation

When confirmation is completed a CO document is generated because of the allocation that occurs. There is no FI document created because the confirmation does not have any direct impact on the general ledger. The order is also debited with additional actual costs stemming from labor on the production order that was confirmed. Because work center master data is tightly integrated with HCM, data regarding working times are transferred to that module. Additional impacts could include other automated steps. One of these is the automation of the goods issue, which normally occurs before confirmation. When this happens, it is called backflushing. We will discuss backflush in more detail shortly. The other possible automated step is a goods receipt posting. The goods receipt is another additional step, generally occurring after confirmation. But as you can see, it can occur automatically as part of the confirmation step. Why is the goods receipt necessary? When production is confirmed, the product must be physically placed in inventory into a storage location. This is a required step in production. Without this step, the value of goods from production is sitting in a Work in Process (WIP) account in the G/L. The value of what was produced must come out of the production order and post to the balance sheet in the G/L, reducing WIP. We will discuss the goods receipt step in more detail next, as it also has significant integration in the SAP S4HANA system.

Goods Receipt

When production has completed and confirmation takes place, the products must be physically and systematically moved to inventory. Whether the goods receipt is automated as part of confirmation or not, several things occur (Figure 8.43). As the products are received in inventory, there is a financial accounting impact. The goods receipt results in the increase of a stock/inventory account in the balance sheet. The value at this this account is debited comes from the standard price of the product in the material master record.

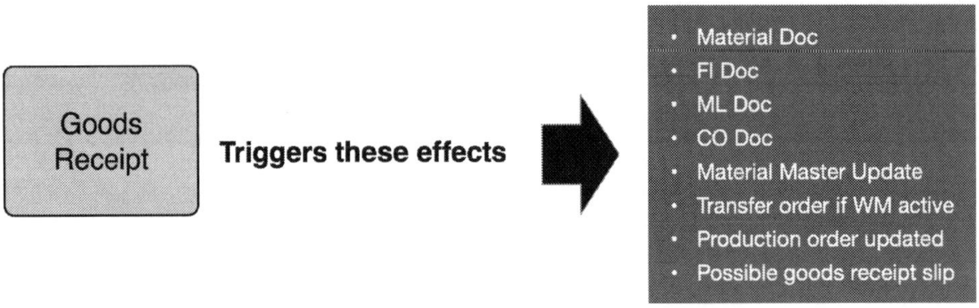

Figure 8.43: Goods Receipt Integration

Technical Completion

During Production Processing, the production order is managed with various statuses. When the order was created, it received the status: CRTD. In this status, there are limitations on processing the order. Recall, executable steps cannot take place until the order is released (Status: REL). Once production is completed, the production supervisor will change the status from REL to Technically Completed or TECO. When the order is in the status TECO, changes to the order are disallowed.

Period-End Activities: Variance Calculation and Settlement

At the end of the accounting period, the accountants want to make sure all costs are properly recorded to their responsible areas so they can close the accounting books. For production, this means first determining the costs remaining in the production order, and second settling those costs to the responsible areas. The first step is the Variance Calculation. Referring to our previous discussion, when the goods receipt is posted, the materials are placed into inventory and the production order is credited using the standard price of the material. This value will be different than the actual costs which were posted to the order during the production process. Therefore, there will be a variance between the actual costs on the production order and the value of what was produced. If we look at the example in Figure 8.44, you will see the actual costs posted to the order as debit postings, and the credit to the order from the goods receipt.

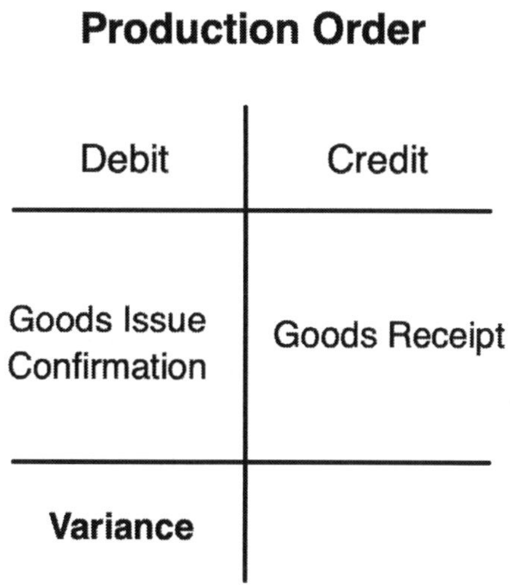

Figure 8.44: Production Order Postings

The variance that is calculated is the difference between the debit/credit side postings. For our purposes, we are going to assume the actual costs to be greater than the value (using the standard price) posted during the goods receipt. There will then be a remaining balance on the debit side, which is the variance (Figure 8.45).

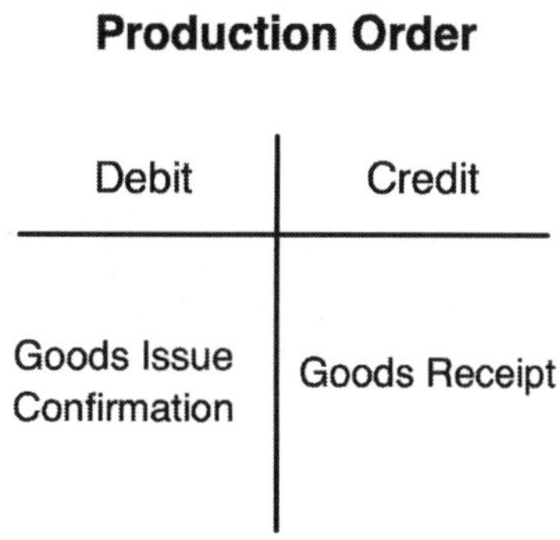

Figure 8.45: Variance of a Production Order

The last step in Order-Related Cost Object Controlling is Settlement. The result of settlement is to settle the balance of the order to zero. For production orders, this means the variance must be settled by crediting the order by the same amount as the variance. In order to settle any Order-Related Cost Object, a Settlement Rule must exist. The settlement rule is maintained in the Header of the production order. In our book and for the certification exam, one hundred percent (100%) of the variance will be settled to the Material Ledger (ML) and a Profitability Segment in CO-PA. In this way, actual costs during goods movements as well as settlement can be tracked in the ML. As a result of settlement, the variance from the additional costs that are settled will also be recorded in Profitability Analysis (CO-PA).

Figure 8.46 depicts all the debit/credit side postings to the production order and the step in which each occur.After settlement, the balance of the order is zero.

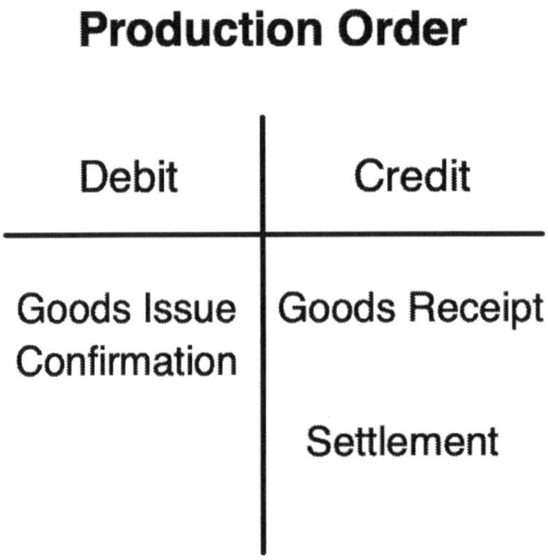

Figure 8.46: Debit/Credit Posting During Manufacturing Execution

<u>Business Completion</u>

To close out our discussion on Production Processing, the production order is set to Business Completion. Business Completion is a status and occurs when all costs and variances on the order have been settled to a balance of zero. At this point, production processing is complete.

It would be worth your while to once again review the Order-Related Cost Object Controlling process. From Figure 8.18, you can easily identify the ways in which manufacturing execution follows the order presented in the image. If you have a good understanding of these steps, as well as the impacts that occur during this process, you will be in a much better position to pass the integration certification exam.

Reporting

SAP S/4HANA provides many reporting features for Production Planning. We have seen a few of these reports already, Stock/Requirements List and MRP List. Other reports that support this part of the business include Stock Overview (Inventory report), Worklists (for planned orders and production orders), and Statistics (for production quantities, materials etc.).

Manufacturing Planning and Execution Summary

As we mentioned at the onset of this chapter, it is very extensive in terms of content. There is a lot of information to cover in the Production Planning module. You should have a much clearer picture of the various planning techniques that are related to this module and the various tools that are available for this purpose. These include Product Cost Planning, Materials Planning using Integrated Business Planning and Material Requirements Planning, and Advanced Planning using Production Planning and Detailed Scheduling.

The planning steps serves as input into production order processing. Planned costs are derived from the Standard Cost Estimate and Procurement Proposals from materials planning serve as the basis for production. Production Order processing also follows the Order-Related Cost Object Controlling process. There are many integrated aspects in this process, which you should now understand.

Chapter 9: Sales and Distribution

Sales and Distribution is the business function that supports the sale of goods (and in same cases services (Chapter 11)) as well as the physical shipment of those goods to customers. This is managed in the Lead-to-Cash business process. Lead-to-Cash processing primarily takes place in the Sales and Distribution module in SAP S/4HANA. However, like other chapters we've covered, there is integration with SAP Cloud solutions to support the process. In this chapter, we will see another SAP Cloud solution, SAP Customer Experience. More specifically, SAP Sales Cloud. As far as S/4HANA, Sales and Distribution is another logistics module so we will see many similarities to things we discussed in other logistics modules. We will address the Enterprise Structure (organizational levels), followed by master data, and then the "best-practice" scenario for the Lead-to-Cash process. At the end of this chapter, we'll also see how Sales and Distribution integrates with Profitability in SAP S/4HANA. We'll also introduce you to Transportation Management, as this also has integration with sales.

It will be important to have a solid understanding of the above mentioned items, but also important to identify the integration that occurs during the Lead-to-Cash process. We will encounter various integrations with both financial and management accounting, as well as inventory management and warehousing. We will also spend some time describing the structure of various documents created during the sales process.

Enterprise Structure

Logistics Organizational Levels

Sales and Distribution is part of logistics in SAP S/4HANA. As with every other logistics module, the four organizational levels in Figure 9.1 are always required. As a reminder, the client is the highest organizational level in SAP S/4HANA and all organizational (enterprise) elements exist within the client. The Company Code represents a legal entity in Financial Accounting where a single set of financial books are maintained for legal financial reporting. As noted above, there is significant integration between Sales and Distribution (SD) and Financial Accounting (FI). The Plant is the key organizational level where data from operational activities are used and maintained. We will address the role of Plants shortly. Finally, the Storage Locations represent data for inventory of materials that will support the sales process.

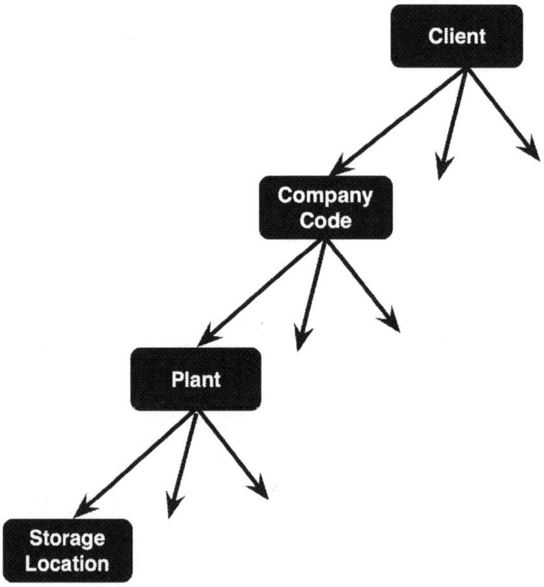

Figure 9.1: Logistics Organizational Levels (Replica of Figure 5.1)

Additional Organizational Levels

Additional organizational levels also exist in SD. The Sales Organization is the organizational level responsible for maintaining terms and conditions associated with sales, as well as managing product liability and rights and recourse for customers. The sales organization can be assigned to only one company code. But it is possible for a single company code to have more than one sales organization assigned to it.

A Distribution Channel represents the means in which products are sold to customers. Examples or distribution channels are wholesale, retail, internet sales, and others. Distribution channels are assigned to one or more sales organizations.

Divisions are another organizational level in SD. The division represent a product line. For example, a computer manufacturer may sell laptops, desktops, accessories, and/or tablets. Each of these would be representative of different lines of products, thus they are considered divisions in SAP S/4HANA. Divisions are also assigned to one or more sales organizations (Figure 9.2).

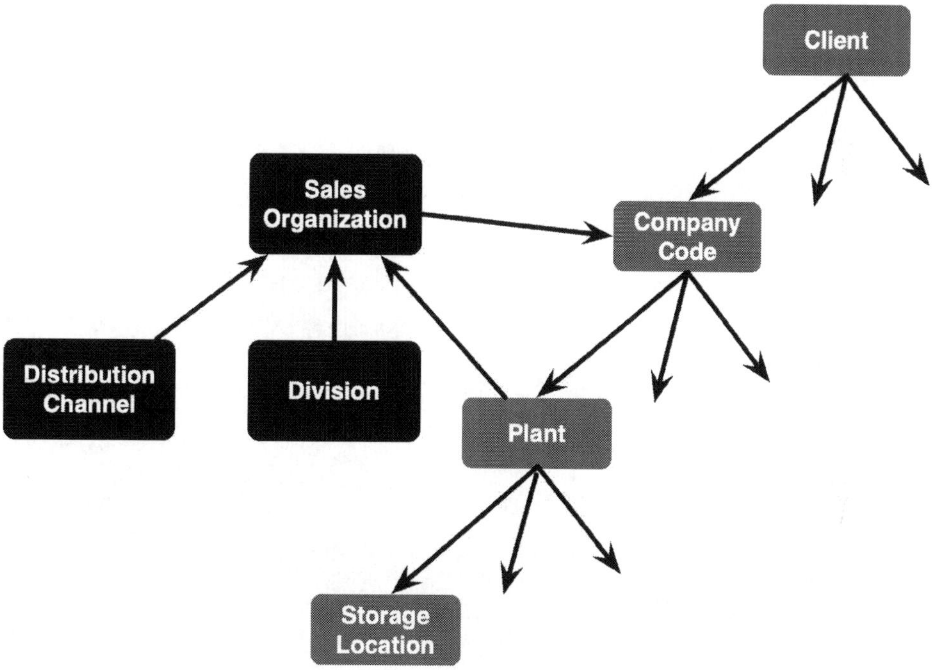

Figure 9.2: Sales Organization, Distribution Channels, and Divisions

Sales Areas are a unique combination of Sales Organization-Distribution Channel-Division. The Sales Areas must be defined by linking the three organizational levels together. They are not automatically derived in the system. Examples of sales organizations can be seen in Figure 9.3. In this image we can see there are two sales organizations, but three distributions channels. Although there are only three divisions, you can see not every possible combination of these three organizational levels automatically creates a sales area. The sales areas must be uniquely defined.

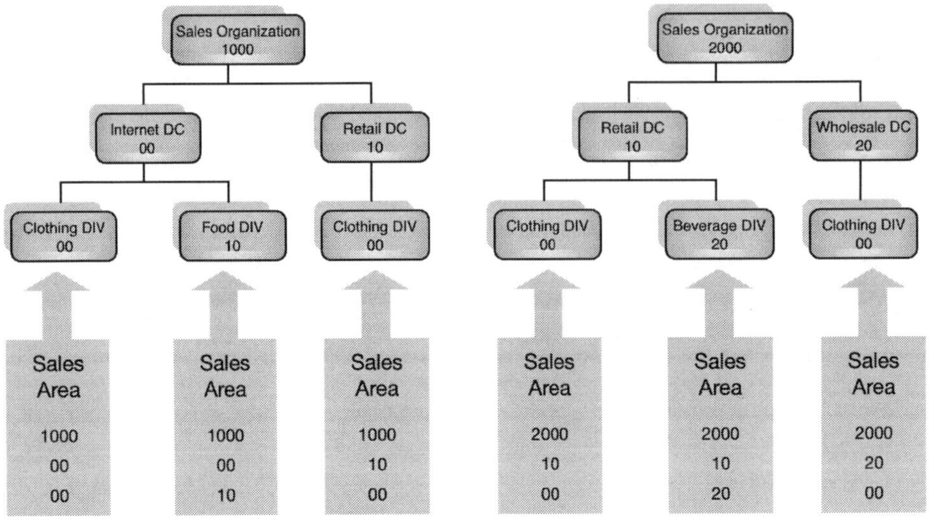

Figure 9.3: Sales Areas

The final organizational level in SD is the Shipping Point (Figure 9.4). A shipping point is a physical location from which shipping activities occur. A shipping point could be an airport, a seaport, or a loading dock among others. Shipping points are assigned to one or more plants and a plant can have more than one shipping point assigned. Assigning the shipping points in this way allows more than one plant to share the same shipping point. i.e. an airport.

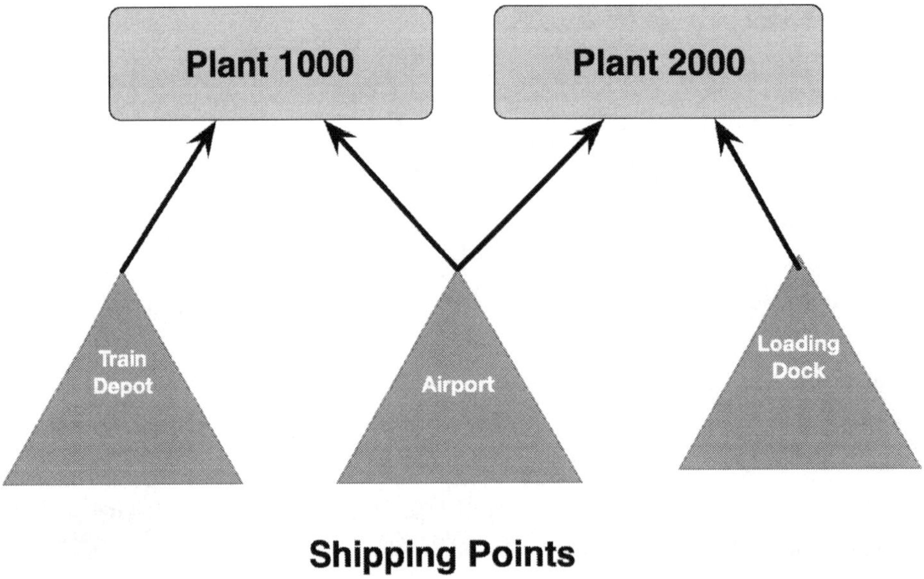

Figure 9.4: Shipping Points

We can also see that Plants are instrumental in supporting shipping activities as Shipping Points are assigned to Plants. But Plants are also assigned to one or more Sales Organization/Distribution Channel combinations. This assignment results in the Plant being considered the "Delivery Plant". Examples of Delivery Plants could be stores or distribution centers.

Best-Practice Scenario for the Lead-to-Cash Process

Our "best-practice" scenario for the Lead-to-Cash process follows a pattern similar to other processes that we've seen thus far (Figure 9.5). We begin with a discussion about master data and we will address all the master data required to support sales. We will then proceed to the next item in the process, which is Pre-sales Activities. During our discussion on Pre-sales Activities we will see how SAP Sales Cloud provides extended functionality to support the process. Sales Order Processing will be next, followed by the Logistics Execution steps involved in shipping products to customer. The process is completed with billing the customer for products shipped and receiving payment from them.

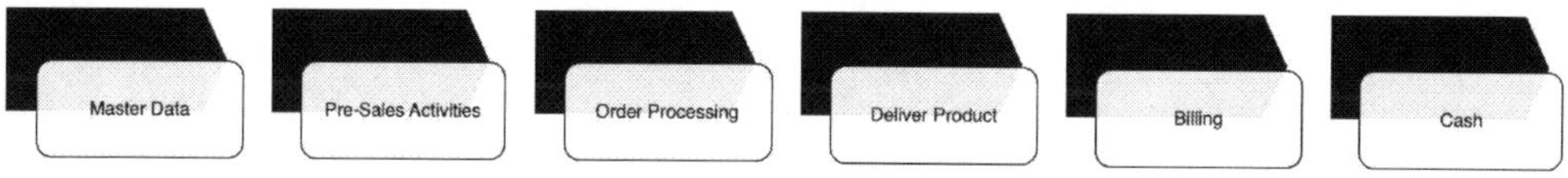

Figure 9.5: Best-Practice Scenario for the Lead-to-Cash Process

Master Data

Material (Product) Master Data

Materials are integrated throughout the SAP S/4HANA system, so it comes as no surprise that material master data is also used in the Sales and Distribution (SD) module. As we have previously seen, material master data is maintained in Views (business functions). Most of these Views are specific to the Plant organizational level. However, in order to sell a material, it is required to maintain the Sales Views for a material. The Sales Views are specific to the Plant organizational level but are also maintained at additional organizational levels. When maintaining the Views for Sales it is also necessary to create the data in the Sales Organization and Distribution Channel organizational levels. Figure 9.6 demonstrates this concept.

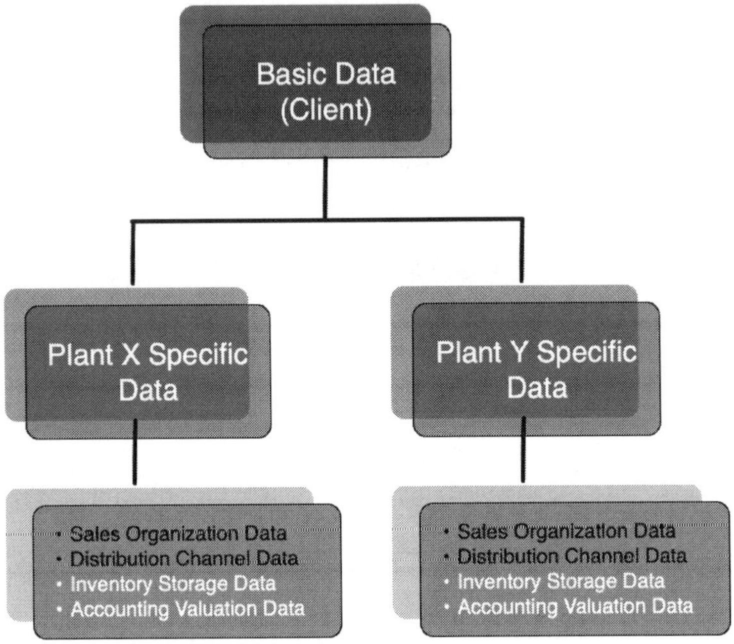

Figure 9.6: Material Master: Sales Views

You may be wondering why the Division is not part of the Sales Views. After all, the Sales Organization, Distribution Channel, and Division make up the Sales Area. The fact of the matter is that the Division is a characteristic of a material and that characteristic does not change regardless of which Sales Organizations or Distribution Channels are used for sales. Thus, the Division is constant and maintained as part of the Basic Data of a material and is stored at the Client Organizational level.

Customer Master Data

As a result of SAP simplifying the data model to develop S/4HANA, maintaining customer master data is similar to how we maintain master data for vendors. Both are now maintained as Business Partners. We discussed this in Chapter 5 when we addressed vendor master data for MM Procurement.

Business Partners fall into one of three categories:

1. Organization
2. Person
3. Group

If a vendor already exists and that vendor is also a customer, there is no longer a need to create a separate master record. Both the vendor and customer are now treated as a single entity, the Business Partner. The Business Partner is maintained in roles. For customers, there are three required roles that support the sales order process. Figure 9.7 shows the Business Partner roles for a customer. You can see from this image that the same Business Partner may also be a vendor.

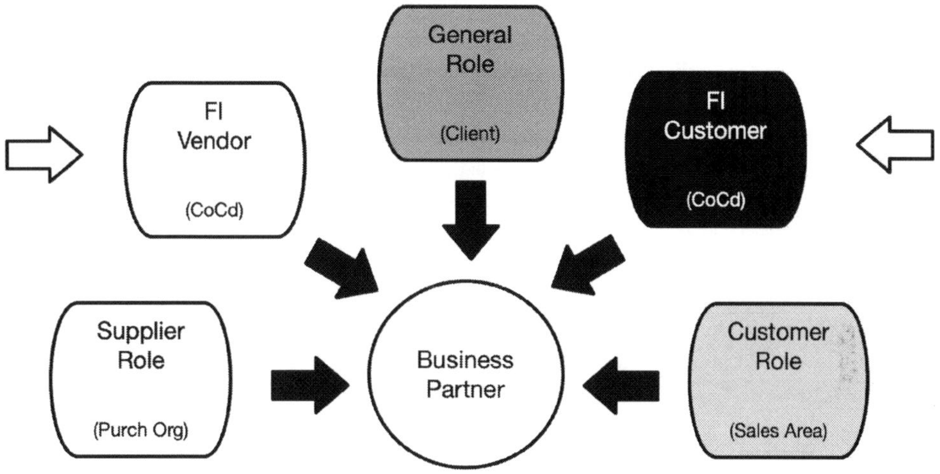

Figure 9.7: Business Partner: Customer

The first role to address is the General Business Partner role, which is maintained at the Client organizational level. This is where information regarding the Business Partner's name, address, and account number are stored. As we have noted when discussing vendors, it's possible to maintain multiple addresses for the same Business Partner.

As we will see shortly, one of the steps in the sales process is Billing, where a bill is sent to the customer. In this step, a direct receivable is created for the customer account, which will also have an impact in the General Ledger. In the Financial Accounting chapter, we described this as the subledger/general ledger relationship. The customer is the subledger account and the general ledger account is called the reconciliation account. The FI Customer role is the role where we link the customer to the reconciliation account. Since the reconciliation account is a G/L account, the postings occur at the company code level. Thus, the information for the FI Customer role is maintained in the company code.

The third role for the customer as a Business Partner is the Customer role. The Customer role is associated with a Sales Area. There is a lot of information maintained in this role. In general terms, we keep Sales Order information, Shipping information, Billing information, and Partner Functions information related specifically to the customer in this role. The sales information includes the information defining how sales orders are processed for the customer. Shipping information includes such things as shipping conditions and delivering plant. Billing information includes Incoterms, tax classifications, and other terms for payment.

The Partner Function requires its own discussion. There are four mandatory partner functions which must be maintained in the Customer role. These mandatory partner functions are listed below:

- Sold-to Party
- Ship-to Party
- Bill-to Party
- Payer

To avoid the risk of making assumptions, let's briefly address the partner functions. If the partner functions are not manually assigned, the SAP S/4HANA system will use the customer account as the default value for the partner function. However, it is possible that the partner functions represent different individuals. For instance, the person who placed the sales order (Sold-to Party) may not be where the order will be delivered (Ship-to Party). Likewise, where the bill is sent (Bill-to Party) and who will pay (Payer) may also differ. Keep in mind, whether the partner functions default to the customer account or are manually assigned, these four are required in the customer master record in the Customer role.

During Sales Order Processing, a sales order is created for a unique sales area and customer. As such, the SAP system can identify the partner functions associated with the customer and include those partner functions to support their relevant activities in the process.

Conditions Master Data

Conditions master data was also used in the MM Procurement process. In sales you will find there are similar conditions. However, these conditions will obviously support the sales process. Conditions appear in sales documents created during the sales order process. Sales documents may include Inquiries, quotations, and sales orders. The conditions in sales can be categorized as the following:

- Prices
- Discounts
- Surcharges
- Taxes
- Freight

Condition classes are used to distinguish between the various conditions noted above. However, conditions also have other features or characteristics. For example, a condition such as discount could apply to an entire sales document or just to one line item in the sales document. This is called the condition level. Scales can also be applied to conditions. An example of scales could be used for pricing whereby the sales price of a material could differ depending on quantities sold. Creating scales for this price would allow a company to offer customers a better price if they purchase in greater quantities. For instance, the sales price for Material X might normally be set at $4 USD. However, scales can be used to create a sales price of $3.50 USD should the customer purchase more than 100 of Material X, and $3.25 USD for a quantity of 250 or greater. Finally, all conditions must be associated with validity dates. Suppose a company is promoting a product and is offering customers a 10% discount on that product for a one week promotional period. It's important to associate the dates for which this discount applies to ensure customers receive that discount as promised, but also to ensure the discount does not extend beyond the promotional period.

Output Master Data

Output is master data used to communicate and transmit documents during the SD Sales process. There are several steps in the sales process where output master data is used. SAP associates different Output Types depending on which document is being transmitted. Most frequently, output in the sales process is used to send confirmations to the customer. The confirmations could be for sales orders (order confirmations) and deliveries (delivery notes). Another example of an Output Type in SAP S4HANA is invoices that are transmitted to customers as a result of billing. The Output Type is captured during the various transactions in the Lead-to-Cash process to in order that the correct document is transmitted to the customer.

Sales and Distribution: Detailed Lead-to-Cash Process

Figure 9.8 is another view of the same process, but with more details. You will notice the steps in our "best-practice" scenario for Lead-to-Cash (Figure 9.5) is essentially the same, but with less context. As we continue moving forward in this chapter, we will address each step in our "best-practice" scenario to include more details.

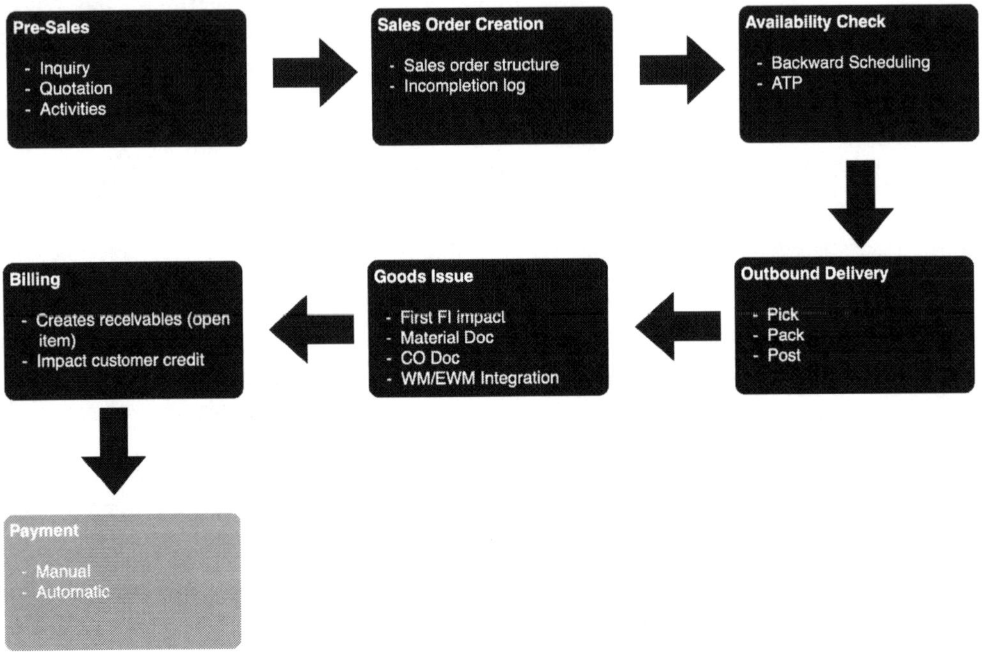

Figure 9.8: SD Lead-to-Cash Process

Like other processes, there are several steps which include integration points. We will look at each step and provide the necessary detail. It will be important to know each of these as well as the correct sequence of steps in the process as we describe them.

We will also see consistency with other processes we've covered. For instance, the first step in every logistics process to have a financial accounting impacts is the first goods movement. This will be no different for the sales. Like the Source-to-Pay process, the payment step in the Lead-to-Cash process also takes place within the Financial Accounting module. It is not a logistics step which is why we have shaded that step in Figure 9.8 differently than the others. Keep these things in mind as we continue with our discussions.

Pre-sales Activities

Pre-sales during the sales process involves documents or activities designed to generate sales orders. Pre-sales activities are such things as marketing campaigns, mail-outs, email marketing strategies, attending trade shows, as well as several other things. Though no formal SD document is necessarily generated during these forms of activities, these activities can result in "leads", which is the potential for increasing the customer base and earning sales orders. Pre-sales documents exist within SAP S/4HANA in the form of Inquiries and Quotations. These two documents can be used as a basis to generate sales orders. It's also possible for an inquiry to be used as a foundation for generating a quotation. Therefore, a difference exists between an inquiry and a quotation. An inquiry could be the result of a customer or potential customer informally inquiring about sales prices for a product you sell. An inquiry document is created in the SAP S/4HANA system to record the information related to the inquiry, including customer information. A quotation is a formal request, typically a result from receiving a Request for Quotation from a customer. In such cases, a quotation document is created in the system to record the relevant information. Since the quotation is a more formal request for terms and conditions, it is not used to create an inquiry. However, an informal request for terms and conditions can be used as a basis for creating a more formal request. Thus, a quotation can be created from an inquiry.

SAP Sales Cloud

SAP Sales Cloud is an SAP Cloud solution and is part of the SAP Customer Experience (CX) portfolio. SAP Sales Cloud plays an important role in Pre-sales Activities. A little bit about SAP Sales Cloud first. SAP Sales Cloud provides a company's sales team with access to information related to sales, customers, stock levels, deliveries, tasks, and other sales-related information from a easy to use mobile app. In this way, members of the sales team can access information and respond in a timely manner to customer requests. Interactions with customers and potential customers can be documented within SAP Sales Cloud. SAP Sales Cloud also integrates with third-party technologies like Google Calendar, Outlook, and others.

In SAP S/4HANA, we identified two documents that are part of Pre-sales Activities. In SAP Sales Cloud, there are three documents which are part of the SAP Sales Cloud Sales Cycle (Figure 9.9). One of these documents is a Lead document. Earlier, we defined a "lead" as something with the potential to increase the customer base, earning sales orders. A Lead document in SAP Sales Cloud is used to record information about such interactions with potential customers. Leads can be created manually or automatically from other systems such as email or by scanning a business card. The idea is to create a formal record containing this information so it can be qualified as having real potential. Once qualified, a sales representative (or group of representatives) can work to convert that "lead" into an "opportunity".

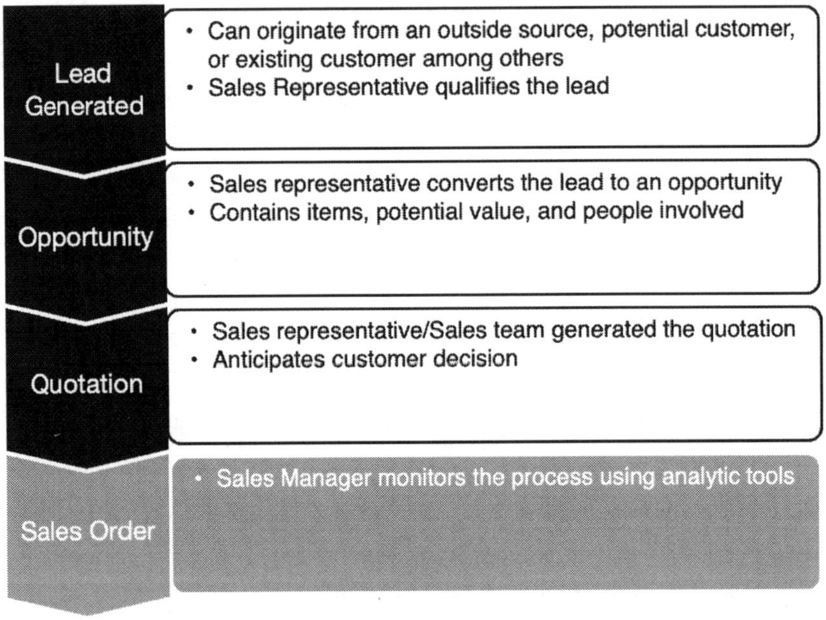

Figure 9.9: SAP Sales Cloud Sales Cycle

When an Opportunity document is created in SAP Sales Cloud from a Lead, they are linked together so any changes to either can be tracked and referenced. The Opportunity document contains important information that supports the sales team in configuring a proposal (Quotation) that can be sent to the customer. The Opportunity document includes items, pricing and value of the opportunity, as well as the different people involved. One of the main benefits of using SAP Sales Cloud is that it provides the sales team with a guided approach to ensure all of the steps are handled properly to advance the process.

The final pre-sales activity is the Quotation document. This quotation essentially functions the same as what was previously discussed in SPA S/4HANA. As a matter of fact, via the SAP Business Technology Platform (BTP), SAP Sales Cloud is tightly integrated with SAP S/4HANA and a quotation document created in S/4HANA can be replicated in SAP Sales Cloud. Likewise, a quotation created within SAP Sales Cloud is replicated in SAP S/4HANA. The quotation in SAP Sales Cloud also integrates with S/4HANA bringing in pricing and availability information into the quotation from S/4HANA.

These three documents, Leads, Opportunities, and Quotations, complete the Pre-sales activities in SAP Sales Cloud. The steps in the SAP Sales Cloud Sales Cycle (Figure 9.9) ends with the creation of the Sales Order. Notice, we shaded this step differently because it signifies a new phase in the Lead-to-Cash process, sales order processing. As you can see, the sales order can be created within SAP Sales Cloud. Although the sales order can also be created within SAP S/4HANA, we are still on the topic of SAP Sales Cloud, so let's briefly address sales order creation from within SAP Sales Cloud.

When a sales order is created in SAP Sales Cloud from a quotation, the information from the quotation is copied to the order. Important pieces of information include the Sales Area, materials (products), and the partner functions from the customer master records. Material availability and pricing is copied from S/4HANA into the sales order. When the user saves the sales order in SAP Sales Cloud, a sales order number is created in SAP Sales Cloud and a second sales order number is created within SAP S/4HANA. All documents within SAP Sales Cloud can be accessed using the Document Flow functionality. Because documents are replicated between SAP Sales Cloud and SAP S/4HANA, the sales team can access and monitor the entire Lead-to-Cash process from within SAP Sales Cloud. This includes shipping and billing processing.

Finally, each step in the SAP Sales Cloud Sales Cycle can be monitored and evaluated using the SAP Intelligent Sales Execution, which provides analytic capabilities.

Sales Order Processing

A sales order is the next document created during the sales process. As a reminder, the previous section explained that a sales order can be created within SAP S/4HANA or from SAP Sales Cloud. Sales order numbers are replicated in each solution. The sales order includes mutually agreeable terms and conditions for one or more products to be sold to a customer. As we noted above, a sales order can be generated from an inquiry or a quotation. But sales orders can also be created using other means. A sales order can be created without reference, meaning it can be created manually without any other documents. Sales orders can also be derived from contracts as well as previous sales orders. See Figure 9.10.

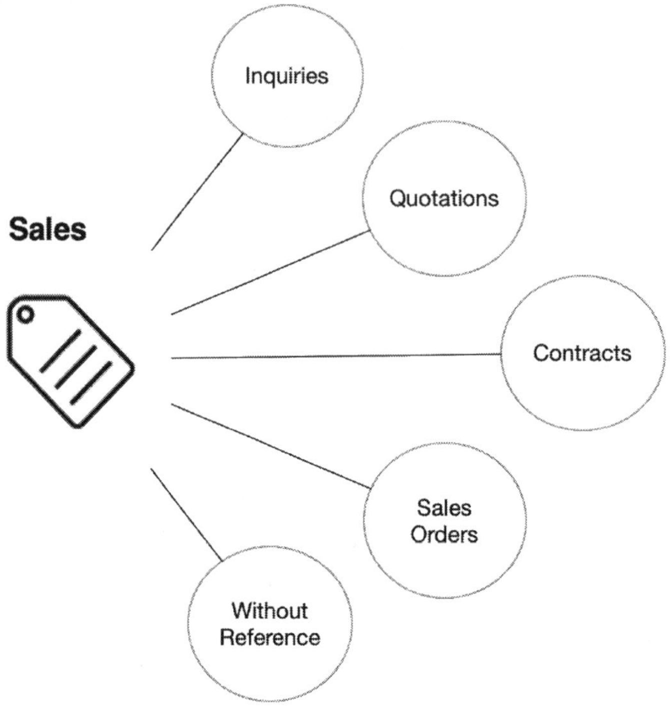

Figure 9.10: Sales Order Creation

The sales order also has a very detailed structure. It includes a Header, Items, and Schedule Lines. The Header of a sales order includes the Partner Function Sold-to Party. The sold-to party is a partner function in the Customer role of the customer master record. Recall, the Customer role is maintained in the Sales Area. When a sales order is created, it is created for a unique sales area. That is, a unique combination of sales organization, distribution channel, and division. As a result, the SAP S/4HANA system can derive the correct Sold-to Party from the Customer role. Additionally, the Header of the sales order includes a reference to the customer's Purchase Order as well as a requested delivery date for the order. When the order is saved, the order number and document date will also be part of the Header data.

As you can see from Figure 9.11, there are three (3) line items in the sales order. Each line item contains a material as well as quantities and a price condition.[1] Pricing is the result of the pricing procedure set in the Customer role of the customer master record. When a sales order is created from a quotation, the same pricing procedure was used in the quotation and is copied to the sales order. However, it is possible to manually overwrite conditions in the sales order. The line item will also contain

[1] It is possible to sell an item with no price. This is called a free goods.

information regarding the Plant from where the materials will be delivered. Each line item in the sales order contains one or more schedule lines. The schedule lines represent the planned shipping dates for the items as well as the quantities to be shipped. The first line item (Branded saw-brush) has two schedule lines, the second line item (Leopard miller) has three schedule lines, and the third item (Psychedelic saw) has only one schedule line.

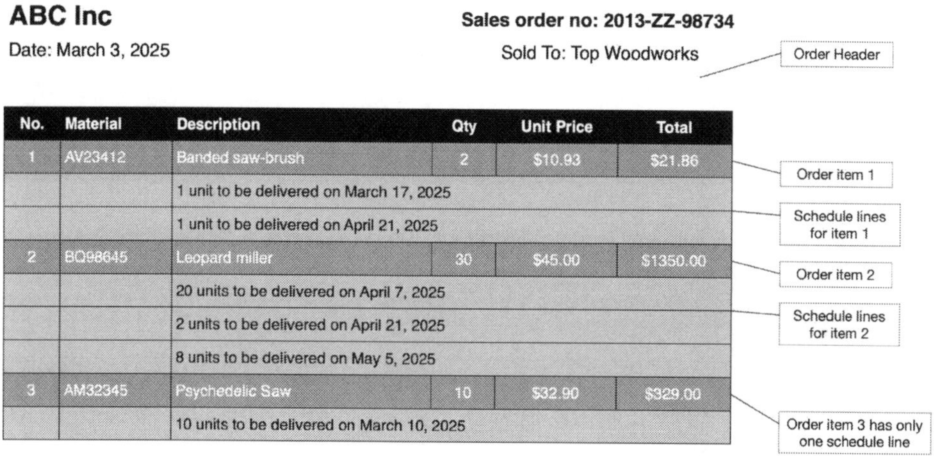

Figure 9.11: Sales Order Structure

The schedule lines play a very important role in a future step of the process, which is the creation of the Outbound Delivery. Therefore, we are going to revisit the structure of the sales order document when we discuss the Outbound Delivery.

But the sales order document has other implications that are worth discussion. For one, the sales order is integrated with output master data. If you think about it, whenever you place an order online you immediately receive a confirmation email with access to your order. When we addressed output master data earlier in this chapter, we recognized the sales order confirmation to be an important aspect in sales.

The sales order also contains an Incompletion Log. The Incompletion Log is a nice tool to validate that all the data needed for the sales order is complete. It not only checks fields in the sales order but can look to other data, such as the customer to ensure there is no missing data in the customer master record which would inhibit further processing of the order. The Incompletion Log can be called up manually from within the sales order or by configuring the system to automatically check for completeness. If data is missing, the SAP Fiori App, "Sales Order Fulfillment Issues" can be used to see which orders have incomplete data. When an order is selected, the

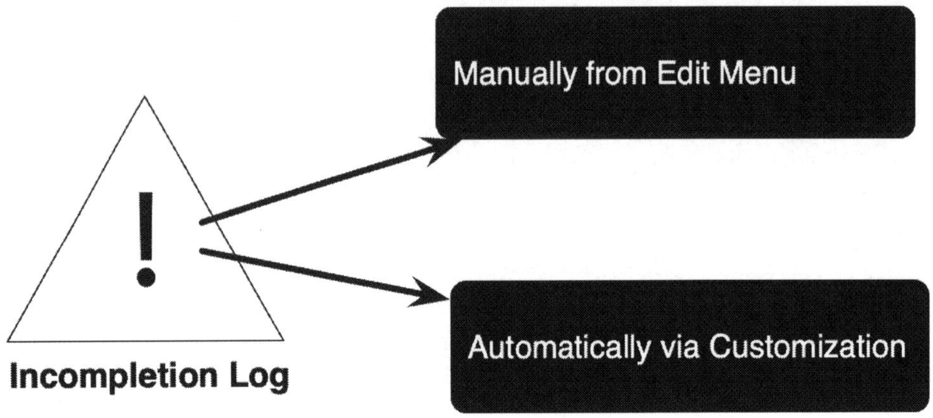

system will point to the missing data so the issues can be resolved (Figure 9.12).

Figure 9.12: Sales Order Incompletion Log

From within the sales order, it is also possible to perform an availability check. The availability check is defined in the material master record. It informs the system which criteria should be used for carrying out the availability check. Many of these settings are created when customizing the SAP S/4HANA system. The availability checks can also consider availability of materials at other plants. The goal is to provide customer with an Available to Promise (ATP) date for the materials in the sales order. The ATP is performed using a backwards scheduling procedure. This quantity is then listed as the "confirmed quantity" in the schedule line(s) for that item. The availability check must occur before the next step, which is to create the Outbound Delivery. The Outbound Delivery initiates the shipping activities and references the confirmed quantity in the schedule lines of the sales order to proceed.

Additionally, sales processing supports material substitutions and exclusions. It is possible to identify substitutes for a material within the material master record. If so, the system can automatically populate the sales order with the substitute material if desired. It is also possible to exclude the sale of certain materials to customers. Materials can be marked as being an excluded material for sale to a customer.

Deliver Product

From the previous sections in this chapter, we have already learned a great deal about the Outbound Delivery. The Outbound Delivery is part of SAP Logistics Execution (LE) and initiates the shipping activities which include the "3 P's" (Pick, Pack and Post). The picking of the Outbound Delivery represents a field in the Outbound Delivery document labeled, “Pick Quantity”. In order to process the goods movement, that field must be populated with the quantity that is being shipped. If warehouse management is active, then the field can only be populated by performing Warehouse Management (WM) or using Extended Warehouse Management (EWM) warehouse tasks. We will revisit those processes shortly. However, if warehouse management is not active, then the user must manually enter a quantity in the Pick Quantity field.

The second “P” (Pack) can be managed in Transportation Management (TM). We will briefly discuss TM towards the end of this chapter. But packing could be as simple as placing products in an envelope for shipment or as complex as using the tools available in TM. The last “P” is Post. This represents the posting of the Goods Issue. The Goods Issue has a great deal of integration points, so it deserves its own section which immediately follows the Outbound Delivery.

The Outbound Delivery document is created by referencing the schedule lines in the sales order. Remember, the schedule lines represent the shipping dates and includes confirmed quantities. Confirmed quantities are important because they are the result of the availability check. The company can only ship quantities that it can confirm as being available. The number of schedule lines for the items in the sales order, and their dates, determines how many outbound deliveries are to be created. If we look at the example of our sales order, we can identify some of the important information in the schedule lines.

Our example in Figure 9.13 shows one of the schedule lines for the 1st item and the schedule line for the 3rd item share the same delivery date. Therefore, these two schedule lines can be shipped together. In this case a single Outbound Delivery can be created for those two schedule lines. The remaining schedule lines in the example above have different dates. This means each of these will need to be shipped separately, requiring their own outbound delivery documents. The sales order in our example will require a total of five (5) outbound delivery documents to fulfill the order. When the last outbound delivery document is created (no schedule lines remain), the status of the sales order changes to “Complete”. The sales order is no longer used to manage any remaining steps in the process. The outbound delivery document now becomes the document of reference for the remaining logistics steps in the sales process. Though the sales order is not used as a reference document after creating the outbound delivery, its status will update with the subsequent steps.

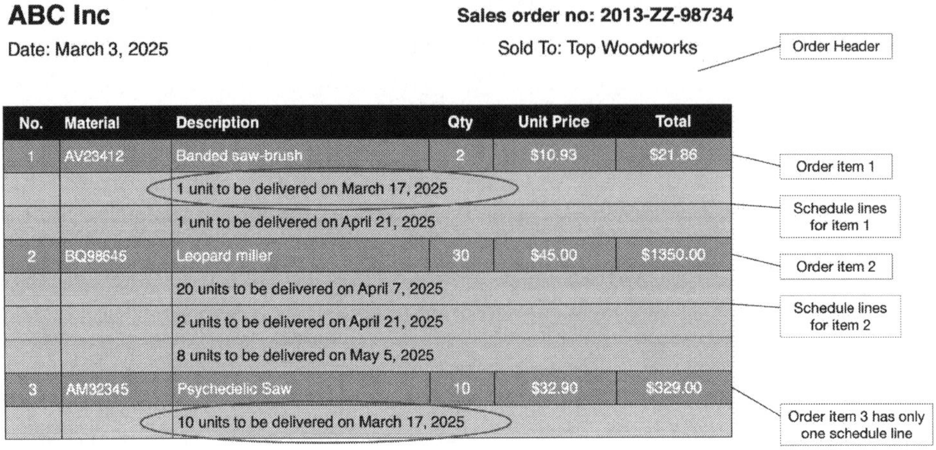

Figure 9.13: Sales Order Schedule Lines

Backorder Processing (BOP)

As you can see, it is possible to split an item in a sales order into separate shipments. This normally occurs when either or both, the requested quantity and/or the requested shipping date cannot be confirmed. This means we are unable to completely fulfill the customer's request on time. We refer to this as Backorder Processing (BOP). Backorder processing involves a strategic approach. Whether we agree with this or not, the truth of the matter is some customers are more valuable than others. Imagine we have two customers, Customer A and Customer B. Customer A has been a longstanding customer, orders from us regularly, and does over $500,000 of business with our company each year. Customer B only orders from us two or three times each year, with a total value of less than $1000. Obviously, it's very important for us to retain Customer A because of their loyalty and level of business. Customer B recently ordered 5 pieces of a product from us and when the availability check is performed, we can confirm all 5 pieces on the requested shipping date. Later, Customer A ordered 10 pieces of the same product. Unfortunately, the availability check results in the confirmation of only 6 of the 10 pieces to be shipped when requested. As a result, BOP needs to take place. Naturally, we want to retain Customer A, so the most logical thing to do is to ensure Customer A receives the 10 pieces they requested. To do this, we may need to take 4 pieces of that product from Customer B and give them to Customer A. We will then have to inform Customer B that 4 pieces of what they requested are now on backorder and we will deliver them at a future date. This is a very simplified view of how BOP works, but it does give us a glimpse into how SAP supports various

BOP strategies. Figure 9.14 explains the different BOP strategies available within SAP S/4HANA.

Win

- Quantities and dates for these customers will always be confirmed.

Gain

- These customers should keep what has already been confirmed. However, it's possible for them to improve.

Redistribute

- Those customers could improve confirmed quantities and dates, but could also lose and do worse.

Fill

- Fill customers will not improve, but are likely to lose confirmed quantities.

Lose

- These customers will lose everything in order to confirm quantities for other customers.
- Lose customers are considered Priority 1 because we take from this customer first in order to satisfy position of others.

Figure 9.14: BOP Strategies

It is also possible to combine items from different sales orders into a single outbound delivery document. For this to be possible, the following must be true for the items in the sales orders:

- Shipping points are the same
- Ship-to Party is the same
- Schedule lines (shipping dates) are the same

Each outbound delivery document is created for a single shipping point. The outbound delivery will also contain information regarding the Ship-to Party. Figure 9.15 depicts the structure of the outbound delivery document. You can see there is data in the Header of the document as well as data in the Items section. The Picking tab in the Item section contains the material to be shipped, the Delivery Quantity, and the Plant. These values are copied from the items and their confirmed quantity in the schedule line of the sales order. The Storage Location can also be copied over it existed in the sales order. Otherwise it is entered manually. The Plant/Storage Location combination is important as the SAP. S44HANA system uses that combination to see if a Warehouse Number has been assigned. If so, then the Pick Quantity cannot be entered manually. If WM is being used, then a Transfer Order is created in WM. Once picking is confirmed on the Transfer Order (TO), the Pick Quantity will copy over from the TO. Figure 9.16 shows the Pick Quantity field with the value copied from the TO

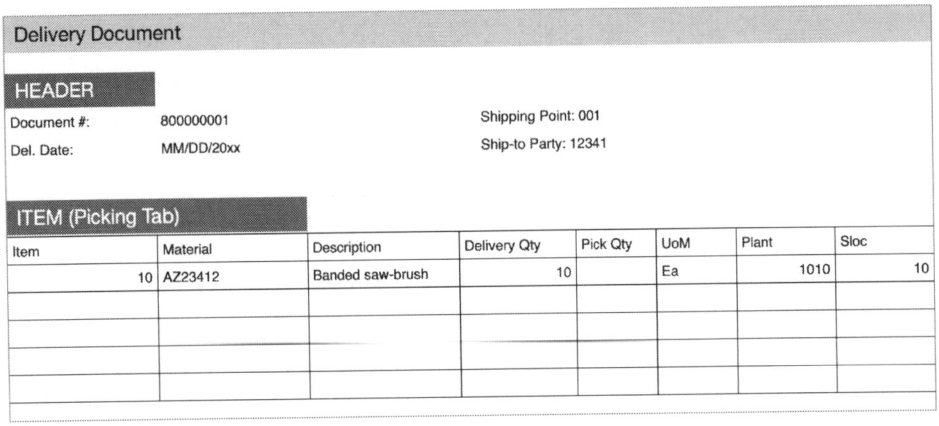

Delivery Document

HEADER

Document #: 800000001

Del. Date: MM/DD/20xx

Shipping Point: 001

Ship-to Party: 12341

ITEM (Picking Tab)

Item	Material	Description	Delivery Qty	Pick Qty	UoM	Plant	Sloc
10	AZ23412	Banded saw-brush	10		Ea	1010	10

Figure 9.15: Outbound Delivery Document Before Picking in WM

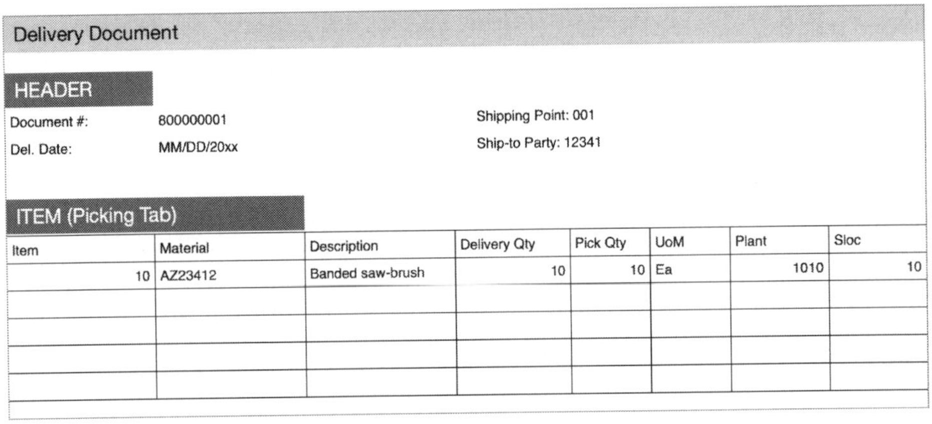

Delivery Document

HEADER

Document #: 800000001

Del. Date: MM/DD/20xx

Shipping Point: 001

Ship-to Party: 12341

ITEM (Picking Tab)

Item	Material	Description	Delivery Qty	Pick Qty	UoM	Plant	Sloc
10	AZ23412	Banded saw-brush	10	10	Ea	1010	10

Figure 9.16: Outbound Delivery Document After Picking in WM

As noted earlier, the Pick Quantity value must be manually entered if a Warehouse Number is not linked to the Plant/Storage Location combination.

If Extended Warehouse Management (EWM) is in use, the Picking and the Goods Issue occur in EWM. The result is the updating of the outbound delivery document to show that the materials have not only been picked but have been issued from inventory. As a reminder of how EWM processes outbound logistics, see Figure 9.17.

Extended Warehouse Management uses Warehouse Tasks to perform the picking step. Warehouse tasks in EWM are also used to perform putaways, internal material movements, goods receipts, and goods issues.

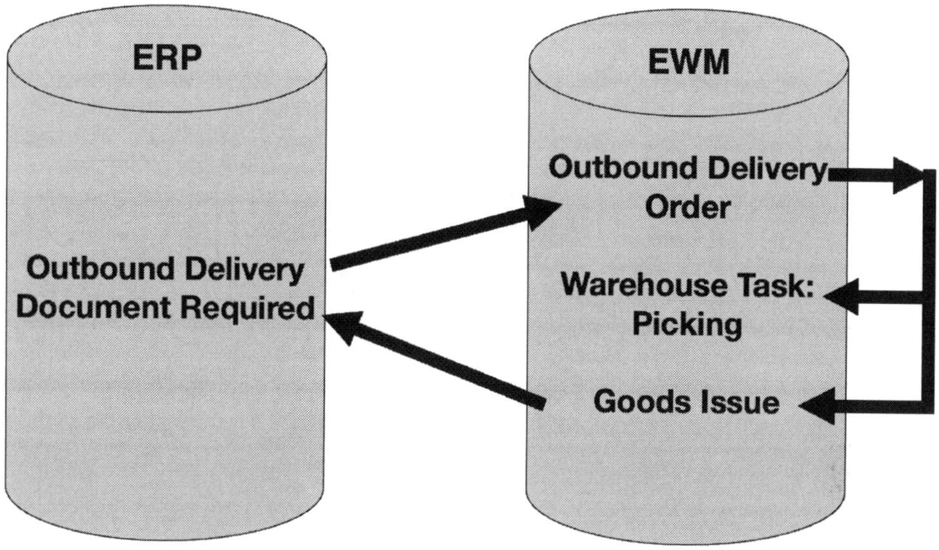

Figure 9.17: Extended Warehouse Management - Outbound Processing (Replica of Figure 7.10)

From a warehouse perspective, it's more than likely there will be several outbound delivery documents requiring items to be picked. SAP S/4HANA uses worklists to create efficiencies and support the collective processing of multiple documents. In the warehouse, this worklist is called a pick list. Other worklists exist in the S/4HANA system. The pick list is not the only worklist in this process. Examples of worklists in the sales process include: Delivery lists, pick lists, and billing due lists (Figure 9.18).

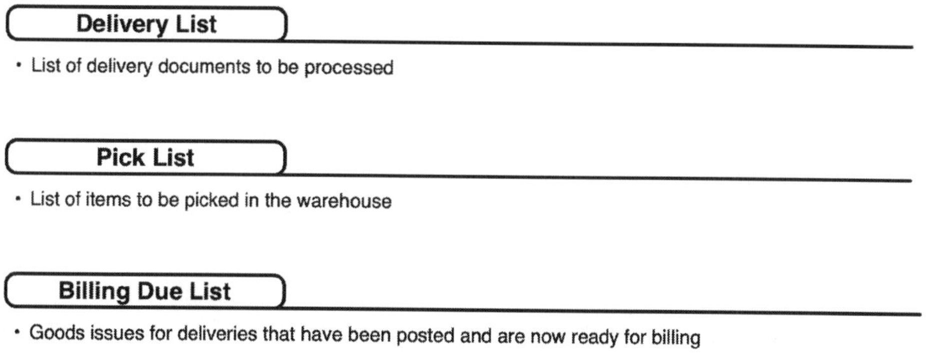

Figure 9.18: Worklists in Sales

As the outbound delivery document is being processed, it is possible to once again use Output master data to send correspondence to the customer. This could include confirmation for shipment (delivery notes) or confirmations of changes in status of the delivery.

Goods Issue

In the sales process, the Goods Issue posting occurs with reference to the Outbound Delivery document (the last "P" - post goods issue). Keep in mind, the status of the sales order may be "Completed", and the Outbound Delivery document is now the document that manages the logistics steps. If EWM is in use, the Goods Issue is posted in EWM from within the Outbound Delivery Order (Figure 9.17).

The quantity issued during this step comes from the "pick" quantity in the outbound delivery document. The company can only issue a quantity that has been picked from the warehouse. The goods issue is the first step in the process that has a financial accounting impact. When materials are issued, they are taken from inventory which will have an impact in the balance sheet in the GL as well as a posting to the Cost of Goods Sold account. All goods movements use the material price for valuation. Figure 9.19 shows what the postings in the GL will look like.

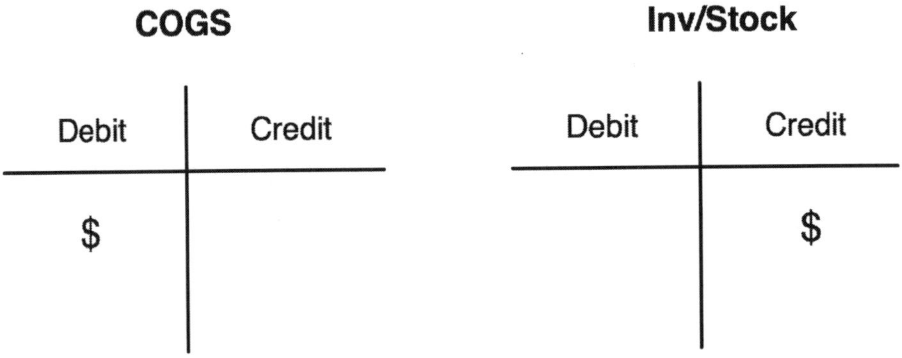

Figure 9.19: Goods Issue - GL Postings

As a result of the goods issue posting, a Material document and a Financial Accounting document FI Doc are created by the system (Material Doc is always generated for a goods movement). Since the COGS account is a Primary Cost/ Revenue Account type, there will also be an impact in the Controlling module and a CO document will be created in parallel (Figure 9.20). All COGS postings from the sales process will go to a Profitability Segment in COPA (PSG). Additionally, a Material

Ledger document is also generated to track the value of the material at the time of the posting

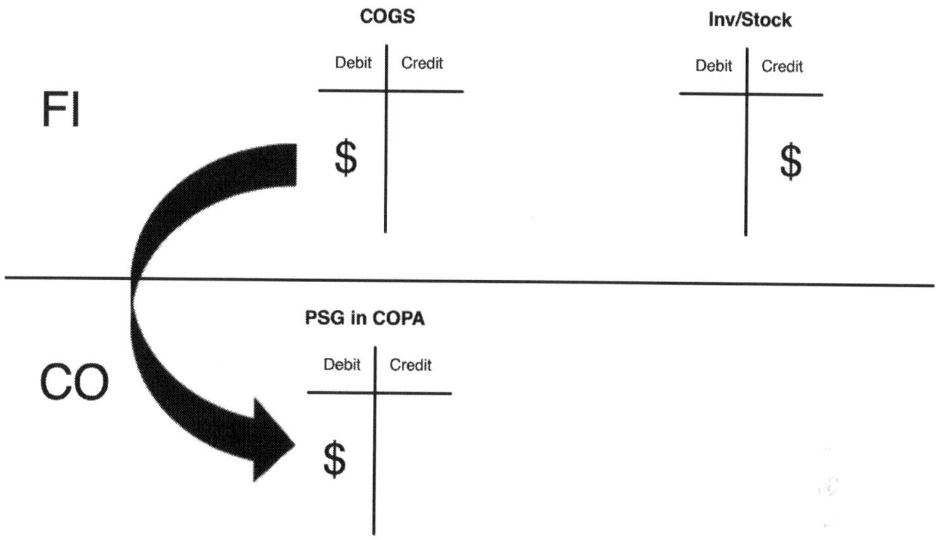

Figure 9.20: Goods Issue - GL Postings CO Impact

There are additional impacts of the Goods Issue posting. At the time of goods issue, the material master record is updated. The quantity and value in the Accounting view are updated and consumption statistics are also posted to the material master. The Billing Due list is also updated, indicating the delivered quantity can now be billed to the customer (Figure 9.21).

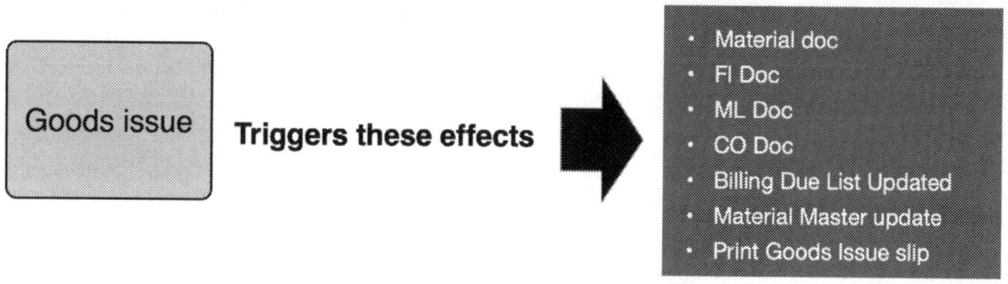

Figure 9.21: Effects of the Goods Issue

Billing

As a result of the goods issue, the delivery is ready for billing. The company will invoice the customer for the quantity issued. The goods issue quantity is stored in the outbound delivery document. Therefore, the billing document is created with reference to the outbound delivery. There is significant relevance to quantities in the Lead-to-Cash process. Figure 9.22 demonstrates important quantities, the documents in which those quantities are recorded, and their relationship to one another.

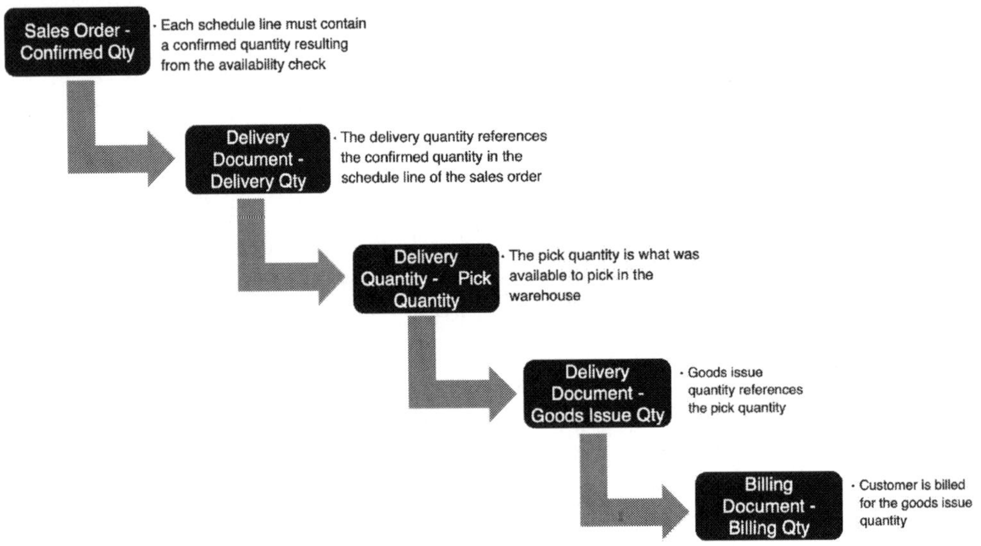

Figure 9.22: Document Quantities

As we noted, it is possible to perform collective billing from the Billing Due list. Optionally, SAP customers can bill individually. Billing in SAP S/4HANA provides the following functionalities:

- Creation of invoices for goods sold or for services
- Transfer of the sales process to accounting for collecting receivables
- Posting customer credit or debit memos
- Cancelling previous billing documents.

Our focus in this section will be on the creation of invoices for customers and the transferring of the process to accounting for collecting receivables from the customer. The result of billing is the creation of a SD Billing document. Like other documents in SAP, the billing document contains a Header. The Header has information regarding the document date and the Payer. Additionally, the billing document has items. The items include the products or services that were billed as well as their quantities. When the billing document is created, it must be sent to the customer. SAP S/4HANA has enhanced output capabilities for billing in SD. The output in this case represents the physical invoice sent to the customer.

Like the creation of outbound delivery documents, it is also possible to combine multiple deliveries to create a single billing document. However, there are criteria which must be met in order to do this.

- Payer must be the same
- Destination country must be the same
- Billing dates must be the same

Once the billing document is created, this triggers the transfer of the process to financial accounting and ends the logistics steps. As a result, the delivery document status is now "Completed". Other integration occurs with the creation of the billing document. A FI document is created in the background showing the receivable from the customer and a posting to revenue. Figure 9.23 shows the financial accounting impact of billing. During billing, a posting is made directly to the customer subledger account. As we learned in financial accounting, it is not possible to post directly to a reconciliation account. The only way to update a reconciliation account is via a subledger account.

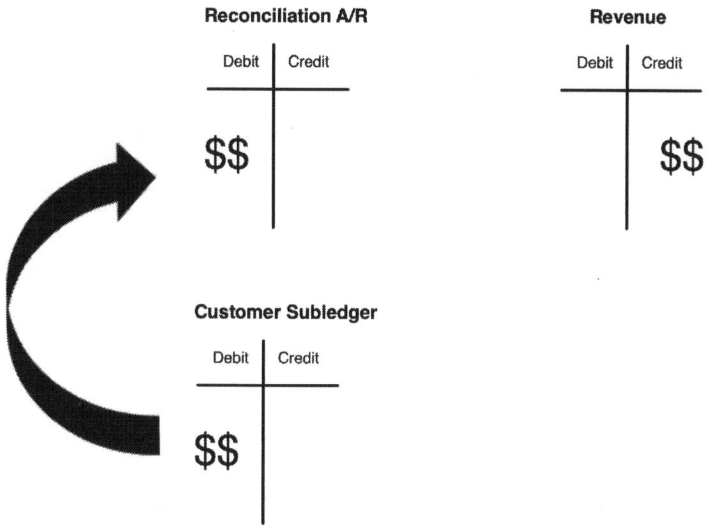

Figure 9.23: Financial Accounting Impacts of Billing

As a result of billing, an open item is created in the customer subledger account. This simply means the customer subledger account does not have a balance of zero. In short, the customer owes us the amount billed. Additionally, there is a posting to the Revenue account, which is a Primary Cost/Revenue account. This posting will result in an update in Controlling as revenue will also post to a Profitability Segment in COPA.

Postings to the Profitability Segment occur during the Goods Issue and Billing. As you can see, the values are likely to be different (though that is not always the case). At the time of goods issue, the posting to COGS and the PSG are valued at the material price. Whereas at the time of billing, the postings to Revenue and the PSG are valued at the sales price. The difference is shown as the profit in the PSG. The posting to the PSG at the time of billing will be recorded in a CO document (Figure 9.24).

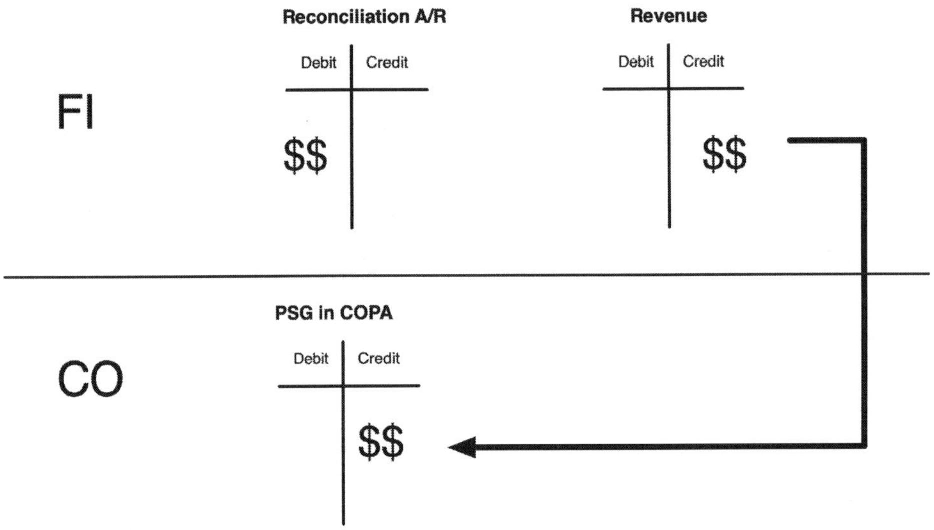

Figure 9.24: Controlling Impacts of Billing

The final impact of billing is an update to the customer's line of credit. When the customer is billed, it will reduce the customer's available credit by the amount billed. The customer credit will be awarded back during the last step in the process, which is the receipt of the customer payment. Figure 9.25 shows all the effects of billing.

Figure 9.25: Effects of Billing

Cash

The last step is the receipt of payment from the customer, completing the Lead-to-Cash process. This step represents the processing of the customer payment to clear the open item in their subledger account. Payment takes place in the FI module and is not considered a logistics step in the process. As we noted above, at the time of payment customer credit is again updated and a FI document will be created to record the transaction (Figure 9.26).

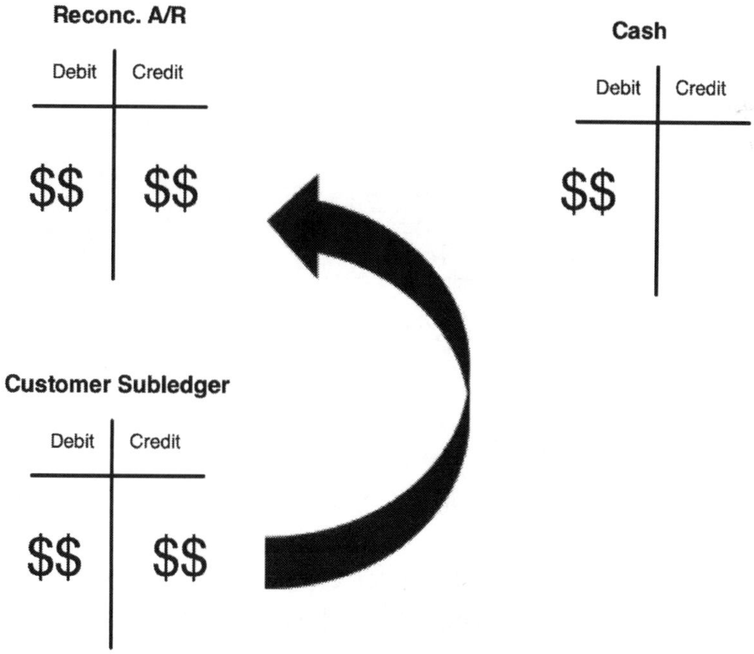

Figure 9.26: Payment

From the image above, we can see the payment clearing the open item in the customer subledger account and simultaneously updating the reconciliation account for receivables in the GL. The posting to the subledger account is offset by the debit to the cash account in the Balance Sheet.

The payment process can be completed manually or using an automatic payment program.

Document Flow

As we saw earlier when we addressed SAP Sales Cloud, there is also a Document Flow in SAP S/4HANA. Throughout the entire process, documents are generated, and their statuses can be tracked and viewed using the Document Flow. The Document Flow can be accessed from the following: Sales Order, Outbound Delivery Document, and Billing Document.

The Document Flow is presented as an indented structure, displaying the relationships and statuses of each document created in the process. An example can be seen in Figure 9.27.

Document Flow		
Customer:	**ABC**	
Document	**Doc #**	**Status**
Inquiry	100000001	Completed
Sales Order	3002	Completed
Outbound Delivery	80000002	Completed
TO WH Picking	12	Completed
GI Mat. Doc	15000001	Completed
Billing Doc	900003	Completed
Accounting Doc	190000001	Cleared

Figure 9.27: Document Flow

Sales and Profitability

In this section we are going to look at profitability. We saw integration with Profitability Analysis during the Goods Issue and Billing steps in the Sales Process. We now want to take a deeper dive into what that means. We are also going to look at profitability at a Profit Center. Recall from the chapter on Management Accounting that Profit Centers are always a statistical object in SAP. To put this in perspective, let's review the areas within Controlling to see where Profitability Analysis and Profit Center

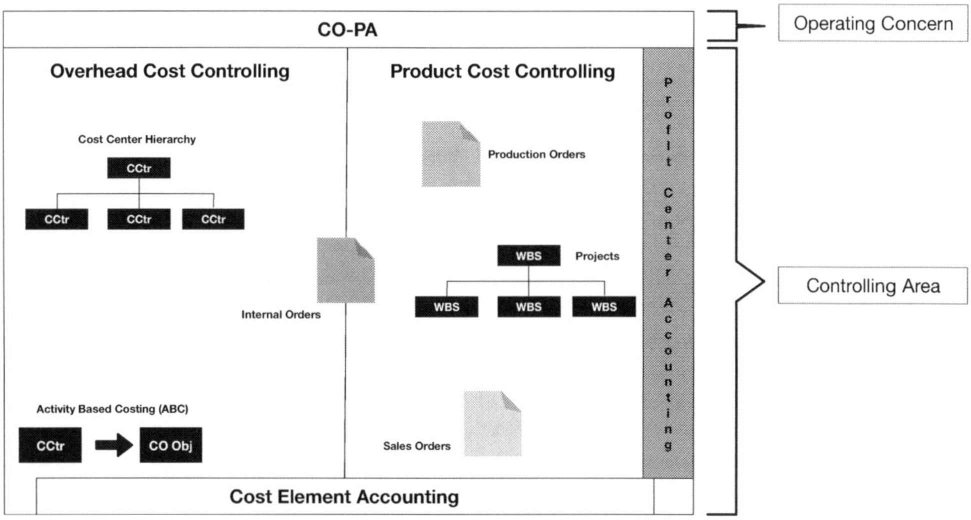

Accounting fall in the overall scheme of CO (Figure 9.28)

Figure 9.28: Areas Within CO (Replica of Figure 4.4)

Profitability Analysis (CO-PA) measures profitability of external market segments, also known as profitability segments. This is information often used by market analysts, strategists, and planners in the enterprise. CO-PA is performed in the Operating Concern organizational level.

Profitability Analysis

Profitability segments are composed of two or more characteristics. Examples of such characteristics include Product, Customer, Country, Sales Organization, Sales Rep, and others. While characteristics make up a profitability segment, key figures are used as measurements for profitability. Key figures include such things as Revenue, Material Costs, and Quantities.

A typical CO-PA scenario would be to analyze the profit of products by customer and country. In this scenario, products, customers, and country define the profitability segment. Key figures such as revenue and cost are used to calculate profit margin.

In CO-PA, profit can be viewed on a Costing-Base or Accounting-Base.

- **Costing-Based CO-PA**
  - Cost of Gods Sold and Revenue are posted simultaneously at the time of billing
- **Accounting-Based CO-PA**
  - Cost of Goods Sold is posted at the time of Goods Issue and Revenue is posted at the time of Billing

Postings to Profitability Analysis can come from a variety of areas within SAP S4HANA. Though we have been discussing the sales process in this chapter, it is important to note that CO-PA can receive cost posting from settlements, overhead costs, assessments, and other forms of allocations.

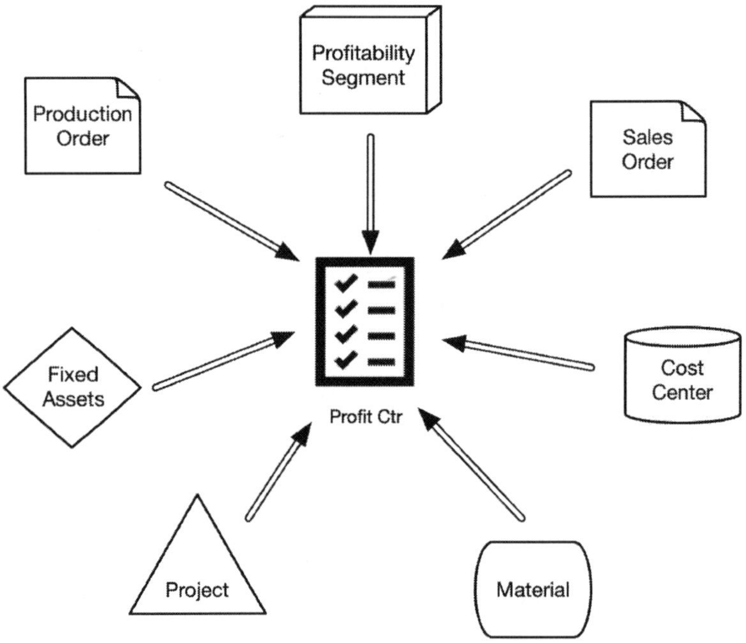

Figure 9.29: Profit Center Integration

Profit Centers

Profit Centers are ALWAYS statistical cost objects in CO. Profit Centers are used to manage costs and revenues for internal areas of responsibility. They can also be used to manage things like return on investment (ROI). Because they are statistical, profit centers receive only information about costs and revenues for which it is responsible. Various objects can be linked to profit centers and these linkages represent how profit centers get their statistical information. From a sales perspective, a sales order and a material can be linked to a profit center. Figure 9.29 shows examples of objects that can send statistical postings to a Profit Center.

Transportation Management

SAP S/4HANA Transportation Management (SAP TM) is a solution to support and manage all aspects of physically transporting materials. SAP TM is available as an embedded solution with SAP S/4HANA. SAP TM is also tightly integrated with EWM as EWM manages more than just the physical warehouse.

From a sales perspective, SAP TM provides SAP customers with better planning and cost-effective management for shipping their products. Figure 9.30 shows the basic steps in SAP TM.

Figure 9.30: Transportation Management

Order Management

Since SAP TM is a solution to support the physical transportation of goods, it can impact more than sales. Various business processes have transportation requirements. Some of those requirements supported by SAP TM include:

- Sales Orders
- Purchase Orders
- Stock Transport Orders
- Returns
- Scheduling Agreements
- Deliveries (Inbound/Outbound)

Regarding the sales process, the Outbound Delivery document managed the "3 P's" (Pick, Pack, and Post). SAP TM provides SAP customer with advanced packing techniques for shipping to create efficiencies while minimizing costs and packing materials.

Transportation Planning

The goal of Transportation Planning is to make the best use of available resources for transportation. Automated planning is available to help optimize resources, freight handling, and transportation routes. An additional capability in Transportation Planning is Driver Management. Driver Management allows SAP customers to manage transportation drivers as Business Partners to help with planning of schedules and availability.

Transportation Execution

Transportation Execution integrates with Extended Warehouse Management to provide support for the following:

- Planning and Execution of Order
- Planning and Execution of Drivers
- Cost Settlement capabilities
- Planning of Arrivals and Departures in EWM

Freight Costing and Settlement

Freight Costing and Settlement in SAP TM allow for automated cost calculations to reduce errors during settlement of costs. Its goal is to enhance accuracies of costs and allocations during transportation.

Analytics and Reporting

With SAP TM embedded in SAP S/4HANA, SAP customers get immediate access to real-time analytics. Dashboards for SAP TM are also available to provide users with the ability to improve response times and planning.

Sales and Distribution Summary

After completing this chapter, you should have a solid understanding of the organizational levels and master data required to support the Lead-to-Cash process in SAP.

The “best-practice" scenario includes the following steps: Master Data, Pre-sales Activities, Order Processing, Deliver Products, Billing, and Cash. You should not only understand the correct sequence but be able to identify the impacts of each step. Keep in mind, we spent a good deal of time going over the Pre-sales Activities and the integration between SAP S/4HANA and SAP Sales Cloud. The documents created during the sales process are also tracked in the Document Flow within both S/4HANA and SAP Sales Cloud. Documents such as Quotations and Sales Orders can be created in either solution, then replicated in the other via the SAP Business Technology Platform (BTP). The main advantage of the integration of these documents between the two solutions is to provide the sales team with the capability of managing all aspects of the Lead-to-Cash process from within SAP Sales Cloud.

We also revisited profitability impacts from the sales process. You should understand what a Profitability Segment is in CO-PA and the objects in SAP that can send information to Profit Centers.

Finally, we were introduced to SAP Transportation Management. SAP TM is now embedded in SAP S/4HANA and is tightly integrated with Extended Warehouse Management. There are several steps in SAP TM that were discussed, beginning with Order Management and concluding with Analytics and Reporting.

Chapter 10: Enterprise Asset Management

The Enterprise Asset Management (EAM) function entails the physical maintenance of fixed assets in an enterprise. In this chapter, our primary focus will be on Plant Maintenance. As we will see, this physical maintenance could result from breakdowns or as an effort to prevent breakdowns of these fixed assets. We will not discuss other functions within EAM, though it is worth noting, EAM is much broader that Plant Maintenance and can be used to manage the entire lifecycle of such assets.

In this chapter we will also revisit Asset Accounting since there is direct integration between these two modules. We will spend a little time detailing how this integration occurs.

Like the chapters prior, it will be essential to be able to identify the various organizational levels, master data and process steps associated with EAM.

Organizational Levels/Enterprise Structure

Enterprise Asset Management (EAM) supports many logistics functions in SAP S4HANA. As such, similar organizational levels required for all logistics processes also apply in EAM (Figure 10.1). In EAM our primary focus will be on the Plant organizational level. Within Enterprise Asset Management (EAM), Plant Maintenance is the business process that involves the physical management of assets owned by the enterprise. As such, we need to identify the various roles the Plant serves in the maintenance process.

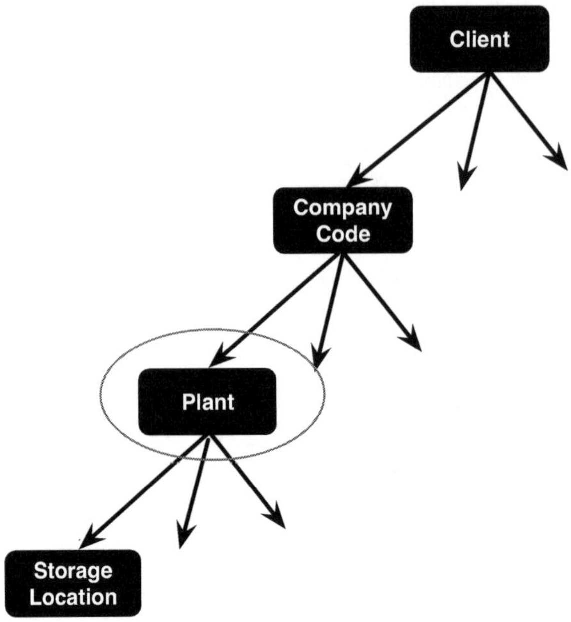

Figure 10.1: Logistics Organizational Levels

In Plant Maintenance, a plant is a "logistics" plant. As the logistics plant, it provides the same functionality as it does in every logistics module. For instance, materials used in the maintenance process are maintained in the plant. Purchasing for services and items needed in the process is also accomplished through the plant. These are logistics related and are handled within the plant.

In addition to these logistics items, plants themselves require maintenance. As an example, if a production facility is designated as a plant, there will obviously be maintenance requirements over time in that plant. It could be scheduled maintenance or maintenance required as a result of breakdowns. A plant requiring maintenance is designated as a "Maintenance Plant".

Finally, the process of performing maintenance must be planned. When maintenance is required, the planning of the maintenance is accomplished via a plant (or plants) designated as "Maintenance Planning Plants". Maintenance Planning Plants are responsible for the planning of maintenance of one or several other Maintenance Plants. It is possible that a Maintenance Plant is also a Maintenance Planning Plant. There are many possibilities for how an enterprise may configure plant maintenance to support their business needs. However, it is more important for you to be able to identify the differences between the roles a plant serves in the maintenance process.

Another organizational level in Plant Maintenance is the Planner Group. A Planner Group represents an individual or a group of individuals whose responsibility it is to plan maintenance. A Planner Group belongs within a Maintenance Planning Plant. Figure 10.2 provides a graphical representation of these concepts.

Logistics Plants

- Performing logistics functions such as procurement, inventory management, etc.

Maintenance Plant

- Plant with maintenance requirements
- Can be many Maintenance Plants

Maintenance Planning Plant

- Planning of maintenance is performed here
- Can be several Maintenance Planning Plants
- Planner Groups exist in Maintenance Planning Plants

Figure 10.2: Role of Plants in Plant Maintenance

Master Data

There are several master data required in Plant Maintenance. We will begin with a discussion on Work Centers, as that is master data with which we have familiarity. After addressing work centers in Plant Maintenance, we will move on to Technical Objects (of which there are three). Finally, we will see how the master data provides integration between Enterprise Asset Management and Asset Accounting.

Work Centers

Work Centers are also master data in Materials Planning and Manufacturing Execution. Work centers provide some essential functionality. They provide information on capacities, scheduling, and costs.

Looking at Figure 10.3, we can see many similarities to what has already been discussed regarding work centers in production. The difference in this case is that work centers are not used to produce products, but rather to repair assets. As you can see, a work center in Plant Maintenance is used for scheduling purposes. Scheduling is contingent on the capacity requirements which stem from operations planned on maintenance orders, not operations from a production routing. Work center capacities are derived from people, machines, or combinations thereof. It is especially important to be reminded, that work centers are associated with a cost center and activity types. These combinations are used to derive activity prices for planning and posting of costs on maintenance orders.

Work Center		
Scheduling • Formulas for scheduling production based on operations requirements in maintenance orders	Capacities • Capacity category (Labor/Machine) • Formulas for calculating available capacity • Capacity usually measured in time contingent on hours of operation available, utilisation, breaks, and number of people/ machines	Costing • Assigned to a cost center • Assigned valid activity types

Figure 10.3: Work Centers in Plant Maintenance (Replica of Figure 8.8)

With regards to the maintenance process, the work center serves several purposes:

1. Main work center for a technical object (master data)
2. Main work center for a maintenance order
3. Work center in a task list header
4. Planned work center for an operation in a maintenance order
5. Performing work center for an operation in a maintenance order

Technical Objects

There are three (3) Technical Objects used in Plant Maintenance: Functional Locations, Equipment, and Assemblies (BOMs).

Technical Objects: Assemblies: (BOMs)

Assemblies are simply another term for Bill of Materials. In manufacturing, BOMs were master data that provided information on the components and quantities required to produce a product. In maintenance, the objectives are a bit different. Instead of supporting the producing of a product, BOMs provide a structured list of components which help plan parts for the maintenance of an asset. BOMs also provide the structure of an asset, so parts can be planned for inventory and for operations in a maintenance order. When creating a BOM for maintenance, it is required to assign the BOM a usage category specific for maintenance. Figure 10.4 describes the roles BOMs play in Plant Maintenance.

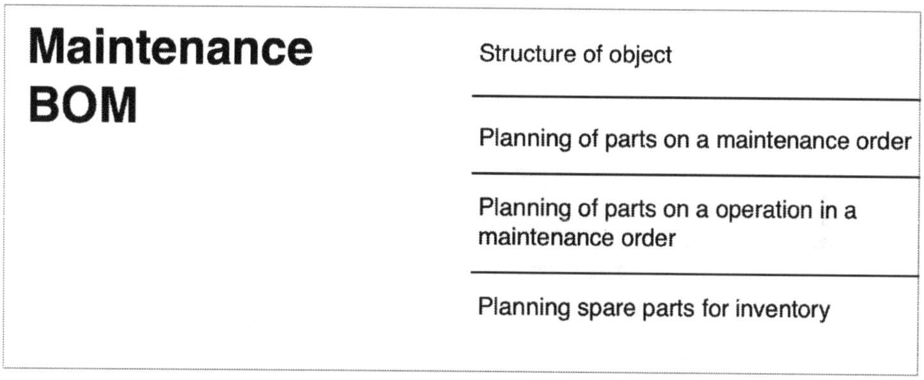

Figure 10.4: Bill of Materials in Plant Maintenance

There are three basic types of BOMs used in Plant Maintenance:

1. Functional Location BOMs
2. Equipment BOMs
3. Material BOMs

Further discussions regarding functional locations and equipment will follow. But we are already aware of material BOMs. Material BOMs are the same as BOMs used in manufacturing of a material, except in the case of Plant Maintenance, its usage is for maintenance.

Technical Objects: Functional Locations

In Plant Maintenance, Functional Locations are master data used to describe what SAP calls the technical system within a plant. Functional Locations are required when users want to gather the following for a technical system:

- Structure of locations

- Recording of maintenance tasks
- Recording of usage over time
- Recording of conditions over time (physical)
- Monitoring of costs for certain locations
- Monitoring of how conditions may affect installed equipment

Functional locations are structured in a hierarchy and its structure can be designed based on one of three criteria. Functional locations can be structured spatially, functionally, or technically (Figure 10.5).

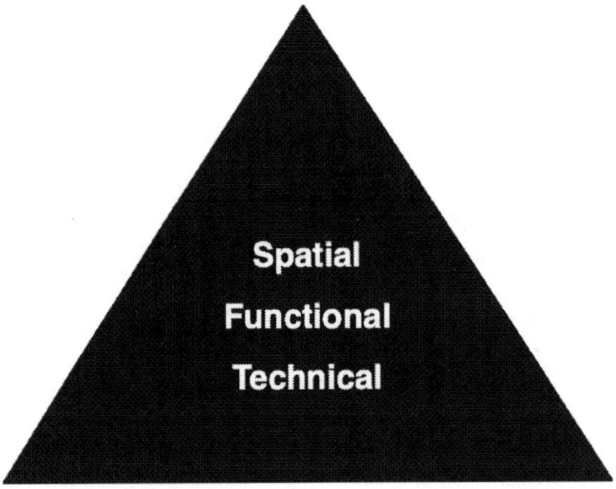

Figure 10.5: Criteria for Structuring Functional Locations

If the functional locations are hierarchically structured based on spatial representation of the plant, it generally involves dissecting the plant into floors, rooms, etc. For instance, a building could be structured based on how many floors there are, the corridors on each floor, and the rooms on each corridor. Each level of granularity would represent a hierarchy level in the structure depicted in Figure 10.6.

Functional locations designed based on functional criteria would produce a different result. For instance, the hierarchy level below the building could be functional departments, such as Accounting, Sales and Marketing, and Administrative. The next level may define on which floor(s) those functional departments exist. Technical criteria are often used in manufacturing facilities or processing facilities. For example, an automobile manufacturing plant may design the functional location based on technical areas within that facility (I.e. wiring, wheel installation, painting, etc.). As you can see, there are several ways in which the functional locations can be designed. However, they are mutually exclusive for the plant. So, whatever criteria is selected, then the

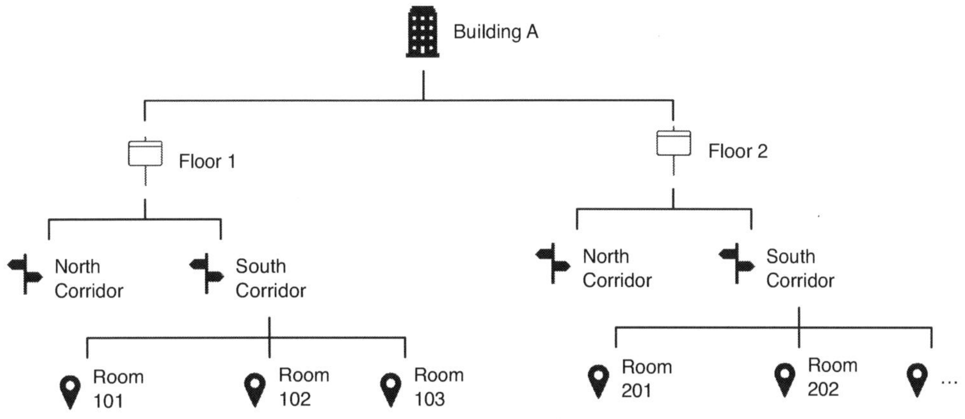

entire hierarchy is designed using that criterion.

Figure 10.6: Functional Location Hierarchy

Functional locations are described using a Structure Indicator. The Structure Indicator has two components: Number of hierarchy levels and a coding mask. If we continue with our example using spatial criteria from Figure 10.6, assuming this represents the entire structure, there would be a total of four hierarchy levels from the building down through the rooms. The next step is to assign a coding mask (or coding template) to the hierarchy. The characters in the coding mask can be alpha (A), numeric (#), or alpha numeric (X).

The highest level in the hierarchy of our example is the building itself. Suppose we assign that level an alpha value, such as "A" in the example. The next level (floors) could get a two-digit numeric value assigned to it. So, Floor 1 could be assigned the value "01", Floor 2, "02", and so on. The corridors (assuming there are only a north and south corridor could be assigned a single digit alpha value, "N" or "S". Finally, each room could be assigned a three-digit alpha-numeric value. Room 101 would simply be assigned, "101".

The coding mask for the Structure Indicator would therefore be: "A-##-A-XXX". Applying the coding mask to our example would produce the following in Figure10.7.

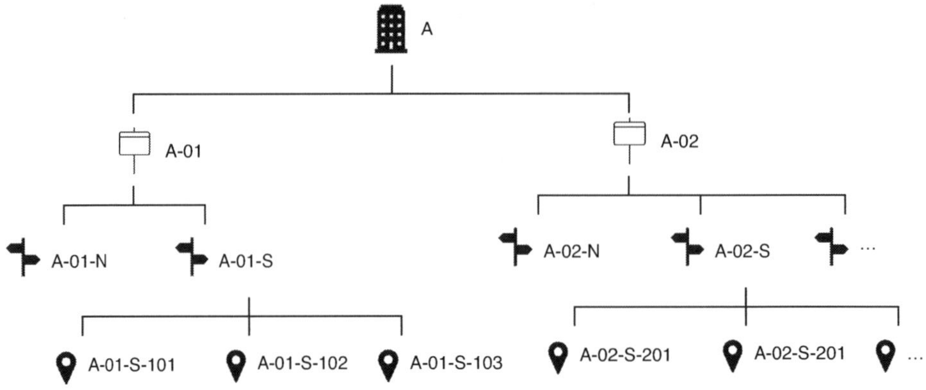

Figure 10.7: Functional Location - Structure Indicator

When creating the master data for a functional location, it is created using the views shown in Figure 10.8.

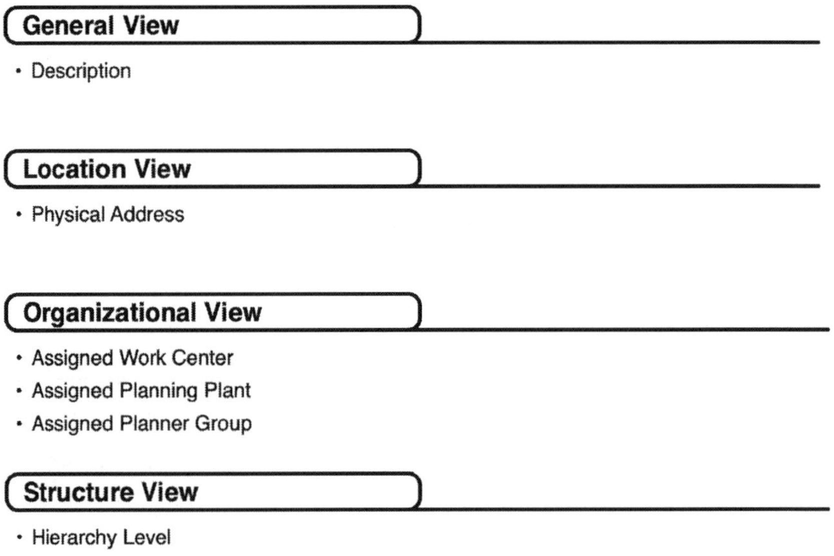

Figure 10.8: Functional Location Master Data Views

Additional information may also be maintained in the functional location master record. It is possible to keep information regarding measurements and counter readings, permits, equipment usage, and links to documents and text.

In the previous section, we introduced the three types of BOMs, one of which is the Functional Location BOM. A Functional Location BOM is simply a BOM that provides the structure of a functional location. For instance, a room in our functional location example has a structure. There are certain types of light bulbs, carpeting, color of paint, ceiling tiles, and other things that may make up the construct of the room. The Functional Location BOM assists the planner groups in knowing what materials to plan when the room requires maintenance.

Technical Objects: Equipments

Equipment is the third technical object used in Plant Maintenance. Equipment are identified as individual objects which require maintenance. Just as there were reasons for maintaining functional locations, there are also specific reasons to maintain equipment master data in a plant.

- Recording of usage of an object over time
- Maintaining data for an object
- Monitoring of maintenance costs for an object
- Monitoring usage of an object in a functional location
- Manage planning and unplanned breakdown and maintenance of an object

The master record of equipment is very similar to functional location master data. The same views exist, but some of the data differs (Figure 10.9).

General View

- Description
- Manufacturer's data

Location View

- Physical Address

Organizational View

- Associated Asset Master Record
- Assigned Work Center
- Assigned Planning Plant
- Assigned Planner Group

Structure View

- Functional Location where installed
- Construction Type

Figure 10.9: Equipment Master Data Views

Equipment, like materials, can also be assigned a serial number. Serialization of equipment allows for inventory functions for equipment and support tracking of equipment by status. This means being able to identify which equipment are new, used, refurbished, or damaged as well as processing goods movements in and out of service and storage.

In the next section, we are going to address the integration of the equipment master record with the asset master record in Financial Accounting. For now, let's look at some of the other data maintained in the equipment master record. In particular, let's focus on the Structure view. It is possible for equipment to be installed in a functional location. If equipment is installed in a functional location, the functional location must be defined in the Structure view. In addition to this, we discussed material BOMs as possible examples of BOMs in Plant Maintenance. If a material BOM is being used to structure a piece of equipment, you must enter the Material Number in the Construction Type field.

If a Material BOM is not being used, then the equipment is managed using an Equipment BOM, which is a BOM unique for that specific piece of equipment.

Master Data Synchronization

There is immediate integration between equipment in EAM and fixed assets in Financial Accounting-Asset Accounting (FI-AA). Recall, EAM is the module used for the physical management of assets. FI-AA is the module used for the financial management of those same assets. In Chapter 3 of this book, we discussed the financial management of fixed assets, but we didn't go into very much detail about the physical maintenance of those assets. From an integration perspective, it makes sense to ensure that for every asset, there exists an equipment master record. The concept of ensuring this occurs is called master data synchronization. It is bi-directional integration. This means that whenever an asset master record is created in financial accounting, an equipment master record is simultaneously created in Enterprise Asset Management, and vice versa. So, if an equipment master record is created in EAM, an asset master record is created in parallel in FI.

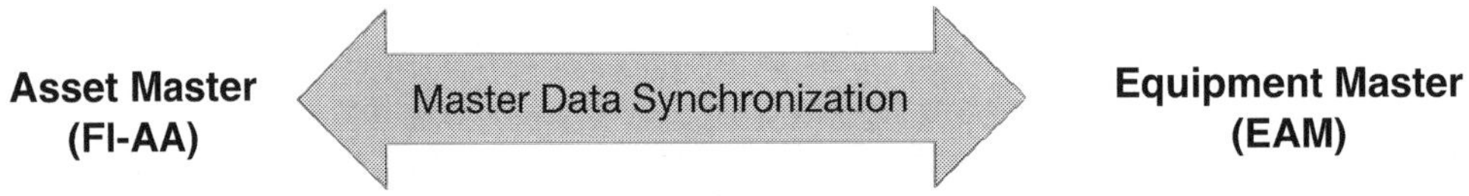

Figure 10.10: Master Data Synchronization

In Chapter 3, we discussed various methods for Asset Acquisition. However, at that time we didn't have the knowledge of Order-Related Cost Object Controlling because we had not yet covered the Controlling module. Internal Orders follow the Order-Related Cost Objected Controlling steps. In Chapter 4, we identified different types of Internal Orders. One example of an Internal Order was an Investment Order. An Investment Order is a form of Internal Order where the costs of the order will be settled to an Asset account. Therefore, it is possible to acquire an asset with an internal order. To make that possible, an asset master record must first be created (an equipment master record in EAM is created in parallel) (Figure 10.10). When the internal order is settled to the asset, that becomes the acquisition value of the asset as well as the acquisition value of the equipment master record (Figure 10.11).

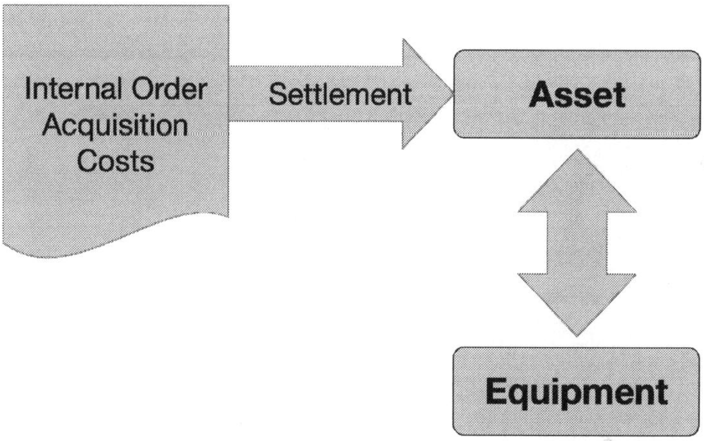

Figure 10.11: Asset Acquisition with Internal Order

As a last note to this section, it is also possible to assign serial numbers to a material to create equipment master data. When a serial number is assigned to a material, it can be managed as an autonomous object for which maintenance can be performed.

Transactions

When is Maintenance Performed?

Maintenance occurs for many reasons. The most notable is to repair something that has broken down or been damaged. We refer to this as "Corrective Maintenance". This means we are correcting an issue that has already occurred. Another reason for planning or performing maintenance is to prevent a break down. This is referred to as "Preventive Maintenance". This is something we do regularly where we live. We frequently clean our houses or apartments. We wash windows, clean floors and plumbing fixtures in the bathrooms etc. The purpose of this is to maintain these things in a manner which will prevent them from breaking down or at the very least, make them last longer. Another option for planning or performing maintenance is "Condition-based Maintenance". In this case we plan and perform maintenance when a specific condition has been achieved. For example, you may decide to change the oil in your vehicle every five-thousand miles. When your vehicle has reaches the five-thousand mile threshold, it is time to change the oil. In a sense, this is done as a preventive measure, yet it's a unique a which differentiate it from "Preventive Maintenance". Finally, there is "Predictive Maintenance". The use of analytics (including SAP Analytics Cloud) can be used to predict when a breakdown might occur. This can be incredibly valuable, especially if it involves a piece of equipment essential to manufacturing. If that equipment fails in the middle of production, that could have serious consequences. The ability to use analytics to predict when the piece of equipment might breakdown affords the the company an opportunity to perform maintenance during a down time which would be far less impactful on the business.

Though all of these are incredibly important, our focus in this book is primarily on the integration of end-to-end business processes. Therefore, we will limit our discussions in this book to the Corrective Maintenance Process.

The Corrective Maintenance Process

We will use the steps in the Corrective Maintenance Process as outlined by SAP to demonstrate Plant Maintenance. In this section, we are going to demonstrate how the Corrective Maintenance Process mirrors Order-Related Cost Object Controlling. As was the case with manufacturing, there are some slight modifications to the basic steps as we know them.

The corrective maintenance process steps and their impacts can be found in Figure 10.12. We can see the sequence of steps in the process are triggered with the "Notification". The notification is a document in EAM that remains in effect and is updated throughout the entire process.

The second step in the corrective maintenance process is "Planning". Here the Planner Group creates the Maintenance Order and is actively engaged in planning of materials and operations to be performed on the order. Based on the system settings, there is integration with MM in this step because the system will generate reservations and/or purchase requisitions for materials and/or services required.

Corrective Maintenance Process	
1. Notification	
	a. EAM Document
	b. PM Integration
	c. Planner Grp Interaction
2. Planning	
	a. Maint. Order is Planned
	b. Planner Grp Interaction
	c. PM/MM Integration
3. Controlling	
	a. Maint. Order is Released
	b. Planner Grp Interaction
	c. PM/MM/HCM Integration
4. Execution	
	a. Goods Movements (Planned/Unplanned)
	b. Technician/Warehouse Interaction
	c. PM/MM/FI/CO Integration
4. Completion	
	a. Order Confirmation
	b. Order TECO
	c. Settlement
	d. Planner Grp/Acct Interaction
	e. PM/CO Integration

Figure 10.12: Corrective Maintenance Process

The third step is "Controlling". Here the Planner Group releases the order, changing its status which will allow the posting of costs to the maintenance order. By now, we hope that it is becoming obvious to you that the maintenance order is treated as an Order-Related Cost Object. Again, dependent on the system settings, reservations and/or purchase requisitions can also be created at the time of release of the order.

The step that follows Controlling is "Execution". During the execution phase, stock materials are issued to the order from inventory or non-stock items are received as a consumable to the order from purchasing. There will be a financial accounting and controlling impact of these movements. This step involves the technician and/or warehouse personnel during the issuing of materials from the inventory.

The final step in the corrective maintenance process is "Completion". Completion involves three parts: Confirmations, Technical Completion, and Settlement. The first part, confirmation, involves confirming actual times for actual work performed on the operations planned for maintenance. During confirmations, additional costs are posted to the maintenance order. These costs are most often related to labor costs allocated from the work centers but can also come from other sources. This is similar to what we saw during confirmation of operations on production orders as well as the confirmation of activities in projects. When the repairs are completed, the status of the order then needs to be changed from "Released" to "Technically Complete" or TECO. Setting the maintenance order to the status TECO is the second part included in the Completion of the order. The order settlement is the third part associated with Completion. This is not the first time we've covered settlement. For maintenance orders, this means bringing the balance of the maintenance order to zero by settling the cost to the responsible receivers(s). Keep in mind, settlement is a period-end activity, which means the order could be settled even if it is still in the process of being managed. Thus, settlement can occur before and/or after TECO.

Referring to the Notification, we again remind you that the notification document is being managed in parallel with the maintenance order. As each step in the process occurs and the order is saved, the notification document is also updated.

Now that we have a conceptual view of the process, it's a good time to demonstrated how the corrective maintenance process is really just another example of the Order-Related Cost Object Controlling Process.

As we can see from Figure 10.13, the Notification is the only step in the corrective maintenance process that has no parallel in Order-Related Cost Object Controlling. All the subsequent steps mirror one another. What does this mean for you? This means you already have a great foundation for understanding the process. You also already know what occurs during each step in Order-Related Cost Object Controlling, making it easier for you to identify integration points. But to be successful, you must be able to recognize how these two processes relate to one another. Recognition is key to understanding this.

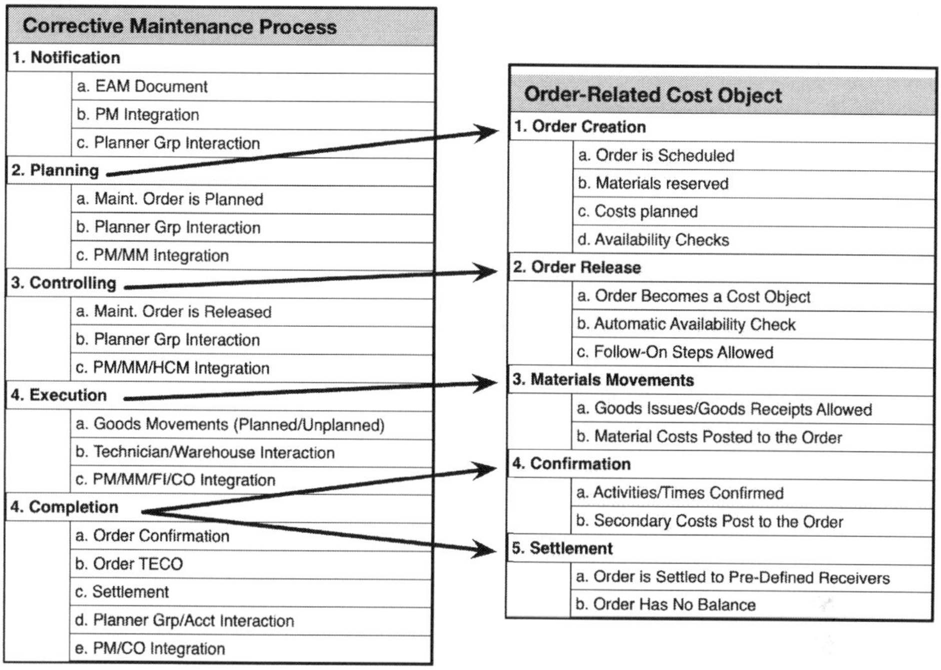

Figure 10.13: Corrective Maintenance Process = Order-Related Cost Object Controlling

Maintenance Notification

The notification generally marks the beginning of the corrective maintenance process. It is a document within Enterprise Asset Management which can be used by the Planner Group to create the Maintenance Order. It's important to know the structure of the Notification document and the various items included within that document (Figure10.14).

From Figure 10.14, we can see that the notification document contains important information used by the Planner Group. In the Header of the document are fields for identifying the Reference Objects. As you can see, the reference objects are the technical object master data elements discussed earlier in this chapter. It is critical to note that an Assembly (BOM) can only be a reference object when either a functional location or equipment is also included as a reference object. The reference object defines the item(s) requiring maintenance. A BOM unto itself does not require any physical maintenance. However, its inclusion as a reference object alongside a functional location or equipment, it provides the Planner Group with the information needed to plan parts for maintenance. You can also see that a reference object is not required in the Header of the notification document, though it is very helpful to include it.

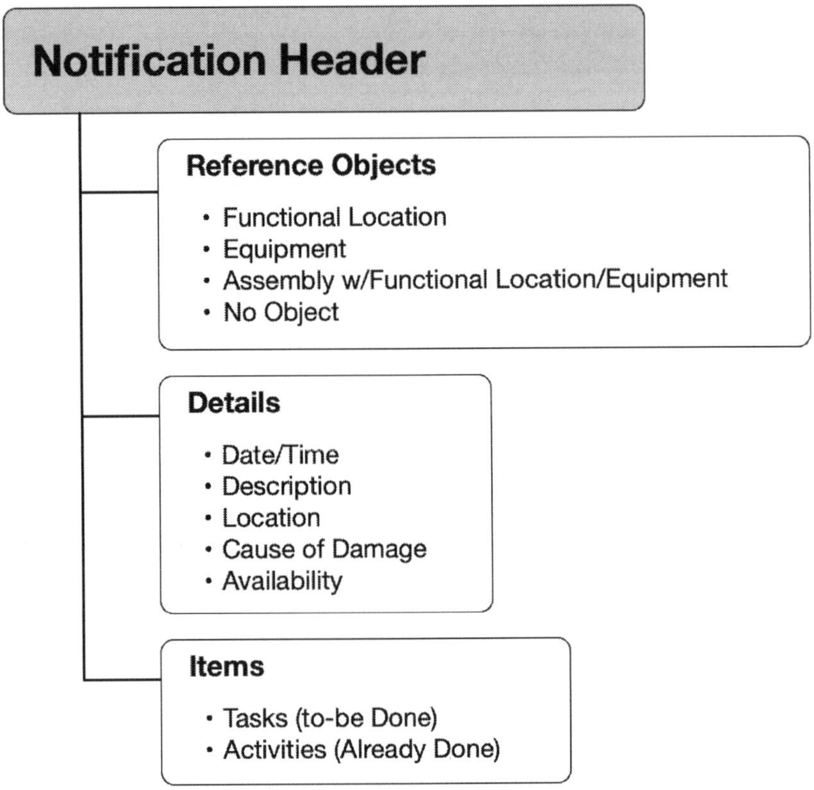

Figure 10.14: Structure of the Notification Document

The header also contains information needed for subsequent planning. The description of the maintenance issue as well as the date and time when the breakdown occurred is also helpful. The availability allows the planner to schedule maintenance when the functional location or equipment is not in use or when the maintenance operations might have the least disruption on business.

The items in the notification provide information on what may have caused the damage or malfunction. Within the items are tasks and activities. Recall, the notification document is updated in parallel with the maintenance order. When operations are planned on the maintenance order, they can be derived from or used to update tasks in the notification. Tasks in the notification represent work that still needs to be performed. The activities identify work that has already been completed.

Maintenance Order

The maintenance order is where the essential planning occurs. This is the second step in the corrective maintenance process, but the first step of Order-Related Cost Object Controlling. There are several methods for creating a maintenance order. For instance, an order can be created from within the maintenance notification. All the data in the notification can then be copied into the maintenance order, reducing data entry errors. But that is only one example. Other examples for creating maintenance orders can be found in Figure 10.15.

Manual Creation

- Notification created after order

From Within a Notification

- All data from notification copied into order

Combining Notifications

- Multiple notifications used to create one order

From a Maintenance Item

- Maintenance item generally related to schedule of planned maintenance

Activity Report

- From confirmation where work is done before the order is created, followed by the creation of the notification

Figure 10.15: Creating Maintenance Orders

The maintenance order also has a structure that is worth noting (Figure 10.16). The structure of the maintenance order is very similar to the structure of a production order, with one exception. The maintenance order contains an Object List.

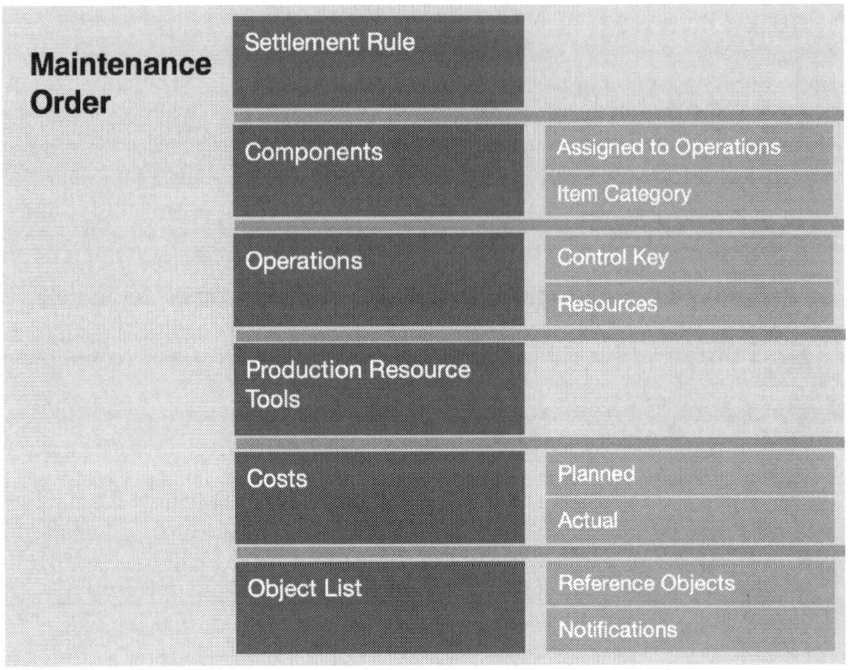

Figure 10.16: Structure of a Maintenance Order

The Object List contains information regarding the objects requiring maintenance. In many cases, this information comes directly from the reference objects within the notification document. In cases where multiple notifications are used to create a maintenance order, the notification numbers become part of the object list.

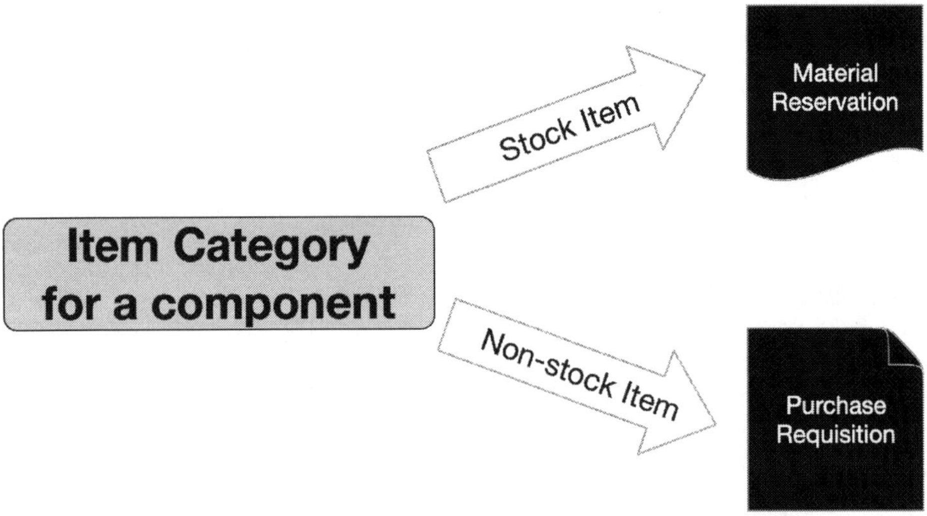

Figure 10.17: Planned Components on a Maintenance Order

Like all order-related cost objects, a settlement rule is required and can be found in the Header of the order. Components (materials) are planned on the maintenance order and like production and projects, material components must be assigned to an operation/activity and receive an item category. As a reminder, the item category is a very important field which informs the system how to process the component. The two item categories you should know are stock and non-stock. Stock items will result in the creation of a reservation for the material at the time the order is created/saved or released (dependent on system settings). A non-stock item will result in the creation of a purchase requisition, also at the time the order is created/saved or released. When a purchase requisition is created, a commitment is also created on the maintenance order. The material price is used to calculate the planned material costs on the order (Figure 10.17).

Operations are planned on the maintenance order and a resource must be assigned to the operations (Figure 10.18). If an operation is internally processed, a work center is assigned. The time planned for the operation is used to reserve capacities at the work center at the time the order is created/saved or released (again, dependent on system settings). The field which defines the resource assigned is the Control Key. Like activities on a project, the control key determines whether the operation/activity is performed internally or externally. As noted above, internally processed operations are assigned to a work center. For external or service operations, the resource is a vendor and the appropriate control key must be assigned to the operation. For externally processed operations, the resource is a vendor and the system will create a purchase requisition at the time the order is created/saved or released. Once again, a commitment is created at this time.

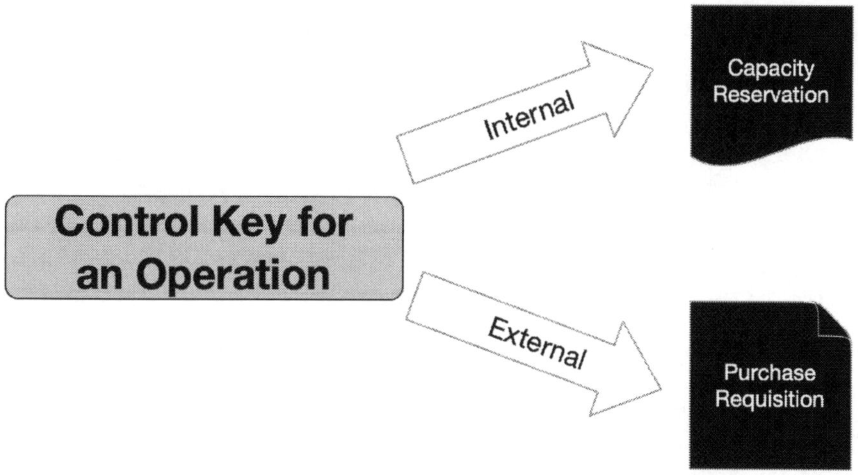

Figure 10.18: Planned Operations on a Maintenance Order

Dependent on the resource for operations, costs are planned. For internal operations where the work center is the resource, the operation is also assigned planned working times and an activity type. It is the combination of the work center and activity type that allows the system to derive an activity price for cost planning. Planned costs for external activities are manually entered in the operation and are often derived from quotations from the vendor or agreements.

The last item in the structure of the maintenance order is the Production Resource Tools (PRTs). PRT's were first introduced in the chapter on manufacturing execution. PRTs are tools needed to perform operations. For instance, if a repair is required on a ceiling light, the technician is likely going to require some form of lift to reach the light. In this case, a PRT might be a ladder.

Controlling - Order Release

Once the order is planned, the next phase is Controlling. It's at this time the order is released. Like all Order-Related Cost Objects, the order must be released before any follow-on activities can occur. The release of the order sets the order as a cost object, to which costs may now be posted. In addition to this, the release always results in an automatic availability check. See Figure 10.19 for information on process actions that may now occur subsequent to the release.

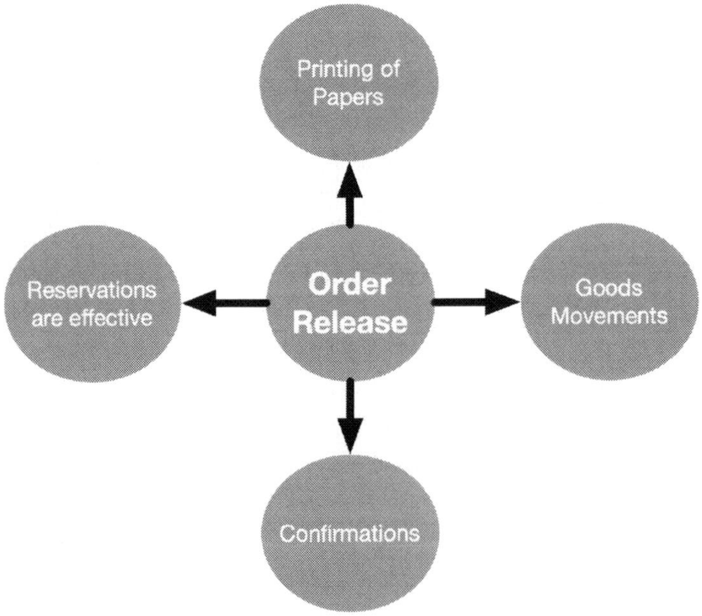

Figure 10.19: Impacts of the Order Release

Execution - Goods Movements

This is the first step in the corrective maintenance process where there is a financial accounting impact and actual cost postings to the order. For components planned on the order, the Item Category determined whether the material was procured from inventory or externally from a vendor using the purchase process. For stock items, the goods movement is a goods issue. The goods issue can be posted directly to the order or by referencing the reservation. For non-stock items, a goods receipt for the purchase order is required. All non-stock items are treated as consumable and the costs will post directly to the maintenance order as that has been identified as the account assignment object in the purchasing documents. When the goods receipt posts, there is no longer a commitment for that item.

It's also very possible during the maintenance process that materials are needed that were not foreseen during the planning step. These materials are considered "unplanned" and goods issues for such material are called, "unplanned withdrawals".

During the execution phase, where goods movements occur, the system will generate a Material Document for each goods movement, as well as a Financial Accounting Document, and Controlling Document.

Completion - Confirmations

There are a variety of options available in EAM for performing confirmations on a maintenance order. In general, the following three items can be confirmed:

1. Times
2. Activities
3. Measurements/Counter Readings

The options for performing confirmations can be seen below in Figure 10.20. As you will see, the Overall Completion Confirmation is an option that can be used to confirm any or all three of the above

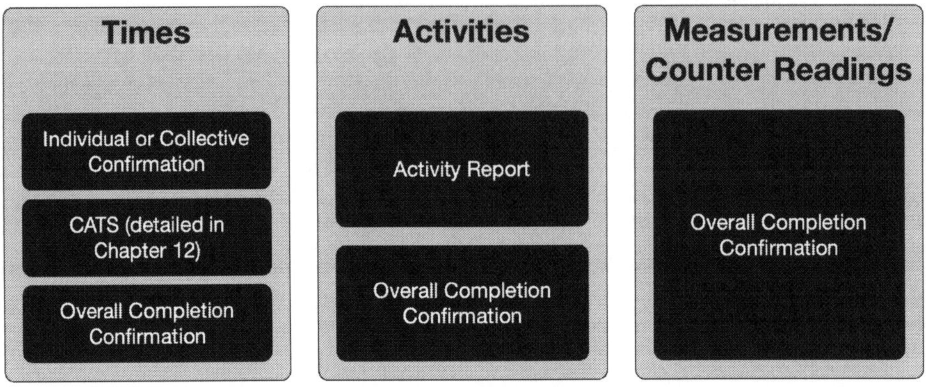

Figure 10.20: Confirmation of Maintenance Order

Since the Overall Completion Confirmation is a versatile confirmation tool, it is worth taking a deeper dive into its functionality (Figure 10.21).

Overall completion confirmation

Header:	Order # 101

Times:

Operation	Actual Times	Work Centers	F	C	N	Plant	Activity Type
10	2 hours	Maintenance	X	X	X	1010	3

Good Movements

Material	Qty	UoM	Plant	Activity Type

Figure 10.21: Overall Completion Confirmation

The Overall Completion Confirmation screen has a Header in which the user can enter the Maintenance Order number. When the order is entered, the operations planned on the order appear in the Times section of the screen. Technicians, planners, and/or management will enter the actual working times for the operation. There are additional options to select to inform the system whether this actual times entered is a final confirmation (F), whether or not to clear any open reservations for capacities (C), and whether or not to inform the system if there is no work remaining for the operation (N).

If materials used on the order have not yet been issued to the order, the Overall Completion Confirmation provides an option to enter the material goods movements in this same screen. This is often used for unplanned components on an order. Finally, there are areas within the transaction to also enter any measurements or counter readings associated with the confirmation. For example, for a maintenance of a vehicle, the technician will want to record the vehicle's mileage in the confirmation. Confirmations also post actual costs to the maintenance order.

Completion - Technical Completion (TECO)

When the repairs or maintenance have been completed for the maintenance order and the technicians and planners are satisfied that everything is done, the status of the maintenance order can now be set to TECO (technically complete). It is very important to note that changing the status to TECO removes the status of Release. In short, this means the order can no longer receive costs and no work can be performed. Figure 10.22 represents the effects of TECO on the maintenance order.

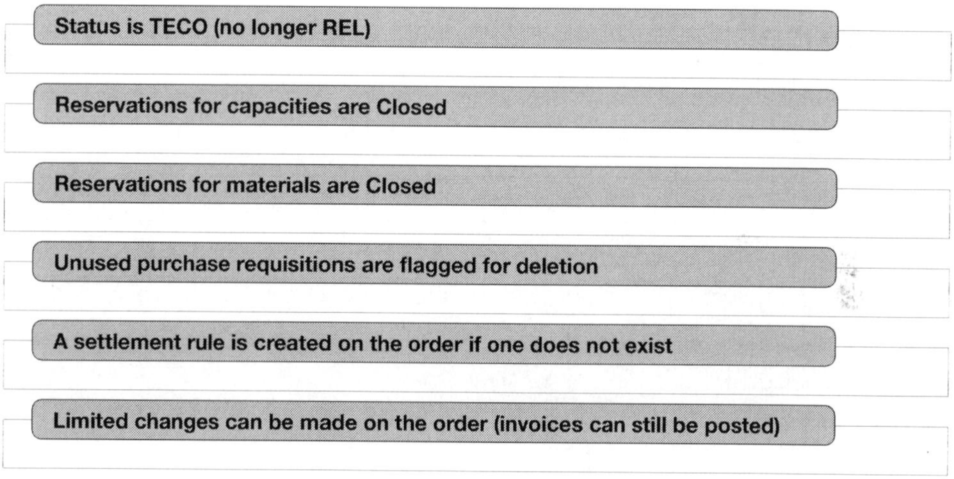

Figure 10.22: TECO Impacts

The notification document is still being managed in parallel with the maintenance order. When the maintenance order is set to TECO, the notification status also changes. The notification status now become NOCO (Notification Complete). The system provides the capability to set the order to TECO independent of the notification. In such cases, the notification status will not change.

It is also possible that after the order has been set to TECO status, it becomes apparent that problems with the repairs persist and more work is required on the order.

In order to be able to perform additional work, use additional materials, and perform additional confirmations, the order must be set back to Released and taken out of TECO status. We refer to this as "reversing TECO". Figure 10.23 depicts the results of reversing TECO.

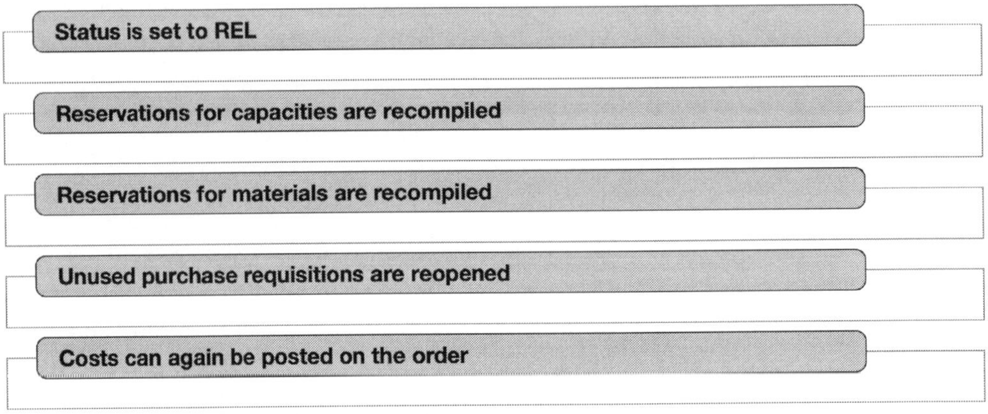

Figure 10.23: ReversingTECO

Completion - Settlement

Settlement is a period-end activity and occurs at the end of the accounting period whether the order is in TECO status or not. At the end of the accounting period, the accountants will want to settle any costs that exist in the order so the books can be closed. When the order is completed and in TECO status, the order is settled at the end of the month and unless TECO is reversed, there is no expectation of any additional costs. After successful settlement, the balance of the order will be zero and no costs will remain. The settlement rule defines who the settlement receiver or receivers are. The process is the same as any other order-related cost object.

Completion - Business Completion

After settlement, and with the understanding that no additional costs or work are necessary, the order can be set to Business Completion. When this happens, the order is closed, and no further processing is allowed. Should future repairs or maintenance be required after Business Completion, the process must start over and a new maintenance order is used.

Enterprise Asset Management Summary

Enterprise Asset Management is the module in which Plant Maintenance takes place. Plant Maintenance involves several logistics activities, so the same organizational levels that we find in all other logistics processes also appear here. But it is the plant that is of most importance in this module. By the end of this chapter, you should now be able to identify the roles that plants can serve in Plant Maintenance. A plant can be a logistics plant, maintenance plant, and/or a maintenance planning plant. Within the maintenance planning plant, we find the planner groups. Planner groups are individuals or groups of individuals who plan maintenance.

Master data includes work centers. Work centers can server several functions in the corrective maintenance process. Other master data include the three technical objects: Functional Locations, Equipment, and Assemblies (BOMs).

You should also be able to explain master data synchronization. This is the integration between EAM and FI-AA (asset accounting). It is the simultaneous creation of the asset and equipment master records that provides the integration. We were also introduced to another method for acquiring a fixed asset. We saw that an internal order can track costs for acquiring an asset and those costs can be settled to the asset to obtain its acquisition value.

The corrective maintenance process was also discussed. You should be able to recognize the steps in the corrective maintenance process and their relationship with order-related cost object controlling. In doing so, you will be able to identify the integration that occurs throughout the process.

Chapter 11: Sales for Service

This chapter brings together concepts from earlier chapters. In the previous chapter (Chapter 10), we focussed our attention on the maintenance of assets owned by our company. In this chapter, we will focus on the sales for service function. Unlike enterprise asset management, this function involves a revenue components as it involves the maintenance of assets owned by our customers. We generically refer to this as "service". However, in this chapter we'll pay specific attention to providing services for products that we previously sold to our customers. Since we will be providing services for our customers, there is also a revenue component to this process, thus we refer to this chapter as Sales for Service. Because of this, we will see concepts from the Lead-to-Cash process from Chapter 9 as well. Additionally, we will also need to manage employees on our service team to provide the services we sell to our customers. Because of this, we'll also revisit concepts from Chapter 6 (Recruit-to-Retire).

There are three SAP solutions which support service. The service focus for each of these are as follows:

- **SAP S/4HANA Service (On-premise)**
  - Planned of services and complex service requirements
- **SAP Service Cloud**
  - Self-service and execution of simple service tasks

- **SAP Field Service Management**
  - Customer self-service, planning and dispatching, mobile field service, integration with Smartforms, and analytics

S/4HANA Service is comprised of two components, Service Management and Sales & Order Management (Figure 11.1).

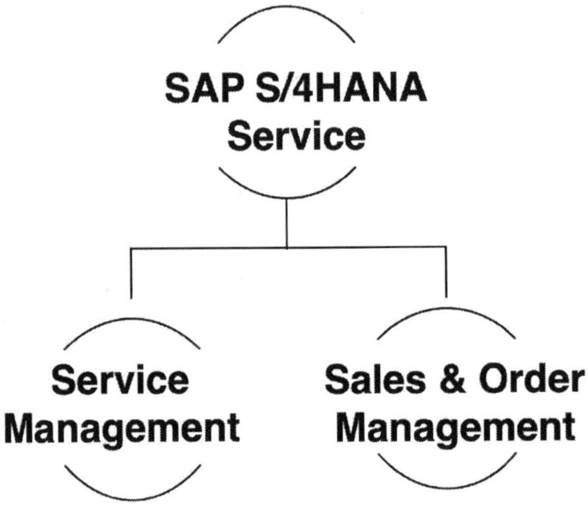

Figure 11.1: S/4HANA Service

Service Management contains a number of different business objects, such as Business Partners, Equipment, Functional Locations, Maintenance Plans, Service Quotes, Service Contracts, and Service Orders. These objects can be created in S4HANA ERP or S/4HANA CRM. The most important aspect of this is that the design of SAP S/4HANA Service mitigates the risk of unnecessary data redundancy. Whether an object is created in ERP or CRM, it can be seen in the other without a need for replication.

Similarly, Sales & Order Management also contain business objects which can originate in ERP or CRM. Such objects include Leads, Opportunities, Sales Quotes, and Sales Orders.

Organizational Levels/Enterprise Structure

We'll begin by addressing the Enterprise Structure components that support the Service business processes steps. The organizational levels associated with this process are copied from Lead-to-Cash (Figure 11.2). You can see from the figure that services requires the same organizational levels. In fact, later we will see some master data that also integrates with Lead-to-Cash. Things such as a price condition, which we learned is unique for a Sales Organization-Distribution Channel combination. Therefore, these organizational levels are necessary for this process.).

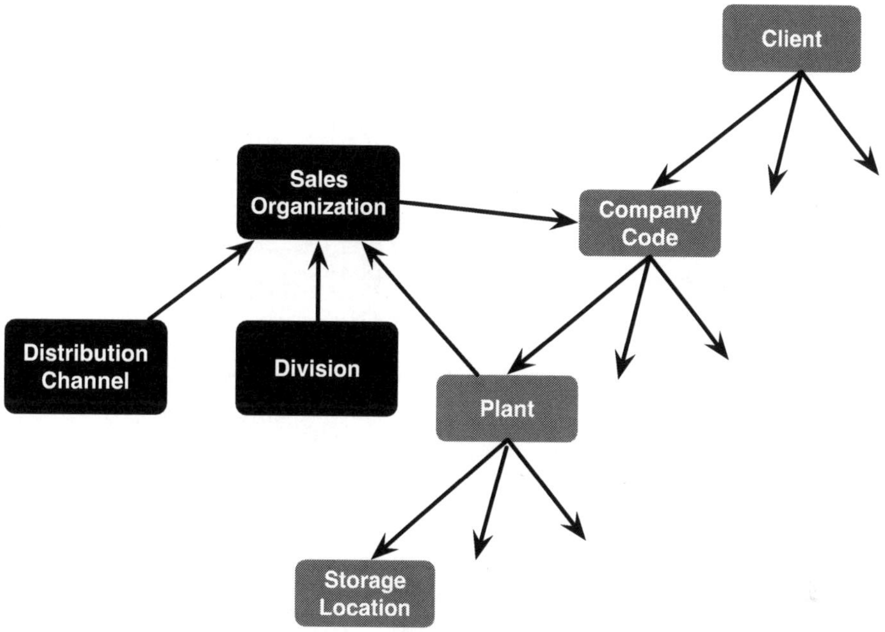

Figure 11.2: Sales Organizations, Distribution Channels, and Divisions (Replica of Figure 9.2)

To support providing services to customers, the organizational levels above are integrated with an Organizational Structure for Services within SAP S/4HANA. The Organizational Structure for Services include Organizational Units (which are structured hierarchically), Positions, and Employees as described in the Recruit-to-Retire process. Figure 11.3 shows what a possible organizational structure might look like. As you can see, the structure is hierarchical with the Sales for Service organizational unit containing two other organizational units, Sales Organization and Service Organization. While the Sales Organization focusses on the sale of goods and services, the Service Organization focusses on customer service and support after the sale. Within the Service Organization, you see two others, Service Administration and Service

Technicians. Each organizational unit contains information such as description, address, validity dates, and hierarchy node. The organizational unit contains positions as well as information about the employees who hold those positions. This hierarchy structure is called the Organizational Model.

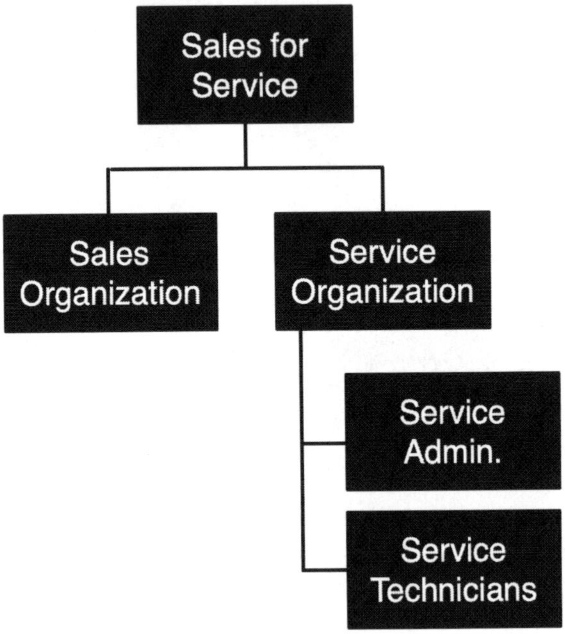

Figure 11.3: Organizational Structure

Best-Practice Scenario for Sales for Service

We'll again offer a "best-practice" scenario for the Sales for Service process. Keep in mind, our view of this process in this chapter is to address services as it pertains to post-sales processing. This is especially important because many of the master data business objects (materials/products and customers) are already available for the Lead-to-Cash process. Sales for Service is simply an extension of the Lead-to-Cash process.

Figure 11.4 shows the items we will be addressing. As we've done with many of our "best-practice" scenarios, we will start by identifying the master data supporting this process.

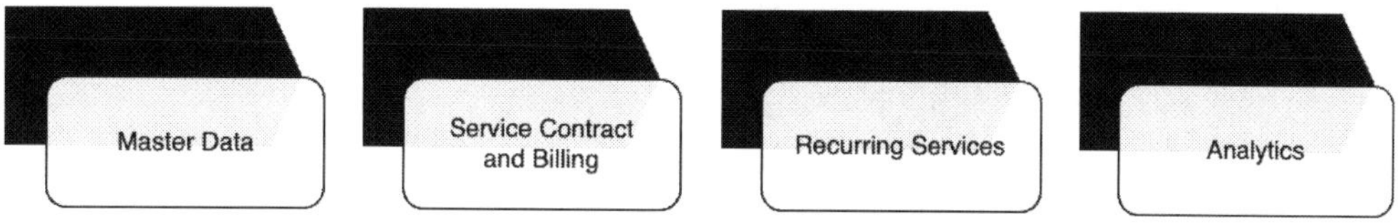

Figure 11.4: Best-Practice Scenario for the Sales for Service Process

Master Data

There are a number of master data that we will cover. Many of these were covered in earlier chapters, but when it comes to Sales for Service, there is some uniqueness associated with them. The master data we will cover includes:

- Materials/Products
- Business Partners
- Conditions
- Technical Objects

Materials/Products

Service Materials/Service Products can be categorized into three main areas based on their functions during the Sales for Service process. This first is generically called, Service Product. This is essentially a service that the company provides, but it is maintained as a material master record. To create a Service Product, it must contain sales views and an Item Category Group for "Service Product". Figure 11.5 shows some of the organizational level and data requirements for a Service Product.

Service Material/Service Product

- Sales Views per Plant, Sales Organization, and Distribution Channel
  - Item Category: Service Product

Figure 11.5: Organizational Level and Data Requirements for a Service Product

The next category of Materials/Products for service is for Planning of Components and Spare Parts. While Service Materials are created as a material master record to describe a service that is performed, other material master data is created to support the planning of components for service orders and spare parts for inventory. These materials represent parts that are required to perform service. Figure 11.6 shows some of the organizational level and data requirements for a material for planning components and spare parts.

Component/Spare Part

- Sales Views per Plant, Sales Organization, and Distribution Channel
  - Item Category: Standard Item

Figure 11.6: Organizational Level and Data Requirements for a Component/Spare Part

The third category of materials for Sales for Service are for materials that are used for the structuring of a Technical Object. Technical Objects in Service are basically the same as those we saw in Enterprise Asset Management. We will talk more about the use of Technical Objects a little later, but for now we are primarily interested in how we categorize materials for the structuring of Technical Objects. Materials can be used in a variety of ways as they relate to Technical Objects. First, a material can be a component in an equipment Bill of Material (BOM). Additionally, Material BOMs can be used to structure parts for equipment. In such a case, a material master record is required. Finally, serialization can apply to a material to create uniqueness and support inventory transactions. Figure 11.7 shows the use of materials for structuring of Technical Objects.

Structuring a Technical Object

- Components in a BOM
- For use as a Material BOM (entry in Construction Type field for the Technical Object)
- Serialization (Material Serial number used as Equipment)

Figure 11.7: BOM's Usage for Structuring a Technical Object

Technical Objects

For Sales for Service, there are four Technical Objects that require discussion. We saw three of these (Functional Locations, Equipment, and Assemblies (BOMs)) in Enterprise Asset Management (EAM). In Sales for Service, we include Material Serial Numbers as a Technical Object. As noted earlier, Material Serial Numbers allow us to treat materials uniquely, like equipment, and it supports inventory management functions.

A brief review of Functional Locations, Equipment, and Assemblies is appropriate here, but for more details on their roles you can refer back to Chapter 10. As a quick reminder, Functional Locations are structured hierarchically and are used to structure the technical system within a plant. Equipment, which represent unique objects, can be installed inside a Functional Location. Assemblies are simply Bill of Materials. Like maintenance, service allows for Functional Location BOMs, Equipment BOMS, and Material BOMs.

Functional Locations, Equipment, and Serial Numbers can be included in documents which support the service process. In reality, this isn't much different than what we saw in EAM. Technical Objects served as reference objects in Notification documents and as part of the Object list in Maintenance Orders. We will see similarities for service documents.

The Functional Location and Equipment master records have four primary views: General, Location, Organization, and Structure. In service, there is an additional view for Serial Number data, should a serial number be assigned to an equipment. In service, important information is needed in some of these views. An example of an equipment master record for service is described in Figure 11.8. You'll see that in the Organization view, we record the "sold-to-party" partner function from the customer master record. This associates the object with the customer for whom we are performing service. Additionally, we enter information in the Structure view for this equipment master record. Like EAM, if the equipment is installed in a Functional Location, that is entered in the "Superior Technical Object" field. It's also possible that another equipment master record serves as a "Superior Technical Object". In such a case, the superior equipment number is entered into that field. The functionality of the "Construction Type" field is exactly the same as in EAM. If we are using a Material BOM to plan components on a service order or for spare parts, we enter the material number in that field.

Technical Object (Equipment)

- Organization View
  - Enter Sold-to-Party (customer) and Partner Function
- Structure View
  - Enter Superior Technical Object if applicable
  - Enter Material Number in Construction Type field if applicable
- Serial Number View
  - Include serial number for the equipment

Figure 11.8: Technical Object Master Data

Business Partners

Business Partners represent the next master data that we need to discuss regarding Sales for Service. By now you should already be familiar with Business Partners. Business Partners are master data as you've seen this in the Source-to-Pay process (Vendors) and the Lead-to-Cash process (customers). Since Sales for Service is really an extension of Lead-to-Cash, customers play an important role as a Business Partner. However, there is much more to Business Partners that we need to cover.

The first thing we need to understand is that there are two types of Business Partners in Sales for Service. A Business Partner can be "internal" or "external". External Business Partners is the type with which we have the most familiarity. Vendors and customers are examples of external Business Partners. In Sales for Service, we can consider an external Business Partner to still be a vendor and/or customer (SAP uses the term, "Account" to also represent a customer). However, an external Business Partner can also be a contact. A contact generally represents an individual that works for a company with which you have a business relationship. As an example, suppose our company has a business relationship with "XYZ Company". A contact is someone at "XYZ Company" that we typically deal with regarding business transactions, such as service. As a reminder, when creating a Business Partner master record, the first step is to select the Business Partner Category (organization, person, or group). "XYZ Company" Business Partner would be created as an organization, while a contact would be created as a person. In the Business Partner master record for the contact, you can link that contact to "XYZ Company". Examples of external Business Partners can be seen in Figure 11.9.

External Business Partners

- Customers (Accounts)
- Vendors
- Contacts

Figure 11.9: External Business Partners

The other type of Business Partner is internal. Internal Business Partners are employees within our company, while external Business Partners are not. In Sales for Service internal Business Partners could be Service Agents, which are representatives within the company who work with customers and provide support. Service technicians is another type of internal Business Partner. A service technician is an employee who performs service activities. Finally, other employees may be needed to support the service process by handling administrative or data entry tasks. We sometimes refer to these as back office employees. Internal Business Partners are not restricted to these three types, but these three give us a good sense of what internal Business Partners are (Figure 11.10).

Internal Business Partners

- Service agents
- Technicians
- Other employees (back office)

Figure 11.10: Internal Business Partners

Since internal Business Partners are employees, there is integration with Human Capital Management/SuccessFactors. As we saw earlier in this book, an employee holds a position and is assigned a unique personnel number as well as specific roles as an SAP user. This data is linked through the "Employee" Business Partner role so their information can be populated in service documents, like service orders and service order templates. This ensures the correct internal Business Partners are properly assigned to the services being performed.

Conditions

Conditions are required master data in Sales for Service. The same conditions which we have seen in previous chapters also apply to Sales for Service and are seen below.

- Price
- Discount
- Freight
- Tax
- Surcharges

All of these are used in the Sales for Service process. As an example, our company could offer one of our customers a discount for a specific service. Likewise, we could have different pricing. Condition types manage how pricing is configured and applied to different documents. For instance, there is a different condition type for price for service orders than there is for service contracts (more on the different service documents later). Some prices can be specific to a material, and some that are specific to a customer/material combination. The same principles apply that we saw in the Lead-to-Cash process. These conditions are specific to a Sales Organization-Distribution

Channel combination. Prices are generally associated with services offered and for spare parts used during service.

Service Contract and Billing

Service Contracts

Often, service is initiated when a customer has an issue that needs to be addressed. It's then when customers typically reach out to request service. Service contracts are used to trigger service without having to wait on the customer to initiate the process. Service contracts offer several benefits. First, it provides efficiencies in scheduling and planning service. Service contracts can also be customized to individual customers to meet their specific needs. And, they also simplify billing because terms and conditions are known in advance and billing plans can be incorporated into the contract.

A service contract is considered an outline agreement between the company and the customer and it includes important pieces of information that define what is included as well as the limitations of the contract. First, the contract is specific to a customer, so customer information is required. It also contains what is covered in the contract as it relates to specific parts and services. The contract will also need to contain conditions for the parts and services that are included, as well as a validity period to define the time parameters for which the contract is valid. Figure 11.11 lists the items that are stored in a service contract.

Service Contract

- Customer Info
- Validity Period
- Service included
- Parts included
- Conditions

Figure 11.11: Main Features of a Service Contract

Service contracts are documents in SAP. As we've seen before, documents are structured with header and item information. A service contract is not all that different, however the terminology deviates a bit from what we have seen in earlier chapters. We know the header of a document as the section of a document which contains information that applies to the entire document. For SAP service contracts, this is referred to as the "Details" section of that document. Details include the following:

- Sold-to-party
- Status
- Validity Dates
- Contact
- Employee responsible (Internal Business Partner)

The other section of the service contract is still called, “items”. A contract can have one or more items in it. Information related to the items include the following:

- Product
- Technical Object
- Conditions
- Service profile (typically a timeframe when service can be performed)
- Response profile (can distinguish priority of service)

Service contracts also include other pieces of information worth noting. Since service contracts include conditions, it’s important to associate the service contract with a Sales Organization-Distribution Channel combination. This is located in the "Organizational Data” tab within the document. Like Maintenance Orders, a Service Contract also has an Object List which links the contract to one or more technical objects that are included in the contract.

Finally, we mentioned one of the benefits of service contracts is that is simplifies billing by including billing plans. A billing plan is simply a schedule for billing that is predefined and included in the contract. It’s typically done on a monthly cycle and the value is typically constant throughout the life of the contract.

Service Contract Billing

Billing Document Request

When preparing to bill for a service contract, it’s a good practice to review the billing plan for the service item from within the service contract. The billing plan will provide an indication as to what has and has not yet been billed based on the billing cycle. Assuming that it is now time to bill the customer, the process is initiated with a Billing Document Request (BDR). The BDR serves as the basis for creating the billing document.

SAP Fiori provides users with an easy to use app to generate the BDR. Upon calling up the Fiori app for the BDR, the user is presented with a field for the BDR Creation Horizon. The user enters a number of days in this field to see if it is time to create the BDR. The purpose of this field to allow the creation of the BDR in advance of the Billing Document, while not creating the BDR too much in advance. For example, if the user enters 28 days in this field, the system will respond as to whether or not it is too early to create the BDR.

In addition to the above mentioned field, the user must also enter the sold-to-party (customer) in the generate BDR transaction. This triggers the system to find the service contract associated with this customer to help determine whether creating the BDR is in line with the billing plan. If everything is correct, the system identifies the Contract ID and BDR document number is generated and saved.

Billing Document

When it is time to create the Billing Document, the user selects the SAP Fiori app for maintaining the Billing Due list. In Lead-to-Cash, we first saw the Billing Due List and described it as a worklist. Worklists in SAP contain a list of items that need to be processed, allowing SAP users the flexibility to process documents individually or collectively. The user needs to see if a BDR exists by calling up the Billing Due List. Once in the Billing Due List transaction, the user will enter values such as a date for billing and sold-to-party customer information. The user will then select "Display Billing List". If the BDR is valid for the customer for the selected date, the billing item(s) from the service contract will appear. The user can then select "Save" to generate the billing document. As with the Lead-to-Cash process, output master data can be used to transmit the invoice to the customer. Though our focus in this chapter is on Sales for Service, it's important not to lose sight that billing will also have accounting impacts as we saw in Lead-to-Cash.

Recurring Services

Recurring services can be triggered under a variety of different criteria. Figure 11.12 shows each of these criteria that could result in recurring service.

The first is time-based recurring services. A time-based recurring service is essentially pre-scheduled service based on a pre-defined timeframe. For instance, imagine you have purchased some type of jewelry with gemstones that are placed in settings. To ensure the gemstones don't fall out of the settings, you may have a regularly scheduled service plan for the jeweller to inspect the settings for quality once each year. This is an example of time-based recurring services.

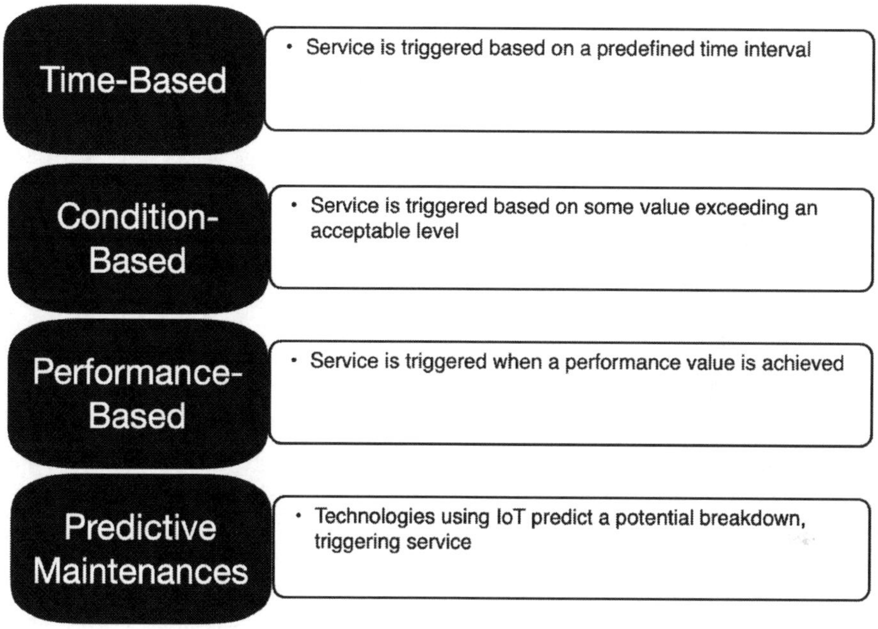

Figure 11.12: Criteria for Recurring Services

Another criteria for recurring service is conditioned-based. Service is then triggered when some condition is met. In most cases this means some value fell outside of acceptable levels. Imagine a home owner who has purchased and installed a water softener system to reduce the levels of minerals in the water. For simplicity's sake, let's assume the water softener system has monitoring capabilities to regularly test the water for levels of minerals. If the levels exceed an acceptable value, then it will trigger service.

A third example is performance-based recurring services. A common example of performance-based recurring services is oil change service for vehicles. I'm sure each of you who own a vehicle plans to have the oil changed on that vehicle at regular intervals. The intervals in this case is the amount of miles (or kilometers) that vehicle was driven since the last oil change service. If that interval is set at five-thousand miles, then service is triggered when the five-thousand mile interval has been met.

Lastly, service can be triggered as a result of predictive maintenance. Use of technologies/sensors that are connected to the internet (IoT) can predict a breakdown before it occurs. In such cases, service is triggered.

If these sound familiar, it's probably because you recall that we covered this in the previous chapter for Enterprise Asset Management. Remember, maintenance is a process we perform on assets owned by our company. Service is really maintenance that is performed on assets owned by our customers. They are very similar in practice.

Figure 11.13 presents the sequence of events for recurring service. We will touch on these in the following sections.

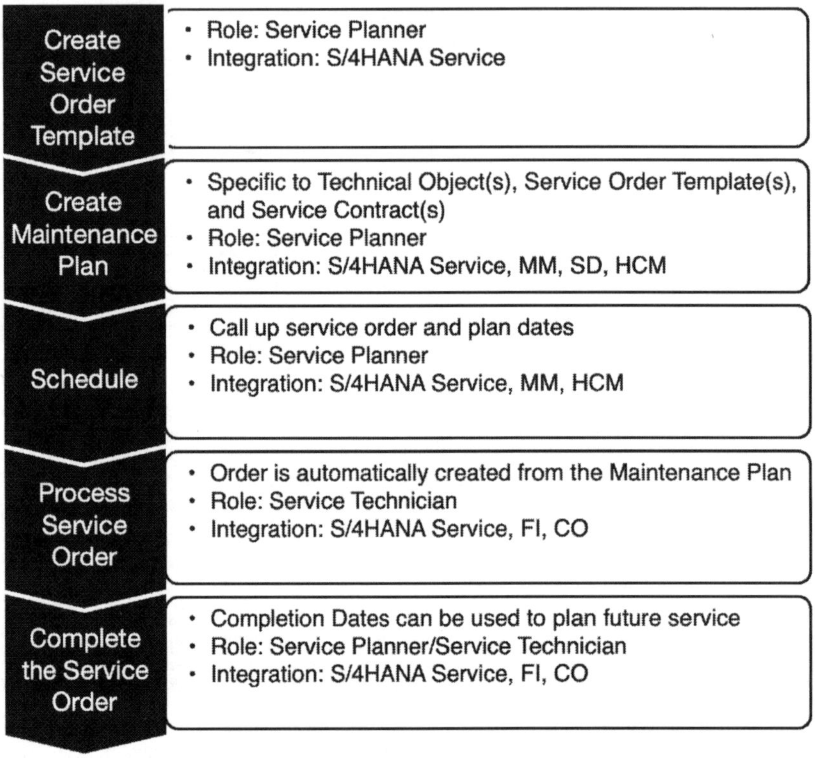

Figure 11.13: Recurring Service Events

Service Order Templates

Service order templates are used to simplify services that are recurring and fairly standard in nature. In this way, the template can serve as the foundation for creating service orders. In such cases, the user selects the appropriate service order template to create the service order and the objects and characteristics from the template will copy over.

Service order templates have a structure similar to contracts. They contain a section for Details (akin to a header) and a section for Items. The information in the Details sections includes the following:

- Template ID
- Description
- Validity Dates
- Status
- Employee responsible (Internal Business Partner)
- Service Employee Group responsible (team of employees)

The Items section provides information on the service(s) that are part of this template and it contains the following:

- Service product
- Spare parts
- Item categories (service items, service parts items, sales items)
- Status

Additionally, Reference Objects (Technical Objects) are also included in the Service Order Template.

Maintenance Plans

Maintenance Plans in Sales for Service has two key components. The items for service, and the planning data for service. Let's start with the planning data. Dates are planned for service in maintenance plans and are generally cyclical, though alternatives exist. With regards to cyclical planning, examples could include annually, bi-annually, monthly, etc. These are considered planned dates. Call dates represent dates that are in advance of planned dates in order to prepare for the service to be performed, essentially serving as a notification to get things started. Therefore, planned data includes:

- Planned dates for scheduling based on cycles
- Call dates to prepare for scheduled service
- Start and end dates based on service contracts

The other component in maintenance plans is the items included in the plan. The following are considered maintenance plan items:

- Technical Objects (Object List)
- Service Contracts
- Service Order Type
- Service Order Template

Scheduling Maintenance Plans

The scheduling of maintenance plans is a straightforward process and includes only a few basic steps. First, the scheduling is generally carried out by the service planner. The sequence of steps for scheduling and their descriptions are shown in Figure 11.14. It's important to note that scheduling is usually carried out as a background process based on the planning cycle. However, it is possible to manually schedule and plan dates.

From Figure 11.14, we can see the scheduling process is pretty simple. It's important to note that the Service Order Template contains information that is copied into the Maintenance Plans making it easy for the service planner to ensure that all the relevant information is also copied into the Service Order. Once service is completed, the service technician will record and confirm the data required to complete the service order. The end date for completing the service can serve as the date for planning subsequent recurring services based on the cycle planning.

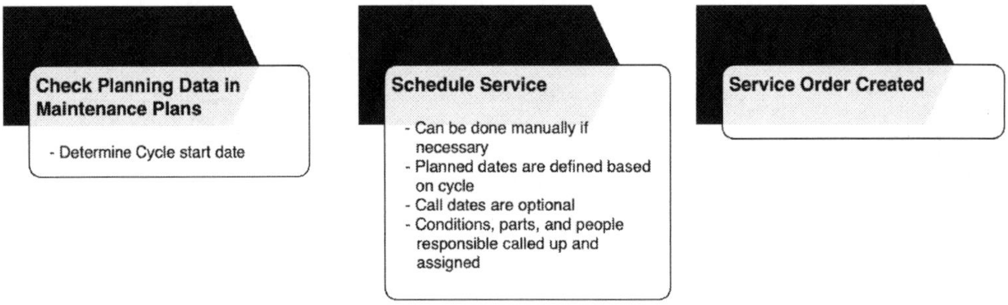

Figure 11.14: Scheduling Maintenance Plans

Analytics

The final items in the "best-practice" scenario in Sales for Service is Analytics. Analytics in the service process provides the company with tools necessary to monitor various aspects such as service issue, master data, service contracts and billing, and recurring services. Reporting and analytics for all of these are available as SAP Fiori apps under

"Service Monitoring and Analytics". From here, users can select the "Service Management Overview" app to get the necessary insights into service. This information can be displayed by selecting the appropriate Sales Organization-Distribution Channel combination. This allows users to select the available service order types and service order items for analysis.

Sales for Service Summary

At the start of this chapter, we emphasized that sales for service incorporates concepts from other business processes, namely Lead-to-Cash, Enterprise Asset Management, and Recruit-to-Retire. This chapter presented us will all three of these elements that are necessary to support service.

We also identified three primary solutions for service, SAP S/4HANA Service, SAP Service Cloud, and SAP Field Service Management. In the intelligent enterprise, it's important to leverage technologies that are best suited to support the business processes. Sales for Service is no different.

The items in our "best-practice" scenario included Master Data, Service Contracts and Billing, Recurring Services, and Analytics. From Service Order Templates, through completion of Service Orders, the process is integrated and supported by various business objects being copied through each stage of the process.

Chapter 12: Project Management

Project management is a business function supported by Project systems (PS) in SAP S/4HANA. PS is a module that can be used flexibly for a variety of business functions. Some SAP customers have used PS for managing projects (most common), while others have used PS to support manufacturing as well as managing budgets and funding. Regardless of how it is employed in an organization, know that SAP PS is a flexible tool that can satisfy many business requirements. However, the content for most of our discussions in this chapter will be built around the foundation of using SAP PS for managing projects. Our objectives in this chapter are to learn how PS as a tool can help SAP customers manage their projects. We will avoid discussion related to managerial decision making on projects and instead focus on how the tool can provide managers with the information they need to make decisions regarding a project.

Project Characteristics

Projects themselves can serve many purposes. There are also several factors that can influence a project. From an enterprise perspective, projects have some defining characteristics. Projects are generally capital intensive and time intensive. They are usually complex in nature and involve many different functional areas. Figure 12.1 depicts the characteristics of projects. Because projects involve various functional areas, projects are tightly integrated to every other modules covered in this book, including Chapters 10 and 11. In addition to these characteristics, projects have a definitive beginning and a definitive end, which means projects have a defined scope.

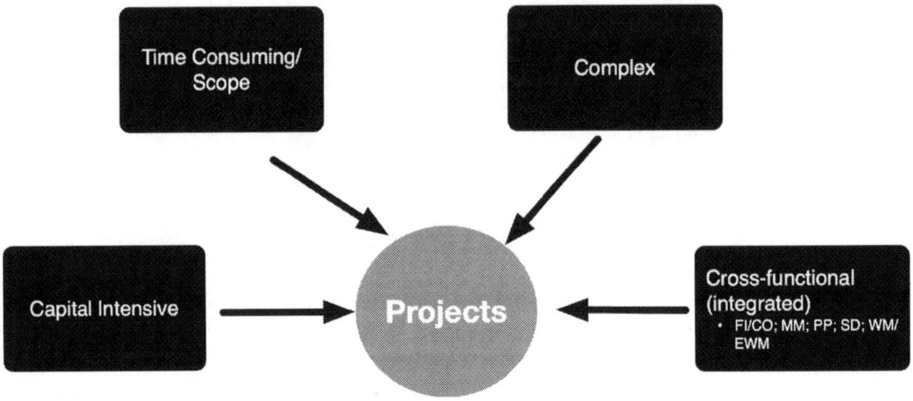

Figure 12.1: Characteristics of Projects

There are also several basic phases of a project, shown in Figure 12.2. The first of these is the Concept phase. During the Concept phase, an idea for a project is defined and presented. There are no formal tasks within SAP PS to be discussed in this phase. For example, a company may consider an internal project for ERP implementation or an organization in the land development industry may have a potential customer inquire if they are interested in paving roads in a new property development. Each of these scenarios would represent the Concept phase of a project.

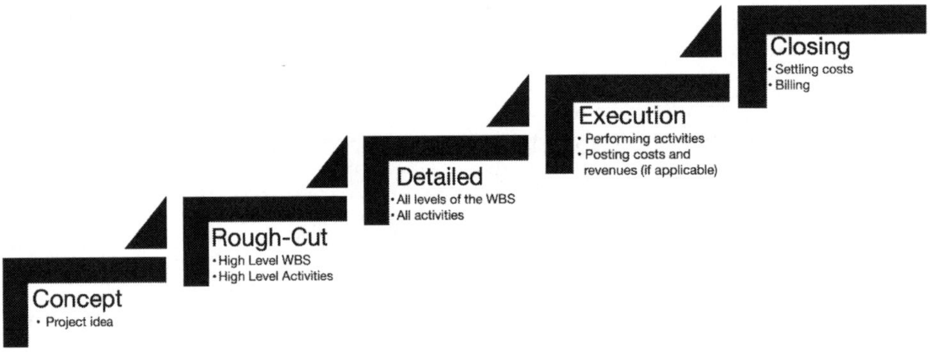

Figure 12.2: Phases of Projects

Let's suppose the company in the land development industry was asked to provide a quotation for paving roads in a new property development. Before they could provide a quotation, they would surely need to have a basic estimation of their costs for such a project. But even after providing the most accurate quotation possible, there is still a risk they won't be awarded the job. Thus, the paving company would not likely invest a substantial amount of time and resources into planning their costs. Instead they would engage in the next phase, Rough-cut Planning. In this phase, they would perform high-level planning of the project to get a "rough" idea of the costs for the project. These costs planned at a high level can then be used to generate a quotation to their customer (SD integration).

We will not go into any more detail on the first two phases of the project. The remaining phases, Detailed Planning through Closing, will be discussed in greater depth in the subsequent sections in this chapter.

Organizational Levels/Enterprise Structure

It is important to understand that SAP Project Systems (PS) has no organizational levels of its own. Because it integrates with all the other modules, the required organizational levels in a project will be derived from the modules with which it integrates.

Master Data

WBS Element Master Data

The Work Breakdown Structure (WBS) of a project is a hierarchical representation of a project and includes all activities to be completed in hierarchical form. Each object in the hierarchy is considered a WBS Element master record. An example of a WBS can be seen below in Figure 12.3. Note the shape of each WBS Element is a triangle. This is the icon SAP uses in S/4HANA to depict WBS Elements.

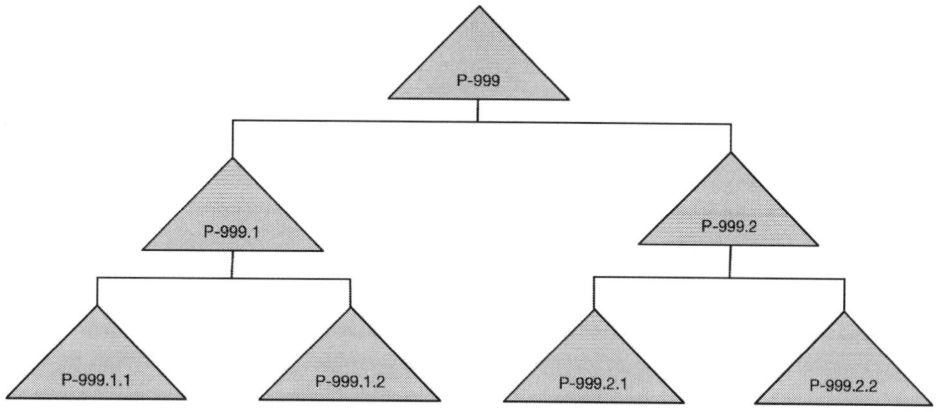

Figure 12.3: Work Breakdown Structure

WBS Element Operative Indicators

The WBS elements have some defining characteristics called Operative Indicators that can be of the following three types:

1. Planning Element
2. Account Assignment Element
3. Billing Element

A WBS elements can be assigned more than one Operative Indicator. If the WBS element will be used for planning costs and/or revenues, it is assigned the Operative Indicator “Planning Element”. If the WBS element will be a true cost collector, then it is assigned the Operative Indicator “Account Assignment Element”. Finally, if revenue is allowed to be posted to a WBS element, it is assigned the Operative Indicator “Billing Element”. Again, the Operative Indicators are not mutually exclusive. A WBS element can be assigned one or more Operative Indicators. It’s important to understand that the Operative Indicators help define how the WBS Element will manage costs and/or revenues associated with the project. A key takeaway here is that the Operative Indicators “Account Assignment Element” and/or “Billing Element” identify the WBS Element as an account assignment object, which was discussed in great detail in Chapter 4. Generally speaking, projects follow the “Order-Related Cost Object Controlling” process, which means a WBS Element must be in “Released” status to be able to received the posting of costs or revenues.

A WBS element can also be statistical. To make a WBS element statistical, we apply the statistical marker to it in the WBS master data. A statistical marker is NOT an Operative indicator. But it allows for statistical postings only for a WBS element for which it is activated.

WBS Element - Functions

WBS elements have several functions. The functions of WBS Elements can be seen in Figure 12.4. It is the WBS Element where we manage costs, revenues, budgets, payments, commitments, dates, and periodic activities. Some of the objects in the figure will be discussed in better detail as we approach the other phases of the project. For now, it’s vital to associate these functions with WBS Elements.

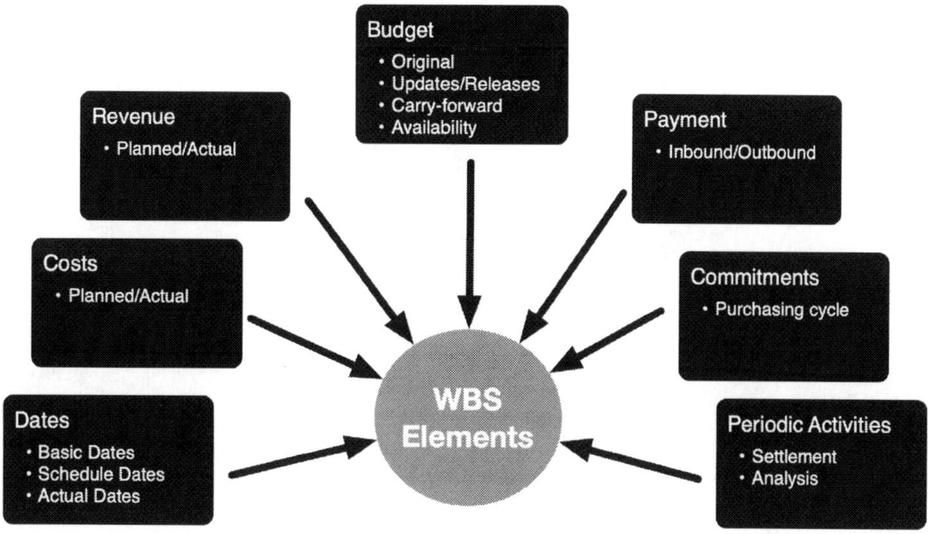

Figure 12.4: Functions of WBS Elements

Activities/Networks Master Data

The operative structure of a project is the Network and the Activities belonging to the Network. The activities define the operative aspects, in other words, the work to be done on a project. To manage the project successfully, the activities are completed in a specific sequence, where one or more activities must be completed before one or more other activities can start. The sequence of activities is what defines a Network.[1] To create this sequence of activities (i.e. Network), relationships are assigned to each Activity master record. The relationships describe which activities are predecessors and successors of each activity. An activity with no predecessors marks the beginning of the Network. Whereas an activity with no successors marks the end of the Network. Thus, it can be said that the Network is formed by assigning relationships to the Activities.

In Figure 12.5, we see a Network (915311) and the associated activities. If we look at the relationships, we can see that Activity 30 has a predecessor (Activity 10) and a Successor (Activity 60). Again, these relationships are assigned in the Activity master records. The icons for activities and networks are also worth noting. Activities are rectangular, while the network is rectangular with a text box as its header. The activity numbers are unique to the network in which they belong. Therefore, there could be more than one Activity 10, but only one Activity 10 in Network 915311.

[1] It is important to note that a project could have more than one network.

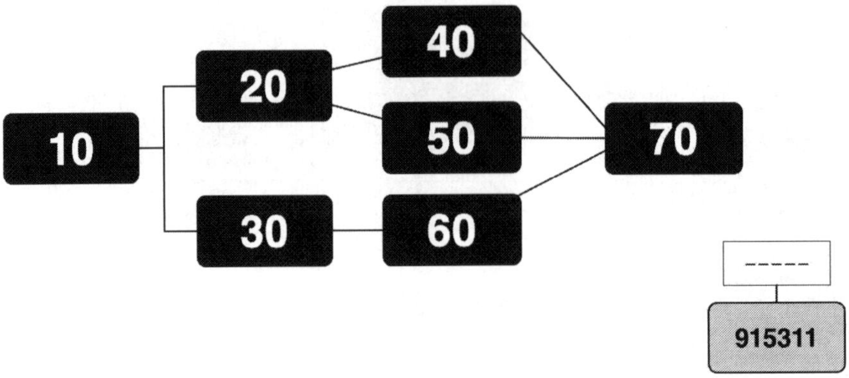

Figure 12.5: Network and Activities

Project Definition: WBS Element/Activities

Activities are assigned to WBS Elements in a 1: N relationship. An Activity can be assigned to only one WBS Element, however a WBS Element can have more than one Activity assigned. Figure 12.6 shows the relationships between WBS Elements and Activities. Also notice there is a new icon in that figure. It is a triangle with a text box above it. This is the icon for the Project Definition. The Project Definition contains all aspects of the project (WBS and Activities) as well as providing default values such as basic dates for the project and other control features.

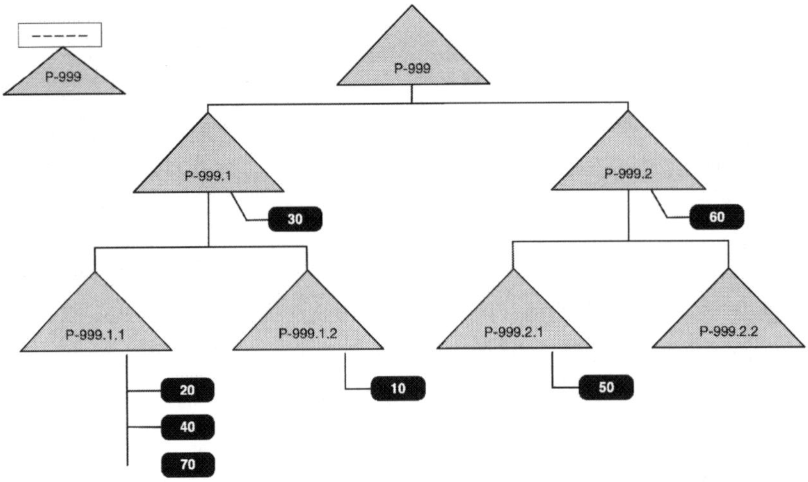

Figure 12.6: Project Definition - Network and Activities

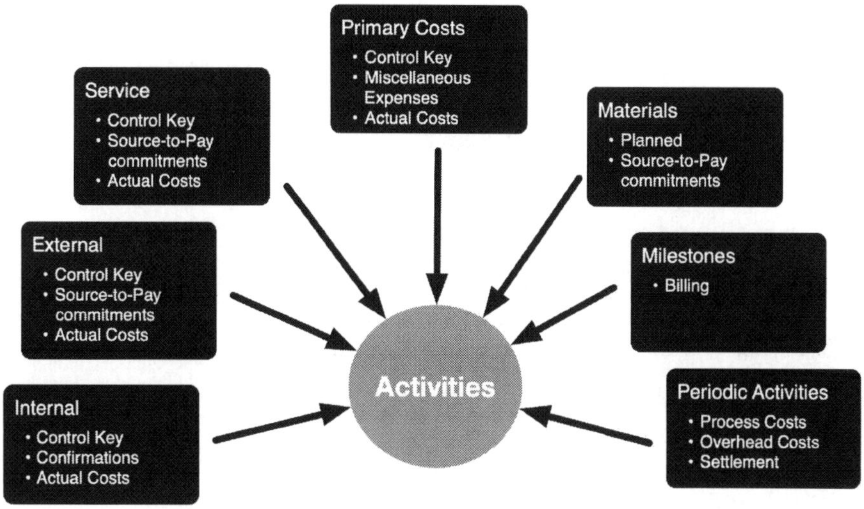

Figure 12.7: Functions of Activities

Activities: Functions

Like WBS Elements, Activities also have some basic functions (Figure 12.7). These functions describe how Activities are used and what can be performed on an Activity. There are four basic categories of activities: Internal, External, Service, and Primary Cost. The Control Key in the Activity master record defines which of these four is assigned to the activity. An internal activity (Figure 12.8) is an activity on the project that is performed internally, meaning a work center is assigned. External and Service activities are performed by a vendor. Because of this, these activities integrate with the procurement process. A Primary Cost activity is an expense on the project that can be managed as an activity. As an example, this could be an expense associated with application fees provided to local agencies for permits, such as those needed for construction.

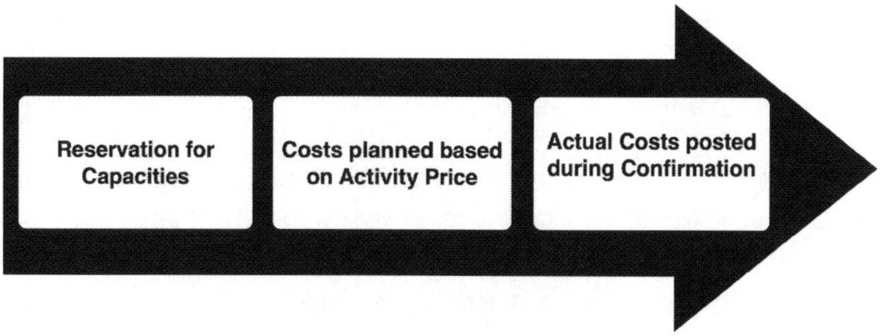

Figure 12.8: Internal Activity Processing

Dependent on the Control Key defining the type of activity, the project will integrate with various modules. To understand how this works, let's assume the Control Key for a given activity defines that activity as internally processed. As noted above, an internal activity requires the assignment of a work center. Therefore, a need exists to plan and reserve capacity for the work center performing that activity. The capacity reservation will occur when the project is created or released (depending on customization settings). Like operations in a production order, the internal activity is also assigned an activity type. Based on the activity type and work center assigned, the SAP S/4HANA system can derive the Activity Price and costs for the internal activity are planned. Actual costs and actual dates will be recorded to the project when confirmation of the activity takes place.

For an external or service activity (Figure12.9), the resource assigned is a vendor. When the project is created or released, the SAP S/4HANA system will create a purchase requisition for the activity. Since the service activity results in creating a purchase requisition, it is treated like a consumable and the SAP S44HANA system will create a commitment for the activity. The Source-to-Pay (S2P) process now manages the remainder of the activity. Actual costs will be posted to the project during goods receipt for an external activity, and during invoice posting for a service activity (other options will be discussed below). A service activity will require actual working times from the vendor and approval of those times to post these costs.

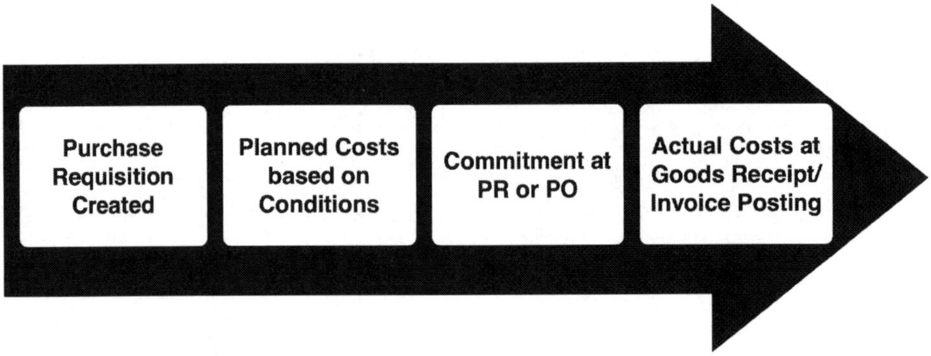

Figure 12.9: External/Service Activity Processing

When materials are needed for a project, they can ONLY be planned for activities (not WBS). Each activity has a component overview. In the component overview, the user can enter a material and quantity needed. Just as a BOM has a field for Item Category, there is also a field for Item Category in each line item of a component. This field is a required entry and informs the SAP S/4HANA system whether the component is a stock or a non-stock item. Because the component is assigned to the activity, when the project is created or released, the SAP S/4HANA system will respond accordingly. For activities with a stock item, the system will create a reservation for that item (Figure 12.10). The planned costs will be based on the material price from the material master record.

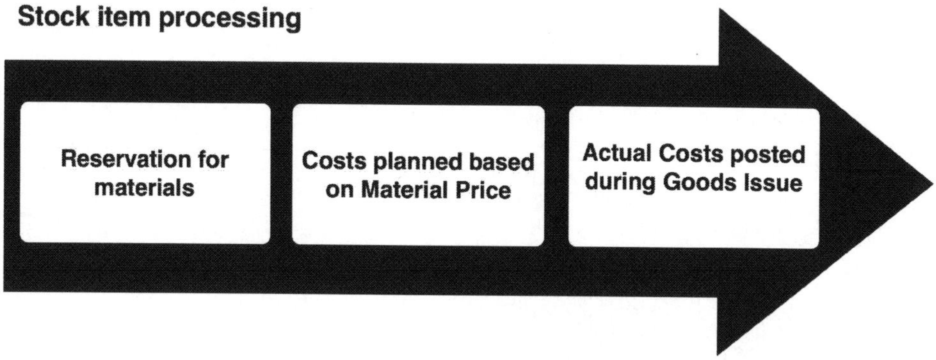

Figure 12.10: Stock Items Processing

For those activities with non-stock items planned, a purchase requisition is created (Figure 12.11). Again, a commitment is created because the non-stock item is always treated as a consumable. Actual costs occur at the time of goods movement. For stock items, a goods issue is required to post the costs from inventory. For non-stock items, the goods receipt from the purchase order is used to post the costs to the project. Additional costs MAY apply at the time of invoice posting if there are any small price differences.

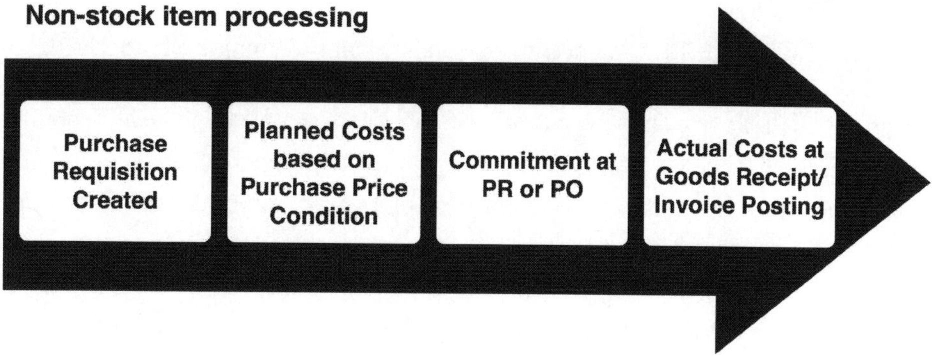

Figure 12.11: Non-Stock Items Processing

Transactions

Project Tools: Project Builder and Project Planning Board

There are two basic tools for managing projects in SAP S/4HANA, the Project Builder and the Project Planning Board (Figure 12.12). Both tools provide similar functionality, however their interfaces differ significantly. The Project Builder provides users with an expandable and collapsible, indented menu for managing WBS elements and Activities on a project. The Project Planning Board is a graphical tool, often referred to as an interactive Gantt Chart for managing WBS element and Activities on a project.

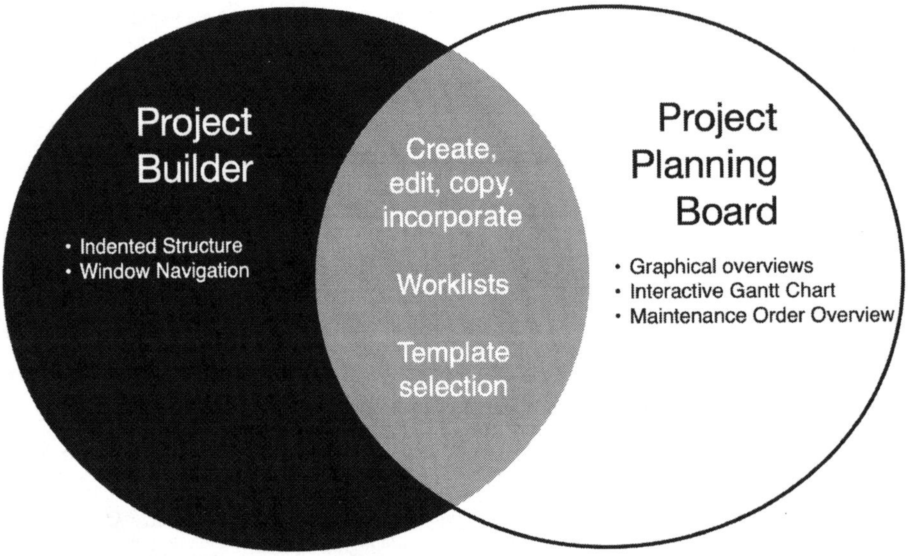

Figure 12.12: Project Builder Versus Project Planning Board

Having both tools available allows users to work comfortably in an environment they prefer. The Project Builder offers an indented navigational feature and when an object is selected from the menu, it appears in a main work area where data can be maintained. A user can call up a template of a project or an existing project and create a new project by copying it. When copying from a template, SAP refers to the template as a Standard Project. When copying from an existing project, SAP refers to that project as an Operative Project. It is also possible to copy aspects of a Standard or Operative project and incorporate or include them into a working project. In addition to this, users can also call up a worklist of recently accessed projects to simplify navigation.

The Project Planning Board offers a more graphical experience for the user. As noted above, the key interface is an interactive Gantt chart where users can call up and work with both WBS Elements and Activities. In addition, the Project Planning Board offers access to graphical overviews of materials, capacities, and cost/revenue information in the project. Like the Project Builder, the Project Planning Board also allows users to call up a template of a project, or portion of a project and create or incorporate by copying it.

Finally, the Project Builder and the Project Planning Board have access to additional graphical tools where users can edit the project. Users can manage the WBS in a Hierarchy Graphic, and the Activities in a Network Graphic.

Project Planning: Detailed Planning

There are many aspects of planning on a project. If you refer to the Phases in a Project shown earlier in this chapter in Figure 12.2, there are two phases for planning: Rough-Cut Planning and Detailed Planning. In this section, our focus will be on Detailed Planning. Figure 12.13 shows the elements involved in detailed planning.

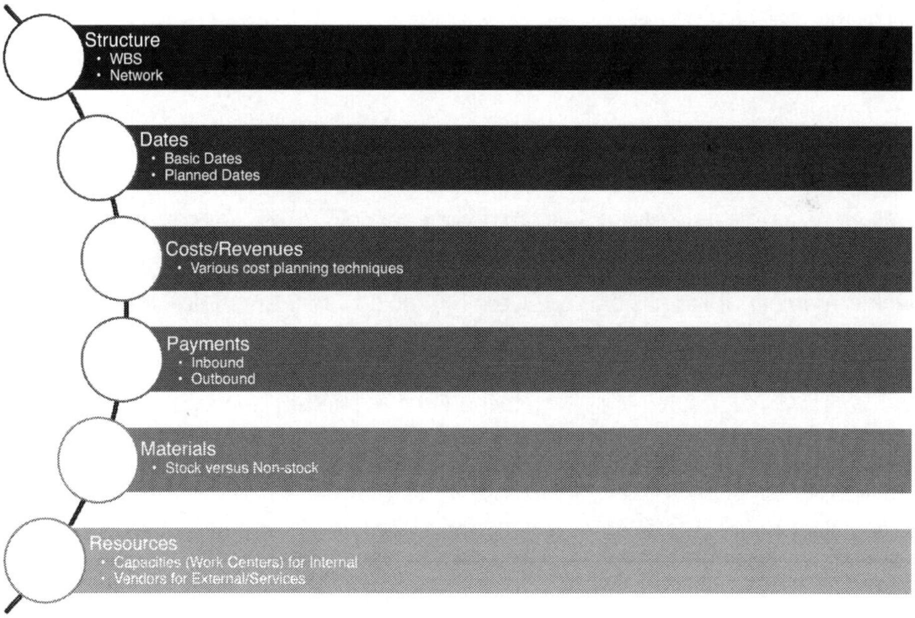

Figure 12.13: Project Planning

Project Structure

The planning of the project structure involves identifying the Project Definition and all the WBS elements, its hierarchy, the activities assigned to them, and the Network in which the activities belong. These aspects were discussed in the Master Data section of this chapter, so we will not provide any additional information on the planning of the project structure. We will also not discuss planning of payments, but you should be aware that planning of payments is an aspect of planning on projects.

Project Dates

The planning of dates on a project includes the Basic Dates. The Basic dates are derived from the Project Definition, in which a start and end date of the project are identified. Each WBS element is then issued a duration time from which the Basic Dates in the WBS Elements are established. Other planned dates will come from the scheduling of the project. Once activities are assigned to the WBS elements, the dates and times associated with completing each of the activities are updated during the scheduling of the project. At this time, the planned dates are extrapolated up the WBS hierarchy. After scheduling the project, the user must save the project for the dates to apply to the project.

Cost Planning

There are several planning options for planning costs on a project. Overall Planning is the least accurate, but still a valid planning technique. In Overall Planning, users provide an overall cost estimate for WBS Elements with the Operative Indicator: Planning Element. It is possible for Overall Planning to be a non-scientific approach to planning costs that could solely rely on intuition.

Another planning option is to plan using Cost Elements. Recall, there are two types of cost elements: Primary and Secondary. Planning using Primary Cost Elements is essentially the planning of costs on WBS Elements based on expenses derived from FI postings. Secondary Cost Elements plan costs that will be allocated to WBS Elements.

SAP S/4HANA also provides project managers with the ability to plan costs by itemizing each cost separately. This is known as Unit Costing. This is perhaps the most detailed planning method because it involves the planning of every single item that will post a cost to the project. It is a detailed and time-consuming method.

Projects can also be planned using planning templates provided within S4HANA. These planning templates are part of SAP Easy Cost Planning for projects.

Additionally, order-related cost objects like production orders, maintenance orders, internal orders, and other projects can be assigned to a project. The costs for these order-related cost objects are planned separately on the objects. When they are assigned to the project, their individual costs are then used to plan costs for the project.

Finally, activities and network costs can be used to plan costs on a project. As we saw earlier, activities can be internal, external, service, or cost activities. The costs can be planned separately for each activity and those planned costs are passed on to the WBS elements to which they are assigned. Likewise, the costs on the activities can be used to calculate planned costs for the entire network. The network is then assigned to a WBS element and can be used to plan the cost for the project in that way.

It is important to note, costs on a project are generally planned from the lowest level WBS elements and rolled up to the highest level WBS element. Also keep in mind, costs can only be planned on WBS elements that have been identified as a Planning Element.

Materials

During our discussion on activities, we learned that materials are planned on activities using the component overview. Each component must be assigned an Item Category to determine whether it will be a stock or a non-stock item. The process for managing each were also discussed earlier and can be reviewed by looking at Figure 12.10 and Figure 12.11. The item category will determine whether the system creates a reservation for the item or a purchase requisition for the item.

Resources

Resources must also be assigned to activities. For internally processed activities, the resource is a work center. For external and service activities, the resource is a vendor. Again, we addressed this in our earlier discussion on activities and the processing of these activities can be reviewed in Figure 12.8 and Figure 12.9. For an internal activity, the system will create a reservation for capacities at the work center. External and Service activities result in the creation of purchase requisitions and commitments. To differentiate between the activities, the Control Key is used. Therefore, it is the Control

Key settings which determine whether a reservation for capacities or purchase requisitions are created for activities.

Projects: Budgeting

Once costs have been planned, they can be used as the basis for budgeting on a project. While costs are planned in the WBS hierarchy from the bottom-up, the budget is distributed from the top-down. There are aspects of budgeting on projects which you should know. The four main aspects of budgeting include:

1. Original Budget. This is the initial budget based on the cost plan
2. Budget updates. From time to time on a project, the budget may need adjustments. It is also possible that budgeted funds may need to be reallocated.
3. Budget Release. The release determines when and how much of the budget gets distributed to the project. All or part of a budget can be released to all or part of the project. The entire budget does not have to be released at once. The release is top-down.
4. Budget carry-forward. It's important to know what happens with a budget when the project spans between fiscal years. If the budget is still made available from one fiscal year to the next, this is considered budget carry-forward.

The tool which manages the aspects of budgeting and funding for the project is the **Availability Control (AVC)**. The Availability Control can also send system messages when a budget is about to be exceeded. In this way, managers of the project can plan accordingly to avoid budget overruns.

Commitments from purchase requisitions and purchase orders are also very important when managing the budget for a project. Commitments count against budgeted funds. Therefore, the commitments created from purchase requisitions and purchase orders are seen in the Availability Control and can be used to warn project managers when the creation of a purchase requisition or purchase order will result in exceeding the budget.

Project: Order-Related Cost Object Controlling

In great part, projects also follow the Order-related Cost Object Controlling steps. Let's review those steps again in Figure 12.14. Here were see the first step is creating the order. When the order is created, costs are planned, the order is scheduled, reservations occur, and availability checks can occur. These are the very same things that happen during the Detailed Planning phase in the previous section. It can be said, the Detailed Planning phase for projects is the equivalent of the creating of the order in Order-related Cost Object Controlling.

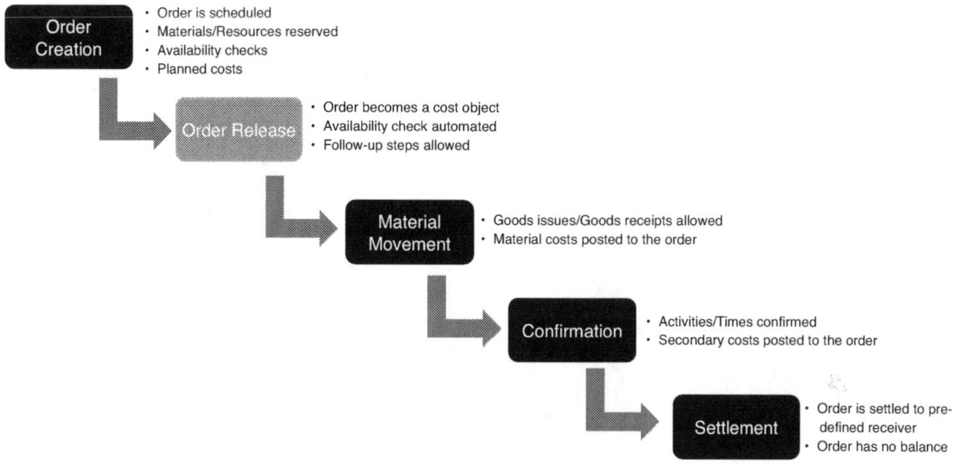

Figure 12.14: Order-Related Cost Object Controlling (Replica of Figure 4.16)

There are other obvious parallels between Order-related Cost Object Controlling and the phases of a project. If we review the phases of the project in Figure 12.15, and compare them to Figure 12.14, we can begin drawing those other parallels.

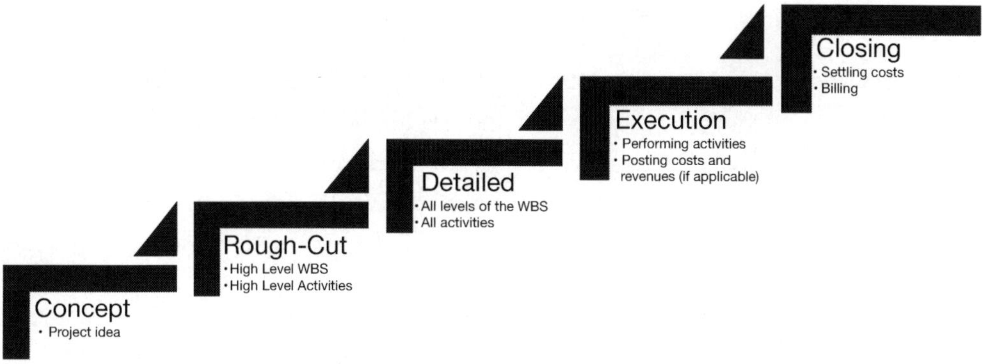

Figure 12.15: Phases of Projects (Replica of Figure 12.2)

From our discussion on budgeting, we can see that budgeting is a result of detailed planning on a project. And once a budget is created and released, the project can then be released. This is the second step in Order-related Cost Object Controlling.

Regarding the release of projects, the manager has the flexibility to release the entire project at one time or parts of the project over time. This means the project manager can choose which WBS Elements to release. Once the project is released, then the Execution phase can begin. It is during the execution phase of the project when goods movements occur as well as confirmations.

Let's review goods movements on projects. During the execution phase, actual costs are posted based on goods movements. Recall, a material planned on a project could be a stock item or a non-stock item. Stock items will require a goods issue from inventory. The materials will be expensed, and costs posted to the corresponding object in the project. If a material is a non-stock item, a goods receipt is posted as part of the procurement process. All non-stock items are treated as consumables, so the account assignment object (project) from the PO will receive the cost posting at goods issue.

Additional costs are posted to the project in the execution phase. These costs can be the result of confirmation from internal activities. When a work center completes an activity on a project, actual dates and times are entered during the confirmation. The costs and dates will then post to the activity and roll up to its corresponding WBS element. External and Service activities will also result in the posting of costs. However, these costs will result from steps in the procurement process as discussed earlier. For externally processed activities, the costs will post at goods receipt for the PO. For service activities, the costs may post when the invoice with working times from the vendor is received and approved.

Cross-Application Time Sheet (CATS)

An alternative for entering working times for internal activities and service activities is CATS. CATS is a tool that can be used internally for work centers to confirm activities by entering actual working times. It can also be used externally, by providing vendors with a CATS account and allowing them to enter their working times in CATS for service activities. There are two basic steps in CATS, Time Entry and Transfer. There are two optional steps seen in Figure 12.16.

Notice the Transfer of times to the target application is a step performed by management. This is the step when actual costs will post to the project, either through confirmation of internal activities or acceptance of times for service activities. There is also a parallel here with Employee Self-Services (ESS) and Management Self-Services (MSS) in Human Capital Management (HCM). The time entry in CATS is an ESS function, while the transfer is an MSS function.

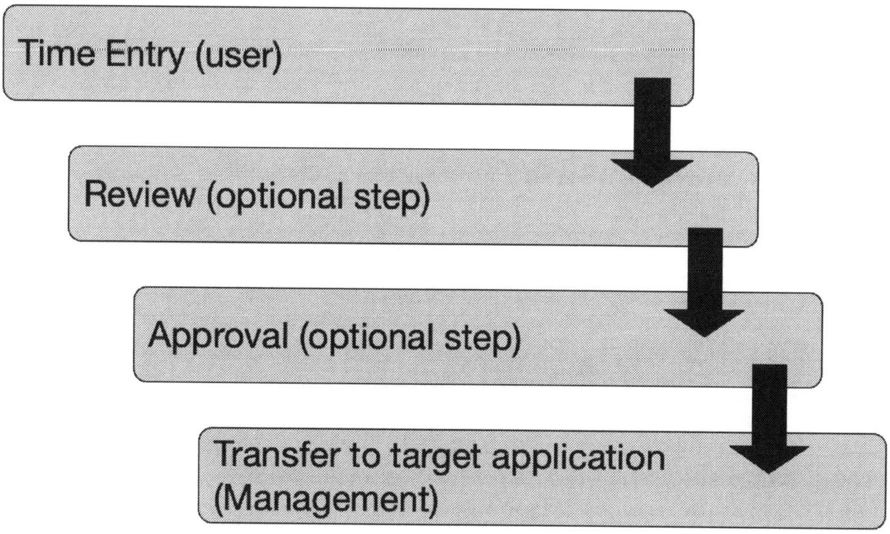

Figure 12.16: CATS Process

While we are addressing HCM, CATS can also be used for employees to enter working times that need to be transferred to payroll. Therefore, CATS can be used for different business applications, thus its name, "Cross-Application" Time Sheet. It is important to know the other application to which times can be transferred. Figure 12.17 provides information on which target applications integrate with CATS.

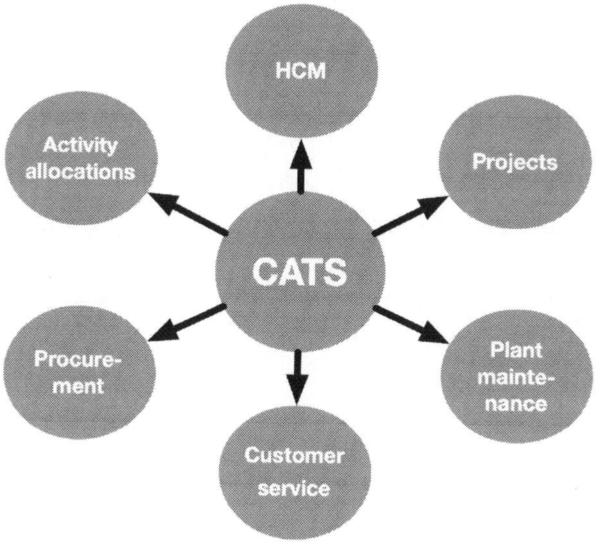

Figure 12.17: CATS Target Applications

Closing

The last phase of the project is Closing. Closing is a periodic activity, which means it takes place at the end of each accounting period, typically end of month. As you can see, this is the phase where Settlement occurs. Settlement is the last step in Order-related Cost Object Controlling and is a period-end activity. There are various settlement techniques. Settlement brings the balance of the cost object to zero. It is possible to settle costs of an activity to WBS elements, WBS elements to other WBS elements, or WBS elements of a project to other receivers. Figure 12.18 depicts possible receivers of project settlement as well as source of costs on a project.

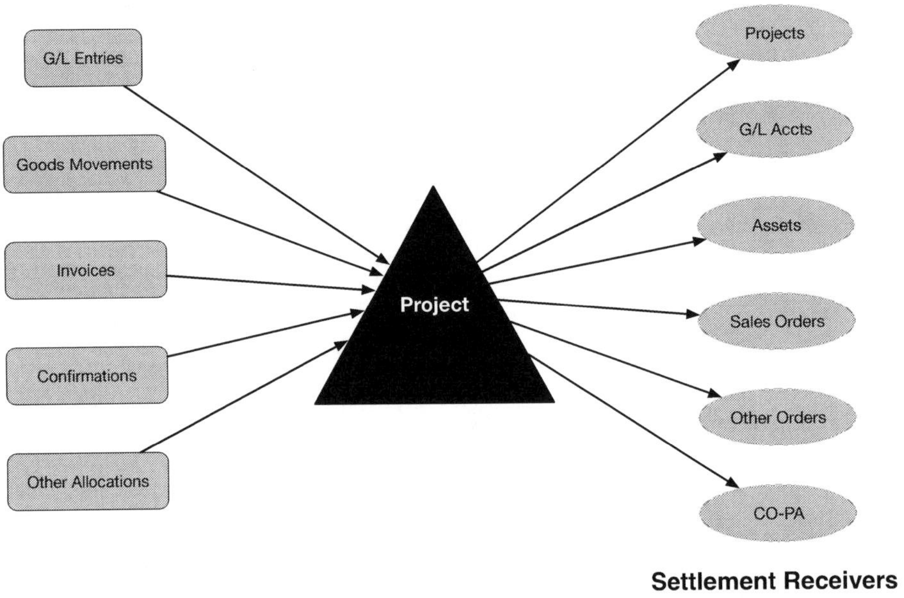

Figure 12.18: Project Costs and Settlement Receivers

We should not leave our discussion on Closing without also mentioning that other activities occur at period-end. Some of those activities include cost forecasting, progress analysis, and interest calculations.

Projects Summary

Project System is a multi-faceted tool in SAP S/4HANA. From a project perspective, projects have numerous characteristics. The most important may be that projects are cross-functional. They integrate with every module in SAP S4HANA Enterprise Management.

The phases of a project in great part, parallel the Order-related Cost Object Controlling process. The master data in a project are derived during the Detailed Planning Phase. The master data include WBS elements and Activities. WBS elements are structured hierarchically, while activities have relationships which form the Network.

The planning of costs on a project serve as the basis for budgeting. Once a budget has been released, the project can be released, and the Execution phase can begin. In this phase, goods movements and confirmations occur resulting in actual costs and dates being posted to the project.

Finally, the last phase of the project is Closing. It is in this phase when the costs on the project are settled.

Made in United States
Orlando, FL
04 November 2026

90201562R00181